MOON WOBBLES AND ECLIPSES IN ASTROLOGY

Looking at the Moon

By

Naomi C Bennett
and
Carl Payne Tobey

BonAmi Publishing

Copyright © 2021 Naomi C Bennett

Published by BonAmi Publishing

All rights reserved. The characters and events portrayed in this book are fictitious. Any similarity to real persons, living or dead, is coincidental and not intended by the author. No part of this book may be reproduced, or stored in a retrieval system, or transmitted in any form or by any means, electronic, mechanical, photocopying, recording, or otherwise, without express written permission of the publisher. Exceptions are granted by a reviewer who wishes to quote a brief passages in connection with a review.

Queries regarding rights and permissions should be addressed to naomibennett360@gmail.com

ISBN-13: 978-1-892134-05-9

Library of Congress: 2021907273

Cover design by: Author

Printed in the United States of America

Other Books by the Authors

Other Books by **Naomi C Bennett**
　　Foundations of Astrology (2014)

Other Books by **Carl Payne Tobey**
　　Astrology for the Millions
　　Astrology of Inner Space
　　Collected Works of Carl Payne Tobey
　　Astrology Lessons by Carl Payne Tobey

Dedication

May the next generation of astrologers benefit from this knowledge. We all stand on the shoulders of those who come before us.

Ancient Egyptian Saying: *"All is Angle"*

"The real voyage of discovery consists not in seeking new landscapes but in having new eyes." - Marcel Proust

"If you want to find the secrets of the universe, think in terms of energy, frequency and vibration." - Nicolas Tesla

Table of Contents

Naomi C Bennett

Introduction	7
History and Myths of Eclipses	9
Moon Wobbles and Eclipses Explained	12

Looking at the Moon by Carl Payne Tobey 1950-51

What are Cycles?	24
What Makes Money Come In?	31
A Controlled Experiment	42
Possible Cyclic Interference	52
Timing Advertising	59
Skill and Luck	63
The Moon at the Time of Marriage	73
The Moon and Vitality	81
A Further Verification	86
Some General Observations	91
Are There Unstable Moments of Time?	100
More Unstable Moments of Time	110
Instability and World War II	118
When Do Great Fires Occur?	128
Instability and the Stock Market	137
Let Us Be Cautious	144
The Turn of Events	152
Loss-Of-Life Through Fire	160
Loss-Of-Life Through Fire, Part 2	169
Loss-Of-Life Through Fire, Part 3	181
Loss-Of-Life Through Fire, Part 4	192
Human Reactions in Emergencies	197
Fires in Hospitals and Institutions	204
Invading the Privacy of a Tradition	210
Planes Crash and Burn	219

Naomi C Bennett

Moon Wobbles-Eclipses with Uranus 1950-2020 227
Major Moon Wobble Events and Famous People 313
Memories of Students of Carl Payne Tobey 375
Tobey System of Astrology 383
About the Authors 395

Introduction

There is extensive history on eclipses since it is one of the oldest observed celestial events that have been recorded over time. However, there are myths and beliefs given to these eclipse events that don't always stand up to scrutiny and research. Carl Payne Tobey was America's first astro-statistician and this book is a reprint of his research that was published in The Astrologer magazine in 1950-51. He intended for this series to become a book called, Looking at the Moon. In consideration of our modern astrological community, I have reproduced Tobey's original work with added research of mine that extend these recorded events from 1950 to 2020 specifically for Moon Wobbles (also called lunar bendings) since these are a less well-known part of astrology.

I have added to his original work to explain the phenomena and to include other astrologer opinions of eclipses for a more rounded perspective of how modern astrologers view these lunar nodes in their work. I then analyze and add my observations of these major events and known people who have significant horoscopes with these squaring Moon Wobbles. The last section are comments from the few remaining astrologers influenced by Tobey along with a review of his entire system of astrology.

Tobey was an early statistician before there were computers or hand calculators. The sheer volume of these tabulations need to be appreciated for the time frame they were created. I have left all of his statistical calculations in the Kindle version of this book but I have edited out much of the rest in the paperback version since it makes for slow reading for most astrologers. The source for these Tobey chapters can be found at the American Federation of Astrologers in Tempe, AZ in their magazine collection. Grant Lewi first published them in 1950-51 for his magazine, The Astrologer.

I give special thanks to the AFA for their efforts to preserve these 20th century records for future astrologers. We have given so much recognition to ancient Hellenistic astrology and Traditional-Medieval astrology that most of today's astrologers have not been trained in these recent discoveries and achievements in the 20th century. More thanks needs to be given to Diane Clarke, another Tobey student, for help in the final editing of the manuscript and making recommendations of what to delete. **Bold** words are my additions to add importance to a statement along with some [clarifying words] that are needed in the material.

The intention of this book is to expand and clarify eclipses and squaring moon wobbles for students and professionals alike, to dispel old myths and hearsay, and to reveal their importance in current events and personal horoscopes.

Naomi C Bennett 2020

History and Myths of Eclipses

Astrology has a long history with the importance of eclipses of major events in world history. Eclipses have been blamed for tragedies, wars, disease outbreaks and the deaths of prominent people. Eclipses only occur when the Sun is conjunct the lunar nodes and the Moon is either new or full. Eclipse lore from many cultures describes eclipses as something eating the sun. The most common lore is that the lunar nodes are dragons, a head for the north node and a tail for the south node. But they have also been a frog, a great bear, a jaguar, a vampire and fire dogs in other cultures.

It was one of the earliest recorded events in Chinese astrology that goes back to 1302 BC. [1] In Chinese legend, two astrologers, Hsi and Ho, were executed for failing to predict a solar eclipse. Historians and astronomers believe that the eclipse that they failed to forecast occurred on October 22, 2134 BCE, which would make it the oldest solar eclipse ever recorded in human history. In China, the emperor was the personification of the Sun on earth. Fearing that the eclipse meant he might die, the emperor would stay out of the palace, eat only vegetarian meals and perform rituals to restore the Sun. Ancient Chinese banged drums and pots to scare the dragon away. In 1302 B.C., Chinese astrologers documented an epic total eclipse that blocked out the sun for 6 minutes and 25 seconds.

The Babylonians, Aztecs and Romans also believed that solar eclipses were bad omens for kings and rulers so they used substitute kings to face the anger of the Gods.[2] They used substitute kings during solar eclipses with the hope that these temporary kings would face the anger of the Gods, instead of the real king. The substitute king was then killed after the eclipse.

The modern world is no longer superstitious about eclipses — except that maybe we should be. Perhaps there are good reasons for superstitions. Eclipse chaser Michael Zeiler said:

> "The reason is quite simple: because it's the most beautiful sight you can see in nature….It's a deeply emotional event, because you feel the

ominous shadow of the moon racing across you. It's a sensory experience. But then the other part of it, too, is that you have the realization that you're looking at the solar system in motion". Astrophysicist Fred Espenak said in 2017, "Trying to explain what seeing a total eclipse is like is like trying to explain what sex is to a virgin. You won't understand it until you see it."[3]

Hindus immersed themselves in water — particularly the Ganges River, which is considered to be purifying — to encourage the sun to fight off the dragon. (Some modern Hindus still take a traditional dip in sacred waters during eclipses.) According to a tale in the ancient Sanskrit poem "Mahabharata," a demon stole an immortality potion and tried to drink it, but the sun and moon reported him to the god Vishnu. Vishnu lopped off the demon's head before the liquid passed his throat, so his immortal head travels around the heavens chasing the sun and moon for revenge. Occasionally it catches one or the other and eats it, but the solar orb falls out of his throat without a body.[3]

In 323 B.C. Alexander the Great died after an eclipse and interestingly, he was born under one. During his career of conquering other countries, he followed his birth eclipse shadow from Rome to Egypt to India where the shadow ended. His greatest success was under his birth eclipse shadow. This was documented by Charles Jayne, a modern American astrologer.

A Spanish friar in the 16th century described a terror-stricken frenzy of sacrificing captives and "men of fair hair and white faces" to the sun during a solar eclipse, fearing that it would never return and that people-eating demons would be unleashed upon Earth.

The Chippewa of North America shot flaming arrows into the sky to rekindle the sun. Ancient Mayans ate a certain type of snake.

Shakespeare mentioned them as bad omens in "King Lear" and "Antony and Cleopatra." John Milton compared the fall of Satan to a solar eclipse in "Paradise Lost."

Christopher Columbus escaped possible death in Jamaica in 1504 by invoking magic to predict a lunar eclipse.

Even into the 19th century, some people believed that you shouldn't breathe the outdoor air during an eclipse. Laundry left out to dry was considered contaminated. Native Alaskans interpreted an eclipse to mean that the sun was sick, so they turned over their pots and cooking utensils to avoid the sun's illness.

The Navajo believed that the eclipse of 1918 over the American Southwest was an omen that foreshadowed the Spanish flu pandemic. Tens of millions died in the following months, including 2,000 Navajo.

In 1919, astronomer Frank Watson Dyson confirmed Albert Einstein's general theory of relativity using calculations based on bending light during an eclipse.[4]

Bill Meridian (who studied under the great 20th century American astrologer Charles Jayne) tells the story that both the Japanese Navy Admiral and US Navy Admiral of World War II were born with the same eclipse shadow that spanned the Pacific Ocean. Both of these Navy men had their careers made under their birth eclipse shadows.

In 2009, financial behaviorist Gabriele Lepori found that stock prices tend to fall on eclipse days.

Since the 1930-50's, Carl Payne Tobey had researched eclipses and found that the square aspect between the Sun and lunar nodes creates events too but without any shadow to see either the Sun or Moon 'eclipsed'. These are the oldest and most observed events in astrology/astronomy and now we have a more modern take on them in this research.

Footnotes
1. https://www.cbsnews.com/pictures/solar-eclipses-in-history/5/
2. https://www.timeanddate.com/eclipse/solar-eclipse-history.html
3. https://www.washingtonpost.com/graphics/2017/lifestyle/eclipse-myths/?noredirect=on&utm_term=.c860044fa497
4. https://www.timeanddate.com/eclipse/solar-eclipse-history.html

Moon Wobbles and Eclipses Explained

Eclipses only occur when the Sun is conjunct the lunar nodes and the Moon is either new or full. More recently, astrologers have noted that the square aspects between the Sun and Lunar Nodes are associated with dramatic events too. Traditionally, these were called Lunar Bendings. Carl Payne Tobey coined a more inclusive term of **Moon Wobble** after extensive research on them.

Tobey was one of the first American astrologers to do statistical research to verify the claims of astrology for Wynn's Astrology Magazine in 1936.[1] He took the Who's Who in Business and hand calculated thousands of birth dates to see if some professions have dominance in particular sun signs. In the prior chapters, he had gotten the national data on fires in the USA from a governmental source. At the first cut of the analysis on the data, he could find no statistical significance. He finally got the idea to only analyze fires with death associated with them. He had hit pay dirt. The factor of the Sun in hard aspect (conjunction, square and opposition) to the Lunar Nodes dominated the occurrence of multiple deaths with fire. He concluded that people can become emotionally panicked during these times and act irrationally. There can be extremes of emotion that cause strong actions to be taken. He noted that wars tend to begin and end during these periods as he watched the major battles of WWII unfold. Charles Jayne also noticed how important these square aspects between the Sun and lunar nodes were in his own research.

It was from this discovery that Tobey coined the term **Moon Wobble** for the hard aspects (0, 90 and 180 degrees) of the lunar nodes to the Sun that is used today by many astrologers. During World War II, Carl noticed that major events in military action occurred not only with the conjunctions (eclipses) but the squares too. He used an orb of no more that 15 degrees (7.5 degrees from either side of the exact partile aspect). In general, the Moon Wobble can last two weeks depending upon whether there are any other planets involved that increases the strength of a Moon Wobble. In general, eclipses are stronger than squaring Moon Wobbles because the Eclipse involves a conjunction-opposition aspect that is stronger than a squaring aspect. But when other planets like Uranus or Mars are involved, the square aspect can be extremely strong.

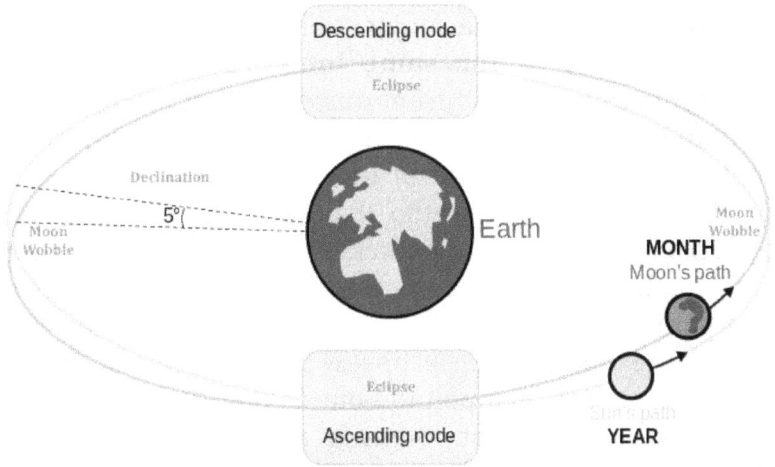

The lunar nodes with the Sun create Moon Wobbles and Eclipses

Moon Wobbles occur approximately every three months when the Sun is conjunct, square or in opposition to the Lunar Nodes, **so there are Moon Wobbles with Eclipses** too. When the Sun is conjunct or opposed to the nodes, there will be a lunar or solar eclipse near this time when the Moon is new (a solar eclipse) or full (a lunar eclipse). The declination of the Moon will determine if the eclipse is total or partial. As with most aspects in astrology, the hard aspects of the conjunction and opposition are the strongest, but the squares manifest too. **It is the square aspect of the Sun to Lunar Nodes that is new in the last century and this research has given us clarity**. The Medieval astrologers did use Lunar Bendings but it was very limited in how it was used. Modern Moon Wobbles are more descriptive of their nature and characteristics. The unexpected can occur and it can produce more extreme characteristics of people since the Moon can possibly be OOB (Out of Bounds). This is an extreme declination beyond 23deg26min—outside of the ecliptic which is the path of the Sun.

In the 1950's, Charles Jayne also noted that approximately 90 days before an eclipse, there is a 'heating up' of activity preceding an eclipse.[2] Without knowing it, he was referring to a Moon Wobble. During the conjunction-opposition, **the Sun and Lunar Nodes are in the same longitude and declination,** which produces an eclipse from our earthly point of view. To have **planetary bodies in double alignment magnifies the effect because it adds another level of exactness**. Astrological theory by Jayne claims that the shadow path of the eclipse will link people and countries together. People born near an eclipse can foreshadow pivotal future events that unfold under its natal eclipse path. Bill Meridian, a financial and mundane astrologer, has written extensively on eclipses[3] since he was a student of Charles Jayne. Meridian pointed out at UAC98 that Jayne noted that Alexander the Great followed his birth eclipse path in conquering the world all the way from Greece to India where his natal eclipse shadow stopped. Recently, many astrologers were concerned about a Solar Eclipse on August 11, 1999 because it occurred with a Fixed Grand Cross of planets which could indicate a major earthquake. The actual eclipse path crossed southern England, through Europe and finished in the Middle East. One astrologer who studied earthquakes properly predicted the Great Turkey quake of August 17,1999 that killed over 17,000.

The length of a Moon Wobble or Eclipse period ranges all over the place by astrologers as to their duration. Some astrologers give a range of six months until the next eclipse. I don't believe in that kind of long-term impact. I think the effects are for the duration of the eclipse period which can be a month to six weeks if there are two lunar eclipses framing a solar eclipse. In my experience, the center of the entire period is the Moon Wobble when the Sun and lunar nodes are in the same degree.

The movement of the Moon is powerful in all major transits as a timing device to set off the events. It's a trigger for the materialization of the tensions into events. So the Moon is a very important timer for all major transits, as the Sun and the Moon can indicate the day of an event. That's why eclipses have so much history and consistency. I believe that the partile aspect of a Moon Wobble is the center of the eclipse period that is the power factor in an event period. If you look at the major events listed below, these are all squaring Moon Wobbles. I added in the strong contributing aspects that set these events apart from the average.

It is commonly believed that the South Node releases energy and the North node receives or absorbs energy. **I haven't found that to be true as much as the nodes indicate a degree of instability or unexpected change that make events come to an apex or peak.** It's also important to track when planets conjunct or square the Lunar Nodes, especially Mars or Uranus which can also create events too. The other planets can be too subtle to produce observable events without close examination. But a long slow transit of outer plsnryd against the Nodes like Neptune, Pluto or Eris can produce events that have these planetary qualities embedded into that time period.

To see which bending the planet occupies in a chart, start with the North Node and move clockwise around the horoscope. If a planet is at the opening square, it is the South Bending. Continuing clockwise around the wheel, if the planet is at the closing square, e.g., 270° from the North Node, it is the North Bending. Kathy Allan believes that "the bending of the nodes may be the most overlooked feature of the horsoscope.[4] Mary Plumb at The Mountain Astrologer Magazine notes these people with planets squaring the lunar nodes:

Web-based political activist and media personality Arianna Huffington (July 7, 1950) has natal Uranus at 6° Cancer, square the North Node at 2° Aries. Uranus is at the North Bending, suggesting that the nature of the planet will be expressed outwardly.

Writer and political activist Arundhati Roy (November 24, 1961) has natal Mercury at 19° Scorpio square the North Node at 21° Leo. Mercury is again at the North Bending, about which Allan writes: "The energy is under the ego's control." (Roy won The Booker Prize for her first book, The God of Small Things.)

Secretary of State Hillary Clinton (October 26, 1947) also has a planet at the North Bending: Natal Saturn at 21° Leo is square the North Node at 23° Taurus.

Actress Drew Barrymore (February 22, 1975) has the Sun at 4° Pisces, square the North Node at 6° Sagittarius. The Sun is at the North Bending, suggesting visibility and manifestation. Her early experiences with drugs and bisexuality are well known, along with her recent award-winning performance as Edith Bouvier Beale in HBO's Grey Gardens.

David Deida (March 18, 1958) is not as well known, but provides an interesting example. Deida is a pioneering yoga teacher who has taught widely on integrating sexuality into spiritual practice. He has natal Mars at 1° Aquarius, at the North Bending, square the North Node at 2° Scorpio.

Michelle Obama (January 17, 1964) has Jupiter 13° Aries square the North Node at 11° Cancer. Jupiter is at the South Bending. We can't know about her interior life, but the suggestion is that the fiery temperament of Jupiter in Aries, although crucial to integrate, is somehow best used internally.

Diana, the Princess of Wales (July 1, 1961), often thought of in her lifetime as the most beautiful woman in the world, has natal Venus in rulership at 24° Taurus, at the South Bending, square the North Node at 28° Leo. It's a bit of an eerie thought to consider her Venus as somehow sacrificed, or offered for the collective.

Vice President Joe Biden (November 20, 1942) has natal Uranus at 0° Gemini, at the South Bending, square North Node at 3° Virgo. Biden is known for his outspokenness [and gaffs], sometimes bringing political trouble. Another way of considering Uranus, the planet of shock and sudden events, at the South Bending: Uranus is also at Biden's natal Descendant at 3° Gemini. His first wife and infant daughter were killed in a traffic accident in 1972. His two sons, although critically injured, made full recoveries.

His Holiness the Dalai Lama (July 6, 1935) has natal Mars at 18° Libra square the North Node at 22° Capricorn at the South Bending. It might be hard to find a better example of someone who has used (a detriment) Mars for spiritual good, or for the good of the collective.[5]

The forgotten but very famous 20th century American astrologer, L. Edward Johndro stated for HoroscopeMagazine:

Payson Weston, the celebrated pedestrian was born on the day of a solar eclipse in Pisces. Thus with his feet (Pisces) did he eclipse many a younger man in long-distance walking contests. Another example was Franz Josef of Austria. He was born on the day of a solar eclipse conjunction Saturn in Leo. Of all royal (Leo) households in modern times his royal house eclipsed them all in deaths and tragedy (Saturn)....

As astrologers we have also seen other hundreds of nativities of failures whose planets, or rather some of them held all the 'grand trines' that some die-hard schools of astrology like to chant about so blindly.

Now the answer to that riddle will never reveal itself to mere scanners of nativities. But it lies there in the eclipses for all to read who, going carefully over the examples to be cited, wisely conclude that no horoscope is complete till it has been overlaid by the near-term eclipses preceding and following the birthdate. This is one of the vital astrological secrets as to which planet or planets, if any, is to be stressed in each nativity. The other vital rule is which mutual aspects are the nearest exact.

One ego-shattering truth is this? Eclipses quite largely define mundane issues for whole groups....men are so born in time as to respond... to some particular cosmic purpose delegated, so to speak, through the eclipses. The importance of our allotted role depends greatly on if and how your nativity ties in with the eclipses (and their) planets in and about your birth year. [6]

The famous weather astrologer, George J. McCormick had much to say about eclipses and the Moon Out of Bounds in 1947:

Abbe Gabriel, Professor of Mathematics, at the Seminary of Caen, Normandy, Frances, an eminent authority on lunar-solar cycles, has made profound researches into the subject and has demonstrated, by reversible graphs, the value of the Moon's nodes in tracing cycles of droughts, floods and extreme cold winters since 762 A.D., depending largely on multiples of the 18.92 year cycle of the nodes and including the Saros and Metonic lunar cycles of eclipses.

Sir John Herschel, in his remarks on "The Weather", in Good Words, for January 1864, commented that an eminent meteorologist, Luke Howard, had some years before employed a weather cycle of nineteen years, based on the circulation of the Moon's nodes. He also took account of the Moon's varying maximum declination as influencing the average of rainfall and the height of the barometer...

The North Node which, with an annual motion of 19°20', rotates backward through the zodiacal signs in a cycle of 18 years, 218 days, 21 hours, 22 minutes and 46 seconds. During this period, it causes the maximum northern declinations of the Moon to move from approximately 28°45' to 18°10' and back. The absolute maximum declination of the Moon is reached when the North Node is at the beginning of Aries and the ephemeral Moon is in either Cancer 0° or Capricorn 0°. The least maximum of 18°10' is reached when the North Node is at the Fall equinox of Libra 0°, with a period of 9 years and about 109 days between these two points. When the node occupies either Tropic, the moon's maximum declination reaches the normal 23°27' just midway between these extremes.

The Node merely provides approximate cyclic timing for anytime, past or future, but eclipses should provide the keys to general causes and timing, whether in natal or mundane charts. Furthermore, with respect to economics, the mutation conjunctions of Jupiter with Saturn, at periods of twenty years and intermediate oppositions between Jupiter and Saturn provide a cycle of 9.93 years that merits serious consideration. When these cyclic positions converge with eclipse points, the climaxes are intensified and may culminate before or overlap the normal cyclic timing point. ...

The eclipses of the Sun are visible in the same place again after 54 years 1 month. It may be pertinent to mention that economists now refer to a major business cycle of approximately 54 years when wholesale prices reach major peaks. L.J. Jensen, of Kansas City, Mo., a recognized authority of long standing in the field of astro-economics, times these peaks as 1865, 1919 and 1973, [2027] respectively. [7]

The very technical Charles Jayne had much to say about eclipses, lunar bendings, occultations and planetary nodes that produce stronger than normal events or human characteristics:

[Planetary Nodes]   Actually, each planet's orbit plane intersects the plane of the Ecliptic to produce the [heliocentric] Planetary Nodes. Very little attention has been paid to them as contrasted with the attention given to the Moon's Nodes. The best astro-statistical researcher in the U.S.A. is the redoubtable Carl Payne Tobey. In 1961 he published a study of 100 hysterectomies in the magazine HOROSCOPE. He found more squares to Mars than expected. He also found that there were more square to the NODES of Mars than there should have been by chance! Those Nodes are at about 19° of Taurus (North) and Scorpio (South). In my own experience Pluto and the sign Scorpio are also linked with such operations. His friend Vernon Clark, M.S., the Clinical Psychologist who had done the famous experiments in the abilities of Astrologers, repeated this experiment twice and each time (with the same number of cases) got the same results that Tobey had gotten. Thus, 300 cases made it very probable that the heliocentric Nodes of Mars are significant. One conclusion that we certainly must draw from this is that the Planetary Nodes are probably as vital as the Moon's Nodes. For instance, Nixon's natal Sun at 20° Capricorn is conjunction both Pluto's South Nodes (within less than 1°) and Saturn's South Node, too (within about 3°), thus giving him, aside from other factors, a Plutonic and Saturnine quality...

[90 Degree Square] ...Mercury and Venus, is an inferior conjunction when the planet lies between us and the Sun). At the second or rare type, the planet is always retrograde. I term all such configurations—ECLIPSES, ALIGNMENTS, OCCULTATION and LINE UPS (the very very rare eclipse of one Planet by another one) —LINCONS, which is an abbreviation of LINEAR CONFIGURATION. **They are by far the most powerful aspects in Astrology. For they combine conjunction and opposition aspects with Nodes. ...They can be quite spectacular, too.** [8]

Dr. Lee Leaman, a very well respected traditional astrologer of today said:

In Ptolemy's wording, any planet square the Nodes is in a critical, that is to say, dangerous position. In Transpersonal system [Dane Rudhyar], the points square the Nodes are also critical but as turning points in the cycle of the Moon. These two views do not contradict....Planets at the bending represent critical issues which can change the flow of life. Since most people are resistant to change the usually response is to build up a rigidity around these planets...planets at any of the critical points (conjunct either Node or at either bending) acquire the character of that placement with respect to the issues represented by that planet. For example, a person with Venus at the bending is someone who will be challenged by issues of love, or generically, women.

The nodal axis is the plane of existence, reduced to a line. The points of maximum latitude, the bendings, produce a line perpendicular to the nodal axis. This figure forms a cross, a primary figure of physical manifestation, as well as reflection of thesis-antithesis. If the nodal axis is the plane of existence, then the bendings are the primary challenge to that existence, which is also a challenge to growth and change. ...

The more appropriate statement may be that the southern latitude person acts as agent of his/her time more than does the northern person. In contrast, the northern latitude person becomes the embodiment of her/his time by acts of personal will. Thus, Lincoln became the hero of the age, not by who he was, nor by manifesting the underlying archetype of his age, but by the courageous application of will and principle to the issue of slavery, on which the country was hopelessly divided...

Southern type Mussolini acted as an agent of fascism, and would never have achieved the power that he had without Hitler's success. Richard Nixon rode Senator Joseph McCarthy's anti-Communism bandwagon to prominence...Barry Goldwater in the early Sixties was the agent for the nation's fear of unbridled conflict with Communism; later he came to represent the conscience of Conservatism...

The Nodes seem to act as a focusing lens for the items ruled by the Houses that the Nodes occupy. [9]

Clelia Romano did a study of 40 charts and concluded there was no difference between the south and north nodes, only that the north nodes maybe slightly better.

"Not taking the Nodes into account is the same as discarding valuable information for understanding the Nativity... to decide ultimately this question is necessary, as in any delineation, to observe in which house the node is in...its depositor and the presence or absence of planets in conjunction with them." [10]

Below is my list for the most dramatic squaring Moon Wobbles in recent times that also involve other planets.

Most Dramatic Squaring Moon Wobbles

Event	Actual Date	Moon Wobble Exact
Challenger Explosion	28 Jan 1986	25 Jan 1986 Pluto sq nodes
OK City Bombing	19 Apr 1995	26 Apr 1995 Uranus Aq with nodes
1stHS shooting 25 Students	21 May 1998	27 May 1998 Mars Cazimi Sun
ColumbineH.S. shootings	20 Apr 1999	8 May 1999
NYC 9/11	11 Sep 2001	24 Sep 2001 op Pluto sq Mars w Ur node

Columbia Explodes	1 Feb 2003	22 Feb 2003
Indonesia Tsunami 275K dead	26 Dec 2004	18 Jan 2005 Mars opp Uranus
London Subway Bus Bombing	7 Jul 2005	11 July 2005 Conj Mars opp Jupiter
Sichuan,China Earthquake Kills 100k, 4.5M homeless	12 May 2008	14 May 2008 Conj Neptune
7.6 quake near Padang, Sumatra 1K dead	30 Sep 2009	19 Oct 2009 Mars conj Nodes
India Worst Floods 100s dead, 1M affected	5 Oct 2009	19 Oct 2009 Pluto sq Nodes
SF-Oakland Bay Bridge failure	27 Oct 2009	19 Oct 2009 Same Moon Wobble
Rio,BrazilWorst Floods 300K w/o homes	4 Apr 2010	8 Apr 2010 Grand Cardinal
IcelandVolcano Erupts EU Flights grounded	14 Apr 2010	8 Apr 2010 Cross Forming
China Earthquake 1100 Dead	14 Apr 2010	6 Apr 2010
BPDeepwater Horizon Worst Oil Disaster	20 Apr 2010	6 Apr 2010 Ju+Ur Pi sq Sa
EgyptArabSpring Peak Mideast Revolt, 99%	11 Feb 2011	20 Feb 2011 sq Uranus Aries
Tsunami & Fukushima Nuclear Explosions	11 Feb 2011	20Feb 2011 sq Pluto Capricorn

Ukraine Revolt	18 Feb 2014	23 Jan 2014 conj Uranus

Footnotes

1. "Who's Who First 20,000 Sun Positions", by Carl Payne Tobey, *Wynn's Astrology Magazine*, August 1936.
2. Bill Meridian quoted Charles Jayne, his teacher for mundane prediction using eclipses at UAC 98 in Atlanta.
3. Meridian, Bill. The Predictive power of Eclipse Paths, Cycles Research 2010..
4. Allan, Kathy, "Re-visioning the Lunar Nodes". The Mountain Astrologer magazine, Feb/March 2009
5. Plumb, Mary, "At the Bending", The Mountain Astrologer Magazine website, February 8, 2010
6. Johndro, L. Edward, "You and Your Eclipses', Horoscope Magazine, June 1937, p. 7.
7. McCormick, George J., 'The Moon's North Node An Important Cyclic Indicator", American Federation of Astrologers Yearbook 1947, pp 11-21.
8. Jayne, Charles A., "A New Dimension in Astrology, Nodes, Eclipses and Other Alignments", The American Federation of Astrologers 1975, pp. 5-6.
9. Leaman, J. Lee, Classical Astrology for Modern Living, Whitford Press 1996, pp. 207-209.
10. Romano, Clelia, The Lunar Nodes – A New Reading of its Traditional Meaning 2009, https://www.academia.edu/15275121/Lunar_Nodes

What are Cycles?

LOOKING AT THE MOON
By Carl Payne Tobey (1950-51)

We are proud to bring to our readers, chapter by chapter, this distinguished and' rigidly scientific demonstration of the influence of cycles on the affairs of humankind. Mr. Tobey, whose Astro-statisics have attracted the attention of men of science, has brought to the compilation and writing of this work the same undeviating accuracy, patience, and fidelity to observed and tabulated fact that has won him a place of foremost importance among the investigators of cyclic phenomena. This book, for which publication is planned in the not-too-distant future, is another milestone in scientific astrology, sure to awaken widespread interest. Readers of THE ASTROLOGER are privileged to see it first. [Grant Lewi, editor]

The cycle with which everyone is most familiar is as simple as night and day, because that's what it is--the rotation of the earth on its own axis. On the side of the earth toward the Sun, it is daytime. On the side away from the Sun, it is night. The fact that the earth rotates and turns on its own axis starts and completes the cycle

For its first definition of the word *cycle*, the Standard Dictionary states: *A period of time, at the end of which certain aspects or motions of the heavenly bodies repeat themselves.*

Every small child becomes familiar with the day and night cycle. It means go to bed and get up. There are many effects of this cycle that are more than human habit. The average temperature is higher in the daytime, lower at night. More babies are born after midnight and before noon than during the afternoon and evening. There are statistics to prove this. The temperature of the human body rises at night. Any doctor will verify this.

At the age of five, the child has become conscious of the annual cycle caused by the trip of the earth around the Sun. This is the seasonal cycle. In the winter, the child can throw snowballs, and has to wear a coat. In the summer he goes swimming. Businessmen find it difficult to sell fur coats in the summer, bathing suits in the winter. The record indicates that stock market crashes and hurricanes have occurred with greater frequency--in the fall of the year. Peaches ripen in late summer, Florida oranges during the winter.

There is nothing complicated about the word cycle, although cycles themselves can be complicated because there are so many of them. There is the old saying that history repeats itself, although it does not repeat itself exactly. It merely follows a similar pattern. There are always variations as well as similarities. We should have no misunderstanding as to what we mean when the term *cycle* is employed. We should keep the day and night cycle in mind. Nights are colder than days, on the average, but winter days are colder than summer nights, because two cycles are involved

The study of cycles is not new, except to a few of our modern educators. It is very old. Roger Babson was plugging the subject before 1920. Economists were ridiculing him until 1929 when economists met with the same fate as 1948 pollsters, but the ancient astrologers were the original students of cycles. They studied cycles before the birth of Christianity. The church fought the study of cycles because of the possible implication of an absolute fate. Because of this opposition, astrology often fell into the hands of the charlatan.

Perhaps the next most important and well-known cycle is that of the Moon, although there are many complicated phases of the lunar cycle. It governs both the rise and fall of the ocean tides and the rise and fall of the ionosphere. Consequently, it has an effect on radio reception. For many years, the New York City Fire Department has maintained that pyromaniacs were active at the full of the Moon. According to Dr. Harlan True Stetson of Massachusetts Institute of Technology, the Moon acts as a trigger in setting off earthquakes.

There is much tradition attached to the lunar cycle, some of which may be false and some of which may be true. Farmers plant by the Moon. Fishermen fish by the Moon. Throughout the southern part of the United States, many people claim that deer feed and fish bite when the Moon is at the meridian or in opposition thereto, directly beneath the observer's position on the surface of the earth.

Little or nothing has been accomplished by modern science to prove or disprove any of these traditions. The academic scientist has often been a man of intolerance. What he does not understand or does not know is easily tossed off as superstition. The individual academic scientist covers himself and soothes his conscience by thinking of himself as a conservative. Charles Fort once wrote that he was a conservative himself at night when he was tired.

The Moon involves a whole series of cycles. One of these is the New Moon cycle, involving the time taken by the lunar object to travel not only all the way around the earth, but a little farther to catch up with the Sun, which by apparent motion has moved about 28 degrees during the interim.

The trip of the Moon from any given point, such as the place of the vernal equinox, around the earth and back to that point, can be regarded as a cycle.

The starting point might also be a moving object such as a planet, or a relatively stationary object such as a fixed star. There is the 18 and a fraction year cycle when eclipses repeat themselves in nearly the same longitudinal positions.

There is a cycle of approximately 346 days, being the time that it takes the sun, by apparent motion, to go from one conjunction with the Moon's north node to another. We are here concerned with the question as to whether these cycles are accompanied by terrestrial effects, whether human behavior is affected.

No one appears to deny the existence of cycles, because no one denies the existence of night and day, or summer and winter. Cycles usually work statistically--or according to the law of averages. There are deviations from the mean. There is an occasional warm day in winter; an occasional cold one in summer, but that is not the rule. On the average, summer days are warmer than winter days. Few cycles can be as clearly defined as night and day, or winter and summer. A curve on a graph may be the net result of a group of cycles-the sum of a series.

The science of statistics is very young, having had its real start in the 1890's. It is based on the mathematical theory of probability--on the calculus of probability. Its growth might have been further retarded had not the proprietors of the gaming houses of Europe been sufficiently interested in knowing more about the public's chances of winning to hire the mathematicians of the day to compute the odds. Throughout Christian history, the pros and cons of astrology have been argued by some of the greatest minds, but their discussions led nowhere, because they lacked the tool with which to penetrate to the truth. The science of statistics is that tool. It could have been used by the astronomers to settle the question, but astronomers of modern times were greatly influenced by Dr. Harlow Shapley, and Shapley preferred dogma.

A certain psychological change has occurred in the minds of men and women over the last twenty-five years. Back in the 1920's, most people scoffed at any such notion as we are about to discuss. And then, something happened. It goes back to the stock market crash of 1929. There had been a great post war prosperity. Values were greatly inflated. The customers' men were having a great day. They were loading stocks onto the butcher and the baker, the farmer and the plumber's assistant. Stocks were bid ever upward. Like the chain letter, it could not go on to infinity. The public had gone beyond available capital, and had borrowed from the banks in order to buy more securities- and then, the inevitable happened. During October and November 1929, men looked at each other. They could not believe what had occurred. All the big men, all the great authorities had let them down. There wasn't any Santa Claus. Stocks crashed nearly every day for a month, and then they crashed some more. Call loans were called, and each time they were called, more distress sales were set off. There came wave after wave of selling. Fortunes were wiped out. There were many varied reactions to the fact. There was an epidemic of jumping from hotel and office windows. This was a new form of suicide, which had its inauguration at that time. Previously, men had shot and hanged themselves. Now, they jumped from windows and splashed on sidewalks below. It was a new innovation.

The old creed was destroyed. There followed a depression. Out of this depression was born the New Deal. In 1932 and 1933, for the first time, astrology magazines began appearing on newsstands. It was not long before the great American News Company had accepted American Astrology Magazine for distribution. With nearly 100,000 outlets, they were able to place this publication within the reach of the public, and the public reached. Today, a half million people in the United States buy astrology magazines each month. Who are these people? Are they the ignorant? They are not. Some of these magazines are subscribed to by some of the most intellectual men and women in the country.

People were thinking along new lines. They were looking for causes in another direction. They were gazing out into space. In his 1932 campaign, President Herbert Clark Hoover had publicly pointed out that he was not an astrologer, that he had been unable to foresee the crash of 1929. On the wall of a home in New York State was a framed letter. It was a letter to an astrologer, expressing thanks for a horoscope computed for the person who had signed the letter. The signature at the bottom of the letter was that of Franklin Delano Roosevelt, who was to become the next President of the United States.

In Brookline, Mass., another development took place after the 1929 crash. A banker looked into the work of a man named Frank Anderson. Anderson had been making predictions relative to stock market movement. The results were rather unusual. The banker told Anderson to get busy and do more research. He furnished $200,000 with which to carry on the work. Anderson set up a statistical organization, and studied the effect of the Moon on stock prices. Today, some of the largest corporations in America pay the Anderson Laboratories $2,000 a year for a graph of the stock market a year in advance. Anderson, however, does not publish his methods.

There has developed a new interest in an old subject. In 1941, a book on astrology emerged from Duke University. Its title was *The Star-Crossed Renaissance*. It was written by Don

Cameron Allen, English professor, who made an investigation of interest in astrology during the Renaissance. One of his conclusions follows:

> "In conclusion, we wish to point out again that the defenders of astrology were not ignorant and superstitious men. Some of the greatest scientific minds of the age believed in the art of the stars. As we look over these books, we notice to our amazement what intelligent writers most of the astrologers are; on the other hand, we are only too often confronted with an anti- astrologer who is both ignorant and dull. There are various reasons for this. To be a ranking member of the astrologer's profession in the in the sixteenth century required a mastery of astronomy and mathematics, sciences in which the stupid never excel. To be an opponent of astrology, one needed only enough Latin to read Pico and abridge his arguments. The underlying reason for the war against astrology had also a share in shaping the character of the defender. The Renaissance debate about the verities of the astrologer's creed has only a small place in the history of rationalism, but it merits a generous chapter in the history of religion. The force that impelled Pico to write his Disputations was the force that inspired most of the writers of the sixteenth century; and when the brotherhood of Christian believers marshals its dogma for an offensive, it takes both courage and intelligence to move against it."

In modern times, there has been a good deal of opposition to astrology because of the belief that it is a cult. The fact is that it has been adopted by many a cult when it should have been investigated by scientists in a scientific and unbiased way.

This is not a book about astrology as a whole. To investigate astrology fully and its almost unlimited number of cycles would require an army of scientists and statisticians. A proper investigation would require several millions of dollars. We merely point out that interest in cycles, astrology and kindred subjects has greatly increased during the last twenty years. Life is filled with unknown factors, and thousands of people are turning their eyes toward distant space with the thought that the causes of many mysteries may lie far beyond the surface of the earth. Relatively, we are not looking a great distance away, a mere quarter of a million miles to the Moon, with a further glance, of ninety-two million miles to the Sun. Astronomically, such efforts come under the head of neighborhood activities. Our data is of a statistical nature. Our conclusions, insofar as they go, are based on statistical principles and laws. Our data is useful data. It can be applied in the daily life of any individual. It holds the hope of making life more efficient. It might be able to shorten the course to a given objective. It is certain that this work only touches the fringe of a subject. There may be a wealth of knowledge waiting for those who will continue investigations along similar lines.

Some scientists may object to this work on the ground that there has been set up no theoretical mechanism to illustrate how the Moon can have its effect upon terrestrial affairs. Practical people are little concerned with theories, particularly since the majority of theories are short-lived. If the Moon does affect people, and if that effect can be statistically and repeatedly demonstrated, the mechanism becomes a secondary matter insofar as this writer is concerned. He will leave the formation of theories to others. We should bear in mind that since the beginning of the Christian era this matter--has been argued pro and con by scientists, with none of the participants lifting a finger to uncover an iota of evidence. Instead, they have piled theory on top of theory. They had tried to upset each other's theories. They have argued between fate and free will. They have jumped from religion to atheism and back again.

Having accepted the diurnal cycle caused by the rotation of the earth on its axis, and having accepted the annual cycle caused by the trip of the earth around the Sun, we now go a step further. We inquire into the possible effects of the Moon in its approximate 28-day trip around the earth.

WHAT MAKES MONEY COME IN?

In 1936, I was studying statistics in connection with a mail order business. Business was obtained by advertising in monthly magazines. In common with any other business, there were fluctuations in volume. These fluctuations interested me. I studied them a great deal. I was interested in determining how long a period elapsed from the time a magazine reached a newsstand until an ad therein reached its maximum of pulling power. In an effort to determine the answer, I encountered complications. The interval varied from one to five weeks with ads appearing in different issues of the same magazine. There was what at first appeared to be a monthly rise and fall in the volume of business, and I had assumed that this rise and fall had definite association with the dates when magazines reached newsstands. The correspondence was out of line. When we took an average figure for the length of time it took an ad to reach its maximum of direct pulling power, peaks of business gradually drew away from the place where they were supposed to be. This presented a problem that was to remain a mystery for a considerable time. There appeared to be a cycle involved, but it did not appear to have a direct relationship to the monthly dates when new issues of a magazine made their appearance on newsstands.

Possible effects of the moon and various traditions connected them with came to mind. There was the thought of new and full moons. The matter was investigated. There was a careful analysis of the figures as they might relate to new and full moons. The result was negative. It didn't fit. Peaks came at new moons, but ultimately, they came at full moons. There appeared to be no correspondence. In consternation, having no idea where to turn next, the matter was dropped.

In 1938, I began a mail order business of my own. I continued to keep records, and I arranged that they be kept in a number of different ways. I did not entirely discard the moon. I continued to keep records of the number of orders received during the various phases of the moon. All of this involved additional expense, but something caused me to follow that course. Records were also kept showing the number of orders received as the moon passed through each sign of the equinoctial zodiac. Having set in motion the keeping of these records, I do not believe that I ever looked at the results during the next two years. I wasn't very confident that they would show anything of interest. I almost forgot about the matter. When the events of life become unsatisfactory in one way or another, irritation often causes one to poke around in some new direction, and the day finally came, when I tabulated the totals of the figures that had been accumulating for an interval of two years. The figures having to do with the phases of the moon appeared to be as meaningless as ever. Turning to the figures relating to the moon in the various signs of the zodiac, my interest was aroused anew.

When I use the term "signs-of-the-zodiac," let me explain what these are. They are twelve divisions of a circle of space, that circle being the apparent path of the sun through the year. This apparent path of the sun is known as the ecliptic. It is the plane in which the signs of the zodiac are measured. This zodiac is entirely a matter of Earth-Sun relationship, and it has nothing whatsoever to do with the stars far out in space.

Some astronomers appear to despise any reference to the signs of the zodiac. They may tell you that these signs of the zodiac mean nothing because they have moved away from the signs of the zodiac signified by the fixed stars, in accordance with the precession of the equinoxes. In one lifetime, this makes little difference. If we were to measure by the fixed stars, however, our annual cycle would ultimately be badly messed up, because winter would ultimately come in the summer time. The western astrologers, for example, have never used the zodiac of the stars. They have knowingly used the zodiac of the equinoxes. They deal with a seasonal cycle. While some astronomers like to believe that the equinoctial signs-of-the-zodiac were named after the constellations, there is no proof of this, and the opposite could well be the truth. It requires the wildest imagination to see the animals in the sky.

It takes in the neighborhood of 25,000 years for one

zodiac to revolve within the other. For our purposes, we are concerned only with the facts as we find them. Even if we were making our measurements within the wrong zodiac, the results would not be affected within one individual's life span. In fact, it is not impossible that our invisible measuring sphere might be nothing other than the magnetic field of the earth. If this were true, it might mean that the position of the magnetic field of the earth is governed by the sun. The zodiac may be something close at hand, something within which the earth rotates. The relevant fact is that when we compared our advertising-result figures with the lunar cycle as it relates to the equinoctial signs of the zodiac, we obtained an interesting result.

On that particular day in 1940 when I finally picked up the experiment where I had left off in 1938, and tabulated the number of orders received while the moon was in each sign of the zodiac, the moon had revolved around the earth about 26 times since we had begun tabulating the results. Before presenting the figures, I wish to point out that there are some legitimate objections to this experiment that were not taken into account, but it must be remembered that at the time when this experiment was conducted, we were on a fishing expedition. We did not know exactly what we were seeking. We were groping in the dark. We had taken a wild shot. The probability that it would hit the mark and bring forth some new truths was remote.

One objection to this experiment lies in the fact that we did not allow for the fact that no mail is received on Sundays, and that mail, as a result, is often very heavy on Mondays. We have some right to assume, however, that this factor will average itself out. The results seem to indicate that it did, for if it did not, there should be a peak at every third sign, and such a peak does not occur. The process of smoothing a curve would also tend to eliminate any defect of this nature. Let us admit, however, that there may have been some defects. We will later produce another experiment conducted under better and more controlled conditions. This first experiment is only a starting point. Its results constituted our first lead. Other tests followed, and we can view these other tests as we go from chapter to chapter

In the following table, we present the names of the twelve signs of the zodiac together with the number of orders received during the times when the moon was in each one of these signs, the figures are as follows:

Aries	434
Taurus	529
Gemini	457
Cancer	411
Leo	376
Virgo	415
Libra	338
Scorpio	336
Sagittarius	412
Capricorn	397
Aquarius	436
Pisces	422

It will be noted that the orders are not evenly distributed through the twelve divisions of space. Taurus has a total of 529, while Scorpio (the exact opposite point) has a total of only 336. Mean expectancy would be 413.5 since the total number of orders received was 4963. Taurus is 115.5 above mean expectancy, while Scorpio is 77.5 below. Fortunately, these figures were begun as the moon entered Aries, so that it was possible to conclude them as the moon left Pisces, and no fraction of a cycle was involved.

From a statistical point of view, would deviations of this magnitude be likely to occur by chance alone? Or do they indicate the operation of some causative factor? This is where the science of statistics and its mathematics becomes useful. .

There is a statistical formula for determining the answer to questions of this nature. But it should be pointed out that in the science of statistics, where we deal with the mathematical laws of probability, there is no absolute proof of anything. There is only relative proof. Theoretically, almost anything--or even anything-might happen by chance alone. We can often compute the odds against an occurrence being due to chance alone, but beyond that we are limited.

I sit at a typewriter. What are the odds against the possibility of the typewriter suddenly turning into a dog?

The materialistically-minded individual will be quick to say that this is an impossibility, and therefore the probability of the occurrence is zero.

A religious person might believe in the possibility of miracles, with the result that he might not accept the theoretical zero. He might say that the probability is an unknown number of ciphers following a decimal point with a "1" or other figure following the ciphers.

We cannot honestly accept the materialist's point of view, because materialism is a form of dogma. We must admit the possibility of all that we cannot prove impossible. Mathematically, we cannot prove that it is impossible for a typewriter to turn into a dog. Physically and biologically such an event appears far beyond the realms of possibility, but actually we can only prove that something is possible. We cannot prove that anything is impossible. In the end, we can furnish absolute proof of nothing, because we can penetrate neither eternity nor infinity. In the end, it is difficult to be absolute in saying that that which we prove is other than a matter of mind. It might be a dream. These are philosophical angles. They are far afield, but we bring them up, to drive home the point that all proof, even though mathematical, is relative. We have to make all acceptances with these possibilities in mind, and consequently all acceptances should be tentative. This is a Fortian principle.

It is possible for an event to happen regardless of the magnitude of the odds against its occurrence. This can be illustrated. Let us suppose that we have a billion and one cards in a sufficiently large container to hold that many. They are well mixed and churned up after which we blindly select one card from the total. The odds against our selecting that particular card were a billion to one. Yet, we select that card against these odds, proving that it is possible.

Coming back to the world in which we live, statistics give us a formula for determining whether statistical results are likely to be due to chance or whether they appear to indicate a causative factor. A familiar term in the study of statistics is Standard Deviation. The statistician usually begins to consider deviations from the mean as having some significance when they are larger than 2.5 times Standard Deviation. Of course that figure is an optional one. Personally, I do not like to take deviations too seriously until they are in the vicinity of 3 times Standard Deviation.

The Formulae for Standard Deviation in connection with a particular experiment for the kind we have at hand is to take the square root of three factors multiplied together: (1) Number of trials; (2) Probability of success; (3) Probability of failure.

By probability of success, we mean the probability of a thing happening in a given way, and by probability of failure, we mean the probability of its not happening in that given way.

The formula is mathematically expressed: $\sqrt{npq}$.

The "n" stands for number of trials, the "p" for probability of success, and the "q" for probability of failure.

When a particular order arrives in the mail, the probability of the moon being in the zodiacal sign, Taurus, for example, is 1/12, because there are 12 places where it could have been. We refer to this as the probability of success, so the probability of success is 1/12. On the other hand, the probability of failure is 11/12, because there are 11 other places where the moon could have been. In the experiment at hand, there was a total of 4963 orders--or trials. Thus, if we want to evaluate the deviation in Taurus, we find Standard Deviation by filling in actual figures in place of 'npq.' The actual figures will be 4963 X 1/12 X 11/12, which multiplied out is 379. Now, we take t-square root of this, which is approximately 19. For this experiment, Standard Deviation is 19. The observed deviation is 115.5. When we divide this figure by 19, we get an answer that is slightly greater than 6.

Our observed deviation is 6 times Standard Deviation, an extraordinary figure, and far above the necessary 2.5 or 3. The indication is that our figures are not due to chance alone.

More important, perhaps, is the fact that our figures appear to present a rather definite pattern. There is the indication of a cycle, because the figures around Taurus are also high, while the figures around Scorpio are low again. On either side of Taurus, we have Aries: 434 and Gemini: 457, as against the two signs on either side of Scorpio: Libra: 338 and Sagittarius: 412. The figures on one side of the zodiac are much higher than the figures on the other side of the zodiac. If we begin in Aquarius, as we do in the following table, we find that we have six high signs followed by six low signs. One half of the zodiac totals 2.689, while the other half totals 2,274. In the following table, the signs in the second column are in exact opposition to those in the first column. Leo is the sign opposite Aquarius, Pisces is the sign opposite Virgo, etc. In each instance, the sign in the first column shows a greater figure than that sign opposite to it in the second column. Note:

Aquarius	436	Leo	376
Pisces	422	Virgo	415
Aries	434	Libra	338
Taurus	529	Scorpio	316
Gemini	457	Sagittarius	412
Cancer	411	Capricorn	397
Total	**2689**	**Total**	**2274**

Column shows an excess of 207.5 above mean expectancy. In this instance, Standard Deviation will be the square root of: (4963 X 1/2 X 1/2) or 35. Our observed deviation is 5.9 times

Standard Deviation, another important and significant figure

We will now smooth this curve that is displaying itself. This can be done by averaging each figure with the ones on either side of it. We can express our action thus: A+B+C divided by 3. This process is also known as applying a 3-moving-average. A moving-average will help to take chance fluctuations out of a curve, assuming that they are chance fluctuations. In this new set of figures, to get the new figure for Pisces, for example, we will add the 436 of Aquarius to the 422 of Pisces and the 434 of Aries, for a total of 1292, which when divided by 3 will give us 43.1 (approximately).

In the following table, we see these figures after they have been placed on a 3- moving-average.

Aries	462
Taurus	473
Gemini	466
Cancer	415
Leo	401
Virgo	376
Libra	363
Scorpio	362
Sagittarius	382
Capricorn	415
Aquarius	418
Pisces	431

It will now be noticed that we have a peak in Taurus and that each sign declines thereafter until we reach the opposite extreme, Scorpio. Then, each sign rises until we are back in Taurus. We drop for six signs, and then we rise for six signs. This becomes more apparent when we place our figures from this last table on a graph. Graph "A" illustrates the point. At the top of the graph are the symbols for the signs of the zodiac, beginning with Aries and ending with Pisces.

"Graph "A" was our first real suggestion that there might actually be a connection between the cycle of the Moon and the cycle of the mail order business. At this point, however, there were many possible objections. If some other cycle conformed very closely to the cycle of the Moon, we might be dealing with that cycle, and our figures might be fooling us. For example, the cycle of the Sun turning on its axis is very close to the same time that it takes the Moon to make this trip around the earth. We had some figures that appeared to mean something, but we could not be too certain of what they meant.

Another thing that puzzled and interested the writer was the fact that the peak of the cycle came with the Moon in Taurus. Why Taurus? It happens that the Sun was in Taurus when the writer was born. Would the cycle be different for some other person? These figures were based on a business that the writer owned personally. As an individual, he was most affected. The manner in which the orders came in affected his income. Would a Scorpio person have the peak in Scorpio--the exact opposite point?

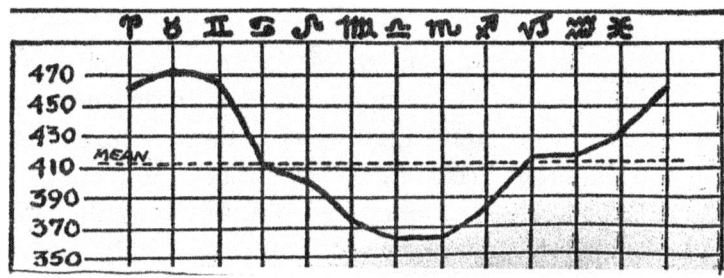

Graph A

There followed a period of general observation. What happened when the Moon passed the opposite area? Many notes were kept. It seemed that a person born in winter was at his best when the Moon was in the winter area of the zodiac, and that this was the negative area for people born in the summer. It seemed that people's luck and judgment were better when the Moon passed through their Sun signs. It appeared that many people were unstable when the Moon was at the opposite extreme from the position of the Sun at the time of their births.

This involves a peculiar factor, one that may be difficult for some to understand, but one very familiar to the astrologers of ancient and modem times.

Why should the longitudinal position of the Sun or any other solar body at birth be of any significance at some later time when the object is no longer there? It suggests the past existing in the present. We have a somewhat similar condition with the camera. The shutter opens and closes. The past is gone, but on the sensitive plate inside the camera, the past exists as it was. We might say that the shadow of the past remains.

Actually, since unknown antiquity, the astrologers have been using time as if it were a fourth dimension of space. They have made their measurements from the position of a body in space at one given time (the present) to the position of a body in space at another time (date of birth) just as if both moments of time were simultaneously existent. Thus, the conception of time as a fourth dimension of space existed several thousands of years before the birth of Albert Einstein or any other modern scientist.

The fact that we cannot understand a fact or a phenomenon does not mean that it is non-existent, although many academic scientists assume that anything they do not understand is non-existent. Charles Fort demonstrated, during his life-time, that a great many scientists, and particularly astronomers, have claimed as nonexistent anything they did not understand, or anything that did not conform to their preconceived or orthodox conclusions. Pre-conceived conclusions (theories) that become orthodox acceptances are a barrier to progress and prevent discoveries, because they prevent or obstruct honest investigation.

At a later date, another experiment, based on data taken from the same business as that considered in this chapter, was conducted, and under more favorable conditions. This first experiment had not been planned carefully. It was merely a fishing expedition. The results were unexpected. The conditions under which it was conducted are somewhat subject to criticism. In the later experiment, there was the opportunity to guard against such conditions. It was possible to consider them in advance. However, the results of this experiment first caused the writer to begin work on an entirely different kind of an experiment, and it is the story of this new and different piece of research that will be discussed in the next chapter.

Let us draw conclusion only with the greatest of caution. We have witnessed an experiment. We have found that orders received in the mail did not arrive with an even flow. We found that they arrived with greater frequency while the Moon was on one side of the zodiac than when it was on the other side.

It is improbable that this was due to chance alone, because deviations are greater than we would expect to happen by chance. Was the Moon, in some unknown way, the causative factor? Was there some other causative factor, and is it a matter of chance that our results fit into the pattern of what we might expect in the event that the Moon might be the causative factor? This is a point that we must watch carefully. Some other cycle might accidentally coincide quite closely to that of the Moon, and it might take a considerable time for the two cycles to draw apart. We have an indication, and we must make further tests.

A CONTROLLED EXPERIMENT

We are proud to bring to our readers, chapter by chapter, this distinguished and rigidly scientific demonstration of the influence of cycles on the affairs of humankind. Mr. Tobey, whose Astro-statistics have attracted the attention of men of science, has brought to the compilation and writing of this work the same undeviating accuracy, patience, and fidelity to observed and tabulated fact that has won him a place of foremost importance among the investigators of cyclic phenomena. This book, for which publication is planned in the not-too-distant future, is another milestone in scientific astrology, sure to awaken widespread interest. Readers of THE ASTROLOGER are privileged to see it first.

When our first experiment, described in Chapter 2, was conducted, we were following a hit or miss technique, hoping that we might learn something of value. Now, we had a definite conception of a cycle, and we set forth to put it to a carefully prepared test. We made a marked departure from our first experiment. We decided to test whether a person is more likely to spend money at one time of the lunar month than at another time. We reasoned that if a person is more prosperous at one time of the month, that will be the time when that person will be most likely to spend money.

A wealthy man might spend five or ten dollars as easily when things were not going his way, but the majority of people are not wealthy. Many live from hand to mouth, spending their money as rapidly as they obtain it. We wanted to know whether people born in the summer spend their money more freely when the moon passes through the summer section of the zodiacal belt or whether those born in winter spend their money more freely as the moon travels through the winter section of the heavens, whether people in general spend their money more freely when the moon passes through the zodiacal sign occupied by the sun at the time of birth.

If we make a test with a large enough number of people, and that group includes some wealthy people, these persons may not be particularly affected, but if the others are affected in their spending, and the group is large enough, the effect upon those who are affected should show in the totals. For a test of this kind, one advantage of the statistical method lies in the fact that an "influence" can be detected, no matter how infinitesimal, provided a large enough sample of trials is examined. Theoretically, although you can go to infinity insofar as the smallness of the "influence" is concerned, you can also go to infinity insofar as the magnitude of the number of trials is concerned. If you are dealing with a very strong influence, a small number of trials may be sufficient to detect it, but if you are dealing with a slight influence, a tendency, then a very large number of trials may be necessary for detection.

Suppose that only ten percent of the people are influenced, in the spending of their money, by the time when they receive money. In an experiment embodying a large enough sample of trials, this ten percent would make itself known by deflecting the totals involving all of the people. Thus, if only some of the people spend their money soon after they receive it, and are thus affected by the lunar cycle, in a large enough number of trials, the effect of their action would become visible.

In this experiment, every trial relates to a different person, and in most cases a different moment of time. Each trial is completely separate and independent of every other trial. From the statistical point of view, they are separate and independent events. They have no relation to each other, and no trial is in any way affected by any other trial. This was not true of the first experiment discussed in Chapter 2, because all trials had a relationship to one individual. We rule out the possibility that we might be dealing with a characteristic of a single individual.

If you were examining a graph, ordinarily, it might be easy to mistake a 27.5 day cycle for a 28-day cycle. An advantage of this experiment lies in the fact that such an error cannot be made. If we find evidence of a cycle, it cannot be mistaken for some other cycle, this is because no single trial has any relation to any other trial. We test for a cycle of a definite length, corresponding with the motion of the moon, and our result has to be either positive or negative.

We divided our experiment into four equal parts that they might be compared with each other. Each experiment consisted of 1200 trials, for a total of 4800 trials. We accumulated 4800 letters written to several publishers by customers ordering astrological material, each letter furnishing the birth date of the individual customer. Each envelope was postmarked, and this postmark enabled us to determine the approximate time when it was mailed. We were enabled to calculate the position of the sun at the time of each customer's birth. We could calculate the position of the moon at the time when the letter was mailed, and calculate the distance of arc in the plane of the ecliptic, from the first position to the second position. Each letter contained money and represented a purchase. A customer had parted from some of his money, usually five dollars, but the range was from three to twenty-five dollars.

Where each individual trial is concerned, we measure the distance of arc from the sun on the day of the customer's birth to the moon at the time when he parted with his money by mail. The moon goes around in a circle. We divide this circle into twelve equal parts. If only chance factors are involved, the moon is as likely to be in one of these segments of space as another. In a large number of trials, we should get fairly equal distribution. We use the signs of the zodiac for purposes of measurement and convenience.

If, on the day when the order was mailed, the moon was in the same zodiacal sign as the sun on the day of the customer's birth, the order was recorded as having the moon in the first segment of space. If it was one zodiacal sign past this point, it was recorded as being in the second segment of space, etc. Thus, if the moon was around to the zodiacal sign previous to the sign occupied by the sun at the time of the customer's birth, it was recorded as being in the twelfth segment of space.

We present a table showing the results of the four separate parts of this experiment, each part being made up of 1200 trials, and we present the totals for the 4800 trials. The four separate experiments can be compared, in order that we may see whether the cycle appears to be operating in each experiment.

In the first column of the table, we have the 12 space segments listed from 1 to 12. In the next four columns, we have the frequency with which the moon appeared in each of the twelve segments of space. The last column represents the totals of the four separate experiments.

POSITION OF MOON WHEN PURCHASES WERE MADE

Space Segment	First Test	Second Test	Third Test	Fourth Test	Total* Four Tests
1	115	110	113	108	446
2	110	108	101	111	430
3	115	97	82	110	404
4	101	96	85	115	397
5	98	92	116	99	405
6	91	97	95	83	366
7	94	100	100	92	386
8	90	106	100	98	394
9	81	90	102	89	362
10	95	100	102	98	395
11	104	100	100	89	393
12	106	104	104	108	422
TOTAL	1200	1200	1200	1200	4800

There are a great many pitfalls in passing statistical judgment, as only the experienced statistician knows, and I want to point out the peculiar part the elements of "chance" can play in work of this kind. Of course, no one really knows what he means when he uses the term "chance." It is a word to fill in a gap. It is the unknown. There is something we do not understand, something we cannot explain, and so, we give it a name. We call it "chance." Having done so, we understand it no better. We have merely identified it. Perhaps we should refer to it as the sum of all unknown factors.

If we look at our first test of 1200 cases, we find that the third space-segment scored 115, equal to the high of any segment. If we look at the third test of 1200, we find that this segment scored 82, the low of all segments. Insofar as this segment is concerned, the first and third tests deny each other's testimony. Thus, it would have been dangerous to pass judgment on either of these figures. To a statistician and his standards of measurement, however, neither figure by itself held statistical significance, and he would not have been misled. For a single figure from one of these space segments to hold statistical significance in a test of 1200 trials, there would have to be a deviation of about 24 from the mean. Our greatest deviation in four tests is 19.

Although we are going to draw positive conclusions from these figures, the above facts indicate that 1200 trials are not a sufficient number for the detection of an influence of the magnitude with which we are dealing. We can make use of tests of that size when we have a series of them that we can compare.

As we look at these figures, there is very definite evidence of our lunar cycle in these several tests. We can see it best by comparing the 12th, 1st and 2nd segments with the opposite segments, the 6th, 7th and 8th. The 12th, 1st and 2nd segments are the top of the cycle, while the 6th, 7th and 8th are the bottom. The 6th is opposite the 12th. The 7th is opposite the 1st, and the 8th is opposite the 2nd.

In each and every instance, a segment at the top of the cycle scores higher than the segment opposite. There is 1 chance in 2 of this being the case if no lunar cycle is operating. In the four tests, the 12th segment is above the 6th each time by the following scores: 106 to 91; 104 to 97; 104 to 95; 108 to 83. The 1st segment is above the 7th by these scores: 115 to 94; 110 to 100; 113 to 100; 108 to 92. The 2nd segment scores above the 8th in the following manner: 110 to 90; 108 to 106; 101 to 100; 111 to 98.

The probability of this being due to chance alone is 1 divided by (2 carried to its 12th power). In other words, there is 1 chance in 4096 that this result is a matter of chance.

In the totals, the 12th scores 422 against 366 in the 6th; the 1st scores 446 against 386 in the 7th; and the 2nd scores 430 against 394 in the 8th. The three high segments score 1298 against 1146 in the low segments opposite. The excess of 98 in the high segment is much greater than the deficiency of 54 in the opposite segments. The deficiency is distributed over a greater area than is the excess. The excess seems to be more concentrated.

We can evaluate this excess of 98. Standard Deviation (explained in Chapter 2) will be the square root of: (4800 x .25 x .75), or 30. The excess deviation of 98 is 3.26 times Standard Deviation, which is definitely considered as being of statistical significance. When we link together this experiment with that described in Chapter 2, our results begin to assume broad significance. In that experiment, if we refer to the 12th, 1st and 2nd space-segments (in that case, Aries, Taurus and Gemini), we have an excess or plus deviation of 179. Standard Deviation will be the square root of (4963 x .25 x .25) or approximately 31. The observed deviation of 179 is about 5.8 times Standard Deviation. If we add the two experiments together, we have a deviation that is 6.4 times Standard Deviation. These are figures that no scientist or statistician can dare ignore if he is to retain his honesty.

Each separate test of the four tests in our second experiment covered in this chapter does definitely tend to confirm the existence of the lunar cycle.

When we completed our first test in Chapter 2, we placed our figures on a three-moving-average. Let us do the same with these figures, in order to determine whether we will find the same kind of a curve.

**MOON POSITION AT PURCHASE
TIME ON 3-MOVING-AVERAGE**

Space Segment	First Test	Second Test	Third Test	Fourth Test	Total Four Test
1	110	107	106	109	432
2	113	105	99	110	427
3	109	100	89	112	410
4	105	95	94	108	402
5	97	95	99	99	389
6	94	96	104	91	386
7	92	101	98	91	382
8	88	99	101	93	381
9	89	99	101	95	384
10	93	97	101	92	383
11	102	101	102	98	403
12	108	105	106	102	420

Our two experiments have produced similar curves, with the apex at the same point. The second shows a flatter bottom. This fact also may be of future significance.

If we look at our smoothed figures in the above 3-moving-average table, we find that in each of the four parts of the experiment, the apex is always on the side toward the 1st space-segment, never on the opposite side. In our totals in the last column of the second table in this chapter, we find that quite a definite curve is in evidence. A test of 1200 trials is rather small for an "influence" of the size of that with which we appear to be dealing. We can get a better picture if we compare the results of the first two tests with the second two tests. This gives us 2400 trials which we may compare with a separate and independent 2400 trials. First we must combine the figures in the following table:

ACTUAL FIGURES

SPACE SEGMENT	1ST & 2ND TESTS	3RD & 4TH TESTS
1	225	221
2	218	212
3	212	192
4	197	200
5	190	215
6	188	178
7	194	192
8	196	198
9	171	191
10	195	200
11	204	189
12	213	212

It should be noted that in the smoothed figures headed "3-Moving Average", any segment that is above the mean (200) in the first column is above the mean in the second column, while any segment that is below the mean in the first column is below the mean in the second column. There is but one chance in 4096 of this being due to chance. The figures in the first column closely parallel those in the second column, never being more than 9 apart, while there is a range of 30 between the high and low figures in the first column, and a range of 26 in the second column.

A better conception of the manner in which the first 2400 trials compare with the second 2400 trials may be obtained if we look at these smoothed figures on the last graph shown.

3DAY-MOVING AVERAGE

SPACE SEGMENT	1ST &2ND TESTS	3RD &4TH TESTS
1	217	215
2	218	209
3	209	201
4	200	202
5	192	198
6	190	195
7	193	189
8	187	194
9	188	196
10	190	193
11	203	200
12	213	208

The eye can now see that the two lines representing the two separate and independent groups of 2400 trials compare very favorably. The two lines run a close parallel. Nor is this graph very far removed in its appearance from that presented in Chapter 2 in Graph "A".

In one test, we found that a man's business was better when the Moon passed through the area of the heavens occupied by the Sun at the time of that man's birth. In a second test, we found a tendency for people to spend their money more freely when the Moon passed through that area occupied by the Sun at the time of each individual's birth.

Speaking from general observation, it has appeared that there are definite times when this lunar cycle does not function, and if an experiment happened to be made, with even a large number of trials, involving such an interval, a negative result might follow. This cycle does not appear to be as simple as our graphs might indicate. By using a large number of samples, it is possible that our tests have averaged out and hidden the existence of certain "interferences" which we believe to exist. In statistical studies, when you find a cycle, it is the exception to the rule which can lead you to your next discovery. **Other experience has convinced us that there are specific times when the lunar cycle fails. We want to know why. One possibility is interference from a solar cycle.** We will discuss that possibility in the next chapter. Another possibility is that the lunar cycle may not function when the Sun is near, or at right angles to, one of the Moon's nodes.

The nodes of the Moon are points in space where the Moon crosses the ecliptic. They move clockwise, and completely circle the zodiacal belt in an interval of a little less than 19 years. Solar and lunar eclipses can only occur at the time of the year when the Sun is near one of the Moon's nodes, with the result that they will occur a little earlier each year. The period from the time the Sun crosses one of the Moon's nodes until it crosses it again is approximately 346 days, or 19 days under a year. We will have reason to consider this 346-day cycle later. Bear in mind that the nodes of the Moon move clockwise, while the Moon and planets move in the opposite direction.

Our first experiment was a fairly accurate prediction of what was to take place in our second experiment, and the first half of our second experiment was an excellent prediction of what happened in the second half. If we can determine just when the lunar cycle temporarily ceases to function, our whole subject will hold greater possibilities of prediction. General observations have led us to believe that the cycle works more drastically sometimes than on other occasions, and that it occasionally becomes inverted for a short interval, throwing a peak exactly where a depression should be. In spite of these short intervals, which have not been eliminated from our totals, the overall picture produces a definite curve that corresponds with lunar motion. We are anxious to know whether a solar cycle interferes with the lunar cycle, as is the case where ocean tides are concerned, and whether the cyclic Sun-nodal relationship interferes with the lunar cycle. In future chapters, the reader will find that these considerations will arise again.

POSSIBLE CYCLIC INTERFERENCE

General observation has caused us to suspect that there are intervals or periods when the lunar cycle is completely thrown out of line, and when it fails to function temporarily. We have certain suspicions as to when these times may be. They are three in number. We will list them:

1--Near the time of the Full Moon.
2--When the Sun is angular (conjunct or square) to the nodes of the Moon.
3--Six months after an individual's birthday.

In connection with the Full Moon, in going through the correspondence of publishers, we long noted that there appeared to be an excess of orders from people who ordered astrological literature around the time of their birth dates. Originally, no attempt was made to investigate this matter, because we assumed it to be caused by the fact that the individual is conscious of the time of the birth date. Habit and custom cause a person to celebrate his birth date. We assumed that people order astrological literature in anticipation of another year of life ahead.

Although high ocean tides follow the Moon, they are higher at the New Moon. We decided to try and determine whether a solar as well as lunar cycle might be involved in our tests, and whether one might interfere with the other.

Following the same procedure followed in our other tests, we tabulated 3600 cases. Instead of using the position of the Moon at the time of the postmark on each envelope and comparing it with the Sun position at the time of birth, we used the position of the Sun at the time of the postmark on each envelope, and compared it with the Sun-position at the time of birth. By this procedure, we were actually testing how much people ordering astrological literature are influenced by the birth date, whether they are influenced consciously or unconsciously. Our 3600 cases were divided into three separate tests of 1200 cases each. We present a table showing the results of the three separate parts of this experiment, each part being made up of

1200 trials, and we present the totals for the 3600 trials. The three separate experiments can be compared. In the first column of the table, we have the 12 space segments listed from 1 to 12. In the next three columns, we have the frequency with which the Sun appeared in each of the twelve segments of space. The last column represents the totals of the three separate experiments.

POSITION OF SUN WHEN PURCHASES WERE MADE

Space Segment	First Test	Second Test	Third Test	Total Three Tests
1	114	121	95	330
2	121	102	96	319
3	113	104	109	326
4	88	106	115	309
5	92	87	89	268
6	81	103	105	289
7	97	101	103	301
8	87	104	101	292
9	95	107	92	294
10	111	82	99	292
11	86	90	100	276
12	115	93	96	304
TOTAL	1200	1200	1200	3600

SUN POSITION AT PURCHASING TIME ON 3-MOVING AVERAGE

Space Segment	First Test	Second Test	Third Test	Total Three Tests
1	117	105	96	318
2	116	109	100	325
3	107	104	107	318
4	98	99	104	301
5	87	99	103	289
6	90	97	99	286
7	88	103	103	294
8	93	104	99	296
9	98	98	97	292
10	97	93	97	287
11	104	88	98	291
12	105	101	97	303
TOTAL	1200	1200	1200	3600

There are rather wide differences in our three tests, but in the totals, the tendency to purchase near the birth date is definitely to be detected. It may be best for us to place these figures on a 3-moving average as we have done with all other tests. It is important that we ultimately determine whether we are dealing with a factor caused by habit and custom, in other words a conscious process, or an unconscious process. The average individual knows when his birth date will occur. He does not know the position of the Moon at the time when he decides to mail an order. In our next table, we present these same figures placed on a 3-moving average.

While there is still considerable in the way of conflict when our three tests are compared, the totals show a definite tendency for an excess of orders near the birth date. One of the important things we wanted to know was whether this excess was spread out, or whether it was concentrated near the birth date. It appears to be well spread out. We have a five-month period that is above normal, and a seven-month period that is below normal. The picture becomes clearer if we look at Graph "C", where the figures in the above table are illustrated. This graph suggests that the excess near the birth date may not be something that is attributable to conscious action. It may be subconscious. A man might be influenced by knowledge of his birth date near the time of his birth date, but it is doubtful whether he would be so-influenced over a five-month period. For example, would a man be likely to purchase in August because his birthday is in the month of May?

If we look at the lower section of our line in Graph "C", we find a bump in the bottom of our curve, as if a second minor peak were attempting to show itself at the half-way mark. We cannot be sure of this yet, until more cases are available. This may or may not be a chance factor. It might indicate a tendency for there to be a secondary purchase period approximately six months after the birth date.

Our main peak is not exactly in the birth-month period. It comes one month after the birthday, but this too might possibly be a factor of chance. A larger sample might bring the peak to the exact birthday month. This, we do not know. We do find a similar apparent cycle that is similar to our lunar cycle curves, and we have the very definite possibility that a solar cycle may interfere with the lunar cycle. If this is the case, we may find that at the full of the Moon, when the earth is between the Sun and Moon, these two cycles maybe fighting or opposing each other. This would explain why the lunar cycle might not function as well at the time of the Full Moon as at other times. We might also point out that the ratio of deviation found in our solar-cycle experiment is not too far removed from that found in connection with our lunar-cycle experiment in Chapter 3. Statistical values would not be too different. In fact, they are very similar.

If the lunar cycle and the solar cycle are opposed to each other at the full of the Moon, the result might be for each to level off the other, or for one influence to cancel the other, with the result that no effect whatsoever might be visible at such a time.

This is not the case with the ocean tides, however. When the Sun and Moon are on opposite sides of the earth, a tide is lifted on each side of the earth and water moves away at the mid-points in between. However, when both the Sun and Moon are on the same side of the earth, there is still a high tide on the opposite side of the earth as well as on the Sun-Moon side. Physicists explain this by saying that the Sun and Moon pull the water from the earth on the side toward the Sun-Moon, and pull the earth away from the water on the side opposite the Sun-Moon.

If we compare the figures in Chapter 3 with those presented in this chapter, we find that with both the solar and lunar cycle, the area just past the birth-Sun point shows a greater excess deviation than the area preceding.

At the beginning of this chapter, we mentioned three types of interval when the lunar cycle does not appear to function.

If there is a solar cycle of type indicated, this cycle would explain two of the three mentioned times when we suspect that the lunar cycle fails to function. Not only might a solar cycle cause interference at the time of the Full Moon, but the high point in the lunar cycle, six months after the birthday, would be at the Full Moon. Thus, two out of three of our listed times when the lunar cycle may not function may be explained by the possible existence of a solar cycle, an individual solar cycle rather than a seasonal solar cycle. At a later point in this work, we will discuss the possibility of additional interference having to do with the Moon's nodes and their relation to the Sun.

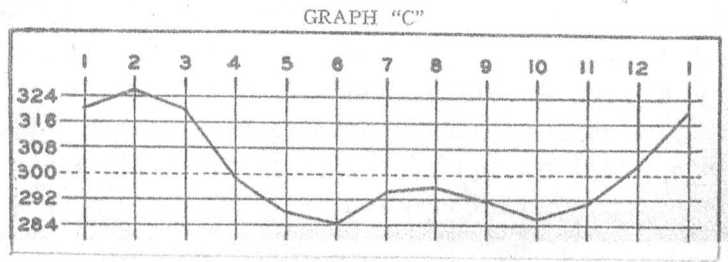

Graph C

It should not be assumed, that because we have mentioned three specific times when we suspect that the lunar cycle does not work, there are no other such times. There maybe many other interferences, but determining these factors is slow and tedious work. They must be taken one at a time. There may be more than one lunar cycle, and the ultimate effect may be the result of a series of lunar cycles which fit together in complex form. Our early preliminary experiments appeared to rule out the possibility of a New Moon cycle, but we may have to come back and consider this further. It is possible that we discarded some of our early experimental data before we gave it proper consideration, because it must be realized that when we originally began this work, and when we had no positive results to guide us, we were floundering. We have now reached a point where we have statistically significant results, and with this foundation, our work must continue in many directions. Ultimately, we must go much further, and even test the possibility of planetary interferences, but at this writing, that would appear to be far in the future, because it will probably take years of work to iron out eccentricities that are brought about by corresponding eccentricities in lunar and apparent solar motion. As we go forward with this work, we are partly guided by our efforts to make our findings useful. We will have much more to say about this practical side of the work in future chapters. Thus far, we have conducted three experiments, which we will refer to as "A", "B", and "C".

We have found that our figures indicate that people spend more money when either the Moon or the Sun is near the position, in the heavens, that was occupied by the Sun at the time of birth.

In one case, we found that money came more easily under similar circumstances, and we assume that these factors are, in some unknown way, linked together. We assume that people spend their money when they have it to spend. We are faced with the fact that this might be more true of poor people than of rich people. We are building up to the hypothesis that people's luck and skill may be affected by the position of the Moon, that a person's stability may be affected, that the unconscious processes of the mind and body may be affected, but there is more evidence to be unfolded.

These experiments are being presented, more or less in the order of their occurrence, because in this kind of a presentation, the reader may better understand why we followed the procedure that was followed. In some respects we will violate this rule, but only for the purpose of dividing experiments dealing with individual action from data dealing with mass action.

In one respect, our procedure is the reverse of that followed by the astrologers, particularly the ancient astrologers. They attempted to understand the parts by first gaining a philosophical understanding of the whole. Any defects in the philosophy of the whole could throw everything out of gear. This was a weakness of the ancient astrology. Some astrologers adopted a philosophy of fatalism, and this colored their entire realm of investigation. Others adopted the philosophy of the church, and this colored their ultimate findings. In each instance, a prejudice formed a part of the foundation, and prevented a clear fact-finding investigation. All of this was in addition to the fact that the ancients did not have the tools that we are using. The science of statistics had not yet been born. It is through this new science of statistics and its mathematical principles that we hope to find out a part of the truth. The whole is too vast for us to hope to approach it. We are not making our approach with any preconceived conclusions. We are investigating· the facts, and we, will accept them as we find them. In such an investigation, it may be necessary for us to alter our views many times as we go along, and as we have heretofore stated, all of our conclusions will be accepted tentatively, with possible future adjustments.

TIMING ADVERTISING

From a practical point of view, knowledge of the lunar cycle might prove very valuable to the advertising business. Cycles are very important where advertising is concerned. A ski resort would not plan to advertise in the summer. The owners know in advance that there will be no snow. They are familiar with the annual cycle and its effects upon the weather. Advertising agencies have men skilled in the art of copywriting. Good copy pulls better than poor copy. Even so, there is much more to the advertising business than good copy. You see a product well-advertised today. It is highly successful. There comes a day when you see the ads no more. The cycle is over. People have stopped buying that product.

I recall an occasion when I ran an ad for the first time and it did not pull very well. Several months later, the same copy was run again. For some strange reason, it pulled very well. The difference in pulling power had nothing to do with the copy, which was the same. What caused the difference? Advertising people have to tune in on the temporary whims of the masses. There are fads.

A friend had been making some experiments with some direct mail advertising. We discussed his experience. He had records of each mailing, and he allowed me to copy from his books the date and cost of each mailing together with the resultant financial return. His records showed 38 different mailings. We computed the return that he received per dollar of expense incurred in connection with each mailing. There was a range from 56 cents to $4.82. The 56 cent figure meant that he lost 44 cents out of every dollar that he spent. The $4.82 figure meant that he made a profit of $3.82 for every dollar spent on that particular mailing. Of course, out of this had to come the cost of the product sold, with which we are not here concerned.

Considering the birth date of the friend who made the mailing, I arranged the figures according to the position of the moon at the time when the mailings were made. The figures thus obtained are presented herewith, and we again follow the same procedure we have followed thus far, splitting the heavens into twelve equal segments of space. In the following table, we show the number of mailings made with the moon in each one of these segments. We show the ratio of return per dollar spent, and we show the same figures on a 3-moving average, as we have done with all other experiments. We will call this experiment "D". The figures follow:

EXPERIMENT "D"

Space Segment	Number of Mailings	Ratio of Return	Ratio on a 3 Moving Average
1	2	3.90	3.60
2	4	2.80	2.85
3	4	1.87	2.57
4	5	3.03	1.89
5	4	.78	2.59
6	3	3.97	1.93
7	3	1.03	2.18
8	4	1.53	1.10
9	3	.75	2.37
10	2	4.82	2.04
11	2	.56	3.16
12	2	4.10	2.85

Now let us see what happens when we place the last column of figures on a graph.

In presenting these figures, we present them for what they may be worth. Actually, they do not lend themselves to statistical analysis. The number of trials is too small. It is just a matter of seeing whether the results conform to the general idea of a lunar cycle as we have been finding it. The above graph indicates that they do. The general curve of the lunar cycle is clearly visible. The apex is exactly where it should be. The bottom of the curve is within one segment of where we would expect it. In a small sample, we cannot expect more than this. There are many firms in the business of direct mail advertising, and it would not be difficult for them to submit our views to broader tests. Knowledge thus obtained might actually be of great value to them. It would be very important to a businessman if he could know that advertising done at a given time might have a dead response, while advertising done at some later time might have a live response. Large advertising agencies might find it profitable to conduct further research along similar lines.

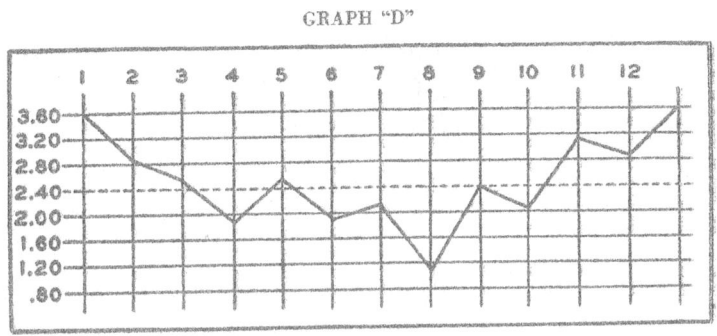

Graph D

It may not seem rational to think that a man born in the summer may be able to gain a better advertising return by advertising when the moon is in the summer section of the zodiac. Neither television nor moving pictures would seem rational to a man born in the year 1700. It is unwise to try and rule out what does not appear rational. Reasoning is often in error. We have now had two experiments that offered evidence that advertising return may be affected by the motion of the moon. With the millions upon millions of dollars that are spent in advertising each year, a method that could time favorable advertising return in advance would be of tremendous value. It might play a part in reducing sales costs.

There is a difference between the experiment presented in this chapter and that discussed in Chapter 2. The experiment in Chapter 2 showed a tendency for advertising return to be higher at the apex of the lunar cycle, while the test explained in this chapter appeared to indicate that mail sent out at the apex of the lunar cycle produced a greater overall return.

From this, we might draw the assumption that any firm doing direct mail advertising could gain greater return per dollar expended by spacing mailings approximately four weeks apart, so that each sales endeavor was timed to go into the mail at the apex of the cycle for the person owning the business.

You may think of the question: Suppose two men born six months apart are in the direct mail advertising business as partners, how will the lunar cycle act for this business? To such a question, we will have to fall back on the technique of public officials, and reply, no comment at this time. We do not know the answer to the question. One would have to find two such partners in such a business and make a test.

SKILL AND LUCK

Bowling is a game of skill. A good bowler gains plenty of practice and has rules that he follows religiously, and yet, elements of luck--for want of a better word--play an important part.

A group of us were watching a good bowler who was having an unusual night. He was scoring very high. At one point, he bent over to the writer and said, "It doesn't make any difference how I hit them tonight; they just fall down".

His statement may have been exaggerated, but everyone recognized that he was having a "good night". A great many people believe that they have good and bad days, and they go to strange lengths sometimes in an effort to find the answer. Yet, even if they go to the weirdest forms of superstition, they are more scientific when they search for an answer than the reactionary, so-called scientist, who merely shakes his head and says, "Tommy-rot".

Getting back to bowling, I have heard men say, "If you hit them right, they go down."

That may be, but they also go clown a great many times when you do not hit them right, and there are plenty of hits that are perfect insofar as the eye can detect when the pins do not all go down. The very best any bowler can do is hit them right *insofar as the eye can detect.*

I have seen a good many strikes occur when the headpin was missed, and on one occasion, I saw a girl's ball touch only the number 10 pin (last pin to the right in the back row), and she made a strike.

With five very poor hits, one evening, I made five consecutive strikes. The pins were falling down almost regardless of how I hit them. These things are the exception and not the rule, but they can be the factors that win or lose close games. I think the element of "luck" is greater than most experts like to concede.

I kept a record of my own bowling games over a period of time. I am not a good bowler, but that will make no difference in this discussion. I accumulated the scores of 443 games. I wanted to know' whether the lunar cycle would have anything to do with my high and low scores.

Dates of games were carefully recorded, and ultimately the scores were mapped out in accord with the position of the Moon at the time when each game was bowled. As in previous experiments, the lunar path was divided into twelve space segments, the first being the zodiacal sign occupied by the Sun at the time of my own birth. Oddly, when the following table is viewed, it will be noticed that no games were ever bowled when the Moon was in the 4th space-segment. One thing or another always prevented me from going bowling when the Moon was in that position. Sometimes, I was just busy with other matters. At other times, I wasn't in the mood. Some time, I hope to bowl with the Moon in that segment so that the record can be complete. The fact that out of 443 games, none was bowled with the Moon in this space-segment is something that I cannot explain.

In 443 games, 62,330 pins were knocked down. This is an average of 140.7 per game. In good bowling company, these would not be scores to write about, but this is not a book about bowling and bowling is not our topic. For our purposes, these scores are as good as a 240 average.

We will call this experiment "E". The following table shows the number of games bowled with the Moon in each space-segment, the number of pins knocked down, the average number of pins knocked down per game, and these same pins-per-game figures on a 3-movingaverage. Let us look at the table.

EXPERIMENT "E"

SPACE SEGMENT	GAMES	PINS	AVERAGE	3-MOVING AVERAGE
1	6	983	164.	150.5
2	44	6522	148.2	151.0
3	54	7601	140.7	144.2
4	00			*
5	25	3597	143.8	139.0
6	56	7422	132.5	135.9
7	13	1707	131.3	133.3
8	55	7481	136.	136.0
9	41	5774	140.8	142.8
10	38	5763	151.6	144.0
11	60	8379	139.6	143.5
12	51	7101	139.2	147.6

* The absence of any figure in the 4th space-segment made it necessary to ignore this space in computing the 3-moving-average. The 3rd, 5th and 6th are averaged instead of the 4th, 5th and 6th.

EXPERIMENT "E"

If we look at the figures in the last column, it is hardly necessary to place them on a graph. They produce a curve that is almost perfectly in accord with all of our other curves. The apex is in the 2nd space-segment, but it is only half a point from the 1st segment. The bottom of the curve is exactly in the 7th segment, where it should be.

I tried very hard to get my scores up when the Moon was at the bottom of this cycle. I couldn't do it. I don't know whether my skill or my luck is better when the Moon is at the apex of this cycle, but something is better. The pins fall down.

There is the question as to whether I might have been unconsciously influenced by my own knowledge of the lunar cycle. Within myself, I cannot take this point seriously, but we will have another experiment involving a person who was not conscious of the lunar cycle. First, however, let us have a graph of the above results.

A lady took up bowling. I asked her to keep a record of her scores and the dates when they were made. A considerable time later, she gave me a record of 300 games she had bowled. This lady was born at a different season of the year from myself, and the lunar cycle will be different for her than for me.

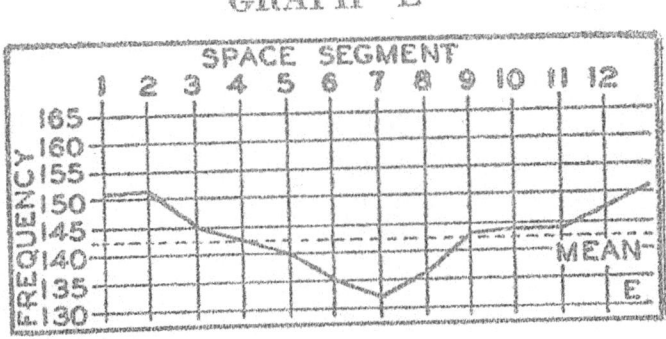

Graph E

In her 300 games she scored 38,396 pins, for an average of 127.99 per game. Using her birth date instead of my own, I have arranged these 300 games according to the space-segment occupied by the Moon at the time when each game was bowled.

Oddly enough, this lady bowled no games while the Moon was in the 4th space-segment, paralleling my own experience. In her case, no games were bowled with the Moon in the 2nd space segment either. Taking the experience of two people, 743 games were bowled without one single game ever being bowled with the Moon in the 4th space-segment. Again, I will have to say that I have no explanation to offer for this.

We will make up the same kind of a table as that used for Experiment "E", using these new scores of the lady bowler, and we will call this Experiment "F".

EXPERIMENT "F"

SPACE SEGMENT	GAMES	PINS	AVERAGE	3-MOVING AVERAGE
1	20	2703	135.1	132.0
2	00			
3	32	4170	130.3	130.1
4	00			
5	22	2753	125.1	127.5
6	35	4453	127.2	125.1
7	17	2092	123.0	126.6
8	65	8425	129.6	125.8
9	40	4993	124.8	125.9
10	19	2345	123.4	125.6
11	34	4370	128.5	127.5
12	16	2092	130.7	131.4

EXPERIMENT "F"

The range of scores is not as great in this experiment as in Experiment "E", but again, no graph is required to see the curve of the lunar cycle. We have the apex in the 1st segment. In the raw figures, the bottom is exactly in the 7th segment, and in the smoothed figures, it is in the 6th. Thus again, our experiment conforms to the general pattern of the lunar cycle. Although these two experiments do not readily submit themselves to statistical analysis, they constitute cumulative evidence. All of our experiments thus far have shown definite evidence of the lunar cycle. By now, we might say that we have found evidence of the lunar cycle in many places. If we had two well-matched bowlers born exactly six months apart, so that one man was at the top of the lunar cycle while the other was at the bottom, it might prove very interesting to see whether, by the use of the lunar cycle, we could predict who would win the majority of the games under those conditions.

The following graph shows the results of Experiment "F".

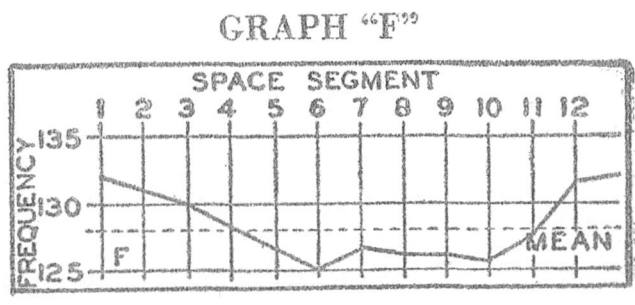

Graph F

All of our evidence indicates the possibility of a lunar cycle affecting people, but it is not a drastic influence, and we must not expect too much of it. Nevertheless, it might be a deciding factor in many instances in life. Small influences can be vitally important when well-known. Gambling houses, bookmakers, banks and insurance companies make fortunes by having a slight preference in the odds.

We must remember that this cycle works statistically. There is no guarantee as to what will happen in any one individual case. The law of large numbers must be applied before the cycle can be found.

Remove one ace from an ordinary deck of playing cards, you might play with this deck for some time and not realize that an ace was missing. If playing stud poker, there is one chance in 221 of getting aces back-to-back when all the cards are in the deck, but with one ace eliminated, there is only one chance in 425. The probability of getting aces back-to-back is almost cut in half when one ace is removed. It is unwise to ignore small influences.

During 1948, the writer played and kept a record of 596 games of Canfield. Otherwise known as Solitaire. This is a game played by one person against a bank or, as in this case, against an imaginary bank. It is not a game of physical skill like bowling. It is mainly a matter of luck how the cards fall, although one can make errors, and his game would suffer from the errors. It might seem preposterous to suggest that the lunar cycle might show itself in scores of Canfield games, but without suggesting anything, our usual technique was applied to the scores of the 596 games, and the scores were arranged according to the space-segment occupied by the Moon at the time when each game was played.

Again, this was an experiment where my own birth date had to be taken into consideration. In the following table, we show the results of our Canfield experiment. We call it Experiment "G". Our table shows six columns.

The first is the segment occupied by the Moon, the second the number of games played with the Moon in that segment. The third and fourth columns show the total points from profitable games and the total points from games which showed a loss while the Moon was in a given space-segment. By deducting the lesser from the greater of these two figures, the fifth column shows the net result plus or minus. The 6th column shows the average per game. We will show these figures on a 3-moving-average in another table.

In presenting this particular experiment, we want to make it clear that we do not regard it as a particularly good test, and it is not one that submits itself to careful statistical analysis, but we are presenting it in order to include all of the evidence. It might prove important in helping to guide us in future experiments. We must again raise the point that the player was conscious of the lunar cycle, and while I do not believe that this fact had any effect upon the results, we must make note of it. We must consider the possibility that the player may have been, in some way; subconsciously affected by his conscious knowledge of the lunar cycle.

EXPERIMENT "G"

MOON SEGMENT	GAMES PLAYED	PLUS TOTALS	MINUS TOTALS	NET RESULT		AVERAGE PER GAME	
1	27	885	615	Plus	270	Plus	10.00
2	71	1725	1465	Plus	260	Plus	3.64
3	84	1480	1480	Even		Even	
4	5	210	95	Plus	115	Plus	23.00
5	68	965	1350	Minus	385	Minus	5.66
6	42	620	860	Minus	240	Minus	5.71
7	38	855	565	Plus	290	Plus	7.63
8	57	840	1380	Minus	540	Minus	9.47
9	45	810	1040	Minus	230	Minus	5.11
10	65	1720	1020	Plus	700	Plus	10.76
11	113	2894	1730	Plus	1164	Plus	10.30
12	81	2710	1800	Plus	910	Plus	11.23

EXPERIMENT "G"

First let us call attention to the fact that only 5 games were played with the Moon in the 4th space-segment, far less than any other space segment.

Here again, we have the factor we ran up against in both of our bowling experiments. When the Moon was in this 4th space-segment other matters took my attention away from the experiment.

If we note the figures in the top half of this cycle, the 10th, 11th, 12th, 1st, 2nd and 3rd space-segments, there are no minus figures in the last column. In the other half of the cycle, which we consider the bottom half, we have two plus and four minus scores. One of the plus scores is based on only 5 games, and can be considered a very unreliable figure. It was originally my intention to play 1200 games, 100 games with the Moon in each space segment, but I never found the time to complete the experiment. Perhaps others will find this· an interesting way to spend their evenings. Following our usual procedure, we now take the figures in the last column and smooth them by the application of a 3-moving-average, containing the following results.

SPACE SEGMENT		3-MOVING AVERAGE
1	Plus	8.29
2	Plus	4.54
3	Plus	8.88
4	Plus	5.78
5	Plus	3.87
6	Minus	1.24
7	Minus	2.51
8	Minus	2.31
9	Minus	1.27
10	Plus	5.31
11	Plus	10.76
12	Plus	10.51

Here we find the plus scores grouped together and the minus scores grouped together. In the following graph, it will be seen that again we have a curve, and the curve conforms fairly well with our previous experiments.

A poker player played poker on 59 different occasions, kept a record of profits and losses as well as dates of the games, and furnished me with the results.

GRAPH "G"

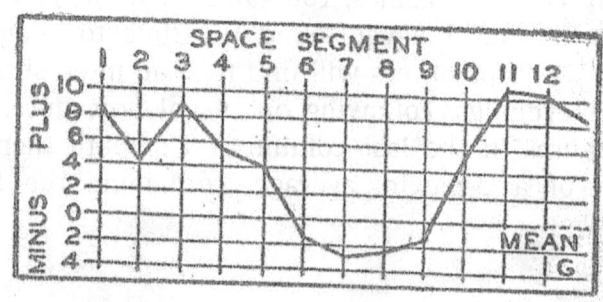

Graph G

Taking into consideration the birth date of the poker-player, his facts were arranged in a table which follows: The first column of the table shows the space segment occupied by the Moon. The second column shows the total winnings of all profitable games played while the Moon was in that position. The third column shows the total losses of all unprofitable games played while the Moon was in that space-segment. The fourth column shows the net result, and the fifth column shows these net results on a 3-movingaverage. This will be Experiment "H".

EXPERIMENT "H"

SPACE SEGMENT	PROFITS	LOSSES	NET RESULT		3-MOVING AVERAGE	
1	$28	$30	Minus	$2	$10.33	Plus
2	57	None	Plus	57	22.33	Plus
3	29	17	Plus	12	20.33	Plus
4	13	21	Minus	8	5.66	Plus
5	23	10	Plus	13	1.33	Minus
6	7	16	Minus	9	.33	Plus
7	25	28	Minus	3	7.33	Minus
8	17	27	Minus	10	1.33	Minus
9	37	28	Plus	9	8.33	Plus
10	35	9	Plus	26	6.33	Plus
11	6	22	Minus	16	4.33	Minus
12	18	42	Minus	24	14.00	Minus

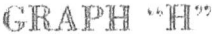

EXPERIMENT "H"

Here, our results are the poorest we have obtained in any of our experiments, but our number of trials is very small, and again, the results do not submit them- selves to statistical analysis. The high point does come within one segment of where it should, but the 11th and 12th segments show losses while they should show profits. If we place our figures on a graph, however, the cycle does appear to be showing up, with the exception of its dip in the last two segments. Actually, the high half of the cycle shows a profit of $53, while the low half shows a loss of $8.

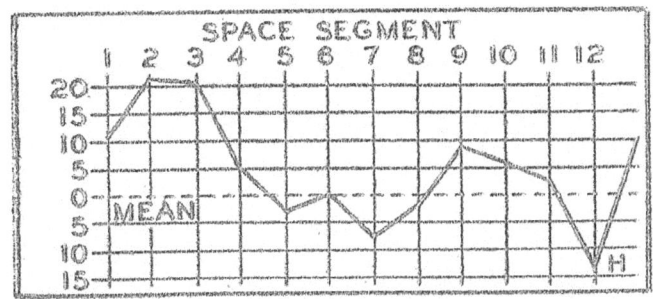

Image Graph H

Even experiment "H" based on a very small number of trials, does show some evidence of conforming to the lunar cycle. In presenting this last experiment involving the factor of luck, we do so mainly to make it clear that all evidence available is included. We have held nothing back, and some scientist reading these findings may want to know whether we have conducted any other experiments without presenting the results.

THE MOON AT THE TIME OF MARRIAGE

You might wonder what caused us to investigate the lunar position at the time of marriage. Data was available. That is the only reason we checked the matter. It is easy to check marriage dates. Most "Who's Who" type of directories give the birth date and the marriage date. However, most birth dates in such directories are those of men.

This experiment is not complete. It will never be complete, for it can always be carried further. As this manuscript is being written, we have checked the Moon at the time of marriage of 4,800 men and 1,200 women. We have followed the same procedure that we have followed with our other experiments.

The methods applied are exactly the same as those applied in the experiment covered in Chapter 3. There we used the date when a person spent money. Here, we use the date when a person gets married, and we measure the distance of the Moon on that date from the position of the Sun on the date of birth. Our first test concerned 1,200 men and 1200 women from European marriage records. This data was furnished to us by a friend, and we were unable to resist the temptation to check the lunar cycle. We had no reason to expect any kind of a positive result. but we checked the matter in order to obtain a negative result if that was what we were to find. What we did find proved interesting, and so, we checked the birth and marriage dates of 3,600 engineers from a directory of engineers, Who's Who in Engineering--1925.

There is a difference in our male and female figures, but our number of females is too small to pass much in the way of judgment. Our female figures are a challenge for further experimentation and may be a key to further enlightenment. We will call this Experiment "I," and we will call our experiment with engineers Experiment "J."

The table headed Experiment "I" shows the results of our experiment with 1,200 European marriages.

EXPERIMENT "I"
POSITION OF MOON AT MARRIAGE

Space Segment	1,200 Males	1,200 Females	2,400 Combined
1	118	97	215
2	106	101	207
3	110	79	189
4	87	83	170
5	92	90	182
6	103	98	201
7	93	104	197
8	89	107	196
9	85	113	198
10	106	120	226
11	106	107	213
12	105	101	206
TOTAL	1,200	1,200	2,400

EXPERIMENT "I"

For the moment, let us ignore the male and female factor and view the totals, because our other experiments did not divide males and females. Let us put our totals on a 3-moving average. The figures will appear thus: 1--210, 2--203, 3--189, 4--180, 5--185, 6--193, 7--198, 8--197, 9--207, 10--212, 11--215, 12--211.

In these figures we find a pattern that has already become familiar. **We find an excess of marriages when the Moon is near the birth Sun position.** It is the same pattern we have found in our other experiments.

If we tabulate the males on a 3-moving average, we obtain the following figures: 1--110, 2--111, 3--101, 4--93, 5--94, 6--96, 7--95, 8--89, 9--93, 10--99, 11--06, 12--110.

If we tabulate the females on a 3-moving average, we obtain the following figures: 1--100, 2--92, 3--88, 4--84, 5--91, 6--97, 7--103, 8--108, 9--113, 10--113, 11--109, 12--102.

GRAPH "I"

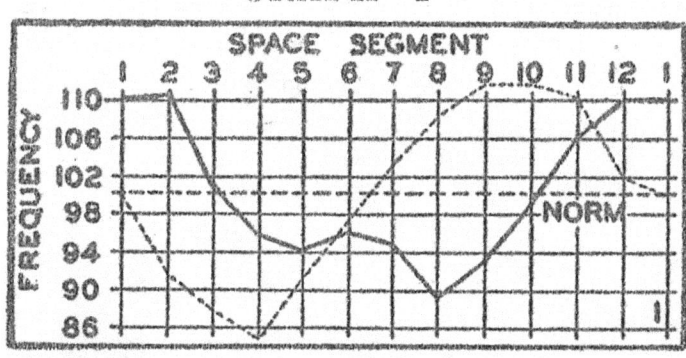

Image of Graph "I"

These figures show a marked difference between males and females. The excess, in the case of females, is not where we have hitherto found it. The whole pattern has shifted by 90 degrees. The main female excess is to be found in the 9th and 10th segments of space. The indication is, if we are to accept these figures as other than chance, that a woman is most apt to marry during the time when the Moon is traveling toward her birth-Sun position, least apt to marry when the Moon is traveling away from the birth-Sun position. An excess of 52 women married while the Moon was traveling toward the birth-Sun position. Standard Deviation is 17.4. The Observed Deviation of 52 is approximately 3 times Standard Deviation, a statistically significant figure.

To find that the Moon affects the marriage date of women suggests that the Moon may have a connection with the menstrual period, but what about the Moon affecting the marriage date of males in relation to their own birth dates? This is something else again.

At the time when this experiment was conducted, further birth and marriage dates of females were not available, and since male data was available, we continued the experiment with males.

We tabulated the lunar position at the time of marriage of 3,600 engineers. Following the same procedure that we have followed in the past, we present the results of Experiment "J" in the following table.

EXPERIMENT "J"
POSITION OF MOON AT MARRIAGE OF 3600 ENGINEERS

Space Segment	First Test	Second Test	Third Test	Total
1	104	96	99	299
2	110	106	109	325
3	115	103	123	341
4	107	108	83	298
5	105	92	106	303
6	78	103	96	277
7	104	101	96	301
8	93	93	103	289
9	104	105	93	302
10	99	90	108	297
11	97	97	94	288
12	84	106	90	280
TOTAL	1,200	1,200	1,200	3,600

EXPERIMENT "J" image

When our totals are placed on a 3-moving-average, we obtain the following figures: 1--301, 2--322, 3--321, 4--314, 5--293, 6--294, 7--289, 8--297, 9-296, 10--296, 11--288, 12--289.

Here, we find an excess in the first, second, third and fourth segments of space. In other words; the cycle has turned, slightly to the east while with females we found it turned slightly to the west, suggesting the possibility, that the cycle as previously studied has been a combination male-female cycle. The figures indicate that females are most apt to marry just before the Moon reaches the birth Sun position, and males just after the Moon passes the birth-Sun position.

Going back to our original figures for engineers, before a 3-moviug-average was applied, we find an excess of 65 in the first three segments of space. Standard Deviation will be 26, so that Observed Deviation is 2.5 times Standard Deviation. By itself, this would be a significant but somewhat doubtful deviation, which might possibly happen by chance alone. Our 1,200 European males also showed an excess of marriages with the Moon in this area, however, and this must be taken into account. The 1,200 European males showed an excess of 34 in this area. Here, Observed Deviation is 2.26 times Standard Deviation, another figure which by itself is somewhat doubtful. However, one of these experiments tends to confirm the other, and when we unite our 1,200 European males with our 3,600 engineers. We have an Observed Deviation of 99. Standard Deviation will be 30. The Observed Deviation is 3.3 times Standard Deviation, well within the realms of statistical significance.

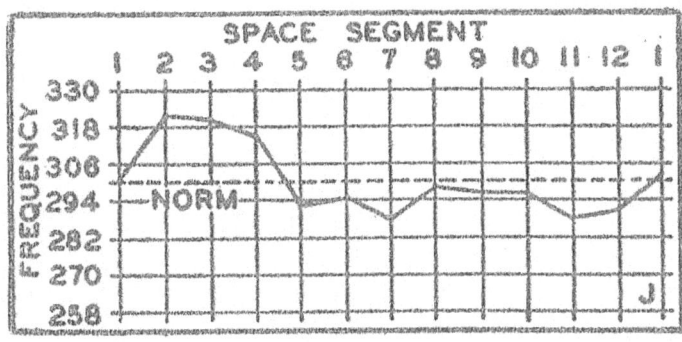

Image Graph J

It should be noted that the deviation of the European males is greater in ratio than the deviation of engineers. This suggests an interesting possibility. The engineers are college graduates. Only a fraction of the European males are college graduates. On the average, college graduates marry at a later age. Our figures suggest the possibility that the influence of the Moon upon marriage may be greater with 'younger people' than with older people.

Our figures definitely tell us that all people are not influenced by the Moon in selecting the marriage date. If we let "n" equal the number of trials and let "d" equal the Observed Deviation, then "d/n" will indicate the ratio of people who are affected by the

Moon insofar as marriage is concerned with our 4,800 males, "d/n" will be 99/4800 or approximately 1/48. We find one person out of 48 affected to the extent that they unconsciously marry according to the Moon's position.

In the case of our European males, "d/n" will be 34/1200 or approximately 1/35. We find that one out of 35 people appear to be affected. In the case of our 3,600 engineers, "d/n" will be 65/3600 or approximately 1/55. We find only one person out of 55 appears to be affected. Where we found a tendency for our European females to marry when the Moon was traveling toward the birth-Sun position, "d/n" will be 52/1200 or approximately 1/23. One out of every 23 females appeared to be affected by the Moon in selecting the time of marriage.

If we take a composite of these figures, we have 6,000 trials, and "d/n" will be 151/6000 or approximately 1/40. Our tests indicate that one person out of every 40 examined was affected by the Moon in the selection of a marriage date.

Now, let us go back and consider our figures in Chapter 3, where we tested the effect of the Moon on the spending of money. There, we dealt with males and females combined. The ratio was approximately 2 females to each male. If we include the cases in the footnote, we find an Observed Deviation of 118 at the top of the lunar cycle, the 12th, 1st and 2nd segments of space. In this test, "d/n" will be 118/6000. This is approximately 1/50. Our test indicated that one out of 50 people were affected by the Moon in the expenditure of their money. These two figures, one out of 40 in the case of 6,000 marriages, and one out of 50 in the case of 6,000 purchases, are not too far apart.

You might argue that this ratio is not great, but it can also be argued that this ratio is tremendous when we consider how great must be the influence of the Moon to affect one out of 50 people to this extent. If the Moon can affect one out of 50 people to this extent, it is reasonable to believe that the Moon affects all people to some extent.

We present two graphs with this chapter. The first shows the results of Experiment "I" on a 3-moving-avera.ge, and the second presents the results of Experiment "J" on a 3-moving-average.

Other than the comment we have already made, we are going to let the figures in this chapter speak for themselves. There were some by-products of this investigation that we are going to mention briefly.

We checked 6,000 birth dates to determine whether more people are born at one phase of the Moon than at another. The result was negative. We found 1,470 persons born on the first quarter, 1,529 persons born on the second quarter, 1,495 persons born on the third quarter, and 1,506 persons born on the fourth quarter of the Moon. The largest deviation here is 30, which is less than Standard Deviation.

We checked 4,800 marriage dates to determine whether more people marry at one phase of the Moon than at another. The results were negative. We found 1,209 persons married on the first quarter, 1,171 on the second quarter, 1,175 on the 3rd quarter, and 1,245 on the 4th quarter. There is an excess of 54 marriages during the half of the time when the Moon is giving the earth its greatest light, but this is only 1.5 times Standard Deviation, an excess that we can expect to happen by chance alone. We dropped both of these experiments as negative, and that phase of the work is not being continued.

We checked the birth dates of 3,600 engineers to see whether they were born with the Moon evenly distributed through the zodiac of the equinoxes. The results were as follows: Aries--296 Taurus--300, Gemini--287, Cancer—310, Leo--297, Virgo--266, Libra--301, Scorpio--288, Sagittarius--319, Capricorn--312, Aquarius--299, Pisces--325. These figures do not appear to hold statistical significance.

We checked the marriage dates of 3,600 engineers to see whether the Moon was evenly distributed through the zodiac at the time of marriage. Here, we obtained a result worthy of further study and experimentation. The frequency with which the Moon appeared in each of the zodiacal signs when the marriage ceremonies were performed was as follows: Aries--287, Taurus--287, Gemini--265, Cancer--294, Leo--290, Virgo--311, Libra--296, Scorpio--293, Sagittarius--322, Capricorn--344, Aquarius--311, Pisces--302.

In the three consecutive zodiacal sign, Sagittarius, Capricorn and Aquarius, we have an excess deviation from the mean of 77. This is approximately 3 times Standard Deviation.

The Moon does not spend an equal amount of time in each sign of the zodiac in a given year, and we must consider this factor as a possible cause of the above figures. This factor will average itself out in approximately 8.25 years, however, and these marriage dates were spread over a good many years. It did not occur to us, to test this zodiacal factor when we began testing marriage dates, but we did record 720 of our 1,200 European marriages with the following result: Aries--53, Taurus--55, Gemini--60, Cancer--54, Leo--60, Virgo--56, Libra--8, Scorpio--56, Sagittarius--61, Capricorn--80, Aquarius--56, Pisces--71. These marriages occurred in an entirely different group of years, but again we find Capricorn at the top.

We present these byproducts as clues for further and more rigid investigation. On the surface, it would appear that marriage occurs with greater frequency when the Moon is in the vicinity of the zodiacal sign, Capricorn. It might not be amiss to mention the fact that the astrologers associate Capricorn with "the established order." Marriage is an "established" institution.

The deviation in Capricorn in the two sets of figures is 3.5 times Standard Deviation. It is not likely that the figure is due to chance, It is unlikely that the deviation is due to the fact that the Moon does not spend an equal amount of time in each zodiacal sign during a short interval. It is probable that the marriage dates were stretched out over sufficient years to overcome this factor, but we have not proved this to be so, and our experiment must merely be considered as an indicator that may furnish a valuable guide for future research, either on the part of the writer or someone else. It is fair to assume that the marriage dates would be stretched out over as long an interval as the birth dates of the same people, and the birth dates of these people did not show any deviation of this kind. If the Capricorn deviation in the test with marriage dates was due to the fact that the Moon does not spend an equal amount of time in the various signs of the zodiac during a short period, then we should have found a similar deviation in the test with birth dates of these people.

THE MOON AND VITALITY

As heretofore stated, the nature of the experiments herein conducted bas been largely a matter of the availability of data. Mrs. Nellie Duff of Findlay, Ohio, was kind enough to mail me a large accumulation of death notices which contained both date of birth and date of death. This data offered us an opportunity of learning whether there might be lowered vitality or lower resistance when the Moon is at the low of the lunar cycle for any particular individual. We reasoned that if this were true, then there should be a higher death frequency at the low point in the lunar cycle.

Following our usual procedure, we tabulated the position of the Moon at death and compared it with the position of the Sun at birth in the case of 2,400 individuals. The result was negative. **We found no indication of any effect from the individual lunar cycle where death is involved. Insofar as this experiment is concerned, the indication is that vitality does not seem to be affected by the individual lunar cycle.**

Dividing the circle of the heavens into 12 space-segments in the same manner as we have continuously done in our other experiments, we will call this Experiment "K." It was conducted in two parts, each part involving 1,200 trials. In the following table, we present the results.

EXPERIMENT "K"
POSITION OF MOON AT DEATH

Space Segment	First 1200 Trials	Second 1200 Trials	Total 2400 Trials
1	92	96	188
2	102	98	200
3	84	118	202
4	94	107	201
5	107	104	211
6	97	90	187
7	102	114	216
8	104	88	192
9	108	99	207
10	96	109	205
11	104	90	194
12	110	87	197
TOTAL	1200	1200	2400

EXPERIMENT "K" image

As the figures indicate, there is no indication of a cycle-rhythm here, and the deviations that do occur are within the realm of what we expect to occur by chance alone. We also tabulated the Moon position in each of the signs of the zodiac, while we were conducting the above experiment, and when we did so, we obtained a rather unusual result. We obtained a great excess of deaths while the Moon was in Capricorn. However, this excess displayed itself mainly in the first 1,200 cases, and to a lesser extent in the second 1,200 cases.

There was an important difference between the first and second groups. The first group were mainly young men, killed in action in the war, while the second group were the general run of deaths including many very old people. Deaths appeared to be much more frequent while the Moon was in the winter section of the zodiac, and least frequent while the Moon was in the summer section of the zodiac. This does not mean that summer and winter enter into the matter. When we refer to the "winter section of the zodiac," we merely mean that part of the zodiac occupied by the Sun during winter. The Moon passes through this section a little oftener than once a month=-thirteen times in a year. But, first let us have the actual figures. We will call this Experiment "L."

EXPERIMENT "L"

Zodiacal Sign	First 1200 Trials	Second 1200 Trials	Total 2400 Trials
Aries	98	104	202
Taurus	98	97	195
Gemini	87	105	192
Cancer	91	105	196
Leo	84	98	182
Virgo	97	85	182
Libra	90	89	179
Scorpio	116	93	209
Sagittarius	108	86	194
Capricorn	141	108	249
Aquarius	99	117	216
Pisces	91	113	204
TOTAL	1200	1200	2400

EXPERIMENT "L" image

These figures are presented for future reference, and we should be very careful about drawing conclusions until the matter is tested under different conditions. The data was assembled by the obituary editor of one or more daily newspapers. Perhaps more deaths were published on days when news was scarce. We do not know. An experiment of this kind should be conducted, using all deaths of a given area. We do not know what ratio-of-all-deaths was included. There might be some unknown factor that caused this excess of deaths with the Moon in Capricorn and the winter section of the zodiac, We cannot conceive of such a factor, but we advise withholding judgment until some other experiment can be conducted under different conditions. We tested the data because it was available.

Some years ago, the writer tabulated birth and death dates from the New York Times. At that time, it was the purpose to see whether a person would be more likely to die near his own birth date than at some other time of the year. We found a great excess of deaths recorded near the time of the birth date.

We passed the data along to Dr. Ellsworth Huntington at Yale University, who made a similar test with data obtained from genealogies. His results were negative. We wrote to the editors of the New York Times, who investigated and found that it was a habit of the obituary editor always to note the birth date if a person died near that time, but not always to do so when the person died at some other time of the year. Our statistics showed a positive result, but they had merely picked up and registered a habit of the obituary editor, just as a radio picks up music from the air.

In this case, the editor would not know the position of the Moon, in all probability, and would not heed it if he did, so that such an error is highly improbable, but there is a wide difference between our first and second groups of 1,200 trials The result is not entirely consistent. Capricorn scored 141 in the first experiment 108 in the second, against a mean expectancy of 100. In the first experiment the winter section of the zodiac (Capricorn-Aquarius-Pisces) scored an excess of 31, and in the second experiment, 38, for a total excess of 69. This deviation is 3.3 times Standard Deviation.

There is another point to be considered, and a very important one. It has no effect on our regular lunar cycle experiments because measurements are taken from twelve different points in the circle of space, but here, in this kind of an experiment, the Moon spends more time on one side of the zodiac than on the other. Therefore, mean expectancy would not be exactly 100.

In the second half of our experiment, 1947 deaths were very heavily a part of our data, and in 1947 the motion of the Moon was very slow in Capricorn, giving a reason for an excess of deaths at that point, merely because with the Moon there longer, there would be more time for deaths in that sign to occur.

However, our big Capricorn excess was not in this data, but in the first half of our experiment which was largely made up of deaths from World War II. These deaths occurred with the Moon's slow-motion pointer back in Virgo. Any excess due to this factor should appear on the other side of the zodiac.

The excess of 41 in Capricorn in the **first 1,200 trials is 4.3 times Standard Deviation a highly significant figure. It would appear to indicate that the death rate among men killed in action was very high when the Moon was in Capricorn.** This, of course would be dependent upon the time when battles occurred. One great battle which occurred with the Moon in Capricorn would account for a great many deaths, and it might be the reason for our results being distorted.

To sun up, we can account for nothing definite insofar as this particular experiment is concerned. We found no evidence of lowered vitality at the bottom of the lunar cycle, and our Experiment "L" merely indicates that the matter should be investigated under different circumstances and under more controlled conditions, when it is entirely possible that a negative result might follow.

The fact that Experiment "K" gave us a negative result in the face of all of our other positive results may be of great help to us in enabling us to learn more about just how this cycle affects us physically and emotionally. **It has been the writer's general observations that the low point in the lunar cycle is not so much a matter of lowered vitality as a matter of emotional instability.** We will have more to say about this later, but along these lines of thinking, we would expect the person who is emotionally unstable to begin with to be more affected in this respect at the bottom of the cycle than a more stable individual.

A FURTHER VERIFICATION

We have covered considerable territory since Chapter II, and now we are going to revert to the subject of that chapter.

There, we found our first hint that an individual's income might be affected in some way by the motion of the moon.

There were weaknesses in the experiment, because it was not conducted under sufficiently controlled conditions. In spite of all this, the graph that appeared as a result of that experiment proved to be the equivalent of a prognostication of the results of other experiments which followed. Lack of time and other circumstances made it impossible to repeat the experiment with new data immediately, and over a considerable interval, records were not maintained. Thus, the further experiment was postponed.

In spite of all this, the graph that appeared as a result of that experiment proved to be the equivalent of a prognostication of the results of other experiments which followed. Lack of time and other circumstances made it impossible to repeat the experiment with new data immediately, and over a considerable interval, records were not maintained. Thus, the further experiment was postponed.

It will be recalled that in Chapter 2, we tested income from a mail-order business owned by the writer and possible association of its fluctuations with the motion of the moon as related to the position of the sun on the date of the writer's birth.

Over a considerable period, records were kept on a weekly basis and they did not lend themselves to a repetition of this experiment.

(First Six Months)

Space Segment	1	2	3	4	5	6	7	8	9	10	11	12
	99	46	30	61	50	85	144	13	75	124	143	93
	206	80	38	105	34	239	82	104	69	66	35	47
	59	77	36	249	114	29	149	40	46	121	47	42
	85	44	164	49	79	12	15	94	24	65	122	142
	107	61	00	92	89	3	3	33	87	86	276	35
	201	129	00	54	192	128	14	40	62	59	61	00
	155	28	65	24	33	47	45	61	28	13	44	32
	105	119	45	70	79	5	00	213	179	51	107	12
	13	184	3		52	105	30	157	69		96	24
	00	18	36			95		00	33		103	30
		327	114			37		00	68		95	68
		97				00		9	17			26
		44				145						
		5										
Total	1030	1259	531	704	722	930	482	764	757	585	1129	551
Days	10	14	11	8	9	13	9	12	12	8	11	12
Average	103	90	48	88	80	71	53	63	63	73	102	46
3-Moving Average	90	80	75	72	80	68	62	60	66	79	74	84

Experiment M

Finally, on October 18th, 1948, the writer decided that daily records must be maintained for the next interval of a year in order to repeat the experiment. Operations were on a five-day week. This time, we made allowances for the fact that the moon would be in some zodiacal signs longer than in other signs and that there would be no mail received at times when the moon was passing through a given sign because of Saturdays and Sundays.

At the end of a year, a table was prepared. This table showed each date, the amount of money received on that date, and the position of the moon by space segment on that day as related to the writer's birth date. This first table is a little voluminous for presentation here and so we omit it and prepare a second table.

In this second table, we place the numbers of the space segments across the top. Then, we take each day's figure in dollars and place it beneath the number of the space segment occupied by the moon on that date. In other words, the figure "144" under "7" means that on a day when the moon was in the 7th space-segment orders received totaled $144. We divide this table into two parts, showing the first and second six-month periods separately. We will call this Experiment "M".

EXPERIMENT "M"
(Second Six Months)

Space Segment	1	2	3	4	5	6	7	8	9	10	11	12
	41	77	120	64	96	8	16	404	88	34	22	27
	57	00	70	137	19	28	60	107	103	60	141	45
	183	77	74	10	49	22	122	51	68	445	129	5
	112	52	13	213	29	36	00	72	71	68	19	00
	15	00	86	52	36	18	6	8	128	389	15	71
	00	90	16	136	53	5	58	20	00	52	3	291
	11	101	120	46	30		50	18	44	63	38	107
	102	31	104	108	5		00	45	29	44	42	38
	15	354	326	13	181		00	86	69	62	33	109
	36	179		46				171		41	9	11
	15			13				44		5	13	78
	00			30				98		00	8	301
	50			15							199	
	117										120	
											166	
Total	754	961	929	883	498	167	312	1124	600	1263	957	1083
Days	14	10	9	13	9	6	9	12	9	12	15	12
Average	54	96	103	68	55	28	34	94	66	105	64	90
3-Moving Average	80	84	89	75	50	39	52	65	88	78	86	72

Second "M" group

In both halves of this experiment, the effect of the lunar cycle is in evidence. Considering the high half of the cycle to be the 10th, l11th, 12th, 1st, 2nd and 3rd segments, the averages in the first half of the experiment total 462 against 418 in the remaining segments which constitute the low half of the cycle. In the second half of the experiment the corresponding figures are 512 for the high half of the cycle against 345 for the low half.

In the first half of this experiment, the first figure of 144 under the 7th segment is far above average for that 7th-low segment. It should be noted that this figure is for November 1st, 1948. There had been an eclipse of the sun during the night,

We can now combine the figures for the first six months with those of the second six-month period, and we obtain the following:

The raw averages (or actual averages) of the top half of the lunar cycle total 483, while the averages for the low half of the cycle total 388. Splitting this into quarters, the two quarters of the top half of the cycle register 245 and 238 against the two quarters of the lower half of the cycle which score 204 and 184.

SPACE SEGMENT	AMOUNT	DAYS	AVERAGE	3-MOVING AVERAGE
1	$1784	24	$73	$78
2	2220	24	92	79
3	1460	20	73	80
4	1587	21	75	72
5	1220	18	68	68
6	1097	18	61	57
7	794	18	42	60
8	1888	24	78	61
9	1357	21	64	80
10	1848	20	97	80
11	2086	26	80	82
12	1634	24	68	74

Combined "M"

It is the feeling of the writer that in any experiment of this kind, an interval of at least six months, and probably one year, should be employed in order to exclude other cycles or factors which may be operating. This cycle is not necessarily visible to the eye when observed on an ordinary graph. It can be completely hidden behind other interfering factors, but when the statistical method is applied, its existence is detected. An astronomer detects objects in space at distances beyond the reach of the human eye, by the use of the telescope. A biologist detects the existence of objects too small for observation by the human eye through the use of the microscope. In the same manner, we detect what is otherwise hidden, by the careful use of the mathematical science of statistics.

We can look at the figures of "M" on Graph "M." Here, we see the familiar curve that we have repeatedly seen in other experiments. The line is a little weak at the 12th segment, but it is above the mean. In fact, at all points our line is above the mean while the moon is passing through what we have already designated as the high half of the lunar cycle. Insofar as the low half of the cycle is concerned, we find our line below the mean in five out of six space segments, the exception being the ninth, which adjoins the high half of the cycle. It should be noted that this graph is based on the 3-moving average figures.

During the high half of the cycle, we took in $11,032 during 138 business days, while during the low half of the cycle, we took in $7,943 in 120 business days. This means that during the high half of the lunar cycle, we averaged $79.94 per day, while during the low half of the cycle we averaged $66.19 per day. This is language that the average businessman will understand. The practical value of knowledge of the lunar cycle becomes evident

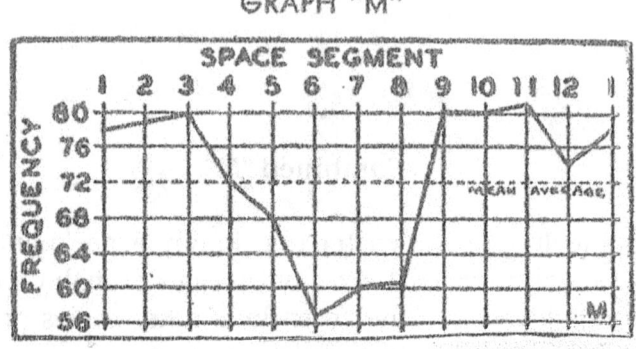

Graph M

Even a skeptical businessman cannot afford not to experiment with such a factor. The salesman might find half of the cycle with those during the low half. For some year, the writer has made a practice of devoting the lower half of the cycle to routine matters that have to be done some time but which do not require particular skill, while devoting the high half of the cycle to important conferences, etc. In such matters, we can only report general observations, but since we have already reported a great deal in the way of statistical evidence; perhaps it is now time to make some general observations, and before going into an entirely new phase of this work, we will devote the next chapter for something in the way of general observations of the writer.

SOME GENERAL OBSERVATIONS

One cannot watch the Lunar Cycle in the lives of everyone around him over a decade without drawing some conclusions which are not based upon statistical analysis. We have reserved this chapter for a bit of discussion. It may prove helpful in directing research of the future.

The writer knows the birth dates of people around him. For much more than a decade, he has carefully observed what has transpired in the lives of people around him at various phases of their individual lunar cycles. He has kept a good many notes, and formulated certain ideas, and before going further with our data, is going to outline some conclusions.

These are not dogmatic conclusions. You are not asked to accept them. You can, however test them out in your own life and environment. Ultimate research will either bear them out or disprove them. We can draw tentative conclusions if we keep our minds flexible, but we must not let these conclusions crystallize into hard and fast prejudgments. We must be ready to alter our views if new and more complete evidence casts doubt upon our tentative conclusions. [Ed. Please apply these principals to all of astrology.]

The writer has developed the tentative conclusion that, on the average, a person is luckier at the top of the lunar cycle (i.e. with Moon in or near your Sun's sign) than at the bottom (i.e. with the Moon in or near the sign opposite your Sun's sign). He is convinced that there is greater emotional stability at the top of the cycle than at the bottom. The emotions appear to get out of hand more easily at the bottom of the cycle. A given event will upset you at one time and not at another time. It has been observed that loss of temper appears to occur more readily at the bottom of the cycle.

The writer has observed many instances of dire consequences resulting from the business judgment men exercised and acted upon at the bottom of the cycle.

As an example, a man had been operating what had been a very successful business for over fifteen years. Within a period of three months, he made three decisions and acted upon them. They were evenly spaced apart, so that each decision was made with the moon in the seventh segment or bottom of his own lunar cycle. Each decision involved expansion. As a result of these three decisions, a year later the business was on the verge of bankruptcy.

A lady had been under a strain for several weeks. She called on the writer to relate her problem and seek advice. As she began to relate her story, she slipped from her chair in a faint. At that moment, the moon was exactly 180 degrees from her birth-sun-position, at the exact bottom of her lunar cycle.

The writer's observation has indicated that more people seem to become ill at the bottom of the cycle. Illness which develops at the top of the cycle appears to be followed by prompt recovery, while illness which develops at the bottom of the cycle appears to be prolonged. On one occasion, the writer was rushed to the hospital with pneumonia. Two days later, at the top of the cycle, he could no longer observe that there was anything the matter with him, and would have left the hospital if permitted to do so by the physician. On another occasion, he was taken with the grippe at the bottom of the cycle. One month later, he was still ill.

The average person may not be able to detect this cycle without tools (statistics), and it should be made clear that the writer does not consider it a happiness cycle. He is convinced that people are not happier at the top of the cycle, but people's happiest moments are not always their most stable moments. Quite the contrary might be true. A drunken man may be happy. He is likely to be less stable. The factor of stability seems definitely involved. A man might buy some worthless wildcat oil stock at the bottom of the cycle, and be momentarily in the-cloud, because of his dream about millions of dollars which he is never going to see. Much of life is unreality because people make it so. The low days in this cycle often appear to be days of illusion. Emotions can blind the individual to true facts. Judgment can become very faulty. Many frustrated people judge a day of illusion as favorable because their dream state offers them momentary happiness, or produces a state of mind which they catalogue as happiness.

We are not seeking illusion. We are attempting to gain facts. We cannot judge the favorability or unfavorability of an event or an interval of time unless we consider its ultimate outcome, and an event can be extended considerably in its time dimension. It can be spread over a considerable interval. The birth of an individual or a marriage is an example. We must view an event in the perspective. We must consider it in the light of its ultimate effect or conclusion. The plan of Benito Mussolini or that of Adolf Hitler might have appeared to have been very successful if analyzed in 1940. If viewed in 1950, far different conclusions would be reached. We are attempting to judge a matter that is very delicate, and it is unwise to leap to conclusions.

We must not expect too much of this cycle. We must not expect it to win an election for an unknown man in a political-machine-dominated community over a very popular machine-backed candidate, even if the moon is at the high point for the first man and the low point for the second man. The writer regards it as probable that the first man would make a better showing than if conditions were reversed, but even that showing may be quite one-sided. He might get 30% of the vote where otherwise he might get 20%, of the vote. This would not elect him to office. It might help to build him up for something in the future. The cycle will not do all the work for you, but the writer believes that it will help. He is convinced that it has helped him. He has had many peculiar and favorable "breaks" as the result of business moves executed with the moon at the apex of this cycle.

The view that people are less stable at the bottom of this cycle is an echo of a very ancient claim.

Far back in history insanity was named lunacy. It has been contended that insane people become violent at the full of the moon. This has frequently been a theme for fiction. Persons working in institutions for the insane have told me that they encounter more trouble at the full of the moon.

Fire marshals mark a big circle around the date of the full moon on their calendars. At that time, they are on the alert for pyromaniacs. We will have more to say about this in a later chapter.

Meanwhile, although we are not dealing with full moons as we know them in this work, the low point in the lunar cycle has a resemblance to the full moon. It is what we might term an individual full moon. Instead of being the time when the earth is between the moon and the sun, it is the time when the earth is between the moon and the birth-sun-position of the individual.

This might beg the question as to whether people born at the full of the moon are less stable than other people. Some astrologers make this claim. My own observations of approximately fifty people born at the full moon leads me to believe that as a group, they are below average in stability. My experience with one individual born at the full of the moon long held me against this view, He is a scientist, and for many years I regarded him as a very stable person, but I ultimately discovered that appearances were very deceiving. His expressed views were purely dependent upon the group he was with when they were expressed. He could lecture and voice certain conclusions at one hall, cross the street to another and express the opposite views because he was with people who wanted to hear the opposite views. Under the influence of alcohol, his views might be anything.

The writer is quite convinced that people are less stable when they are at the low point in the lunar cycle. This is a conclusion he will alter whenever broader investigations cast doubt upon the claim, but all of his evidence and experience points in this direction. When a person is unstable, that person's judgment is not good. For years, the writer has made a practice of exerting caution at the bottom of his personal cycle. He tries not to jump into things. He attempts to bide his time. as it were. He delays decisions and action. Important moves and decisions are made at the top of the cycle.

It is possible that unstable people react to this cycle more radically than stable people. We have not defined the word stability. The dictionary identifies the word with equilibrium. We think of stability as that which does not change easily. The writer thinks of a man as stable when he has conscious control of his thoughts and actions, when he is not blown about, so to speak, by the cosmic winds. People of genius are often unstable people and have some very unstable moments. **It has been the writer's conclusion that stable people are less stable at the low point in the lunar cycle, and that unstable people are radically stable at such a time.**

Most of us are even working for improved welfare and for improved conditions in the future. The man who is working for wages is doing so to improve his financial condition at the end of the week. His financial status will be better if he works than if he does not work. It has been the writer's experience that what is begun at the top of the lunar cycle works out more satisfactorily than what is begun at the bottom of the cycle. From this point of view, the cycle appears to have implications concerning the future. Of course, if a man's judgment is better at the top of the cycle, action at that time would appear to be better guided, but the writer is not convinced that this is the whole answer. There would still appear to be a factor of luck, or whatever you wish to call it, involved. How else account for the statistics which indicate that the writer's business is better, on the average, at the top of the cycle?

A peculiar tendency has been noted. Temporary reversals in the cycle seem to indicate long-term reversals.

For business to suddenly throw a peak at the bottom of the cycle appears to indicate that a downward trend lies ahead.

For business to dry up at the top of the cycle appears to indicate that a long-term upward trend lies ahead, In the normal course of events, if a man's business is prospering and going forward, it seems to run in accord with the lunar cycle. This appears to be a healthy indication, but just before the business trend changes, the lunar cycle suddenly goes haywire and fails to function. When all periods, good and bad, are averaged, the cycle still appears to work from a statistical point of view.

Back in a prior chapter, we listed three other occasions when the cycle does not appear to work as we expect it. **Two of these might be explained by the possible existence and interference of a solar cycle. The third was when the sun is near or square (90 degrees) to the moon's nodes.** This is a matter that will be treated later, but it is the writer's view that these periods are also unstable moments of time. Occasions when the sun is near the moon's nodes are also the occasions when eclipses of the sun and moon occur. **The writer has found marked exceptions to the general trend near the time of eclipses and when the sun was square the nodes.**

At the time of an eclipse, the earth is partially or completely cut off from the rays of the sun or the moon, depending on whether it is a solar or lunar eclipse. The rays of the moon are reflected rays which are cut off by the earth itself. We do not know how necessary these rays may be to our stability, but the claim that eclipses are milestones in human destiny and terrestrial affairs is as ancient as known history. This is something we will discuss at length later on. Let us emphasize that we do not expect the lunar cycle to work well at the time of an eclipse, but we are not sure that the eclipse itself is a factor. **Perhaps it is merely the close proximity of the sun to the node of the moon. How else can we account for the fact that we find similar conditions, to be discussed later, when the sun is square to the node, and when there are no eclipses or related phenomena.** No attempt has been made to eliminate these intervals from our statistics. They have not been excluded, for as yet, this has been a problem that we have not been prepared to face.

Entirely aside from these factors, we find that the lunar cycle works more radically in one month than in another, and the results which have been presented are those which are obtained when all periods are grouped together. On one occasion, we may find that our peak comes a couple of days ahead of schedule, while on another occasion it will be later. When these various occasions are added together and averaged, however, the peak appears to find its way into the first segment of space, or a point very near thereto.

Before contemplating this book, the writer wrote a short manuscript about this cycle, multigraphed it, and sold it to the public showing the high and low dates in the lunar cycle for the individual. Today, something over five thousand people purchase and use these dates. Very few of these people ever write about their personal experiences. Their interest is indicated by the fact that at the end of a year, they come back to have the dates calculated for another year. It was found in the beginning that people were seeking a happiness 'cycle', and it was necessary to be emphatic in pointing out that the lunar cycle is not a happiness cycle. Actually, we often find a person very happy at the bottom of the cycle because of over-confidence and the misinterpretation of facts. It is true that we constantly get a certain number of letters from people about the cycle, but few of these letters contain data that could be used as scientific evidence.

A gentleman wrote that the cycle did not work in his life. He was urged to give facts upon which this conclusion was based. His next letter was apologetic. He had based his judgment on a single event. He was an accountant, and on a day when the lunar cycle was at its apex for him, accountants arrived from the home office unexpectedly for the purpose of inspecting his books. He was caught off guard and unnerved, and when he wrote his first letter, he was badly worried about the possible outcome. During the interval between the man's first and second letter, he had received a communication from the home office commending him on the excellent condition of his accounts and thanking him for the good job he was accomplishing. He had altered his judgment as to the day being unfavorable. There have been many enthusiastic and complimentary letters, but these are not taken too seriously in the fear that the writer may be trying to be nice rather than scientific.

Here is a woman who tells of beginning a long journey at the bottom of her individual cycle. She relates how everything went wrong. She missed connections, became ill, and completely failed to accomplish the purpose of her journey.

An important man in a distant city telephoned me. He had a business proposition that could hardly be ignored. The moon was at the very bottom of my own individual cycle. It was near the bottom of his own cycle, as I afterward learned. I did not make the trip at that time. I delayed the journey for two weeks and arrived in the other city at the top of my own lunar cycle. The man's business proposition completely petered out, but I made a very important contact while in the other city which proved profitable. This contact would not have been made had I left earlier.

Let us suppose that we have two men who are partners in business, and that they are born exactly six months apart. Matters become complicated. The high point in the cycle for one partner is the low point for the other. How will this work out? We have not had an opportunity of observing such a partnership in business, but we have observed a number of marriages where the mates were born six months apart. Although no real conclusions have been drawn, these people seem to go their separate ways. Perhaps they belong to different churches. There appear to be wide differences of views and opinions. Such cases may furnish an interesting topic for future research.

We might wonder how the lunar cycle would work in the case of a corporation involving many individuals. Not having had the opportunity of making any statistical investigations or even general observations along these lines, we are unable to offer any light.

The writer could enumerate many experiences of individuals to demonstrate how the lunar cycle has worked in specific cases in a very peculiar way, but each and every reader of this book has the opportunity to study this cycle as it relates to his or her own life and environment. It is the writer's view that this can be done profitably, but it is wise to diversify. Do not put all of your eggs in one basket. Do not risk everything on one single high point in the cycle, and do not let your judgment be influenced one way or the other by any specific event. Strike the average. Study and record your experiences with the cycle for a minimum period of a year. We believe that you will find the cycle helpful, but you must test it for yourself. Avoid prejudgments. Gather ample evidence before you draw any conclusions whatever. Remember that the writer has been studying and testing this cycle for more than a decade, and his views still have not completely jelled. They have to be adjusted from time to time. When you do draw conclusions, make certain that they are only tentative conclusions. Be ready to alter them in the face of additional evidence. Remember that the exceptions to the rule are vitally important, because a study of these can carry us higher in understanding peculiarities and eccentricities of the cycle's functioning.

ARE THERE UNSTABLE MOMENTS OF TIME?

A young man stood on the ledge of a tall building on Fifth Avenue in New York. From windows, police tried to coax him back. Below in the streets, there were masses of humanity, watching. It was one of the great city's most dramatic moments. For hours the newspapers had been telling the story of the young man on the ledge. "Sportsmen" in the street were betting as to whether he would really jump after all.

Then, he leaped and it was all over.

On the following day, newspapers casually mentioned the fact that it had been the young man's birthday.

No newspaper made mention of the more subtle fact that not only was it the young man's birthday, but this birthday coincided with an eclipse of the Sun that was occurring on the other side of the earth. These two events seemed to be too remote for consideration as part of a pattern.

Perhaps there is nothing about which we know less than we know about time.

The noted psychologist, Karl Jung, has expressed the view that time has quality, and that whatever is born at a given moment of time possesses the characteristics of that moment of time.

Ancient literature contains many references to events that coincided with eclipses of the Sun and Moon. Ancient astronomers (who were also astrologers, before astronomy grew out of astrology) were of the belief that eclipses of the Sun and Moon were often accompanied by unusual terrestrial occurrences. Some modern astronomers know of no way in which this can be true, whereupon they utilize their characteristic art of prejudgment and declare that it is not true.

The writer suggests that there maybe unstable moments of time, when the unusual occurs with greater than ordinary frequency. His life experience appears to point in this direction. Life may go on from day to day in dull fashion, and then, within a short interval, a whole series of events occur. Life is filled with mysteries that science has not yet explored.

The writer further suggests that many of these possible unstable moments of time may be cyclic and may coincide with a cycle of approximately 346 days which can be divided into four parts of approximately 86.5 days, this cycle being the relationship between the Sun and the Moon's node.

It takes the Sun approximately 346 days to go from one conjunction of the Moon's north node to another. From the time of conjunction, it takes 86.5 days for the Sun to reach a point 90 degrees (one quarter of a circle) from the node. In another 86.5 days, the Sun will have conjoined the south node. It will be 90 degrees past that point in another 86.5 days. After the next 86.5 day period, it will again have conjoined the north node of the Moon.

The writer suggests that these four points mark the center of some of our suggested unstable moments of time. Let us look further. Back in the days of the old *New York World* [newspaper], a friend occupied an important editorial position on that publication. This friend had shown interest in the suggestion that unusual occurrences happen when eclipses take place near the time of one's birth date. For this to occur, the Moon's node has to be near the subject's birth Sun position.

Some months hence, such an eclipse was to occur on this friend's birth date. It was the subject of some joking as to what might occur on that day. The approaching eclipse and birth date were watched with a great deal of interest.

There was a startling announcement. *The World* was to be sold and combined with the *New York Telegram*. A vast number of old newspapermen were thrown out of work, my friend among them. It was the end of *The World* for him. It was also the end of the newspaper business for him. Ultimately, he entered another profession. This startling event occurred on his birthday, and on the day of an eclipse of the Sun.

My own first marriage ended in divorce which was granted on my wife's birthday, and on the day of an eclipse of the Sun.

Charles Fort was impressed by the great amount of coincidence in life. He asked, "What if it should not be coincidence?"

In the history of ancient China, there is the story of two astronomers who were executed because they failed to predict an eclipse of the Sun and thus warn the populace of this important omen.

Great national and international developments would appear to have a habit of occurring within a week or ten days of the time of eclipses of the Sun and Moon.

On April 9th, 1865, General Lee of the Confederate Army surrendered to the northern forces. On April 10th, there was an eclipse of the Moon. On April 14th, Abraham Lincoln was shot. On April 15th, he died. On April 20th, the Sun crossed the Moon's node. On April 25th, there was an eclipse of the Sun. On April 26th Booth, Lincoln's assassin, was shot and killed.

On March 14th, 1867, the Sun crossed the Moon's node. On March 20th, there was an eclipse of the Moon. On March 30th, the United States purchased Alaska from Russia.

On July 11, 1870, the Sun crossed the Moon's node. On July 12th, there was an eclipse of the Moon. On July 19th, the Franco-Prussian War began. On July 18th, the doctrine of Papal infallibility was adopted by the Ecumenical Council in Rome.

On March 24th, 1885, Louis David Riel started his rebellion in northwest Canada. On March 25th, the Sun crossed the node. On March 30th, there was an eclipse of the Moon.

On September 2nd, 1885, the British, under General Kitchener, defeated the Mahdi's army and ended his rule in the Sudan. On September 8th, there was an eclipse of the Sun. On September 18th, the Sun crossed the node.

On January 11th, 1889, the Sun crossed the Moon's node. On January 17th, there was an eclipse of the Moon. On January 29th, Crown Prince Rudolf of Austria and Baroness Marie Vetsera were found assassinated.

[We are purposely making no note of great fires that occurred during these suggested unstable moments of time, because they will be treated in another chapter. We are taking our dates from the World Almanac, and it should be noted that for many specific years, that publication notes no outstanding dates or occurrences.]

The Park Place disaster in New York, killing 64 persons when a building floor collapse occurred on August 22nd, 1891. On August 24th, the Sun squared (90 degrees) the Moon's nodes.

On June 27th, 1894, the Sun squared the Moon's node. Five days later, on July 2nd, President Cleveland sent Federal troops into Chicago to battle strikers. Many died in conflict. Property damage was great. [ed. The Pulman Strike and birth of Labor Day.]

On February 22nd, 1896, the Sun crossed the Moon's node. On February 28th, there was an eclipse of the Moon. On February 29th, King Menelik of Ethiopia attacked the Italians, taking them by surprise at Adowa. The Italians lost 3600 white and 3000 native troops, killed and wounded.

On April 12th, 1898, the Sun squared (90 degrees) the Moon's nodes. On April 21st, diplomatic relations were broken between the United States and Spain. On April 22nd, the Cuban Blockade was declared. On April 24th, Spain declared war. On April 25th, the United States declared war. On May 1st, Dewey destroyed the Spanish fleet in Manila Bay.

The battles of San Juan and El Caney were fought from July 1st to 3rd. The battle of Santiago and the destruction of Admiral Cervera's fleet occurred on July 3rd. An eclipse of the Moon occurred on July 3rd, and the Moon crossed the node on July 9th.

On April 25th, 1902, the Sun crossed the Moon's node. If the writer may be facetious with this inclusion, he was born on April 27th, 1902. On May 7, 1902, there was an eclipse of the Sun. On May 8th, St. Pierre, Martinique, was destroyed by the eruption of Mt. Pelee. Over 30,000 lives were lost.

On April 6th, 1903, the Sun crossed the Moon's node. On April 12th there was an eclipse of the Moon. The Kishinev massacre of the Jews occurred on April 19th and 20th.

The first Wright Brothers plane flight at Kitty Hawk occurred on December 17th, 1903. The Sun squared (90 degrees) the Moon's nodes on December 25th.

The World Almanac for 1907 mentions only that Carrie Nation made her first hatchet raid on saloons in Kansas on January 24th of that year. The Sun crossed the Moon's node on

January 23rd. An eclipse of the Sun occurred on January 14th, and eclipse of the Moon on January 29th.

The year 1912 marked the greatest sea disaster which had ever occurred up until that time. It involved the loss of 1517 lives. On April 11th of that year, the Sun crossed the node. On April 14th, on her maiden voyage, the great steamship Titanic struck an iceberg in the North Atlantic. On April 15th, the ship sank. It was said that the band played, Nearer My God to Thee, as the ship went down. There was an eclipse of the Sun on April 17th.

On October 5th, 1912, the Sun crossed the node. On October 8th, the Balkan War began. On October 10th, there was an eclipse of the Sun.

King George of Greece was assassinated on March 18th, 1913. There was an eclipse of the Moon on March 22nd. The Sun crossed the node on March 24th.

August 1914 was a month of history. World War I began. Stock Exchanges closed. There was a series of preliminary events, but on August 16th, the British Expeditionary forces landed in France. On August 20th, the Germans occupied Brussels. On August 21st, there was an eclipse of the Sun. The Sun crossed the node on August 29th. The battle of the Marne lasted from September 6th to 10th. Perhaps we should also mention that on August 15th, the first ship passed through the Panama Canal.

On February 14th, 1915, occurred an eclipse of the Sun. On February 16th, the Sun crossed the Moon's node. On February 18th, Germany began her official submarine blockade of Great Britain. On March 1st, the British began a blockade of Germany. For general events of that year, the World Almanac records but one date. The Panama-Pacific International Exposition opened at San Francisco on February 20th.

May of 1915 was marked by the sinking of many vessels by German submarines. Of these, however, the most outstanding was the sinking of the Lusitania on May 7th. There were 1195 lives lost, and of these, 124 were Americans. The Sun squared the nodes on May 13th. No more sinkings appear to rate listing by the World Almanac until August 19th, when the Arabic was sunk. On August 10th, the Sun crossed the Moon's node. On the same day, there was an eclipse of the Sun. On August 17th, the Galveston hurricane killed 275 people.

On April 24th, 1916, the Sun squared the Moon's nodes. On that date, there was a rebel uprising in Dublin. Patrick H. Pearse and others were executed on May 3rd. Sir Roger Casement was hanged on August 3rd, four days after the eclipse of the Sun on July 30th. The Sun had crossed the node on July 21st. There was an eclipse of the Moon on July 15th. The first battle of Somme lasted from July 1st to 10th. The second battle of Somme lasted from July 14th to August 5th. Captain Fryatt was executed on July 27th.

This interval was not without excitement in the United States. Three days before the lunar eclipse, on July 12th, 1916, there was a Preparedness Day parade in San Francisco, which was accompanied by a great explosion, thus beginning the long drawn out Tom Mooney case. Remember that the solar eclipse was on July 30th on the eastern coast of the United States on that day. The Black Tom explosion took place with a loss of $22,000,000.

The events that led the United States will be a subsequent chapter, because they need more thorough treatment than we are offering in this chapter. However, there was an eclipse of the Sun on January 23rd, 1917, and nine days later, on February 1st, Germany began her unrestricted submarine warfare, which caused the United States to break off diplomatic relations on February 3rd.

On April 5th, 1917, the Sun squared the nodes of the Moon, and on April 6th, the United States declared war on Germany.

There was a solar eclipse on June 19th, 1917. The first American troops landed in France on June 26th, 1917. On July 2nd, the Sun crossed the Moon's node. On July 4th (birthday of the United States) there was an eclipse of Moon.

On December 7th, 1917, the United States declared war on Austria. On December 14th, there was an eclipse of the Sun, On December 23rd, the Sun crossed the Moon's node. The United States took over the control of the railroads on December 28th. There was an eclipse of the Moon on that day. We might also add that Congress passed the 18th Amendment (Prohibition) on December 18th, 1917.

The armistice was signed on November 11th, 1918. The German fleet surrendered on November 21st. There was an eclipse of the Sun on December 3rd, United States troops entered Mainz on December 6th. The Sun crossed the node of the Moon on that date. American troops crossed the Rhine on December 13th. There occurred an eclipse of the Moon on December 17th.

On June 14th of that year, the Sun had crossed a lunar node. On June 24th, there was an eclipse of the Moon. The mass murder of the Czar of Russia and his family is reputed to have taken place twelve days later, on July 6th. The constitution of the Soviet Republic regime was adopted on July 10th.

From July 10th, 1919, various countries were ratifying the Versailles Treaty, but on November 17th of that year the Sun crossed the Moon's node, and on November 19th, ratification was defeated in the United States Senate. There was an eclipse of the Sun on November 22nd.

The years 1920 to 1923 were rather quiet. On October 27th, 1920, there was an eclipse of the Moon. On October 29th, the Sun crossed the Moon's node. On November 2nd, Warren Harding was elected President, thus ending the wartime administration of Woodrow Wilson and the Democratic party. On November 10th, there was an eclipse of the Sun. Here was a President elected near the time of the eclipses. He was elected on his birthday. He died in office.

On March 3rd, 1923, there was an eclipse of the Moon. Early in March, there was a revolt in Bavaria which ended on March 9th, when the Beer Putschists marched in Munich. This revolt was organized by General Ludendorff and another whose name was little known. He was wounded. His name was Adolf Hitler. On March 12th, the Sun crossed the Moon's node, and on March 17th, there was an eclipse of the Sun.

On August 14th, 1924, there was an eclipse of the Moon. On August 15th, the Sun crossed the node. On August 16th, the Allies and Germany accepted the Dawes Reparation Plan. On August 18th, French troops began evacuation of the Ruhr. The

Agreement was formally signed on August 30th, 1924. There was an eclipse of the Sun on that day.

Newspaper-wise, the story that took public attention in 1924 was the Leopold and Loeb case. These two young men of means kidnapped, mutilated and killed Robert Franks, 13, on May 22nd, four days after the Moon crossed the square of the node on May 18th.

Politically, the most important event of the year came on Election Day, November 9th, 1924, when two of the states elected women governors. Nellie Taylor Ross was elected Governor of Wyoming, and Miriam (Ma) Ferguson was elected Governor of Texas. The Sun squared the nodes on November 10th.

On January 20th, 1925, a storm in Missouri, Southern Illinois and Indiana killed more than 830 persons, injured 3,800, and caused property loss of over ten million dollars. On January 24th, there was an eclipse of the Sun.

The greatest news story of 1925 was the Scopes Trial. On July 20th, 1925, there was an eclipse of the Sun. John T. Scopes was prosecuted for teaching evolution in Tennessee. His prosecutor was none other than William Jennings Bryan, many-times candidate for President on the Democratic ticket. Scopes was found guilty on July 24th. Two days later, on July 26th, William Jennings Bryan died suddenly. The Sun crossed the node on July 28th. There was an eclipse of the Moon on August 4th. On August 5th, two Nine Power Treaties of the Limitation of Armaments Conference were ratified in Washington by the United States, France, Japan, Italy, Great Britain, China, Portugal, Belgium and Holland.

America went crazy in 1927. A young man had flown the Atlantic alone. Charles A. Lindbergh was welcomed back to the United States by President Calvin Coolidge on June 11th, 1927, New York City put on its greatest celebration of all time on June 13th. There was an eclipse of the Moon on June 15th and Lindbergh was welcomed in Brooklyn on June 16th. He flew his Spirit of St. Louis to St. Louis on June 17th. The Sun crossed the node on June 20th. There was an eclipse of the Sun on June 29th.

On March 23, 1927, Cantonese troops shelled the burning Standard Oil plant, killing several foreigners. The Sun squared the node on March 24th. The most sensational murder case of that year was that of Albert Snyder by his wife, Ruth, and Judd Gray, her lover. The murder occurred on March 20th.

On February 11th, 1929, the Papal State, extinct since 1870, was recreated under the name of the State of the Vatican City. On February 14th, the Sun squared the nodes.

On May 9th, 1929, there was an eclipse of the Sun. I noted at the time that this was the birth date of an outstanding New York banker who was heavily involved in market operations of the stock of Radio Corporation of America. Knowing the man personally, I was in a position to know many facts that have never become public. He was also a key national figure. He began widely expanding his stock market interests. The fall of the year brought the greatest of all stock market crashes, the most radical part of which became most disastrous by November 1st, when there was another eclipse of the Sun. At this time, the New York banker committed suicide. On that same day, Albert B. Fall, former Secretary of the Interior was sentenced to a year in jail and a fine of $100,000.

The London Naval Reduction Treaty was signed on April 22nd, 1930. The Sun crossed the node on April 23rd. The writer's birthday is April 27th. There was an eclipse of the Sun on April 28th. The writer will long remember this eclipse. He made an important change in his life on April 28th, joining up with a new firm. From the window of his new office, he watched the eclipse. Everything looked like a perfect setup, but within a month, partners in the firm could not agree, and the firm was dissolved.

Things were happening in South America. Governments were being overthrown one after another, winding up with the overthrow of the Brazilian government on October 24th. The Sun had crossed the node on October 17th, and there had been an eclipse of the Sun on October 21st. There was also an eclipse of the Moon on October 7th. The British dirigible, R-101, was destroyed with 47 deaths on October 5th.

We have not completed our submission of data relative to events which occurred during what we have suggested as the unstable intervals of time which appear to accompany the angular relationship of the Sun and the Moon's node, eclipses, etc., but we were closing an era in 1931 to begin a new one in 1932 and 1933. We will treat this new era in the next two chapters. There were other events worthy of notice which did not coincide with the factors. We have been employing. It must not be forgotten that there are other possible causative factors, however, others that we have not mentioned up to this time of this book. We are not expecting a perfect score. We are merely suggesting that there may be unstable moments of time, and that some of these unstable moments of time may have an association with the Moon's node-Sun relationship. There is much more data to be considered, however.

MORE UNSTABLE MOMENTS OF TIME

Astute observers may already have noticed certain characteristics of the type of events we have been recording as having happened during what we have suggested as unstable moments of time. Over centuries, knowledge of eclipses could have been regarded as military information. What occurs during these intervals does not appear to be in line with the laws of probability. The unexpected and the improbable seem to happen. The status quo is disturbed. Events are exciting. They gain attention. They are what newspapermen write about, and what the rest of the people think about. These events often appear to be subject to subsequent unexpected developments, as we will later point out. As events, they are not individual unrelated events. They are like part of a chain. The thread of destiny appears to run through them, just as World War II could not be said to be unrelated to World War I.

What would be the probability of Abraham Lincoln being assassinated within five days after General Lee's surrender, with an eclipse separating the two events?

What would be the probability of William Jennings Bryan dying within two days after he succeeded in convicting John T. Scopes, both events being close to the eclipses?

The spectacular is involved, and we are reminded of the view of the noted psychologist, Karl Jung, who said that **time has quality, and that whatever is born at a given moment of time has the characteristics of that moment of time.**

It is the suggestion of the writer that **there is a time of stability when the status quo is not easily disturbed, and that this time is when the Sun is 45 degrees from one node, 135 degrees from the other. Society is balanced. The pendulum is at rest, so to speak.** It swings neither to the right nor to the left. The Sun moves away from this point of stability, and there is a slight movement to the symbolical pendulum. **The Sun moves toward either the zero or the 90 degree point, which acts as a point of maximum disturbance.** As the Sun moves toward either of these points, there is a gradual increase of excitation. **The zero and 90 degree points mark the intervals of greatest**

instability when the status quo is most likely to be disturbed. Our original lunar cycle was approximately 28 days. This is a longer cycle, averaging approximately 86.5 days. This cycle can completely upset the earlier cycle in its functioning. It supersedes it.

We do not know how many other cycles there may be which interfere with these two and bring about exceptions to the rule. There may be many. Nevertheless, we have shown that from 1865 to 1931, the most celebrated events of history conformed with this pattern. We will show that this tendency did not stop with 1931. We have a grave problem in deciding whether eclipses of themselves are of any significance. That is why we have listed both the dates of the eclipses and the dates when the Sun crossed the node [Ed. CPT coined the term Moon Wobble]. **There is no eclipse when the Sun is 90 degrees from the node, and we appear to find these intervals also important. We find that important events of history seldom occur when the Sun is in the area near 45 degrees from the node. We suggest that judgment is doubtful during the intervals of suggested instability.**

We pointed out that the Sun squared the nodes on April, 12th, 1898. Diplomatic relations were broken with Spain nine days later. The last chapter shows a series of events till May 1st. The World Almanac lists no further events until July 1st, a complete lull of two months. Why the lull? When the Sun was crossing the point 45 degrees from the node, nothing but routine preparations were taking place. Nothing was reaching any climax. On May 1st, the Sun was 70 degrees from the node. It crossed the 45 degree point on May 26th. Everything began popping from July 1st on, when the Sun was within 9 degrees of the node and approaching it.

The archduke of Austria and his wife were assassinated on June 28th, 1914, with the Sun 63 degrees from a node going toward the 45 degree point of stability. There was a lull. Nothing important happened. Nations only talked, but on July 28th, a month later, with the Sun leaving the area of stability, Austria declared war on Serbia. The Sun was 33 degrees from the node- past the 45 degree area-heading for the interval of instability.

Russian troops invaded Germany on August 2nd, with the Sun 28 degrees from the node. British forces landed in France on August 16th, with the Sun 14 degrees from the node. The Germans occupied Brussels on August 20th with the Sun 10 degrees from the node. The Sun crossed the node on August 29th. The battle of the Marne lasted from September 6th to 10th. After that, there appears to have been another lull.

This same tendency can be noted on other occasions, but this method of observation is unsatisfactory because it allows no statistical evaluation. Nevertheless, let us go further in listing events that did occur during our suggested intervals of instability.

We illustrated how Charles Lindbergh reached his place of greatest honor near the time of the crossing of the node by the Sun, and near the time of two eclipses. Let us follow Lindbergh a little further. Leading up to the solar eclipse of March 7th, 1932, the Lindbergh baby was kidnapped on March 1st. On March 17th, the Sun crossed the node. On March 22nd, there was an eclipse of the Moon. Throughout the entire month of March, the public mind was centered on little else than the Lindbergh kidnapping. Until the last day of February, attention had been entirely centered on the Japanese attack at Shanghai, but thereafter, you could find nothing about it in the newspapers. Had anyone wanted to get the American attention away from what was happening in China, they could not have conceived of a better plan.

On September 10th, 1934, Bruno Richard Hauptman was arrested, and was found to possess some of the ransom money, and although the evidence failed to bring him to the scene of the alleged murder, he was convicted of murder amid a wave of mass hysteria. During the trial, Lindbergh testified that he recognized Hauptman's voice as the voice of the man to whom he had tossed $50,000 over a cemetery wall. There were two other facts that did not appear in the court record of the case. During the trial, on February 3rd, 1935, there was an eclipse of the Sun. Lindbergh's birthday was February 4th. Lindbergh's testimony against Hauptman was given on or close to his birthday and close to an eclipse of the Sun, within a degree of his natal Sun. The Sun had crossed the node on January 21st.

Among learned people, and particularly among lawyers, there was a feeling that the Hauptman trial was a monster. It was conducted, not in the solemn atmosphere of the usual courtroom, but in the atmosphere of a county fair. All that was lacking was a band. On other occasions, the trial would have been called a lynching, but it was a tribute to the name of Lindbergh during an eclipse near his birth date.

The writer has always felt that the Lindbergh legend died with his testimony, and with the eclipse within a day of his birthday. He had testified that he recognized a man's voice that he had heard but once, after three long years.

There was dissatisfaction, despite the fact that it was the dissatisfaction of a minority, a thinking minority.

Persons in high places believed that there was more to the case than Bruno Richard Hauptman. These persons included the warden of the state penitentiary in Trenton, Governor Harold G. Hoffman of New Jersey, Clarence Darrow, and Evalyn Walsh McLean who spent over $100,000.00 on the case. In a conversation with the writer, Governor Hoffman said, "Do you realize that every person who was present in the Lindbergh home on the night of the kidnapping is either dead or out of the country?" Lindbergh and his family had just slipped out of the country to live in England. On April 3rd, 1936, Hauptman was electrocuted in the Trenton prison. The Sun had squared the nodes on March 28th, six days before. Lindbergh stayed in Europe. In Germany, he mixed with the Nazis and accepted one of their medals. Many Americans were horrified; particularly those who had shouted for Hauptman's blood the loudest, on the grounds that he was a German and probably a Nazi.

The Lindbergh legend was over. Never again did the name of Lindbergh have the same magic over people's hearts.

Aside from the Lindbergh kidnapping, the greatest story of 1932 was the Seabury Investigation in New York. They were after James J. Walker, mayor of New York City. Late on the night of August 31st, there was an eclipse of the Sun, and on the following morning, Mayor Walker resigned from office. This resignation was to be of great significance over the years, because from that moment on, Tammany Hall began to crumble and its power diminished. The Sun crossed the node on September 10th.

These two stories are typical of the kind of event we find associated with this lunar node-Sun relationship, typical of what we mean when we refer to our cycle of social instability. We repeat ourselves. **The unexpected and improbable seems to occur. Events are exciting. The status quo is disturbed. Who would have dreamed that the Lindbergh baby could have been kidnapped?** Who would have expected the resignation of James Walker, the most popular and colorful mayor that New York ever had, and the subsequent crumbling of Tammany Hall?

Looking over the World Almanac we find another event. We find that on March 12th, in Paris, Ivar Kreuger, Swedish "match king" committed suicide on March 12th, five days after the eclipse of March 7th, heretofore noted.

On June 4th, there was a revolution in Chile. The Sun squared the nodes on June 12th.

On November 8th, 1932, Franklin D. Roosevelt was elected President of the United States. That date does not conform with one of our periods of instability, but wait. We will have more to say. That date was near the high point in the lunar cycle for F. D. Roosevelt and near the bottom for Herbert Hoover, whom he defeated.

The next eclipse was that of the Sun on February 24th, 1933. The Sun crossed the node on February 26th. Things began to happen on February 14th, when Governor Comstock of Michigan ordered all banks in that state closed. Banks in other states were closing by the hundreds, and on March 4th, Franklin D. Roosevelt took office. He declared a national bank holiday and all banks closed on March 6th. Conditions were stabilized and banks reopened on March 15th, as the Sun moved away from the Moon's node. Again, this interval marked one of the greatest periods of chaos and instability we had ever known.

On February 27th, three days after the eclipse and one day after the Sun crossed the node, another historic event occurred on the other side of the Atlantic. The German Reichstag was destroyed by fire. On March 5th, two days before the eclipse, the

Reichstag, which was later to place Adolf Hitler to power was elected. The next eclipse was a solar eclipse on August 21st, 1933.

On August 12th, an army revolt caused Cuban President Machado to resign and flee. Carlos Cespedes became Provisional President on August 13th. The Sun crossed the node on the same date as the eclipse. A second revolt on September 5th placed Ramon Grau San Martin in office. He remained in office until January 18th, 1934, twelve days before the eclipse of January 30th, 1934. The Sun did not cross the node until February 8th. His term began 15 days after one eclipse and lasted until 12 days before another.

On May 25th, 1933, the Sun squared the node. On May 27th, the United States Supreme Court declared the National Recovery Act unconstitutional. On November 16th, 1933, the Sun again squared the node. On that day, the United States established diplomatic relations with Russia.

On January 30th, 1934, The birthday of President Roosevelt and also of the German Republic, there was an eclipse of the Moon. The Sun crossed the node on February 9th. There was an eclipse of the Sun on February 14th. On January 31st, the U.S. Government reduced the gold content of the dollar. The Social Democratic (Nazi) uprising in Vienna, Linz, and other places, took place from February 12th to 15th. On February 17th, King Albert of Belgium fell from a cliff and was killed.

There was another dramatic episode. The F.B.I. had declared John Dillinger as public enemy Number One. He was captured in Tucson, Arizona, on January 25th, five days before the eclipse.

There was a lunar eclipse July 26th, 1934. The Sun crossed the node on August 2nd. There was a solar eclipse, on August 10th. On July 1st, Franklin Roosevelt left on the cruiser Houston for Hawaii. He reached Portland, Oregon on his return trip on August 3rd, and returned to Washington. That comment is merely to let the reader know where he was.

On July 25th, in Vienna, the Nazis seized the building used by the cabinet and assassinated Chancellor Engelbert Dollfuss. This occurred on the day before the lunar eclipse. On August 2nd, when the Sun crossed the node. President von Hindenburg died.

On August 19th, nine days after the solar eclipse, the German people approved the consolidation of the offices of President and Chancellor in a single Leader-Chancellor. Adolf Hitler was head man, six months after an eclipse on the birthdays of both President Roosevelt and the German Republic!

There was another dramatic episode. John Dillinger had escaped from jail at Crown Point, Ind., on March 3rd. He was shot to death by F.B.I. agents outside a movie theatre on July 22nd, four days before the lunar eclipse.

On January 5th, 1935, there was an eclipse of the Sun. On January 19th, there was an eclipse of the Moon. On January 21st, the Sun crossed the node.

On January 6th, the U.S. Supreme Court upset the Agricultural Adjustment Act. On January 13th, the Saar Territory, taken from Germany by the Versailles Treaty, voted to return to German ownership.

A check on The World Almanac does not appear to mention very much in the way of excitement as accompanying three eclipses that occurred during the summer of 1935. Over in England, however, a romance was attracting a vast amount of attention. Folks were trying to watch the Prince of Wales and a companion named Mrs. Simpson. The birth date of the prince was June 23rd. On June 30th, there was an eclipse of the Sun. On July 15th, the Sun crossed the node. We see no significance to events at this time other than the fact that the eclipse was close to the birth date of the prince.

On December 25th, there was an eclipse of the Sun. On January 3rd, 1936, the Sun crossed the node. On January 8th, there was an eclipse of the Moon. Geocentrically speaking, the eclipse of December 25th was almost exactly opposite the birth-Sun position of the Prince of Wales. On January 20th, King George V of England died. He was succeeded by his eldest son, the Prince of Wales, who was never to be crowned.

On June 19th, there was an eclipse of the Sun. It might be mentioned that this was the approximate birth date of Mrs. Wallis Simpson. On June 25th, the Sun crossed the node. On July 4th, birth date of the United States, there was an eclipse of the

Moon. During late July and August, the node crossed the birth-Sun position of the new king.

On July 11th, Adolf Hitler signed a treaty with Austria and promised to recognize the Austrian frontier. The revolt against Spain's Republican government began on July 17th. In England there were preparations for the coronation. On October 27th, Mrs. Simpson was divorced in her preparation to marry the king.

On December 13th, there was an eclipse of the Sun. This was the birth date of the Duke of York. On December 11th, the new king abdicated and the Duke of York became King George VI. On June 3rd, 1937, Mrs. Simpson and the dethroned king, now the Duke of Windsor, were married. On June 8th, 1937, there was an eclipse of the Sun. On June 6th, the Sun had crossed the node. The outlook for the new king was World War II.

Let us also mention that on December 16th, 1936, three days after the eclipse of December 13th, the Inter-American conference for the Maintenance of Peace adopted the collective security convention, the non-intervention protocol, and the resolution calling upon republics that had not already done so to ratify existing peace treaties.

A rather interesting development took place on May 14th, 1938. Scientists uncovered King Solomon's long-vanished seaport, where he built and operated ships and smelted copper at the northern end of the eastern arm of the Red Sea. May 14th was also the date of an eclipse of the Moon. The Sun crossed the node on May 18th.

On November 2nd, 1938, Germany and Italy awarded 4,000 square miles of Czechoslovakia to Hungary. The Hungarians marched in on November 5th. There was an eclipse of the Moon on November 7th. On November 10th, the Sun crossed the node. On November 12th, the German Government decreed a fine of a billion marks on Jews. In this chronology, we are headed for the year 1939, the year when World War II began.

INSTABILITY AND WORLD WAR II

In the presentation of data in the last two chapters of this work, we did not establish a norm. We did not show that the frequency of events occurring during our suggested intervals of instability is anything other than chance might allow. The size of a newspaper is not determined by the amount of available news. It is more likely to be determined by the amount of available advertising. Headlines are not always an indication. On 365 days of the year, newspapermen find something to write about, and they fill their columns. If there isn't a war, or if a king doesn't die, the news columns can be filled with news which might not be printed otherwise. The attack of the Japanese on Shanghai was big-headline news until the Lindbergh baby was kidnapped. Thereafter, it didn't rate any front page space whatever. Yet, it cannot be denied that the type of historical event we have been enumerating as having happened during our suggested intervals of instability contains something of the unusual and the sensational. Ultimately, we will have to more carefully define the character of the type of event which appears to recur during our suggested unstable intervals.

We have encountered the odd coincidence of sensational circumstances developing at the time, or subsequent to, eclipses occurring near the birth dates of people involved or entangled. It is important that the reader realize that such phenomena recur only at intervals of 19 years, for it takes between 18 and 19 years for the lunar node to travel all the way around the ecliptic. At the end of 19 years, new moons recur in approximately the same celestial longitude, and because the lunar nodes are also again near their previous positions, eclipses usually occur on or near the same dates.

It must be realized that in the majority of cases we have presented. we did not know the birthdays of the principals involved. Therefore, the significance of the cases we have presented is greater.

World War II began in 1939. It was generally recognized that one man, more than any other, was responsible for this war. He was Adolf Hitler, whose birthday was April 20th. On April 19th,

1939, there was an eclipse of the sun. The war did not begin at the time of this eclipse, but on April 27th, the British House of Commons authorized conscription. On April 29th, the sun crossed the node. In New York on April 30th, the World Fair opened. On May 2nd, Molotov became Commissar of Foreign Affairs in Russia. There was an eclipse of the moon on May 3rd. On May 7th, a military pact between Hitler and Mussolini was announced. On May 11th, fighting broke out between Japanese and Soviet troops near Lake Bor and lasted for six months, On May 17th, the King of England began a tour of Canada and the United States.

On April 20th, Hitler's birthday, the south node of the moon was 9 degrees of arc from Hitler's birth-sun position. It moves very slowly. The south node crossed the place of Hitler's sun either in September or the first few days of October, according to published astronomical data, which can be slightly inaccurate due to the fact that published positions of the nodes are average positions and do not show a slight bobbing back-and-forth motion of the nodes.* Hitler invaded Poland on September 1st. Great Britain declared war on September 3rd. This day marked the exact top of the lunar cycle for Adolf Hitler. It was near the bottom for the British king.

On September 27th, Russia invaded Poland. On September 28th, Warsaw fell to the Germans. There was not much left to the war in Poland. From here on, it was a mop up. On October 10th, Hitler spoke before the Reichstag, saying, "I have given expression to our readiness for peace. Germany has no cause for war against the Western powers. They have recklessly provoked a war on the flimsiest grounds. If they reject our readiness for peace, Germany is determined to take up the battle and fight it out-this way or that." A phase of the war had ended. There was an eclipse of the sun two days after Hitler's speech on October 12th, 1939. On October 23rd, the sun crossed the node. There was an eclipse of the Moon on October 28th. Before leaving 1939, let us also mention that the sun squared the node on February 3rd, Pope Pius XI died on February 10th.

From here on, through the winter of 1939-40, the war in Europe began to take on the term "phony war." England and

France, the countries that egged Poland into the war against Hitler, confined their war-making activities to reporting that scouts had raised their heads to see what the enemy was doing.

Then came April of 1940. On April 7th, there was an eclipse of the sun. On April 8th Hitler began the invasion of Denmark and Norway. On April 10th, the sun crossed the node. The position of the moon as this invasion began was approximately the same as on September 1st, 1939, when Hitler invaded Poland. From the lunar cycle point of view, however, we have pointed out that this cycle is undependable when the sun is near or square to a lunar node.

On July 8th, 1940, the sun squared the node. On July 9th, the Duke of Windsor was appointed Governor and Commander-in-Chief of the Bahama Islands [Ed. To move the Duke away from Europe and the War]. On July 14th, Estonia, Latvia and Lithuania were annexed by Russia.

From the time of the April 7th, 1940, eclipse, Hitler never stopped marching until he had swept over Norway, Denmark, Netherlands, Belgium and France. Things wound up on July 9th (day after sun squared the node) when the French Parliament voted itself out of existence.

September 27th, 1940, was an important day, because the Axis powers took action that was later to bring the United States into the war. As we look back now, this was an act of self-destruction on their part. Germany, Italy and Japan signed a ten-year pact to assist one another with all political, economic and military means "when one of the three contracting powers is attacked by a power at present not involved in the European War or in the Chinese-Japanese conflict." Four days later, on October 1st, there was an eclipse of the sun. On October 4th, the sun crossed the node.

We arrive in 1941. There was an eclipse of the moon on March 13th, 1941. The Sun crossed the node on March 23rd. There was an eclipse of the sun on March 27th. An event of great importance to the future destiny of the Axis powers occurred on March 10th. President Roosevelt signed the Lend-Lease Bill. On the day of the solar eclipse, March 27th, 17-year-old King Peter was enthroned as king of Yugoslavia. On June 19th, 1941, the sun squared the node. On June 22nd, Germany invaded Russia.

On September 5th, 1941, there was a lunar eclipse. On September 15th, the sun crossed the node, and on September 21st, there occurred a solar eclipse. On August 25th, Great Britain and Russia invaded Iran. This country accepted their terms on September 9th. Somewhat of an incident occurred on September 22nd. A United States government ship, flying the flag of Panama, was sunk by a submarine off Iceland.

On December 7th, 1941, Japan attacked Pearl Harbor. On December 8th the United States declared war on Japan. On December 9th, the sun squared the node. On that day, Japan began its invasion of the Philippines. On December 10th, the British battleship Prince of Wales, and the cruiser Repulse were sunk off Malaya. On December 11th, the United States declared war on Germany and Italy. On December 12th, Japan occupied Guam.

We will not attempt to further enumerate the vast parade of other events which occurred during this interval. The writer counted 85 different declarations of war that took place in December.

Our next interval of suggested instability came in March 1942. On March 3rd, there was an eclipse of the moon. On March 4th, the sun crossed the node. On March 16th, there was a solar eclipse. On March 5th, Tokyo announced that Jap forces had occupied Batavia in Java. On March 8th, Japan invaded New Guinea. General Douglas MacArthur arrived in Australia on March 17th.

On May 30th, 1942, the sun squared the node. On the 30th and 31st, Great Britain made a mass raid with 1,130 planes on Cologne, Germany. This is the first item we find where the war was being taken to Axis territory. The battle of Midway took place on June 4th, 5th and 6th. This was Japan's first defeat of the war. On June 5th, the United States declared war on Bulgaria, Hungary and Romania. On June 7th, Japan invaded the Aleutians.

Our next interval of suggested instability arrived in August, 1942. There was an eclipse of the sun on August 12th. There was an eclipse of the moon on August 26th. The sun crossed the node on August 27th. There was another eclipse of the sun on September 10th.

The United States attacked Guadalcanal on August 7th. US. Marines established a beachhead on August 8th. A great naval battle between Japanese and American ships took place on August 9th. On the French coast, on August 19th, British, American, Canadian and Free French forces landed on the mainland and attacked Dieppe. On August 22nd, Brazil declared war on Germany. The naval Battle of the Eastern Solomons was fought on August 23rd. On August 25th, the Duke of Kent, brother of King George VI, was killed in an air crash. On September 10th, the British announced the invasion of Madagascar. On September 15th, the U.S. aircraft-carrier Wasp was sunk.

After the above period, there is a lull. Fighting was a continuation of operations already begun. On November 7th landing operations in North Africa began. There was a major naval engagement in the Solomon Island area on November 12th to 15th, the Battle of Guadalcanal. On November 22nd, the sun squared the node. From November 13th to 31st, New York Harbor was blocked by German mines. On November 23rd, French Admiral Jean Francois Darlan announced that French North Africa had come under Allied control. On November 27th, the French fleet was scuttled at Toulon.

There occurred an eclipse of the sun on February 4th, 1943. The sun crossed the node on February 14th. An eclipse of the moon took place on February 20th. There was a series of developments beginning on January 17th and lasting till February 16th, and then the World Almanac mentions no war events until April.

Iraq declared war on January 17th. On January 18th, the 17-month siege of Leningrad was broken. The Russians took 31,000 prisoners. Chile broke relations with the Axis countries on January 20th. U.S. Army Air Force began bombing of Germany on January 27th. Brazil joined the United Nations on February 6th. The windup offensive on Guadalcanal occurred on February 14th. Soviet forces occupied Kharkov on February 16th.

On May 12th, the sun squared the node, and it was announced that organized resistance in Tunisia was ended.

There was an eclipse of the sun on August 1st. The moon crossed the node on August 9th, and there was an eclipse of the moon on August 15th. With this August 1st eclipse; everything went to pieces in Mussolini's Italy. Mussolini and not Hitler, had been the original dictator. On July 19th, Rome itself was bombed by the U.S. Air Force. On July 25th, six days before the eclipse, Mussolini was toppled. King Emmanuel announced Mussolini's resignation. Badoglio succeeded him. The August 1st eclipse was close to the birth date of Mussolini. On August 15th, forces landing in the Aleutians discovered that the Japs had evacuated. Technically, Italy remained in the war until October 13th, but without Mussolini, it wasn't the same kind of war. It was a matter of bargaining for peace.

In the general news, we note that on the day of the August 1st eclipse, Harlem riots caused a million dollars worth of damage and five deaths.

On November 5th, the sun squared the node. This does not appear to be a very important period, although the Russians recaptured Kiev on November 6th.

There was an eclipse of the sun on January 25th, 194-4. The sun crossed the node on January 28th. Records do not indicate this as a very important interval, although there was one event that captured the public's attention. U.S. planes destroyed the Abbey of Mount Cassino on February 3rd.

On April 22nd, two days from the birthday of Hitler, the sun squared the node. Neither does this appear to be a very important period, but let us point out that for the first time since the beginning of the war, when the node was crossing Hitler's birth-sun position, the node was again involving this birth date. The node had moved approximately 90 degrees since the beginning of the war in 1939. In May and June, it actually squared Hitler's birth-sun position. Watch developments.

On July 20th, 1944, there was an eclipse of the sun. On July 19th, Hitler was burned and bruised at his headquarters by a bomb, set off by a would-be assassin. The volume, *The Last Days of Hitler*, lays great stress on this date, and tells us that this event was practically the end of the war for Hitler. From that day on, his spirit was gone. He had no confidence. He was a nervous wreck.

The sun also crossed the node on July 20th. From then on, Hitler was a changed man who lived in the shadow and fear of defeat. His only partner now was Japan. Mussolini, although still alive, was powerless. Japan was far away and slipping.

We have skipped a very important event. June 6th, 1944, was 'D' Day. It does not conform to the pattern. This long planned venture did not occur during one of our intervals of suggested instability. In fact, on that date, the sun was between 44 and 45 degrees from the node, the exact center of our period of stability, rather than our period of instability. The writer is not going to attempt to interpret this one way or the other on the grounds that it was a single event, and therefore, it does not lend itself to any form of statistical analysis. Of course, the last three chapters do not actually lend themselves to statistical analysis. We have merely been holding a parade of events. Yet, it has been an impressive parade. Nevertheless, we have reached no definite conclusions. The writer is just as open-minded as his most open-minded reader. He has merely presented evidence for consideration. He has asked for no verdict. He not only admits but calls to your attention the fact that the evidence is circumstantial. He suggests the possibility of an 86.5 day cycle. He draws no definite conclusion. Having made that point clear, can we go on with the parade?

The bombing of Hitler was not the only event that accompanied the July 20th crossing of the node by the sun. Allied armies were moving forward on all fronts, closing in. Throughout the summer, Germany was retreating across France. U.S. Troops landed on Guam on July 19th. Little countries that had taken up sides with the Axis were being knocked out of the war one by one. By September 4th, Finland had quit. Bulgaria was out of the war by September 9th. By September 10th, American shells were falling on German territory.

On October 16th, 1944, the sun squared the node. For the most part, the fall was merely a continuation of Allied victories that had begun in the summer, but on October 22nd it was announced that US troops had landed in the Philippines. This began the invasion. Otherwise, it is difficult to pick out significant dates during the remainder of 1944. It was one continued forward march for the Allied forces on all fronts. Before leaving 1944, however, let us take note of the fact that in the United States, at Port Chicago in California, 322 persons were killed by the explosion of two monition ships on July 17th. Note that this was within two days of the date when Hitler was injured by an explosion, three days from the sun's crossing of the node and an eclipse.

There was an eclipse of the sun on January 14th, 1945. The sun had crossed the node on January 9th. This was the last eclipse to occur in the lives of Franklin D. Roosevelt, Adolf Hitler or Benito Mussolini. On January 9th, General Douglas MacArthur, with Sixth Army troops, landed on Luzon in the Philippines, and began the invasion of that main Island. On January 11th, the Germans began a general withdrawal on the Western front. On January 13th, the Russians opened their winter offensive and advanced to within 71 miles of German territory. They took Warsaw on January 17th. Hungary was out of the war by January 20th. By January 26th, Allied troops were advancing into Germany from the west.

On all fronts, the forward march continued. U.S. Forces were getting closer to Japan. By February, they were bombing Tokyo and other parts of Japan at will. Berlin and other cities were soon bombed every night by thousands of planes. The Axis was crumbling under the greatest military attack known to history.

On April 3rd, the sun squared the node. On April 1st, U.S. troops landed on Okinawa, and were within 352 miles of the Japanese home islands. On April 12th, with U.S. troops within 60 miles of Berlin, Franklin D. Roosevelt died. Organized resistance in Germany was as good as over, although the final official surrender did not come till May 15th (New York Time). Benito Mussolini was executed on April 28th, and Adolf Hitler is supposed to have ended his own life on April 30th.

Only the Japanese phase of World War II remained, and that not for long. Japan was now alone, all of her partners were gone. On June 25th, there was an eclipse of the moon. On July 1st, the sun crossed the node. On July 9th, there was an eclipse of the sun.

Organized Japanese resistance on Okinawa ended on June 21st. By July 4th, U.S. planes based on Okinawa were bombing

Japan. Japanese naval resistance appeared to be over. During these months, the moon's north node was crossing the birth-sun position for the birthday of the United States. Japan's position was now hopeless. It was mainly a matter of terms. Could she bargain? The atomic bomb was dropped on August 6th. The sun was 36 degrees beyond the node. This date did not conform to one of our suggested intervals of instability, Japan surrendered on August 14th, with the sun 45 degrees from the node. The point of stability rather than a point of instability.

On December 19th, 1945, there was an eclipse of the moon. The sun crossed the node of December 23rd. On December 21st, General George S. Patton Jr., one of the most colorful American figures of the war, died. On December 15th, the United Nations had chosen the United States as its permanent seat. There was an eclipse of the sun on January 3rd, 1940. On January 10th, the first assembly of the United Nations opened in London.

Also of interest during the period covered by the above paragraph were the facts that Shinto was abolished as the national religion of Japan on December 15th, and the World Bank was set up on December 27th, 1945.

On November 23rd, 1946, there was an eclipse of the moon. On December 4th, the Sun crossed the node. On December 8th, there occurred an eclipse of the sun. On December 11th, John D. Rockefeller Jr. offered an $8,500,000 plot of land in mid-town Manhattan as the site of the U.N. World Capital. The offer was accepted on December 12th.

On November 12th, 1947, there occurred an eclipse of the sun, and the sun crossed the node on November 16th. On November 13th, the U.N. General Assembly approved a U.S. proposal for an all-year-round "Little Assembly" to cope with issues arising while the parent body was in recess.

Upon the death of F. D. Roosevelt, Harry S. Truman had become President of the United States. There was glee in the Republican camp, where Truman was considered a pushover. His defeat in the election in the fall of 1948 was a foregone conclusion. The American Labor Party had turned against him. In the south, the Dixiecrats had turned against him. All the pollsters forecast his defeat. On election night, the head of the Secret

Service is reputed to have gone to New York to take over the guarding of the new President, Truman's opponent.

On October 28th, 1948, the sun crossed the node. On November 1st, there was an eclipse of the sun. On November 2nd, the United States held its Presidential election, and on the following day, it was discovered that Harry S. Truman was going to continue in office. This event again emphasizes the element of the unexpected.

*Editor's note: The true lunar nodes 'oscillate' more than the mean lunar nodes that is an averaged position. These two measurements can vary by a degree which becomes important when these lunar nodes change signs. It can be up to a month's difference between the two measurements of the mean node versus the true node. This needs to be studied more since so many astrologers are mislead by the term 'true node'.

WHEN DO GREAT FIRES OCCUR?

Have you ever noted that fires seem to occur in a series? You read of one unusual fire, and it is quickly followed by another, or so it seems.

It has appeared to the writer that newspapers are filled with stories of fires during our suggested intervals of instability.

Some time after earlier chapters of this work were prepared, the writer ran across the possibility of another cycle, a cycle that still relates to the nodes of the moon. **This cycle, however, relates to the longitudinal distance between the lunar nodes and the planet Uranus.**

Now, Uranus is far away, and no physicist of crystallized ideas will ever be able to understand how this factor could be of any importance. The modern physicist or the modern astronomer is no more of an expert on this subject, however, than Napoleon was an expert on television. Consequently, we are not concerned with the crystallized views of any group. We have new evidence to consider.

From one crossing of the planet Uranus by the north node to another requires a few days more than 15 years. Break this cycle into four parts as we did with the cycle involving the sun and the lunar node, and we have an interval of approximately 3.75 years. It is here suggested that the effect of this cycle is similar to the suggested effect of the sun-node cycle. We had no data on this factor at the time when Chapters 11 to 13 were prepared.

The evidence presented in this chapter was selected by outsiders. We have merely taken a record of all the great fires that are presented in the World Almanac.

These fires were in the nature of conflagrations. They were of sufficient significance to have been written into history by the mentioned publication. We are using all fires listed. We are omitting explosions, except where the explosion was followed by a great fire. We are dealing primarily with fire, and nothing else. In most of these fires, there was heavy loss of life in addition to great property damage. One fire only was omitted, and that because we were unable to learn the exact date of the fire. Only the year was given.

We are going to list these fires, and in each case, we are going to state the distance from the closest lunar node to the sun on the day of the fire.

We are also going to state the distance from the nearest lunar node to the position of the planet Uranus on the day of the fire.

While we are about it, we will also list the phase of the moon, and we will do this by breaking up the moon cycle into 12 parts. The first part is when the moon has passed the "new" but is still within 30 degrees of the sun; the second part or phase will be when the sun and moon are from 30 to 60 degrees apart and separating, or, going toward the "full." Thus, phases six and seven will indicate that time when the moon is near the "full".

For the sake of brevity, we will use abbreviations. The node-sun relationship will be abbreviated as **"NS"**. The node-Uranus relationship will be designated as **"NU"**. The phase of the moon will be abbreviated to **"MP"**. These symbols, with accompanying information, will follow each file as it is individually listed. Thereafter, we will be able to sum up our results.

On December 16th, 1835, a fire in New York City ravaged 17 blocks and destroyed 674 buildings including the Stock Exchange, Merchants Exchange and the Post Office at a cost of 20 million dollars. NS-37 degrees; NU-87 degrees; MP-11.

(Hereafter, we will eliminate the word degrees, but NS and NU will always be expressed in degrees of geocentric longitude.)

On April 27th, 1838, fire destroyed 1158 buildings in Charleston, S. C. NS-23; NU-78; MP-2.

On May 3rd, 1851, a fire in San Francisco began and destroyed 2500 buildings within a three-day period. NS-78; NU-89; MP-2.

On June 22nd, 1881, fire in San Francisco destroyed 500 buildings. NS-27; NU-84; MP-10.

On October 5th, 1858, the Crystal Palace, where the World's Fair in New York had been held in 1853, was destroyed by fire. NS-35; NU-87; MP-12.

In Quebec, Canada, on October 13th, 1866, fire destroyed 2500 buildings. NS- 18; NU-10; MP-2.

The great Chicago fire began on October 8th, 1871, and burned until the 11th. There were 18,000 building destroyed at a loss of $196,000,000. NS-71; NU-40; MP-10.

The great Boston fire occurred on November 9th, 1872. 776 buildings were destroyed. NS-17; NU-61; MP-4.

On December 5th, 1876, 289 lives were lost in the Brooklyn Theatre fire. NS-88; NU-21; MP-9.

The Hotel Royal in New York City burned on February 6th, 1892, with the loss of 28 lives. NS-86; NU-15; MP-4. On July 8th, 1892, 600 lives were lost in hotel fire at St. Johns, New Foundland. NS-63; NU-12; MP-6.

The Windsor Hotel fire, with the loss of 45 lives, occurred on March 17th, 1899. NS-82; NU-26; MP-3.

On June 30th, 1900, docks and ships at Hoboken, N. J., burned with a loss of $10,000,000. NS-29; NU-0; MP-2.

The Park Avenue Hotel fire in New York City, with loss of 21 lives, took place on February 2nd, 1902. NS-86; NU-42; MP-10.

The Iroquois Theatre fire in Chicago occurred on December 30th, 1903, with the loss of 602 lives. NS-84; NU-135; MP-5.

The Baltimore fire destroyed 2500 buildings on February 7th, 1904. NS-42; NU-89; MP-10.

The San Francisco earthquake and fire, which resulted in the loss of 452 lives, began on April 18th, 1906. NS-70; NU-39; MP-11.

On January 13th, 1908, 169 persons were killed in the Rhodes Theatre fire at Boyertown, Pa. NS-8; NU-0; MP-5.

On March 4th, 1908, 174 children and 2 teachers died in the Lake View School fire at Collinwood, near Cleveland, Ohio. NS-62; NU-4; MP-1.

Fire destroyed a great part of Chelsea, Mass., at a loss of $6,000,000 on April 12th, 1908. NS-76; NU-8; MP-5.

On March 25th, 1911, the Triangle Shirtwaist factory fire took the lives of 145. NS-38; NU-77; MP-11.

On June 25th, 1914, a great part of Salem, Mass., was destroyed at a loss of $12,000,000. NS-66; NU-28; MP-1.

Fire following the Black Tom explosion in Jersey City caused a loss of $22,000,000 on July 30th, 1916. NS-8; NU 20; MP-1.

On May 17th, 1923, 76 persons died in the Cleveland Rural School fire at Camden, S. C. NS-68; NU-0; MP-1.

The Cleveland Clinic Hospital burned on May 15th, 1929, with the loss of 124 lives. NS-3; NU-42; MP-3.

On April 21st, 1930, 320 convicts died in the Ohio State Penitentiary fire. NS-3; NU-21; MP-10.

The German Reichstag burned on February 27th, 1933. NS-0; NU-43; MP-2.

On September 11th, 1940, fire and explosions killed 51 persons at the Hercules Powder plant at Kenvil, N. J. NS-68; NU-44; MP-12.

The Cocoanut Grove fire in Boston, in which 491 persons perished, took place on November 28th, 1942. NS-85; NU-87; MP-8.

One hundred persons were killed in the Knights of Columbus Hotel fire at St. John's, Newfoundland, on December 12th, 1942. NS-69; NU-87; MP-3.

The Ringling Brothers and Barnum & Bailey Circus fire killed 107 persons at Hartford, Conn., on July 6th, 1944. NS-15; NU-48; MP-7.

On June 5th, 1946, 61 persons died in the La Salle Hotel fire in Chicago. NS- 8; NU-4; MP-3.

On December 7th, 194-0, 121 persons perished in the most disastrous hotel fire in history, that of the 15-story Winecoff Hotel in Atlanta. NS-3; NU-9; MP-6.

Beginning October 23rd, 1947, forest fires destroyed a large part of Bar Harbor, Me., and several other communities causing $30,000,000 damage. NS-26; NU- 31; MP-4.

There is nothing in these figures to show any excess of fires at the full of the moon. Only one of these fires was attributed to arson, however, and therefore, this should not give us reason to refute the theory of former New York Fire Commissioner Brophy, who only maintained that pyromaniacs worked at full moon.

These figures do show an excess during the first and last quarters of the moon. If we refer to these two quarters as the dark of the moon, there were 23 fires during this absence of light, while if we refer to the second and third quarters as the dark of the moon, there were only 11 fires, There were 13 fires during the first quarter against only 3 in the third quarter.

Now, Let us repeat our "NS" figures which indicate the distance from sun to node at time of each fire. They are: 37, 23, 78, 27, 35, 18, 71, 17, 88, 86, 63, 82, 29, 86, 84, 42, 70, 8, 62, 76, 38, 66, 8, 68, 3, 3, 0, 68, 85, 69, 15, 8, 3, 26.

If we divide these figures into six groups of fifteen degrees each, they will score as follows:

0-14....	*******	7
15-29....	*******	7
30-44....	****	4
45-59....		0
60-74....	********	8
75-89....	********	8

Note that we have nothing between 45 and 60 degrees.

Now let us do the same with the "NU" figures, those designating the distance from the planet Uranus to the nearest node. The figures are as follows: 87, 78, 89, 84, 87, 10, 40, 61, 21, 15, 12, 26, 0, 42, 85, 89, 39, 0, 4, 8, 77, 66, 20, 0, 42, 21, 43, 44, 87, 87, 48, 4, 9, 31.

If we divide these figures into the same six groups of fifteen degrees each, they will score as follows:

0-14....	*********	9
15-29....	*****	5
30-44....	*******	7
45-59....	*	1
60-74....	***	3
75-89....	*********	9

The pattern is similar, and there is no known reason why it should be. Note that in this case, only one fire occurred while Uranus was between 45 and 60 degrees from the node.

If we combine these two sets of figures, they will look as follows:

```
0-14. . . . ****************  16
15-29. . . . ************      12
30-44. . . . ***********       11
45-59. . . . *                  1
60-74. . . . ***********       11
75-89. . . . *****************  17
```

Thus, we find greater frequency of fires when either the sun or Uranus is near or at right angles to the nodes of the moon, such times 'being the periods that we have suggested as intervals of instability. However, because we appeared to find instability at both the zero and 90 degree points, we had assumed that the interval of maximum stability would center at 45 degrees. These figures indicate that it lies from 45 to 60 degrees, with its center around 52 degrees.

We do not know why fires occur in accordance with our cycle of instability. The German Reichstag fire was arson. It occurred with the sun exactly on the node. It was not a case of a pyromaniac, however. It was the act of a political group, it did not occur at the full of the moon.

In these figures, we included no fires that were not in the World Almanac. As this chapter was being prepared, fire in a Philadelphia asylum killed 9 persons on March 30th, 1950. This fire was the work of a confessed pyromaniac. The full moon occurred on April 2nd. This fire will conform with our theory. The sun was 2 degrees from the node. Uranus was 84 degrees from the node. On the following day, March 31st, 69 escaped from a fire in the Manhattan State Hospital on Wards Island. **These two fires occurred with both the sun and Uranus near our suggested points of instability.** And, why two asylum fires in two days? The newspapers were filled with news of fires at this time, a number of them including loss of life.

It is the view of the writer that these suggested intervals of instability are dangerous times for important action. Things do not turn out as you might expect. You are apt to

run into unexpected circumstances and developments. If this should prove true, advance knowledge of these periods would be valuable. Advance knowledge is easily supplied.

In originally associating spectacular events with eclipses, the writer did nothing the astrologers had not done for many centuries before him-perhaps several thousands of years before him. He had read the literature of the astrologers before embarking on this venture. Some modern astronomers have laughed at the astrologers, and have considered them unscientific. Nothing is more unscientific than prejudgment, a characteristic of organized astronomy. The ancient claims may have been partly true and partly incorrect. **The ancient astrologers, even back in the most ancient civilization of India and China, attributed great significance to the nodes of the moon. The north node was called the dragon's head; the south node, the dragon's tail. The dragon's head was supposed to be a fortunate influence while the dragon's tail was an unfortunate influence. For the most part, the writer has not found any cause for such a conviction, although <u>most of the U.S. wars came about with the dragon's tail near the birth-sun position of the United States</u>. For the most part, the writer doubts whether there is any difference in the two nodes. Both seem to bring about instability when near the sun or Uranus.**

We should mention that if Mercury or Venus are used in place of the sun or Uranus, somewhat similar results will be obtained. This is a fact that we discounted however, due to the fact that these two bodies are always close to the sun, with the result that if the sun is near to, or at right angles to, the Sun, Venus and Mercury are apt to be also. Similar tests were made with Mars, Jupiter, Saturn, and Neptune. The results were negative.

Sea disasters and earthquakes were tested to see whether they occur with greater frequency during our intervals of suggested instability. We found that they did not. It is odd that what were probably the two greatest sea disasters in history did conform to our pattern. It may be only coincidence that both the

Titanic and the Lusitania went down during our periods of suggested instability.

It may be that great masses of people are unstable and impatient during these periods just enough to bring about a series of unusual occurrences. It may go beyond that. The phenomena may be of a nature that is beyond our current understanding, because of our lack of more complete knowledge of Man and the universe in which he lives. Nature often operates in accord with patterns. All snowflakes have six sides. Man is created according to one pattern, and reproduces that pattern, without knowing how, in his offspring. An elephant is created according to a different pattern, and recreates his offspring according to that pattern, without knowing how nor why. For some strange and mysterious reason, the events of life may have to follow a given pattern until we better understand them. By knowing more about heredity, man brings about the production of better cattle.

During a limited period of years in our earlier citation of history, some may argue that because Hitler had dabbled in astrology, he planned his course in accord with these factors, a very unwise thing to do, but Hitler didn't shoot Lincoln. He didn't push that young man off the Fifth Avenue window ledge. It is easier to accept Mrs. O'Leary's cow than to claim that Hitler started the Chicago fire. Hitler didn't buy Alaska from Russia, He didn't start the Franco-Russian War, and he didn't vote for Harry S. Truman in 1948. Nations were following these patterns before Hitler was born and after he died.

One factor we have not taken into consideration in this investigation is the current distance between the moon and the earth. In this connection, there is another cycle involved. When the moon is closest to the earth, its longitudinal motion is greatest. When it is far away, its geocentric longitudinal-motion is slower. At times, its daily motion will be less than 12 degrees, at other times more than 15 degrees. Its point of perigee is when the moon is nearest, and its motion most rapid. Its point of apogee is when the moon is farthest away and its motion slowest. These two points move in the opposite direction from the nodes, completing the circle in eight and a fraction years. It is the writer's hunch that these points may also be a factor in upsetting our regular lunar cycle as discussed in earlier chapters. This will be taken up in the future.

Our earlier reviewed evidence has indicated that climactical periods in the U.S. history appear to occur when eclipses take place near July 4th, which is the birthday of the United States. On that date, the sun is approximately 12 degrees of Cancer in the equinoctial zodiac. Eclipses in this area can occur only when the moon's nodes are passing through the area. This happens twice in any nineteen-year interval, when the north node passes through the area, and when the south node passes. **It is interesting to examine the periods when the south node, or dragon's tail, passed through the Cancer area.**

Such a year was 1823 when the Monroe Doctrine was declared. The next transit of this node through this area came in 1842 at the time of the Dorr Rebellion. The next movement of the node through this position was accompanied by the Civil War in 1861. In 1880, we find little of importance while the node passed, although President Garfield was shot on July 2nd, 1881, before the node was too far away. There had been an eclipse on June 12th.

The south node reached this area again in 1898, and the Spanish-American War followed. In 1911, the passage of this node was accompanied by World War I.

Had this pattern been completely followed, World War II would have begun in 1935, which was the time it did begin from one point of view. It was in 1935 that Hitler began his expansion to the west. It was then that he broke the Versailles Treaty, ordered conscription, occupied the Saar Territory, and began the expansion of the German army. Within a year, he reoccupied the Rhineland Zone, breaking the Locarno Pact. He also formed the Rome-Berlin Axis.

In all of this work, we may be exploring only a very small part of a very large and complicated pattern.

INSTABILITY AND THE STOCK MARKET

If we have found a key to these periods of instability, the question is bound to arise: Do they relate to the stock market? Where else do we see such drastic effects of instability? Propounding the question is much more simple than answering it. The answer is not that simple.

Previous chapters of this work were prepared prior to June 25th, 1950. On that date, the Sun squared the node. The planet, Uranus, was 87 degrees from the node. Here was a time when two of our cycles of instability, the Sun-node cycle and the Uranus-node cycle were coinciding. A number of my friends were watching the papers to determine whether there would be any excess of fires at that time. Alas, there was no room on the front pages of the newspapers for fires. The North Koreans attacked the South Koreans.

The most exciting event of 1950 occurred as the node became square to both Sun and Uranus merely repeating the pattern that has been occurring for centuries, adding another bit of evidence to chapters 11 to 14. Stocks crashed.

However, the greatest interval of instability, insofar as stocks were concerned, did not occur within what we would term our period of greatest instability. The stock market crackup was not a matter of action, It was reaction. On other occasions the stock market would anticipate international action, and its erratic nature would be displayed before the event. If we were to compare our last June, 1950 period of instability with the period that followed it, we would find that stocks were more unstable in July. Yet we cannot deny that the Korean crisis coincided perfectly with our suggested period of instability, and it would be difficult to deny that the stock market crack-up that followed had no connection with the Korean crisis. Regardless of this, if we are technical, the greatest interval of instability in stocks did not coincide with our suggested period of instability. Other timing factor marked only the beginning of stock market instability. Thereafter, increased in intensity.

As we look over past years, we find similar circumstances. The result is that a statistical test of the possible effects of our suggested periods of stability upon the stock market would appear to show negative results. We do not have the answer although we may have part of it. A major turn in the market has often occurred at one of these times, but that is not always true. It is not even a general rule. Major world events seem to have a habit of following our 86.5 day Sun-node cycle, yet not all such events are accompanied by instability in the stock market.

We checked the daily range of stocks during these suggested unstable intervals from 1911 to 1921. By the term daily range, we mean the difference between the high and low price of the day. We are paying no attention to the direction in which stocks moved. We are concerned with whether they were moving or standing still. For this experiment, the New York Times industrial averages were employed.

In the following table, we have divided time into two parts, stable and unstable, and we have used as the unstable periods, those times when the Sun was within 15 degrees of the conjunction or square of the lunar node. We have compared these with the remaining intervals. We have listed the average daily range of stocks during each interval.

If we average the figures in column two for unstable periods and compare them with figures in column three for stable periods, we will find that the unstable periods average $1.01 against $.93 for stable periods. This is a

Dates	Unstable	Stable
1-21 to 2-18-1911	.67	
2-20 to 4-13-1911		.41
4-17 to 5-16-1911	.72	
5-17 to 7-14-1911		.58
7-15 to 8-12-1911	.68	
8-14 to 10- 9-1911		.88
10-10 to 11- 8-1911	.64	
11-9-11 to 1-3-1912		.70
1- 4 to 1-27-1912	.57	
2- 1 to 3-27-1912		.53
3-28 to 4-26-1912	.82	
4-27 to 6-22-1912		.60
6-24 to 7-24-1912	.52	
7-25 to 9-19-1912		.48
9-21 to 10-18-1912	.63	
10-19 to 12-14-1912		.78
12-16-12 to 1-13-1913	.57	
1-14 to 3- 8-1913		.66
3-10 to 4- 7-1913	.57	
4- 8 to 6- 5-1913		.50
6- 6 to 7- 3-1913	.79	
7- 7 to 9- 1-1913		.48
9- 2 to 10- 2-1913	.52	
10- 3 to 11-26 1913		.45
11-28 to 12-24 1913	.49	
12-26-13 to 2-18-1914		.69
2-19 to 3-20-14	.55	
3-21 to 5-16-14		.55
5-18 to 6-16-14	.33	
6-17 to 7-30-14		.86
7-31 to 12-11-14	Stock Exchange Closed	
12-11-14 to 2-1-1915		.65
2- 2 to 3- 2-15	.51	
3- 3 to 4-27-15		.95
4-28 to 5-28-15	1.46	
5-29 to 7-26-15		1.02
7-27 to 8-25-15	1.51	
8-26 to 10-23-15		1.48
10-25 to 11-20-15	1.97	
11-22-15 to 1-14-1916		1.06
1-17 to 2-11-16	1.18	
2-14 to 4- 8-16		.93
4-10 to 5- 6-16	1.16	
5- 8 to 7- 5-16		.94
7- 6 to 8- 5-16	.71	
8- 7 to 10- 4-16		1.10
10- 5 to 11- 1-16	1.47	
11- 2 to 12-26-16		1.62
12-27-16 to 1-25-1917	1.23	
1-26 to 3-21-17		1.16
3-22 to 4-20-17	1.11	
4-21 to 6-16-17		1.08
6-18 to 7-17-17	1.04	
7-18 to 9-13-17		.96

Dates	Unstable	Stable
9-14 to 10-11-17	1.13	
10-15 to 12- 8-17		1.34
12-10-17 to 1-5-1918	1.44	
1- 7 to 3- 2-18		.86
3- 4 to 4- 2-18	.67	
4- 3 to 5-29-18		.77
5-30 to 6-29-18	.66	
7- 1 to 8-26-18		.50
8-27 to 9-25-18	.54	
9-26 to 11-20-18		1.20
11-21 to 12-20-18	.97	
12-21-18 to 2-13-1919		.77
2-14 to 3-14-19	.93	
3-15 to 5-10-19		.89
5-12 to 6-10-19	1.46	
6-11 to 8- 8-19		1.65
8- 9 to 9- 6-19	1.63	
9- 8 to 11- 1-19		1.67
11- 3 to 12- 2-19	2.42	
12-3-19 to 1-26-1920		1.40
1-27 to 2-24-20	1.85	
2-25 to 4-20-20		1.76
4-21 to 5-20-20	1.85	
5-21 to 7-17-20		1.04
7-19 to 8-18-20	1.34	
8-19 to 10-15-20		1.19
10-16 to 11-13-20	1.40	
11-15-20 to 1-7-1921		1.29

difference of but 8 cents, but it is 8 cents per day for every day over an interval of ten years. From a practical point of view, this figure is of no value. From a statistical point of view, it is questionable. Thus, we have not found anything of practical value insofar as this cycle is concerned in the stock market.

Nevertheless, the matter should not be dropped here. We are publishing these figures because of their possible usefulness to further research in the future.

Moon phases were also checked. We divided the new Moon cycle into twelve parts, beginning and ending with the new Moon. We checked average daily movement of stocks for the same interval of ten years. From 1911 through 1915, we found that the average daily range was .684 during the waxing Moon and .722 during the waning Moon. From 1916 to 1920, we found the average daily range to be 1.111 during the waxing Moon and 1.188 during the waning Moon.

The manner in which the average daily range scored for the twelve phases of the Moon was as follows:

Moon Phase	Average Daily Range 1911-1915	Average Daily Range 1916-1920
1	.697	1.088
2	.656	1.133
3	.707	1.099
4	.701	1.096
5	.667	1.198
6	.676	1.053
7	.651	1.148
8	.684	1.265
9	.736	1.203
10	.728	1.153
11	.768	1.233
12	.767	1.120

As the figures indicate, the stock market was more active during the 1916-20 period than during 1911-15. There is nothing conclusive about these figures, but they do show stocks about 6 per cent more active during the waning Moon--or to be more accurate, they show the daily range to be 6 per cent greater during the waning Moon. The difference is not sufficiently great, however, to allow anything in the way of forecasting. We present the figures for what they might be worth in connection with other work accomplished in the future.

The daily range of stocks while the Moon was in the various signs of the zodiac was also checked. The result was not marked. The first five-year period did not conform too well with the second five-year period. The results are indicated in the following table.

These figures are not very useful. They have not hit the bull's-eye. They give us no secret formulae by which we can predict market movement or even stock market stability. Nevertheless, the writer feels that there is far

Moon Sign	Average Daily Range 1911-1915	Average Daily Range 1916-1920
Aries	.773	1.188
Taurus	.703	1.204
Gemini	.743	1.201
Cancer	.717	1.185
Leo	.626	1.174
Virgo	.680	1.189
Libra	.698	1.181
Scorpio	.728	1.263
Sagittarius	.674	1.187
Capricorn	.713	1.138
Aquarius	.681	1.209
Pisces	.736	1.145

more to be learned in this connection. Anyone who has lived close to a stock market panic such as that of 1929 knows that there is something cosmic about it. The feelings of millions of people are swept by a great cosmic psychological tide. Many of the major moves of the stock market over the last 25 years have been accurately called by some of the astrologers, studying planetary positions and aspects. Those same astrologers have been wrong on other occasions, but they have been more right than anyone else. If their methods have been imperfect and defective, they have been less imperfect and less defective than those of the college professors, the economists and the Wall Street experts.

In tabulating the work presented in this chapter, we occasionally came to a very radical stock market interval that appeared right in the middle of one of our periods of stability. We examined the planetary timetables, and we usually found some extraordinary lineup of planets, on several occasions a conjunction or opposition of Mars and Uranus. I am expressing a personal opinion now, but it is an opinion based on over 25 years of general observation. I think the key to mob psychology as manifested in the stock market and elsewhere lies beyond the surface of' the earth, yet within the solar system, but the amount of statistical work necessary to bring it out into the open would be stupendous. The cost would be tremendous. Only the government or some very large institution could afford it. There are too many factors to be checked. It is outside the scope of this work which we have tried to confine to the Moon itself.

I was much amused by an incident that occurred back in 1929. It was summer. Stocks were at their all-time top. The nation was prosperous. Everyone was happy. **A reporter for the *New York Post* traveled to Hoboken to interview an astrologer. He came back and wrote a humorous article about his interview. This astrologer predicted dire things ahead. In October, there was to be the greatest of all stock market crashes.**

In October, the greatest of all stock market panics occurred. In itself, this was not at all amusing, but the amusing thing was that neither the reporter nor the newspaper ever referred to the prediction when printing the news of the panic which followed. Instead, they gave great space to the explanations of economists as to why they were wrong. The astrologer died without honor.

LET US BE CAUTIOUS

Here and there in this work, the writer has expressed an opinion, but for the most part he has attempted to let the facts speak for themselves. Where he has expressed opinions, he may be wrong. The reader is asked to bear this in mind. The reader is also asked to be careful not to be dogmatic in drawing his own conclusions.

The study of cycles is new--in a sense--and yet it is very old, because the human race, animal and plant life have been adjusting to cycles as far back as we know. Primitive man worked in the daytime and he slept at night. He went on doing this throughout his entire life. Back in the most ancient of times that we know anything about, there were astrologers who studied cycles. They believed that when a planet reached a certain point in the heavens, a given type of event recurred, and that people born when a planet reached a given point had certain characteristics that were also possessed by people born the last time the planet passed that point, and the many times before when it passed.

A new school grew up from the astrologers' ranks, there emerged astronomers. The astrologer used his knowledge of space, matter and motion as an interpretative art. The astronomers dropped the interpretative art. They condemned the astrologers. In part, this was merely the march of Christianity. Astrology was feared. The Christian doctrine taught free will, and it was feared that the study of cycles implied fate. No happy medium could be reached. It was one dogma or the other, and as a result there was division. The two dogmas carried in different directions. Power was long on the side of the astronomers. Even today, in the world of astronomy, a young astronomer of today is safest if he follows the dictates of the older men who dominate the profession. If there is any doubt about the truth of this statement, it is only necessary to point to an interesting fact. One such fact will suffice. Many more could be presented.

Connected with the Hayden planetarium and the American Museum of Natural History is a Junior Amateur Astronomers Association. About a decade ago, a noted and highly connected astronomer spoke before this group. His topic was astrology. He proposed cooperation between astrologers and astronomers in statistical research to determine the true facts behind some of the cyclic claims of the astrologers. The writer sat in the audience and heard the talk. With the astronomer who delivered it, he later visited in the home of a mutual friend and discussed his talk of the earlier part of the evening. Some days later, he mentioned to the astronomer that his talk had been recorded by a court stenographer and was to be published.

This information set off a bit of excitement, Publishers were called on and told that they had no right to publish the talk. It was the private talk of the astronomer who had made it, and any publication would be subject to legal liability. Meanwhile, an entirely different talk, which said about the opposite of what the man actually said, was published in *Sky* magazine at Harvard. It was purported to be the original address actually delivered, and was so represented by the publication.

It might be very difficult for the writer to believe such a story did he not know it first hand. There are many more such facts, for many a young astronomer has come to the writer with his troubles. Usually, it is a case of losing his job unless he agrees to conform to the crystallized dogmas that have become a part of modern astronomy. When an astronomer speaks in public, he has to stop and ask himself, "Is it safe to say this?" Over many years, the result of this was that astrology often fell into the hands of the charlatan. Any sincere investigator was certain to be classed a charlatan by the astronomical profession.

Cycles continue to operate, and now we find the astronomers slipping back to the study of cycles. We find Harlow Shapley himself bound up in an organization for the study of cycles.

If I were going to make a prediction, I would predict that the worlds of astrology and astronomy will ultimately reunite. There are influential men in the world of astronomy who will never break away from their dogma, but that dogma will go when they leave, and they have to leave. All men die. These men will pass on, and when they go, their dogmas will go with them. There will come a day when today's dogma no longer rules the astronomers.

My plea is for impartial investigation by organizations with the equipment to investigate. It took one person ten years to accumulate the statistical data that appears in this book. A large organization could accumulate much more multitudinous data in far less time. This work is preliminary. It is only a starting point. We are far from our goal. Cycles are highly complicated.

Before me is an interesting graph showing the mail order business on a day-to-day basis over the period of the last two years. The graph is based on a five day week and is run on a five-day moving-average. There are no Saturdays and Sundays on the graph. The five-day moving-average has the effect of eliminating from the line any fluctuations that are due to the day of the week. Business is usually best on Mondays. The graph shows us what the line would look like if all days of the week were of equal significance.

It was a study of this graph that caused me to select the title for this chapter. There are sections of this line where I would defy anyone to find the lunar cycle with a naked eye. Yet, mathematical analysis will show that it is there. By eliminating the mathematical analysis, I could prove to your satisfaction that the lunar cycle is not there. The reason for this is that there appear to be so many different cycles operating. For example, beginning in April, 1950, and running through the summer, there is a series of waves in this line which indicate another cycle. They average 18 days in length. I know of nothing that would create an 18-day cycle, and if I go back prior to April, 1950, there are no such waves.

If you throw a stone into a tranquil body of water, you will create similar waves. If you throw a larger stone, you will create bigger waves. These waves ultimately peter out. Sometimes we find what appear to be cycles that peter out--cycles perhaps created by some disturbance like the stone falling into the water. The night and day cycle, caused by the rotation of the earth on its own axis, does not peter out insofar as we know. If the power that turns the earth on its axis ever gives out, it will. We must consider the possibility of cycles that peter out and cycles that do not peter out, in which event, the cycles that peter out make it more difficult for us to discover the cycles that do not peter out.

So well do we know the diurnal, or night-and-day, cycle that we have mechanisms that turn lights on and off when it gets light and when it gets dark. That is an example of the usefulness of the knowledge of cycles. On the whole, however, our combined knowledge of cycles is so limited that we will do well to be very careful in drawing conclusions.

Take our 86.5-day cycle. It is probable--or at least possible--that there is some biological factor in man that varies with this cycle. If they searched for it, biologists might find this factor. Is there an increase in emotionalism? Does adrenalin flow more freely at such times? Why do world leaders suddenly act at such times, with no knowledge of any such cycle? This work marks the first time such a cycle has ever been mentioned. **The astrologers were dealing with part of the cycle when they associated eclipses with world events, but their eclipses, did not explain many events which occurred when the Moon's node was square the Sun, which was the missing factor in this cycle insofar as the astrologers were concerned.**

The philosophy of the new school of thought relative to cycles is an interesting one. This school does not prove cause. It is concerned only with the length of cycles. The reason for the failure to probe cause is obvious. Astronomers are involved. What if they should discover that their cycles are caused by the movement of bodies in space? This would disprove their crystallized claims. That would not do. There would be red faces.

The new school of cycles usually assumes them to be uniform or symmetrical. The waves of cycles are seldom uniform. The day-and-night cycle is only equal day-and-night at the equator, and most of the people live elsewhere. Nights are longer in winter. Days are longer in summer. When we deal with the day-and-night cycle, we always consider cause. We consider the rotation of the earth on its axis, and we consider the tilt of the earth and its path around the Sun. The earth doesn't travel in a circle. It travels in an ellipse. If cycles are caused by solar bodies moving in space, those cycles would not be uniform. All planets, as well as the Moon, travel in eclipses.

Astronomers have felt greater security in dealing with sunspots as a causative factor. The ancient astrologers did not deal in sunspots. What causes sunspots?

The sunspot cycle is believed to be 11.3 years. It takes 11.8622 years for Jupiter to go around the Sun. There is a discrepancy of .5622 years. The sunspot cycle is slightly more rapid than the cycle of Jupiter. Jupiter is the largest of all planets of the Sun. What would be the effect if sunspots were caused by Jupiter. Would not other planets interfere with the cycle?

In Sunspots in Action, Dr. Harlan True Stetson, astronomer of M.I.T. states:

"The fact that periodicities in the sunspot curve do not agree with periods of revolution of the planets about the Sun does not appear to me as necessarily excluding planetary influences. An important point which seems to have been overlooked thus far in all such investigations of tidal action is the effect of the Sun's rotation and that of any natural period of oscillation of the solar atmosphere."

Actually, the sunspot cycle varies greatly. The figure 11.3 is only an average established over a long period of years. On one occasion, the cycle may be 9 years, while at another time it may be 18 years. It is not a perfectly functioning cycle like night and day. Estimates can be far off. So long as we do not know what causes the sunspot cycle, that will be true.

If we live in a world of cause and effect, there must be a cause for cycles. We know of nothing terrestrial that could cause some of the cycles with which we are familiar. No one ever thought of an 86.5 day cycle as possibly being associated with the Moon. We have shown that an 86.5 day cycle is .75 of the 346 day cycle, and that it takes 346 days from one crossing of the Sun by the Moon's node to the next. Thus, in seeking a cause for an 86.5 day cycle, we have actually taken into consideration the relative motion of three bodies in space, the Sun, the· Moon and the Earth. Despite its non-statistical nature, the evidence of this cycle which we have put forth is very impressive, and this evidence may be the ground work for the ultimate collection of evidence of a more valuable nature.

Very small influences can sometimes have gigantic effects. For example, suppose we have a perfectly balanced steel plank or girder, each side carrying one ton. A pea might have sufficient effect, when added to the ton-weight on one side, to upset the equilibrium and cause everything to crash.

Where cycles are concerned, there are thousands of possible planetary-group factors which might operate toward upsetting the factor of balance. Yet, it is possible to investigate all of these factors whenever mankind decides that it should be done. The main reason that it has never been done is found in the fact that the dogmatic astronomical organizations gave all of the answers without investigation.

Research is often retarded because people are reasonable. Because we reason, we form conclusions before we investigate. Conclusions should follow investigation. Too frequently, the opposite procedure is accepted. If reason tells us that something is not true, we do not investigate it. We go through life making mistakes that are based on reason. First we decide that thus and so is probably a fact. Then, we investigate to prove our preconceived conclusion. Fortunately, we do learn when our investigations disprove our reasoning.

It would not have been reasonable for the writer to have investigated an 86.5 day cycle based on the relationship of the Moon's node to the Sun. What is the Moon's node? Merely a point in space. How could it be of either importance or significance? Points in space, however, can be both. I can think of a point in space that is very dangerous. It is where a certain highway crosses a certain railroad. The writer's reasonability would have prevented him from investigation the point in space called the Moon's node. Such an investigations would be foolish. Discovery that this point in space might have significance was an accident. Most discoveries are accidents, because we are reasonable.

Because of tradition and because of the existence of an actual physical phenomenon, it was more reasonable to investigate eclipses. It was noted that many great fires had occurred near the time of an eclipse. The results were placed on a graph to determine whether the frequency of fires would run to a maximum at the time of eclipses. Since eclipses occur only when the Sun is near the Moon's node, measurement was made from the Moon's node as an approximation instead of from the eclipse itself. Reason implied that fires might run to a maximum when the node was close to the Sun, and to a minimum when the node was at its greatest distance from the Sun--90 degrees. The result was neither expected nor reasonable. **Frequency of fires ran to a maximum when the node was farthest away from the Sun also.** Immediately, new light was shed on our study of historical events. We had listed a series of vital historical events that did not happen near the time of an eclipse.

Pearl Harbor Day had interested us the most. Like many other days -on our list of exceptions, it conformed to this new pattern. What about the eclipses? Were they of any significance at all? As yet, we do not know, but doubt has been born.

We found this 86.5 day cycle, not because we were smart, but because we stumbled on it. We conceived a possibility that appeared to have some semblance of reasonability, enough to cause us to make an investigation. Further research may prove that there was no basis to our original contention. We may find that we started out to prove one thing and actually proved something quite different. The history of science is filled with such instances. Organized astronomy would never have discovered such a cycle because organized astronomy is more reasonable than the writer. Organized astronomy can only reason within the limitations of its preconceived dogma, but it is very reasonable within that limited sphere, and within that sphere it must remain until the death of its present-day leaders. Organized astronomy would never have investigated the possible effects of eclipses upon world history merely because such an effect had been claimed by the ancients. The astronomer bolsters himself up constantly by trying to convince himself that he is a more intelligent being than the ancients. Were he to discover his true relationship to the broader scheme of things, it might be a blow to his pride from which he could not recover.

In work of this kind, we can progress only with limited speed because of our limited horizons. This may not apply to you and to me as much as it applies to the world of astronomy, but it applies to us never the less. It applies to ail of us to an extent. For generations, we have been taught to think in a certain way. We are not to be cured overnight. Occasionally, we are freed from our mental enslavement to a certain extent by such an humorist as Charles Fort who can sit well back, see us in the perspective and laugh at us.

If we have been drawing conclusions, forgive us. Our purpose is to emphasize the great need of caution in drawing conclusions, and in so doing, if we have fallen into the error of lack of such caution, we emphasize our point to an even greater degree. Even when our evidence becomes overwhelming, we can afford to look further. Chances are we missed something.

THE TURN OF EVENTS

As one might gather from reading [the prior chapter], the writer was preparing to close the manuscript of this book when that chapter was written. And then, something happened. We ran into one of our own suggested intervals of instability. The result was such that we might have gone back and rewritten some of the chapters of this book. But it is more graphic to leave those chapters as they were originally prepared. If we have made mistakes, let this demonstrate them rather than conceal them. We can learn by making mistakes if we don't cover them up.

We have already pointed out in an earlier chapter that during the serialization of this work, The Korean War broke out at the exact top of our 86.5 day cycle on June 24th, 1950 when the Sun squared the nodes. On September 11th, 1950, there was an eclipse of the Sun. On September 21st, the Sun crossed the node, and on September 25th, there was an eclipse of the Moon. This entire period was marked by sudden changes in world affairs.

From June 24th till September 11, the Korean War was a constant advance by North Korean or Communist forces until the United Nations forces were about to be pushed off the peninsula. On September 11th, the day of the eclipse, Communist forces reached their point of farthest advance. They were stopped.

On September 15th, United Nations forces began landing behind the Communist lines. Within three days, 40,000 troops were landed at Inchon. Over 200 ships took part in this landing. On the east coast, other troops landed above Pohang.

On September 19th, Indo-Chinese Communists began an attack on the French in Indo-China. When the Sun crossed the node on September 21st, it was announced that United Nations forces had entered the Korean capitol of Seoul. On September 25th, while the surface of the Moon was actually darkened by the earth's shadow, there was a dramatic announcement by General Douglas MacArthur that Seoul had been captured. Thereafter, until the 1st of November, North Korean forces were marching in the opposite direction. They were retreating up the peninsula, until they were but a few miles from the Manchurian and Russian border. Then, their resistance stiffened, but between September 11th and 25th, the whole course of the Korean War had changed.

All this had nothing to do with the course that this manuscript was taking. Something else did. On September 13th, 1950 the writer swung around quickly in his desk chair in his New York office. He cracked his ankle against an open desk drawer. A very slight affair, but on September 20th, as the sun was about to cross the node, he was rushed to the hospital. Infection had set in, far inside the foot, in the nerve tissue. It has been noted elsewhere in this book that illnesses which begin at the bottom of the individual lunar cycle are of a prolonged nature. The injury was September 13th. The low point in the writer's individual lunar cycle was on September 15th.

After eight days in the hospital, the swelling and inflammation disappeared, and on September 28th, the exact date of the apex of the writer's individual lunar cycle, he was allowed to leave the hospital and go home.

He was still unable to walk except to hobble across the room. Days passed and there seemed to be no further improvement. Knowing that he was headed now for another bottom in his individual lunar cycle, the writer endeavored to be careful. Particularly did he watch October 12th and 13th, because these days marked the next bottom of the cycle. On October 12th, the foot began to swell. It was swollen on the 13th. The writer decided not to report this to the physicians until the 14th, in order to see whether there would be natural improvement after the low point in the cycle had passed. On the 14th, the swelling had disappeared. Otherwise, the foot was sore and it did not improve. It was still impossible to walk other than across the room. I was very weak. My strength did not come back.

The next high point in my individual lunar cycle would be on October 25th. I decided to be patient until that time. On Sunday, October 22nd, I was so weak that I retired at 7:30 pm, immediately after dinner. At 9:30 pm, I awoke. I was completely refreshed. I felt as though I had had a full night's rest. I no longer had any desire to sleep. I decided to go into the living room and smoke a cigarette. Suddenly, I realized that I had walked from the bedroom to the living room normally. My strength was back. My foot was perfectly normal. All soreness had left. On the following day, I went back to work, and put in a good normal day's work.

There had been an interval of 41 days when I was unable to walk, and therefore an invalid. Those days had their effect upon the subject matter of this book. They were days with nothing to do, and so, I delved more deeply into some of the figures. While I was ill, I received a call from Frank Anderson of the Anderson Laboratories in Boston, who was accompanied by M. A. Bridegman of the Engineering Department of Improved Risk Mutual.

I had unsuccessfully tried to obtain figures on fire frequency for the entire United States. I had consulted the corporations most likely to possess such data, but their data was not complete. Being at home with nothing to do, this failure was bothering me, and I told my troubles to Mr. Anderson and Mr. Bridgham. They came to my rescue. They informed me that the necessary data could be obtained from the National fire Protection Associate in Boston. This enabled the writer to test further the 86.5-day cycle and its relation to fires. That investigation will be the subject matter for a future chapter but meanwhile the new data lad to a discovery that caused us to go back the review some of our other data where we had reported negative results.

In an earlier chapter, the writer asserted that the 86.5-day cycle had been tested in connection with shipwrecks or disasters at sea, and that the results were negative. We will not reconsider that statement. It is true that there does not appear to be a greater frequency of sea disasters during out suggested intervals of instability, but let us look at some figures.

From 1833 to 1899 inclusive, the World Almanac lists 240 ships lost at sea, with a loss of life of 31,762. In the following table we have four columns. The first column represents the distance of the lunar nodes from the sun in degrees of arc. The second column shows the number of ships lost during each 15 degree period. The third column show the number of humans lives lost during each 15 degree period. The last column gives an average of the number of human lives lost per ships destroyed.

DISTANCE NODE TO SUN	SHIPS LOST	LIVES LOST	AVERAGE LOSS OF LIFE PER SHIP
0-15 degrees	40	6,998	175
15-30 "	37	4,295	116
30-45 "	30	4,298	143
45-60 "	78	7,650	98
60-75 "	29	4,394	151
75-90 "	26	4,127	158

Shipping Loss-of-Life 1833-1899

As the above figures indicate, there is no tendency for more ship disaster to occur at the 0 or 90 degree points. In the last column, showing average-number-of-lives-lost-per-ship, however, we find the highest figures at 0 and at 90 degrees. Let us proceed further. Let us take the period 1900 to July, 1914, bring us up to the opening of World War I.

DISTANCE NODE TO SUN	SHIPS LOST	LIVES LOST	AVERAGE LOSS OF LIFE PER SHIP
0-15 degrees	6	3,282	547
15-30 "	17	2,664	156
30-45 "	10	1,737	173
45-60 "	12	652	54
60-75 "	2	290	145
75-90 "	11	3,710	337

Shipping Loss-of-Life 1900-1914

Here again, we have no high frequency of sea disaster at the 0 and 90 degree point, but the average number of lives lost in each disaster rises sharply at these points. We have carried these figures up to the beginning of World War I and we have stopped there temporarily, because we do not get similar results when naval records are taken into consideration. This begs the question as to whether or not governments supply true and accurate data on ships and men lost during war times. We know, for example, that the U.S. Government did not give out true information on losses at the time of the Pearl Harbor attack. We also find that records coming out of China do not conform to the pattern found elsewhere, and here again, there is the strong possibility that facts have not been reported accurately. If we take the World Almanac records for the duration of World War I, we will obtain the following results:

DISTANCE NODE TO SUN		SHIPS LOST	LIVES LOST	AVERAGE LOSS OF LIFE PER SHIP
0-15	degrees	6	1,881	313
15-30	"	8	4,425	553*
30-45	"	12	3,186	265
45-60	"	7	1,697	242
60-75	"	12	2,942	245
75-90	"	9	2,134	237

Shipping Loss-of-Life WW I

The report of the sinking of one French warship with a loss of nearly 3,000 men is responsible for this high figure.

It will immediately be seen that these figures are quite different from the first two tables presented, and they do not conform to the same pattern. Much of the loss of life was due to war circumstances, and we are left with the question as to whether government representations were true or accurate. Only 54 ships are included in the list. Two shipwrecks in China with 1,500 lives lost were also included in the above figures. Now, we can look at figures for the interval between World War I and World War II.

In these figures, our 15 degree area does not show up, but the record includes a storm where seven small ships were wrecked with a loss of 22 lives. The inclusion of these figures greatly alters the totals. The 90 degree area is at the top.

The reliability of this entire record is open to question on any number of grounds. In the case of many of these disasters, the cause of the wreck is not mentioned. The records should be separated into groups

DISTANCE NODE TO SUN	SHIPS LOST	LIVES LOST	AVERAGE LOSS OF LIFE PER SHIP
0-15 degrees	15	610	40
15-30 "	8	1,189	148
30-45 "	10	2,190	219*
45-60 "	8	1,629	203
60-75 "	7	1,052	150
75-90 "	5	1,455	291

1,000 lives lost on a Chinese ship.

Shipping Loss-of-Life WW I & II

showing loss through fire, storm and other causes. As this is written, more accurate records are not available. In the above figures, the point of greatest loss of life is in that area from 75 to 90 degrees, which is one of our points of instability. We have no record of ship losses after World War II. Only 10 ship losses are mentioned during the World War II period, which is too incomplete to consider. We will have the following totals:

DISTANCE NODE TO SUN	SHIPS LOST	LIVES LOST	AVERAGE LOSS OF LIFE PER SHIP
0-15 degrees	61	10,890	178
15-30 "	62	8,148	131
30-45 "	50	8,225	164
45-60 "	98	9,931	101
60-75 "	38	5,736	151
75-90 "	42	9,292	221

Consolidated Shipping Loss-of-Life, no War

These figures show greater loss of life during non-war periods than during our suggested intervals of instability, when the lunar node is from 0 to 15 degrees, or from 75-90 degrees, away from the Sun. Chinese figures are included in the above, and the difference might be more marked if they were excluded. However, we are not in a position to prove that Chinese figures are inaccurate. It is merely a suggested possibility. It is probable that if you listed the sea disasters that you remember, they would nearly all fall within our intervals of instability. The Titanic, the Lusitania and the Vestris all occurred during periods of instability.

Nevertheless, we are forced to call your attention to the fact that we regard this entire list as somewhat on the unreliable side. It is published here, mainly because of its similarity to other results that are to follow. Neither should we lost sight of another fact, that life at sea could be divided into two eras, before and after wireless and radio. Still another consideration: The number of lives lost in any sea disaster is dependent upon the size of the ship and the number of people aboard. Also, there are several instances in these records where a single storm caused the loss of a number of ships. The loss of these individual ships did not constitute separate and independent events. They were all related to the same storm. Therefore, good statistics would demand their exclusion. However, our results might be even more marked could these various factors be cleared up. The amazing fact is that our results conform to a pattern despite these difficulties. The results do conform to a pattern. We find the pattern elsewhere. Our original data came from the World Almanac. It was probably never intended for such a statistical purpose.

Despite all the above considerations, it is important that this data does conform to a pattern, because in the next chapter, we are going to have data that has been more carefully collected by a very reliable agency, and we will see our pattern appearing again.

LOSS-OF-LIFE THROUGH FIRE

We have shown that fires listed in the World Almanac tend to occur during our suggested intervals of instability. Although we were being cautious when this data was presented, we did state in Chapter XVI that frequency of fires ran to a maximum during our periods of suggested instability. It had been our intention to guard against so definite a statement until such time as a greater amount of data was available, for the World Atlas fires were those where loss-of-life was severe.

The National Fire Protection Association, hereinafter referred to as the N.F.P.A., maintains records of all fires of over $250,000 loss in the United States, Canada and Alaska, and that organization has furnished case histories of all such fires occurring from 1943 to 1949 inclusive. This enables us to experiment on a much wider basis, and to test out whatever conclusions we may have drawn from the World Almanac fires. Perhaps we should pause long enough to pay tribute to the excellent loss-prevention work that the N.F.P.A. is doing. One can gain an education in this field from reading the case histories.

The N.F.P.A. estimates that probably 11,000 people lose their lives annually through fire, but nowhere are records of these losses maintained. No governmental or private agency properly records this information. Statistics have not advanced to that point. One might think that fire insurance companies would have a central gathering agency to accumulate such data, but there is no such agency. Our most outstanding cases of loss-of-life are included in the N.F.P.A. data, but the number of fires is small when compared with the estimated whole. In 1943, there were 103 fires where property loss was over a quarter of a million dollars. 116 people lost their lives in these fires. This is only one percent of the total loss-of-life. Nevertheless, the data is of very great value in conducting an experiment of a nature never conducted before. The following table gives us essential data on these 103 fires of 1943. We have separated the fires into six groups, according to the distance from the Moon's node to the Sun when the fires occurred. We have listed the number of fires occurring when the Moon's node was at any given distance from the Sun. When we refer to the Moon's node, we refer to the nearest node. We have noted the number of fires resulting in loss of life, the number of people killed, and the average number of deaths per fire.

DISTANCE SUN TO MOON'S NODE	NUMBER OF FIRES	FIRES RESULTING IN DEATH	NUMBER KILLED	AVERAGE DEATHS PER FIRE
0 to 15 Degrees	16	4	47	2.937
15 to 30 "	18	1	3	.166
30 to 45 "	21	4	29	1.381
45 to 60 "	13	2	10	.769
60 to 75 "	13	2	3	.230
75 to 90 "	22	6	24	1.090

In the above table, we find 18 fires during our periods of instability (0 to 15 degrees and 75 to 90 degrees) against an average expectancy of 34 1/3, which is fairly close. Ten of the 19 fires resulting in loss-of-life occurred during our suggested intervals of instability, against an average expectancy of 6 1/3. There were 71 persons who died during these periods against an expectancy of 38 2/3.

We are using a very wide orb around these centers of suggested instability, and one-third of our fires and deaths should normally fall in these areas. From a statistical viewpoint, this method should prove of value until the limits of the area can be more closely examined. It is our belief that instability decreases gradually as we leave the centers of these areas.

Let us look more closely at these 19 fires where loss-of-life results. The first such fire took place on January 7th, 1943, at Mayfield, Ky. The Enterprise Tobacco Warehouse burned. One employee lost his life when he entered the building to regain some personal property. The Sun was 41 degrees from the node. This was not during one of our intervals of instability.

The center of our first such unstable period was on February 14th, 1943, when the Sun crossed the node. On February 13th, at Dawson Creek, B. C., a construction company garage burned, and a dynamite explosion killed five persons. The Sun was 1 degree from the node.

Four days later, on February 18th, 29 persons lost their lives when a bomber crashed into a building of the Frye Packing Co. at Seattle, Wash., and caused a costly fire. On the same day, fire destroyed 33 hatcheries at Bishopville, Md. Although no people were killed and our records are not affected, 60,000 chickens and over two million eggs were burned.

The next fire was on the line. We do not know the time of day when the fire occurred. If it took place in the A.M., it would fall within the tentative limits we have set for our periods of instability. If it occurred in the P.M., it would not. To be safe, we have placed it outside the area. It occurred on March 1st, 1943. Three men died as the result of a fire in a chemical plant in Bristol Township, Penna. We have recorded the incident with the Sun 15-plus degrees from the node.

Between this date and our next period of instability, there were only two fires where loss-of-life occurred, and the total loss-of-life was only three persons. One woman was burned to death in a Binghamton, N. Y. apartment on March 19th (Sun-to-node: 35 degrees), and two employees of a rubber-heel plant in Baltimore, Md., died in a fire on April 16th (Sun-to-node: 65 degrees).

The Sun squared the nodes on May 11th, 1943. Twenty people died in four fires during May.

On May 1st, a clerk, knowing there was a fire in the building, entered a metal works plant in Kansas City and was burned to death (Sun-to-node: 79 degrees). On May 11th, 6 persons were killed and 24 injured as the result of a fire and explosion in a chemical plant at South Charleston, W. Va. (Sun-to-node: 90 degrees). On May 20th, 12 persons were killed in the crash and burning of a bomber in Chicago (Sun-to-node: 81 degrees). On May 24th, a watchman was burned to death in a cotton-warehouse fire at Galveston, Texas (Sun-to-node: 77 degrees). All of these fires fall within our period of instability.

Between this and the next interval of instability only one person died in any of the listed fires, On May 30th, a watchman was burned to death as three war plants burned at Seattle, Wash. (Sun-to-node: 71 degrees).

The Sun next conjoined the node on August 8th, 1943. While the node was within 15 degrees of the Sun, 13 people died in two fires. One of these died as the result of an explosion at the Welbilt Stove Company in New York on July 28th (Sun-to-node: 11 degrees). Twelve were killed by an explosion of solvent vapors at the plant of the Congoleum Nairn Co. at Kearny, N. J. on August 19th (Sun-to-node: 11 degrees).

There was only one fire where anyone was killed between this and our next period of instability, but loss-of-life was heavy. Twenty-five persons died in an explosion at the Norfolk, Va., Naval Air Station on September 17th, 1943 (Sun to-node: 41 degrees). Because this is a marked exception to our own cycle, the writer feels that he should point out that the planet, Mars, was 4 degrees from a conjunction of Uranus, a configuration that astrologers associate with fires and explosions.

During the next interval of instability, four persons lost their lives in two fires. The Sun squared the nodes on November 4th, 1943. On October 24th, at Easton, Penna., a severe explosion followed by a 6-hour fire destroyed a large portion of the Easton Gas Works, and killed three men (Sun-to-node: 79 degrees). On November 8th, when an army warehouse burned at Oakland, Calif., one fireman died (Sun-to-node: 85 degrees).

During the remainder of the year, three more fires involving loss-of-life occurred. The first killed a fireman at Atlantic City on December 4th (Sun-to-node: 58 degrees). Nine men were killed in an explosion and fire at the Phoenix Naval Store Co. at Gulfport, Miss., on December 9th (Sun-to-node: 52 degrees). Again, we must mention that **Mars had retrograded** (an apparent motion of a planet caused by the actual motion of the earth) back to within 5 degrees of a conjunction of Uranus. Two lives were lost in a fire at Wildwood, N. J., on December 25th (Sun-to-node: 35 degrees). Mars was now within one degree of a conjunction with Uranus.

In our earlier discussion of fires, we also mentioned the distance between the Moon's node and the planet Uranus. On January 1st, 1943, Uranus was 86 degrees from the nearest lunar node, within the area of suggested instability and leaving it about May 28th. Sixty-one of our deaths occurred prior to that date.

Leaving 1943 and entering 1944 when there were 121 fires of over $250,000 loss, we find that 18 of these fires involved loss-of-life. Eight of these occurred within our periods of instability and 10 were outside of such areas. In the 10 fires outside of our periods of instability, the death toll was 21 persons, as against 327 persons who died in 8 fires during our intervals of instability. The following table sums up 1944.

DISTANCE SUN TO MOON'S NODE	NUMBER OF FIRES	FIRES RESULTING IN DEATH	NUMBER KILLED	AVERAGE DEATHS PER FIRE
0 to 15 Degrees	27	4	178	6.592
15 to 30 "	27	5	10	.074
30 to 45 "	17	2	2	.117
45 to 60 "	15	1	2	.133
60 to 75 "	11	2	7	.636
75 to 90 "	24	4	149	6.208

On January 12th, 1944, fire destroyed a business block in Toledo, Ohio. One fireman was trapped and died. (Sun-to-node: 16 degrees). This fire was just outside of our area of instability. Mars was now 1 degree from Uranus.

The Sun crossed the node on January 27th, 1944. On February 8th, 3 workmen lost their lives when fire destroyed the prefabricating manufacturing plant of the National Homes Corp.

near Lafayette, Ind. This fire was within one of our areas of instability. (Sun-to-node: 13 degrees). Mars was 5 degrees from Uranus.

On February 18th, 4 men died when a dust explosion wrecked portions of the Larabee Flour Mills at Kansas City, Mo. This occurrence was not during one of our intervals of instability. (Sun-to-node: 24 degrees). **Mars was 9 degrees from Uranus.**

On March 27th, a Sears, Roebuck fire at Fort Wayne, Ind., resulted in heavy losses. Two weeks later, part of the remaining walls collapsed and killed 6 persons. The fire did not occur during our interval of instability. The deaths did. We have not placed the incident in our unstable area, but that is where it probably belongs. It would raise the number of deaths in the 75 to-90-degree area to 155, and lower them in the 60 to 75-degree area to 1. At the time of the fire, the Sun was 64 degrees from the node. At the time of death, the Sun was 78 degrees from-the node.

The Sun squared the nodes on April 22nd, 1944. On May 3rd, two guests lost their lives in the burning of the Modesto Hotel in Modesto, Calif. This fire was within our period of instability (Sun-to-node: 78 degrees).

On June 12th, 1944, one man died at Boston in the fire of a tent manufacturing building (Sun-to-node: 38 degrees).

On July 4th, 1944, one day before the beginning of our next interval of instability, one fireman had a heart attack and died at the burning of a military property near Fairfield, Ohio (Sun-to-node: 15 to 16 degrees).

The next two days were very unusual, and perhaps we should mention that there was an eclipse of the Moon on the night of July 5th to 6th. A line drawn from the Moon to the Sun would pass through the earth. If extended beyond the Sun, it would almost pass through the planets Venus and Mercury. A line drawn from Mars to Jupiter would also practically pass through the earth. If we were thinking in terms of possible lines of force, this was a strange setup.

On July 5th, 2 employees died in the burning of a Produce Warehouse in Cincinnati. On July 6th, 165 persons lost their lives at Hartford in the Ringling Bros. & Barnum & Bailey Circus fire.

On the same day, an oil refinery burned at Oil City, Penna., and 8 men lost their lives. On July 5th, the Sun was 14 degrees from the node, and on July 6th, the Sun was 13 degrees from the node.

Here were four fires involving loss-of-life in three days as against six fires involving loss of life in the first six months of 1944. Not only were three of these fires definitely within our arbitrary limits of our period of instability, but they coincided with these other very unusual lineups of the planets. We don't feel that we should omit mention of these additional factors. What if we are dealing with lines of force that upset the emotions of people, make them unstable, so that they fail to do the right thing in an emergency? Here is an extraordinary example of loss-of-life through fire. Why didn't these fires occur at the very center of our period of instability? Did the eclipse and other planetary line-ups weigh them to one side?

From this to the next interval of instability, there were three fires involving loss-of-life, and total deaths amounted to six people. Three men lost their lives when a steamship pier burned at Hoboken, N. J., on August 11th. (Sun-to-node: 23 degrees). On September 11th, two workers were killed by explosion and fire at the National Foundry & Machine Company, St. Louis, Mo. (Sun-to-node: 55 degrees). One man died in a fire at the fur storage plant of Balch Price & Co., New York City, on September 28th. (Sun-to-node: 71 degrees).

Our next period of suggested instability came in October 1944, and 147 people died in three fires. The Sun squared the nodes on October 16th. One man died on October 4th as the result of fire at the plant of the Spaulding Fibre Co., Inc., at No. Rochester, N. H. (Sun-to-node: 78 degrees). On October 20th, explosion and fire at the East Ohio Gas Co. in Cleveland took the lives of "not less than 130 people." (Sun-to-node: 85 degrees). This was also the date of superior conjunction of Sun and Mercury. On the following day, 16 men lost their lives during a ship and pier fire at Los Angeles. (Sun-to-node: 84 degrees). Here is another case of extraordinary loss-of-life in two fires coming within a day of each other.

The next two months brought only 2 deaths in as many fires. On December 3rd, a group of buildings burned, at

Cowansville, Que. An occupant of one building died from a heart attack. (Sun-to-node: 39 degrees). At the burning of a railroad pier in Newport News, Va., on December 17th, one man died. (Sun-to-node: 24 degrees).

On November 29th, a grain elevator operated by Rosenbaum Bros., Inc., in Chicago burned, and although the loss was nearly two million dollars, there was no loss-of-life, so that the fire does not form a part of our record. However, the N.F.P.A. calls attention to the fact that this same company had a similar fire oil May 11th, 1939, when the loss was $3,500,000, and on that occasion, the fire resulted in the loss of 9 lives. It is interesting to note that the 1939 fire did fall into one of our periods of instability. The Sun was 13 degrees from the node.

Loss-of-life through fire during these two years of 1943 and 1944 conforms with our periods of instability very well. Let us total our two tables and see how the two years look when added together.

COMBINED DATA ON FIRES OF 1943-1944

DISTANCE SUN TO MOON'S NODE	NUMBER OF FIRES	FIRES RESULTING IN DEATH	NUMBER KILLED	AVERAGE DEATHS PER FIRE
0 to 15 Degrees	43	8	225	5.232
15 to 30 "	45	6	13	.288
30 to 45 "	38	6	31	.815
45 to 60 "	28	3	12	.428
60 to 75 "	24	4	10	.416
75 to 90 "	46	10	173	3.761

The N.F.P.A. figures indicate 464 persons killed by fire during these two years. We should expect one-third or 155 of these deaths to occur during our periods of suggested instability.

Actually, 398 deaths occurred during these periods. We should expect two-thirds of the deaths to occur during the more stable periods. Thus, against an average expectancy of 309, we have only 66 deaths during the stable areas. Total fires resulting in death were 37. We should expect 12 1/3 of these (one-third) within our intervals of instability. Actually, 18 occurred during these periods.

If we were to stop here, we would have an impressive case, but let us see how these fires fitted into the pattern of our suggested periods of instability in future years.

LOSS-OF-LIFE THROUGH FIRE Part 2

Like a piece of machinery that suddenly acts up, our 86.5 day cycle was not functioning in 1945, but its effects were outstanding in 1946. At least, that's what our figures appear to indicate. However, in 1945, when our cycle did not appear to be working, the death rate caused by fire was very low, while in 1946 it was very heavy. The N.F.P.A. lists 163 fires of over $250,000 loss in 1945 and 187 in 1946. Deaths listed in 1945 were 142 against 493 in 1946. Death ratio per-listed-fire in 1945 was only .871, while in 1946, the figure was 2.636.

If we tabulate our fires for 1945 in the same manner that we did for 1943 and 1944, they will appear as follows:

DATA OF FIRES DURING 1945

DISTANCE SUN TO MOON'S NODE	NUMBER OF FIRES	FIRES RESULTING IN DEATH	NUMBER KILLED	AVERAGE DEATHS PER FIRE
0-15 degrees	39	4	24	.615
15-30 "	29	4	32	1.103
30-45 "	27	6	62	2.296
45-60 "	31	3	4	.129
60-75 "	14	2	16	1.142
75-90 "	23	2	4	.174

Let us review the 21 fires where loss-of-life did occur during 1945.

The Sun crossed the node on January 8th, 1945.

On January 7th, fire in the Milner Hotel in Lima, Ohio, resulted in two deaths. One guest was standing on a window ledge on the fifth floor. He was practically enveloped in flames and a life net was spread by firemen, who called on him to jump.

He did so, but the force of his fall broke the net, and he fell through to the cement walk. He died several hours later, and the attending physician stated that his death was probably the result of third-degree burns rather than the fact that the life net had failed. Another woman jumped and hit an iron railing on the way down. She was lifeless when she hit the net. On January 9th, two firemen were killed by a falling wall when the Lee Brothers storage warehouse burned in Harlem, New York City. On January 13th, a million dollar fire was started by a drinking party in Philadelphia, and one man was killed. All of these fires fall within one of our period's degrees, and on January 13th, 5 degrees.

From January 27th to March 6th, which period does not include one of our intervals of instability, there were nine fires resulting in loss-of-life. Fifty-nine lives were lost. We have no explanation to offer for these fires. They do not conform to our suggested pattern; and we note the period as an exception to our rule.

On January 27th, one man died in a fire at the Richards & Browne Co. warehouse in Brooklyn, NY The Sun was 20 degrees from the node.

On January 31st, 16 children died in the burning of a baby home at Auburn, Me. (Sun to node: 24 degrees.}

On February 5th, 17 people died in a New York Harbor fire. (Sun to node: 30 degrees.) On February 9th, two people died in the Vierling Steel Works fire in Chicago. (Sun to node: 34 degrees.)

On February 15th, two employees were found dead after a fire at the Columbian Iron Works, Chattanooga, Tenn. (Sun to node: 40 degrees.) On the same day, four persons were killed in the burning of an airplane hangar at Sydney, N. S.

On February 24th, one fireman was killed in an armory fire at Portland, Me. (Sun to node: 90 degrees.) On March 6th, 16 deaths were evenly divided between two fires. Eight people died as the result of the crash and fire when a cargo plane crashed into a hangar near Dayton, Ohio. Eight people also died in a fire aboard the S.S. Green Hill Park at Vancouver, B. C. (Sun to node: 61 Degrees.)

From March 6th to July 18th, there was no loss-of-life in any of the large loss fires listed by the N.F.P.A. This period carried us through two of our intervals of instability as well as one period of stability between them.

From July 18th to August 23rd, 54 people died in five fires. Again, this period does not conform to our suggested pattern. We might mention, however, that Mars conjoined Uranus in August. The conjunction was exact on August 17th.

One person died on July 18th in a scow fire at Halifax, Nova Scotia. (Sun to node: 17 degrees.)

On July 28th, 14 people were killed when a B-29 crashed into the Empire State Building in New York City, starting a difficult fire. (Sun to node: 27 degrees.)

On August 7th, 22 people died in the burning of Grain Elevator No. 5 of the Saskatchewan Terminal at Port Arthur, Ontario. (Sun to node: 38 degrees.)

On August 13th, 15 people died in the burning of the Export Box and Sealer Company in Detroit. (Sun to node: 44 degrees.) On August 23rd, two employees were killed in a fire at the Iron Fireman manufacturing Company at Portland, Oregon. Sun's distance to the Moon's node: 54 degrees.)

Although we have no explanation, we would like to point out that the two fires having greatest loss-of-life during the first six months of 1945 were only five days apart, while the two fires resulting in greatest loss-of-life during the summer were only six days apart, with the third largest loss-of-life fire occurring within ten days of one of these two fires. Yet, we had an interval of 133 days with no loss-of-life in large-loss fires. Also, the interval between the two largest loss-of-life fires was almost exactly six months. By apparent motion, the Sun moved 179 degrees between these two dates. The earth moved within one degree of exactly half way around the Sun. According to our 86.5 day cycle, both of these heavy loss-of-life fires were late.

The Sun squared the nodes on September 27, 1945.

On September 14th, three firemen died in a fire at the plant of Smith, Davidson & Wright in Vancouver, B. C. (Sun to node: 76 degrees.) On September 20th, one man was trapped and died in a fire in Building 92 of the Packard Motor Company in Detroit (Sun to node: 83 degrees).

From September 20th to December 23rd, only one person died in any large loss fire. On November 3rd, a watchman died in a fire at the Gwinn Milling Co., Columbus, Ohio. (Sun to node: 51 degrees.)

The sun crossed the node on December 22nd, 1945. On December 24th, the well-reported Hartford Christmas Tree fire occurred at the Niles Street Convalescent Hospital, and 19 persons lost their lives. (Sun to node: 3 Degrees) Although it will not form part of our records, we will mention that on December 23rd, a great many small animals and birds were burned to death in a circus fire at Mullins, S. C

As 1946 opened, **the planet Uranus was approaching the lunar node. It was within 15 degrees of the node by January 2nd, 1946. It was within 15 degrees of the node throughout the year.** Therefore, it is interesting to note that deaths through large-loss fires leaped from 142 in1945 to 493 in 1946. It should he noted that one hotel fire in 1945 involved loss-of-life (Milner Hotel, Lima, Ohio, on January 7th, 1945) and that it occurred during one of our periods of instability with the Sun within one degree of the node, because the year 1945 became a year of great hotel fires.

The year 1946 and its Joss-of-life through fires fitted into the pattern of our suggested periods of instability very well. Let us pause and look at a table of 1946 large-loss fires.

DATA ON 1946 FIRES

DISTANCE SUN TO MOON'S NODE	NUMBER OF FIRES	FIRES RESULTING IN DEATH	NUMBER KILLED	AVERAGE DEATHS PER FIRE
0-15 degrees	25	8	239	9.560
15-30 "	33	4	44	1.333
30-45 "	36	6	54	1.500
45-60 "	28	5	22	.786
60-75 "	31	4	59	1.903
75-90 "	34	4	75	2.206

[Uranus at this time was on its own node—13.5 degrees Gemini—and the Moon's node was at this point in October and November, 1946. G.L.]

As the reader will see, the two areas of instability, 0-to-15 Degrees and 75-to-90 degrees, score far out in front of all other areas for 1946. It might be well to make note of the fact that one of the greatest causes of fires getting out of hand is failure immediately to notify the fire department. Many people will hold up notification of the fire department until after they try to control the fire themselves. This factor was probably the cause of very great loss-of-life during 1946. Let us study the pattern of 1946 fires more closely.

Two men died from burns on January 13th, when a plane crashed and caught fire near Wichita, Kas. (Sun to node 25 Degrees.) On January 18th, 17 died in the fire and crash of a passenger plan, near Cheshire, Conn. (Sun to node: 31 degrees.)

On January 23rd, one employee was trapped and burned to death when a textile plant burned at Brewer, Me. (Sun to node: 35 degrees.)

On January 28th, ten persons died in the burning of a hangar at Tinker Field near Oklahoma City, Okla. (Sun to node 41 degrees.)

On February 3rd, the first hotel fire of 1946 occurred, but only one person died. This fire was in the Congress Hotel in Chicago. It is interesting to note that there were four fires in this hotel within 12 hours, "three probably attributable to careless smoking." Isn't it odd that all these fires from careless smoking should occur on the same day? The loss amounted to $281,000. (Sun to node: 48 degrees.) None of the above mentioned fires occurred during one of our sola node periods of instability. Thirty people died in the above fires.

The Sun squared the nodes on March 16th, and that date marked the center our first period of instability in 1946. Three days later, 26 persons died when an Army C-47 transport plane exploded in flight, crashed and burned on a snow covered mountain 11 miles from Truckee, Calif. No reason for the explosion was released by Army authorities, if they knew. (Sun to node: 87 degrees.) On March 22nd, two people were killed in an industrial fire at Gadsden, Ala. (Sun to node: 84 degrees.) Both of these fires occurred within one of our intervals of instability.

Although there was no loss-of-life, it is interesting to note that on April 9th, at Bolivar, Tenn., an insane asylum burned. A 1918 Model "T" Ford was the only piece of fire-fighting equipment in the area. Yet, 400 inmates were led safely from the building with no-loss of life. (Sun to node: 65 degrees.)

On April 10th; at Monessen, Penn., the Senior High School was virtually destroyed by fire 30 minutes after the students had been dismissed. When the fire had been subdued, the body of the 64-year-old janitor was found under the debris. Loss of $300,000. Call it coincidence, but on the same day, in Butte, Montana, the High School burned with a loss of $425,000, and no loss of life. (Sun to node: 64 degrees.) On April 17th, four airmen lost their lives when an Army bomber exploded in the air, crashed and burned near Andrews Field, near Ritchie, Md. (Sun to node: 56 Degrees.) On April 30th, seven were killed when the *USS Solar* burned, following a munitions explosion at the Naval Ammunition Depot at Earle, N. J. (Sun to node: 43 degrees.)

Let us pause to make note of the fact that thus far into 1946, the greatest loss-of-life in any one fire occurred during: our first period of instability. 26 deaths with the sun

87 degrees from the node, or 3 degrees from the center of the interval of instability.

There was no loss of life in any of the large-loss fires during May, 1946. The center of the next period of instability was on June 11th, 1946, when the Sun crossed the node. Also, on June 1st, **the planet Uranus was within four degrees of the node and going toward it.** On June 8th, the Sun was between Uranus and the earth. There were three bad hotel fires during this period of instability. Loss-of-life was heavy.

On June 5th, Chicago had its second hotel fire of 1946. The first one (Congress Hotel) had not occurred during one of our periods of instability and only one person died. Now, the great LaSalle Hotel fire: Sixty-one persons died. The loss was $2,260.000.

On June 7th, Hamilton, Ontario, had a $950,000 school fire, but there was no loss-of-life. On June 9th-four days after the LaSalle Hotel fire--the Canfield Hotel fire occurred at Dubuque; Iowa, and 19 persons died in the fire: (Sun to node: June 5th--7 degrees; June 7th--5 Degrees; June 9th--3 degrees.) On June 12th, 12 crew members were killed when an Army B-29 crashed and burned near Gatlinburg, Tenn. (Sun to node: 1 degree.)

June of 1946 had its third great hotel fire on the 21st. A $535,000 fire in the Baker Hotel at Dallas, Texas, resulted in the death of 10 persons. (Sun to node: 9 degrees.) On June 25th, three persons lost their lives when the Staten Island Ferry Terminal burned in New York. (Sun to node: 13 degrees.) During this period of instability, 105 persons had died in five large-loss fires.

On July 9th, 25 lives were lost in the flaming wreckage of an Army B-17 "Flying Fortress" near Holyoke, Mass. (Sun to node: 28 Degrees.) On July 11th, five died in the fire and crash of a "Constellation" near Reading, PN. Sun to node: 30 Degrees.) On July 18th, an Anny C-47 crashed and burned near Goodland, KN., and 14 persons died. (Sun to node: 37 degrees.) On July 25th another hotel fire took place, the fifth of the year. Although there was no loss-of-life, there was a loss of $321,000) when the Broadway Hotel burned at Oakland, Calif. (Sun to node: 44 degrees.) On July 29th, two died when a Navy Corsair crashed onto the Naval Air Station flight line. (Sun to node: 48 Degrees.) On August 1st, a Navy B-24 crashed and burned, killing 12 occupants near San Diego, Calif. (Sun to node: 51 degrees.)

Now let us pause long enough to make an observation. In June, loss-of-life was due mainly to hotel fires. In July, it was due to plane crashes and fires. **We must remember that Uranus was crossing the node, and during July, the planet Mars was squaring both Uranus and the node.** For many years, astrologers have claimed that mechanical accidents accompany angular aspects of Mars and Uranus, Mars reached the exact square of Uranus on July 24th.

On August 5th, 1946 three persons died in a tanker fire al Jacksonville, Fla. (Sun to node: 55 degrees.)

From June 27th to August 24th, which was a solar period of stability rather than instability, 61 people died in these fires. During our next period of instability, which is half as long, 47 people died in two plane-crash fires. This is a ratio of 22.5 deaths per plane, as against a ratio of 11.6 during the previous stable period, **although neither period can be considered as very stable due to the close proximity of Uranus to the node.**

On September 5th, a plane crashed near Elko, Nevada. Loss is given as $250,000. A brief report mentions no deaths, and so no deaths appear in our records. Loss-of-life seems probable, however, because the report states that fire occurred immediately upon ground contact. This incident was within one of our periods of instability, as were the two cases following. (Sun to node: 86 degrees.)

On September 15th, twenty-one Royal Canadian Air Force men died when a C-47 A crashed and burned at Estevan, Sask. (Sun to node: 83 degrees.) On September 18th, a trans-Atlantic plane crashed and burned near Gander, Newfoundland, and 26 people died. (Sun to node: 80 degrees.)

On October 2nd, 11 died when an Army B-29 crashed and burned near Battle Mountain, Nevada. (Sun to node: 65 degrees.) On October 3rd, 39 died when an American Overseas Airline plane crashed and burned near Stephenville, Newfoundland. (Sun to node: 64 degrees.) Also on October 3rd, eight died in a fire at the Sun Oil Company refinery at Marcus Hook, Penna. We might again observe that in addition to Uranus being close to the node, Mars was square to Saturn. On November 13th, a transport plane crashed on White Mountain near Burbank, California. Eleven persons were burned beyond recognition. (Sun to node: 21 Degrees.) On November 19th, six people were killed in a laundry fire at Greenville, SC (Sun to node: 15 degrees.) This fire was a day away from our next interval of instability.

Now, we enter our last period of instability of 1946. We are in for more excitement. We have more hotel fires with even greater loss-of-life. The Sun crossed the node on December 4th.

On November 29th, one man lost his life in a meat processing plant at Charlottetown, P.E.I. (Sun to node: 4 degrees.)

On December 6th, there was a near disaster, when a $1,500,000 fire occurred in a Veterans' Hospital at Peterborough, Ont. There had been a very carefully prearranged plan should fire ever occur. It did occur and 228 patients were safely evacuated.

On the following day, however, a delay in reporting a fire in the Winecoff Hotel in Atlanta, Ga., resulted in the death of 122 persons. The fire was discovered at 3:15 a.m., but for some reason was not reported until 3:42 a.m. This was the sixth great hotel fire of the year. (Sun to node: 4 degrees.) On the following day, eleven people died in the Saskatoon Hotel Fire in Saskatchewan.

Why should these two hotel fires come so close together? Why did hotel fires group themselves in June in the same manner, and why did they do this on each occasion when both the Sun and Uranus were conjunct the node? Here were seven hotel fires in 1946. The eighth occurred on December 22nd at the Kentucky Hotel in Louisville. This fire was outside of our period of instability. The Sun was 20 degrees from the node. There was no loss-of-life.

Note that these periods of instability recede in the calendar at the rate of about 19 days each year. **Note that the great summer fires of 1944 occurred in July. In 1946, they had moved back into June. We have four of these unstable periods constantly moving backwards in the calendar at the approximate rate of 19 days per year. At the end of 1946,**

Uranus was going away from the node, but they were still but eight degrees apart.

Now, let us combine the figures of 1945 with those of 1946. The 0-to-15 degree period is far out in front, as it was for the combined figures of 1943 and 1944. The 75-90-degree area has not stood up in these figures. It was very high in the 1944 figures. Let us now combine the following figures for all four years 1943 to 1946 inclusive. The results follow:

COMBINED DATA OF FIRES OF 1945 AND 1946

DISTANCE SUN TO MOON'S NODE	NUMBER OF FIRES	FIRES RESULTING IN DEATH	NUMBER KILLED	AVERAGE DEATHS PER FIRE
0-15 degrees	64	12	263	4.109
15-30 "	62	8	76	1.226
30-45 "	63	12	116	1.841
45-60 "	59	8	26	.441
60-75 "	45	6	75	1.666
75-90 "	57	6	79	1.386

DATA OF FIRES 1943 TO 1946

DISTANCE SUN TO MOON'S NODE	NUMBER OF FIRES	FIRES RESULTING IN DEATH	NUMBER KILLED	AVERAGE DEATHS PER FIRE
0-15 degrees	107	20	488	4.560
15-30 "	107	14	89	.831
30-45 "	101	18	147	1.455
45-60 "	87	11	38	.436
60-75 "	69	10	85	1.232
75-90 "	103	16	252	2.446

In this combined table, we find that both of our instability areas rate at the top. Out of a total of 1,099 deaths, we should expect one-third or 366 in the two unstable areas. Actually, 740 deaths occurred in these areas. This is more than double expectancy. Although we also find more fires in these areas, the excess is too slight to be of statistical significance. Now, suppose that we consider only those fires where there was loss-of-life, and take the ratio of deaths in those fires by themselves instead of the ratio of deaths to all fires. We will obtain the following figures:

DISTANCE SUN TO MOON'S NODE	AVERAGE DEATHS PER FIRE
0-15 degrees	24.4
15-30 "	6.3
30-45 "	8.1
45-60 "	3.4
60-75 "	8.5
75-90 "	15.7

Combined Fire Data Loss-of-Life Only

It would seem that such figures must mean something. The question is, what do they mean? We find more people killed during the combined unstable areas, but the number of people killed is dependent upon the number of people in a building when the fire occurred. Danger of death in a school fire is greater during school hours. Danger of death in a theatre fire is greater in the evening than during the morning. Fire in a hotel is more dangerous when everyone is asleep.

If a human factor is a cause of the high death rate during our suggested intervals of instability, then all fires where the death toll was not due to a human factor should be excluded from our test, but in the great majority of cases, we do not really know whether a human factor was involved. The real evidence is often burned. Also, it isn't really fair to compare a warehouse fire with a hotel fire.

LOSS OF LIFE THROUGH FIRE Part 3

The years 1947 and 1948 complicate our evidence of the 86.5-day cycle. They might be taken as evidence against the cycle, but we choose to view the matter differently. Exceptions to the rule are quite often the keys with which we unlock the next disclosure of nature. There is a possibility that the exceptions to the rule, in those years when appearances do not indicate that the cycle is working, may be fitting themselves into a pattern, and that pattern may be indicating some other cycle which we have not yet discovered.

It is a single marked exception to the rule that really upsets our figures, but there are other, less important exceptions, and these exceptions appear to be conforming to some pattern that we do not yet understand. We call it a pattern because on three different occasions we find unexplained groups of fires involving loss-of-life where two such unexplained groups fall almost exactly six months apart.

Bear in mind that our 86.5-day cycle can produce a similar phenomenon. It can, or has appeared to, produce groups of fires 173 days apart on the average. Half of a year is 182.625 days. In the case of our group exceptions, we use the term half-a-year only as an approximation. We might be off by as much as 15 days. The close proximity to half-a-year is suggestive. It suggests that our relationship with the Sun is involved, because only the earth's relationship with the Sun is involved with the interval of a year. If the Sun is between us and a fixed point in space on a given day, six months later, we will be between the sun and that fixed point in space. If the point in space is not fixed but is moving, the six month interval would be altered in accordance with the motion of the point in space. These are views for future consideration.

Our great exception to the rule was the Texas City disaster. Loss-of-life was very great. On April 16, 1947, 500 people were killed when two shiploads of ammonium nitrate exploded, injuring 3,000 people and causing property damage of $67,000,000. Prior to that time, scientists did not know that ammonium nitrate would explode when in contact with flame. It had never exploded before. A week later, ammonium nitrate also exploded in France.

Thus, this fire does not fall in the same realm with such fires as the Winecoff Hotel where 122 persons died because hotel employees delayed reporting the fire for 27 minutes. If, in this cycle, we are dealing with a factor of human failure--carelessness, panic, etc., then we would not expect the Texas City disaster to conform to the cycle. There are a great many other of our fires that we would not expect to conform and in any event, we would not expect all such fires to conform, even when human failure is the cause, for we would be dealing with an indirect effect. Instability can have its effect in many directions. If we find instability having its effect upon loss-of-life through fire, that in itself is remarkable, but let us look at the loss-of-life record for 1947.

On January 15th, there was one death connected with the burning of the Peerless Paper Mills at Oaks, PN (Sun to node: 45 degrees.) On January 20th a DC-4 crashed and burned at Oakland, CA Although there was one death, twenty escaped. (Sun to node: 51 degrees.) On January 27th, near Albuquerque, NM, fire-at-impact destroyed a B-29. Eleven of twelve occupants died. (Sun to node: 59 Degrees.) On February 4th, four died in a fire resulting from a collision between a train and a gasoline truck-trailer at Kingsburg, CA (Sun to node: 67 Degrees.) These fires were not within one of our Sun-node periods of instability.

The Sun squared the nodes of February 26th, 1947. On February 20th, Los Angeles, Calif., experienced a costly group fire. Burning of the O'Connor Electroplating Corp. plant damaged 116 buildings, resulted in a property loss of $3, 500,000, injured 140 and killed 17. (Sun to node: 84 degrees.) On March 2nd, 4 died in a Chicago restaurant fire, while a fireman died of a heart attack in a group fire at Wilkes-Barre, PA (Sun to node: 85 degrees.) On March 9th, 3 deaths resulted from a million dollar fire and explosion at the Cities Service Gas Co. at Blackwell, Okla. (Sun to node: 78 degrees.) These fires occurred during one of our suggested Sun-node periods of instability.

On March 13th, 3 died in a dormitory fire at Cazenovia, N. Y. Eighty students were safely evacuated. (Sun to node: 73

Degrees.) On March 25th, 111 were killed in the Centralia Coal Co. at Centralia, Ill. (Sun to node: 61 Degrees.) The Texas City disaster occurred on April 16th. Sun to node: 38 Degrees.)

We have no further data on the Centralia fire, but these two large loss-of-life fires, with 611 deaths are in bad conflict with our Sun-node cycle, although they do fall within an unstable area of the Uranus-node cycle.

The Sun crossed the node on May 24th, 1947.

On May 11th, 4 died in the crash of a Trans World Airlines plane near Cape May, NJ. The words, " ... maneuvers . . . not properly performed," would indicate human failure. (Sun to node: 13 degrees.) On May 13th, near Pittston, PA, the Ransom County Home and Hospital burned. Three hundred mental patients were safely evacuated, but one died of a heart attack. (Sun to node: 11 degrees.) On May 22nd, a C-97 crashed, exploded and burned near Dayton, Ohio, with a loss of five lives (Sun to node: 1 degree.) On May 29th, at New York, a DC-4 crashed and burned during takeoff. Forty-three persons were burned to death. (Sun to node: 5 degrees) These 53 deaths occurred during our period of Sun-node instability.

On June 22nd, 11 died in the *SS Morkay* ship fire in Los Angeles, Calif. (Sun to node: 29 degrees.) On July 11th there was one death in the Liberty Coach Co. fire in Syracuse, N. Y., while 3 died in the G. Whitaker & Co. fire at Peterborough, Ont. (Sun to node: 48 Degrees.) On July 21st, 4 died in the Westland Oil Co. fire at Minot, ND (Sun to node: 59 degrees.) On July 24th, there were two deaths in a multiple occupancy hotel property fire at Susanville, Calif. (Sun to node: 62 degrees.) These fires were not within one of our instability areas.

On August 21st, 1947, the Sun squared the nodes.

On September 1st, 31 people died as the result of a fire caused by the crash of two trains on the Canadian National Railroad at Dugald, Manitoba. Grain elevator and oil storage tanks burned. (Sun to node: 79 degrees.)

On September 9th, 23 deaths resulted from the S.S. Island. Queen fire at Pittsburgh, PA (Sun to node: 70 degrees.)

On September 15th, near Aberdeen, Md., 23 died when a B-17 caught fire in flight and fell into Chesapeake Bay. (Sun to node: 64 degrees.) On September 24th, 12 died in a collision and fire of two ships near Iroquois, Ont. (Sun to node: 55 degrees.) On October 11th, there was one death in the Burlington Fruit Co. fire at Burlington, Iowa. (Sun to node: 28 degrees.) On October 12th, Buffalo had one death in the Standard Oil Co. fire. (Sun to node: 37 degrees.) The Maine forest fires occurred from October 16 to 25th. Two hundred fifty thousand acres were burned. Over 1200 homes were destroyed. Sixteen persons died in 9 major fires, "due primarily to an abnormal period of dry, warm weather." (Sun to node: 23 to 32 degrees.) On October 24th, near Bryce Canyon, Utah, fire in flight aboard a DC-6 resulted in fatalities to all 52 occupants. "Fire is attributed to ignition of gasoline on heater during fuel transfer operation." (Sun to node: 24 degrees.) On October 25th, the Penna Products Co. fire at Cleveland, Ohio, resulted in 2 deaths. (Sun to node: 2.) degrees.) None of these fires occurred within one of our periods of instability.

The Sun conjoined the lunar node on November 16th, 1947.

On November 10th, 2 died in the crash and fire of a E-29 near Oklahoma City, Okla. (Sun to node: 6 degrees.) 011 November 18th, 5 were killed when a Constellation crashed and burned near New Castle, Del. (Sun to node: 2 degrees.) On November 28th, two firemen were killed by a wall collapse at the N. Y. Plumbers Specialties Co. fire in New York City. (Sun to node: 13 degrees.) On November 30th, there were 9 deaths as the result of a crash and fire when a DC-4 overshot the landing field near Seattle, Wash., striking an automobile. (Sun to node: 14 degrees.) Also on November 30th, one man died in a fire at the Michigan Gas Storage Co. at Marion, Mich. These fires were within our period of instability.

On December 5th, 3 employees were killed in a fire at the Haertel Products Co., Minneapolis, MN (Sun to node: 21 degrees.) On December 15th, 2 deaths resulted from the Celanese Corp. fire at Newark, N. J. (Sun to node: 32 degrees.) On December 16th, near Tucson, Arizona, 12 crew members of a B-29 died in a crash fire soon after take-off. (Sun to node: 33 degrees.) None occurred during our periods of instability.

Now, we can look at a table of 1947 fires.

DATA ON 1947 FIRES

Distance Sun to Moon's Node	Number of Fires	Fires Resulting in Death	Number Killed	Average Deaths per Fire
0 to 15 Degrees	32	9	72	2.250
15 to 30 "	30	4	68	2.266
30 to 45 "	45	14(a)	532	11.822
45 to 60 "	33	7	33	1.000
60 to 75 "	37	6	152	4.108
75 to 90 "	33	5	56	1.697

(a)The Maine forest fire is included as 9 fires of separate and independent origin.

The above figures make it quite obvious that our 86.5-day cycle had no confirmation in the 1947 records. Yet, violations conform to a pattern in that they are spaced six months apart. In the spring, greatest loss-of-life came on April 16th. The Maine forest fires broke out six months to the day later, on October 16th. Greatest loss-of-life came on October 24th (52 deaths at Bruce Canyon, Utah). In Chapter 19, we pointed out that in 1945, the two greatest loss-of-life fires of that year, which did not conform to our 86.5-day cycle, came six months apart, almost to the day.

We enter 1948, when the death ratio was down. Greatest loss-of-life through fire came on July 17th, with the Sun 75 degrees from the node, within an area of instability.

Nevertheless, 1948 had two periods when loss-of-life was above average for the year, and again these two periods were approximately six months apart, and again they did not conform with our 86.5-day cycle. One such period came from early in mid-March while the other came in late August and early September. Each period came just after one of our suggested periods of instability. As yet, we are at a loss for an explanation of this pattern.

The *N.F.P.A. Quarterly* for January 1949 states: "*It is regrettable but true that adequate statistics on deaths and injuries in fires are not at present available from any source .... It is quite possible that our present estimate of approximately 11,000 deaths from the fire in the United States annually is conservative.*"

In so far as property loss was concerned, 1949 showed the heaviest loss on record from large-loss fires. The death rate was way down, however. The N.F.P.A. points out that inflationary prices may have been responsible, in part, for the large property loss figures.

The Sun squared the nodes on February 8th, 1948.

The first large-loss fire of 1948 did not come until January 30th. It was the only hotel fire of the year involving loss-of-life. Three people died when the Jesse Welden Inn, a 75 room hotel at St. Albans, Vt., burned. The sun was 81 degrees from the lunar node, and consequently this fire fell within one of our periods of instability. On February 1st, one death resulted from the burning of the First Reformed Church ($335,000 loss) in Schenectady, NY (Sun to node: 83 degrees.) On February 4th, 2 were killed in a truck terminal fire of Retail Merchants Delivery, Inc., in Columbus, Ohio. (Sun to node: 86 degrees.) On February 10th, one death resulted from a fire at the New Jersey Floor Covering Co., in Trenton, NJ (Sun to node: 87 degrees.) On February 20th, 2 died in the Jackson Building fire in Pittsburgh, PA. (Sun to node: 77 degrees.) All of these fires fell within our period of instability.

From March 6th to April 12th, which was not one of our suggested unstable intervals, 45 people died in seven fires. On March 6th, 5 were killed in a fire at the Interlake Chemical Corp. at Waltham, Mass. (Sun to node: 61 degrees.) On March 10th, a DC-4 crashed, burned and killed 12 in Chicago, while at Asheville, N. C., 9 were killed in the Highland Hospital fire. (Sun to node: 56 degrees.) On March 15th, 7 died in a fire at the International Harvester Co. near Louisville, Ky. (Sun to node: 51 degrees.) On March 18th, a B-29 crashed and burned near Tampa, Fla., killing ten. (Sun to node: 48 degrees.) On March 19th, there was one death in a fire at the Waterville Textile, Ltd., at Waterville, Que. (Sun to node: 47 degrees.) On April 12th, one death resulted from the Crucible Steel Co. fire in Jersey City, N. J. (Sun to node: 23 degrees.) Here was the first group of loss-of-life fires that did not conform to our cycle. There was to be another group six months later.

The Sun crossed the nodes on May 4th, 1948.

On May 15th, one died in the fire of the Boston Consolidated Gas Co. at

Everett, Mass., and there was one death in a fire at the United Automotive Supplies Co. at San Francisco, CA (Sun to node: 12 degrees.) On May 17th there were 10 deaths in the Koppers Co. fire at Kearny, NJ (Sun to node: 13 degrees.) These fires were within our period of instability.

On June 2nd, a fire at Price Bros. & Co., Ltd., Priceville, Que., resulted in 1 death. (Sun to node: 30 degrees.) On June 5th, 5 died near Muroc, Calif. when a YB-49 "Flying Wing" jet bomber crashed and burned. (Sun to node: 33 degrees.) On June 8th, one death resulted from the Hillcrest Country Club fire at Los Angeles, Calif. (Sun to node: 36 degrees.) On June 23rd there was one death as result of fire at the Putnam Tool Co. in Detroit. (Sun to node: 51 degrees.) On July 3rd, two died in a fire at the Carnegie-Illinois Steel Co., Chicago, Ill. (Sun to node: 60 degrees.) On July 6th, there were 4 deaths in a fire at the Lyle Ranchflour Co., Seattle, Wash. (Sun to node: 64 degrees.) None of these fires was within one of our periods of instability.

We entered our next period of instability on July 17th, and on that day 43 people died when a DC-6 crashed and burned near Mount Carmel, PA. This was the largest loss-of-life fire of the year. The Sun squared the nodes on August 1st. On August 12th, a B-29 crashed and burned shortly after take-off near Topeka, KS and 5 died, while another B-29 crashed and burned shortly after take-off at Roswell, NM, and 13 died. A DC-4M also crashed and burned at Sydney, Nova Scotia, but there was no loss of life. (Sun to node: 78 degrees.) These 61 deaths occurred during one of our periods of instability.

Deaths continued after this period was over, and here is the exception to our rule that follows the March exception, six months before. On August 20th, 17 were killed when a B-29 crashed and burned shortly after take-off near Rapid City, SD. (Sun to node: 71 degrees.) On August 24th, 16 were killed when a B-29 crashed and burned at Honolulu. (Sun to node: 67 degrees.) On September 7th, 17 were killed in a fire at the E. J. Brach · & Sons factory in Chicago, Ill. (Sun to node: 52 degrees.) On September 20th, 2 died when a B-45 jet bomber crashed and burned near Alpaugh. CA (Sun to node: 39 degrees.) On September 28th, 3 died when a B-29 crashed and burned during the landing at Shemya, AL. A DC-4 was also burned in New York, but there was no loss of life. (Sun to node; 31 Degrees.) On October 6th, 9 were killed when a B-29 exploded in air near Waycross, Ga. (Sun to node: 23 degrees.)

On October 18th, fire at the Michigan Consolidated Gas Company at Melvindale, Mich., accounted for one death. (Sun to node: 11 Degrees.) On October 19th, there was one death from fire at the Seeger Refrigerating Co. at Evansville, Ind. (Sun to node: 9 Degrees.) This was the last unstable period in 1948.

On November 13th, six died when a C-47 crashed into a B-50 and resulted in fire at Ladd Field. Alaska (near Fairbanks). The C-47 was taking off. (Sun to node: 17 degrees.) On December 6th, there was one death in Joseph's Department Store fire at Fremont, Ohio. (Sun to node: 42 degrees.) On December 9th, fire at the Kansas Power and Light Co. at Tecumseh, Kan., resulted in 9 deaths. (Sun to node: 45 degrees.) On. December 16th, one death accompanied fire at the Cattani Cotton Gin at Wheeler Ridge Cutoff, CA (Sun to node: 52 · Degrees.)

Now, we will place these fires in the US for the other years in order to see same kind of a table that we have made the results for 1948.

DATA ON 1948 FIRES

Distance Sun to Moon's Node	Number of Fires	Fires Resulting in Death	Number Killed	Average Deaths per Fire
0 to 15 Degrees	39	5	14	.359
15 to 30 "	34	4	16	.470
30 to 45 "	39	6	13	.333
45 to 60 "	43	9	67	1.558
60 to 75 "	59	5	44	.745
75 to 90 "	54	8	70	1.296

Although maximum deaths actually occurred during the time when the Sun was in the area from 75 to 90 degrees from the node, the ratio of deaths did not reach the top in that area. Now, let us unite this table with that for 1947.

DATA ON 1947-1948 FIRES COMBINED

Distance Sun to Moon's Node	Number of Fires	Fires Resulting in Death	Number Killed	Average Deaths per Fire
0 to 15 Degrees	71	14	86	1.211
15 to 30 "	64	8	84	1.312
30 to 45 "	84	20[a]	545	6.488
45 to 60 "	76	16	100	1.351
60 to 75 "	96	14	196	2.041
75 to 90 "	87	13	126	1.448

[a] This figure may be incorrect, because we do not know whether all nine Maine forest fires of 1947 resulted in death, or whether just some of them so resulted.

As is apparent the overall figures for these two years argue against, rather than for, our 86.5-day cycle, but if we are correct in our suggestion that the cycle deals only with human instability, such results are to be expected in some years so long as we have no way of dividing deaths due to "human failure" from deaths due to factors that are not human in nature. We can now sum up our figures for a six-year period, and we will have the following results:

DATA ON 1943-1948 FIRES

Distance Sun to Moon's Node	Number of Fires	Fires Resulting in Death	Number Killed	Average Deaths per Fire
0 to 15 Degrees	178	34	574	3.224
15 to 30 "	171	22	173	1.011
30 to 45 "	185	38[b]	692	3.767
45 to 60 "	163	27	138	.846
60 to 75 "	165	24	281	1.703
75 to 90 "	190	29	378	1.989

[b] See comment relative to possible incorrectness of this figure at foot of previous table.

At first glance, this table might appear to completely upset our suggestion of an 86.5-day cycle, but actually, it is just one incident that has appeared to make it do so. In our last column of figures (Average Death Per Fire), for the area 30-45 degrees, we have the figure 3.767. If the Texas City disaster were not included, this figure would drop to 1.038, and we would have a curve with the high point at our two points of instability. It is really the Texas City disaster alone that has upset our figures, and that was not a fire with loss-of-life due to human failure.

There is another peculiarity about these figures. The years when our cycle made its best showing were those years when public buildings and places of assemblage were burning. Later, we will represent our figures eliminating warehouses and commercial buildings. **When our figures are confined to theatres, hotels, places of amusement. and places of assemblage, quite a different story is going to be told**. For the present, however, we are including all fires presented by the N.F.P.A. We are making our figures as complete as it is possible to make them from present-day, available records.

What about our Uranus-To-Moon's node cycle during these years?

From May 28th, 1943, to January 2nd, 1946, Uranus was in stable relationship to the moon's node, meaning that it was between 15 and 75 degrees away from the node. During this interval, there were 545 deaths connected with large-loss fires listed by the N.F.P.A. This was 545 deaths in 950 days, or a ratio of .573 deaths per day. From January 2nd, 1946, to April 23rd, 1947, Uranus was within 15 degrees of the moon's node, or in unstable relationship. During that time, 1,149 people lost their lives in large-loss fires listed by the N.F.P.A. This was 1,149 deaths in 476 days or a ratio of 2.413 deaths per day. **This means there were four times as many deaths-per-day during the Uranus-node unstable interval.**

For the remainder of 1947, there were only 257 deaths or 1.015 per day, and during 1948, there were 224 deaths, a ratio of .612 per day.

These figures offer strong testimony for our 3.75-year cycle of instability. It is interesting to note that although the frequency of fires increased after we left our Uranus-node interval of instability, the number of deaths decreased.

NOTE: Since the 86.5-day cycle of Sun-node relationship was first suggested in this series, we have passed three high points of instability in the cycle which have been accompanied by outstanding world events. On June 24th, 1950, the sun squared the nodes, and the Korean War broke out. On September 21st, the Sun crossed the node, and in September the whole course of the Korean War changed. The Inchon landings took place, and on September 21st, U. N. Troops entered the capital of Seoul. The Sun squared the nodes on December 15, 1950. As we left November and entered December, the whole course of the Korean War was changing again as the Chinese Communists entered the battle against U. N. forces, and on December 15th, President Truman addressed the people of the U. S., announcing that he was declaring a National Emergency on the following day.

LOST-OF-LIFE THROUGH FIRE Part 4

The number of large-loss fires in the United States, Canada and Alaska dropped from 268 in 1948 to 218 in 1949. Deaths in such fires increased from 224 in 1948 to 398 in 1949. Despite the fact that the greatest loss-of-life-fire of the year failed to conform with our lunar node-Sun cycle, the death ratio reached its maximum while the Sun was within 15 degrees of the lunar node, thus adding additional evidence to substantiate our Sun lunar-node cycle.

Let us start out with our table of 1949 large-loss fires. The same type of table that we have presented in previous chapters.

DATA ON 1949 FIRES

Distance Sun to Moon's Node	Number of Fires	Fires Resulting in Death	Number Killed	Average Deaths Per Fire
0 to 15 Degrees	19	4	89	4.684
15 to 30 Degrees	42	7	122	2.904
30 to 45 Degrees	41	7	44	1.073
45 to 60 Degrees	31	6	50	1.613
60 to 75 Degrees	41	4	32	.780
75 to 90 Degrees	44	6	61	1.386

On September 17th, 1949, The *S.S. Noronic* burned at its pier in Toronto, Canada, and 104 people were killed. The Sun was 23 degrees from the lunar node. Thus, this fire, the greatest loss-of-life fire of the year, did not conform to our Sun-lunar-node cycle. It did conform to the Uranus-lunar node cycle, but more about that later. Let us heed the actual cause of death as stated by the N.F.P.A. The ship burned at its pier with heavy loss-of-life "because of lack of automatic protection and alarm system, vertical fire bulkheads, enclosures around stairway openings, and any prearranged emergency evacuation and fire defense plan. Large quantities of combustible materials used to subdivide passenger cabins and to form corridors, light wood interior finish, and combustible furnishings and fixtures contributed fuel to fast spreading fire. Delayed alarm to fire department."

Let us point out that with the exception of the delayed alarm to fire department, none of these factors was dependent upon what anyone did or failed to do on September 17th, 1949. This will become important in a later chapter.

Let us now point out that on August 23rd, 1949, the planet Uranus came to within 15 degrees of squaring the nodes, and from that date on, we were in one of our Uranus-to-lunar-node unstable intervals. Out of 34 fires involving loss-of-life, 13 occurred prior to August 23rd and 21 occurred after that date. Out of the 398 deaths, 149 occurred before August 23rd and 249 occurred after that date. Prior to August 23rd, the death ratio was .634 per day. For the remainder of the year, the death ratio was 1.9 deaths per day. Thus again, we find confirmation of our Uranus-to-lunar-node cycle:

Now let's review the 1949 loss-of-life fires.

On January 19th, 11 people died as the result of a collision and fire off the New Jersey coast when a Coast Guard ice breaker and a 10,000-ton tanker collided. (Sun to node: 89 degrees.) On January 21st, the Orton Hotel in Wilmington, N. C., burned with loss of two lives. (Sun to node: 88 degrees.) On January 28th, one employee was killed by an explosion at the People's Gas Light and Coke Co. in Chicago. (Sun to node: 81 degrees.) These three fires were within one of our sun-to-lunar-node periods of instability.

On February 27th, nine were killed in a college dormitory fire at Kenyon College in Gambier, Ohio. (Sun to node: 49 degrees.)

On March 4th, seven firemen were killed in the F. W. Woolworth & Co. 'fire at Charleston, S. C. (Sun to node: 44 degrees.) In a group fire in Palmyra, N. Y., on March 25th, one life was lost. (Sun to node: 21 degrees.) None of these fires were within one of our intervals of instability.

On April 4th, tragedy struck at Effingham, Ill., when the St. Anthony Hospital burned and 74 people lost their lives. (Sun to node: 12 degrees.)

On April 16th, one death resulted from the Sears Roebuck fire in Mobile, Ala. (Sun to node: 1 degree.) Both of these fires were within one of our periods of instability.

An employee was killed by an explosion at the Hardesty Chemical Co., near Dover, Ohio on May 4th. (Sun to node: 20 degrees.) On May 25th, one airman was killed in a B-29 crash and fire near Biggs Force Base in Texas. (Sun to node: 41 degrees.)

On June 23rd, four firemen were killed in a fire at the California Refining Co. in Perth Amboy, NJ (Sun to node: 70 degrees.) These fires were outside of our intervals of instability.

On July 12th, the crash and burning of a C-46 in the Santa Susanna Mountains in California took 35 lives. (Sun to node: 89 degrees.) This disaster was at the center of one of our intervals of instability.

Two died in a coalmine fire in Springfield, Ill., on August 15th. (Sun to node: 57 degrees.) We are listing the next fire only because the N.F.P.A. listed it, and it probably does not belong in this data.

On August 25th, in the Greenland Sea, battery trouble ultimately resulted in the explosion of hydrogen gas. There were seven deaths, but most of them were deaths of members of the rescue squad, and they were drowned, and not burned to death. (Sun to node: 46 degrees.)

There was one death when a B-29 burned near Wellpinit, WA, on August 29th. (Sun to node: 42 degrees.)

On August 31st, 10 died when the U.S. Navy PMB Flying Boat crashed and burned off San Diego, Calif. (Sun to node: 40 degrees.) An explosion at the Hiram Walker distillery in Peoria, Ill., on September 13th resulted in two deaths. (Sun to node: 27 degrees.)

On September 15th, an explosion at the Southeastern Indiana Power Co. in Rushville, Ind., resulted in two deaths. (Sun to node: 25 degrees.) On the same day, there was one death in a B-26 crash and fire near Fort Worth. Texas.

On September 17th; the burning of the *S.S. Noronic* occurred im Toronto, with the loss of 104 lives. (Sun to node: 23 degrees.) These fires were all outside of our lunar-node-to-Sun cycle of instability.

On September 26th, a B-29 crashed and burned near Talihina, Okla., with loss of 13 lives. (Sun to node: 14 degrees.)

On October 2nd, one fireman died as a result of a fire at the Pioneer Hi-Bred Corn Co., near Champaign, Ill. (Sun to node: 7 degrees.) These two fires fell within one of our Sun-to-lunar-node periods of instability.

A B-29 crashed and burned near Hamilton, Bermuda, killing 11 on November 3rd. Although this is listed by the N.F.P.A., it is outside the limits of the United States, Canada and Alaska. (Sun to node: 26 degrees.)

Another B-29 burned near Brownsville, Ind., on November 11th, killing two. (Sun to node: 35 degrees.)

A third and fourth B-29 collided, crashed and burned near Stockton, Calif. on November 16th, with loss of 18 lives. (Sun to node: 40 degrees.)

A fifth B-29 burned near Tampa, Fla., killing 5 on November 18th. (Sun to node: 42 degrees.)

A DC-6 crashed and burned in Dallas, TX on November 29th, and 28 people died, (Sun to node: 54 degrees.)

On December 2nd, one death resulted from the Loraine Hotel fire in Sapulpa, OK (Sun to node: 57 degrees.)

On December 3rd, 3 died as the result of a dormitory fire at the University of Oklahoma at Norman, Okla. (Sun to node: 58 degrees.)

A bowling alley fire at Union City, N. J., resulted in one death on December 12th. (Sun to node: 67 degrees.)

Twenty-one deaths resulted from an explosion at Swift & Co. in Sioux City, Iowa, on December 14th. (Sun to node: 69 degrees.) On December 15th, 6 died in a B-29 crash and fire at Roswell, N.M. (Sun to node: 71 degrees.) None of these fires occurred within one of our Sun-lunar-node intervals of instability.

On December 22, a B-50 burned near Savannah, Ga., killing 11. (Sun to node: 78 degrees.) On December 25th, one death resulted from a group fire in Hyndman, Pa. (Sun to node: 81 degrees.) These two fires did occur within one of our Sun-to-lunar-node intervals of instability.

As this chapter is written, the 1950 records of the N.F.P.A. have not been published, and so, the data of 1950 will have to be reported at a later date.

Now, we can sum up our data on fires for the years 1943 to 1949 inclusive, and we will have the following table:

DATA ON 1943-1949 FIRES

Distance Sun to Moon's Node	Number of Fires	Fires Resulting in Death	Number Killed	Average Death Per Fire
0 to 15 Degrees	197	38	663	3.365
15 to 30 Degrees	213	29	295	1.385
30 to 45 Degrees	226	45	736	3.257 (1.044)
45 to 60 Degrees	194	33	188	.969
60 to 75 Degrees	206	28	313	1.519
75 to 90 Degrees	234	35	439	1.876

Beside the 30-to-45 degree area, we have added the figure 1.044 as the death ratio per fire. This is the death-ratio figure that would apply if the Texas City disaster were excluded from this data. **Thus, we see that the maximum death ratio would occur at the two extremes (0 to 15-degrees and 75 to 90-degrees) if this one disaster was excluded.** The question is should this case be excluded?

In this data, 1270 fires have been included. In 208 of these, there was loss of life. In these fires, 2,634 people died.

The above figures show that we have no significant increase in the frequency of fires during our periods of instability, and no significant increase in the frequency of fires resulting in death, but we do appear to have an increase in the ratio of deaths per fire. **Our figures have also indicated an increase in the death ratio when the planet Uranus, was conjunct or square the lunar node, but no increase in the frequency of fires.** The Texas City disaster, which was our one great exception to the rule in so far as our Sun-to-lunar node cycle is concerned, was actually within one of our Uranus-to-lunar node periods of instability.

Now that we have been able to conclude that there is no increase in the frequency of fires, or in the frequency of fires resulting in death, during our periods of instability, we are prepared to take another forward step in determining why the ratio of deaths should increase during these intervals of instability. That will be the subject of our next chapter. We must keep probing to get closer and closer to the truth, whatever that may be.

HUMAN REACTIONS IN EMERGENCIES

If you are a good observer, you may have noticed an interesting fact about our record of loss-of-life through fire. The excess of deaths during our intervals of instability seems associated with fires in public buildings. We can narrow this down further, and say buildings where people are in unfamiliar surroundings. Again, we can narrow it, and say such buildings if there are no fire drills.

In studying newspaper accounts of fires during our periods of instability, we have noted a number of fires in homes when there were guests. The family escaped, but the guests were burned to death.

All of this suggests the conclusion that the entire excess of loss-of-life in fires which occur during our intervals of instability may be due to the psychological factor of confusion, with resultant panic.

If you awaken in the night to discover that your surroundings are on fire, and you are in your own home, you know your way to safety. You know the location of all exits and how to reach them. Action is likely to be subconscious and automatic. You may find yourself out of the building and safe before you are fully conscious of what is happening.

On the other hand, if you awaken in strange surroundings to discover that the building is on fire, automatic, subconscious action does not necessarily follow. Conscious planning becomes necessary at a time when moments are precious. You must think things out before you act. If the fire occurs during one of our suggested intervals of instability, confusion may be much greater, because you are less stable. If you are in a public building, like a hotel, a large number of people may become confused, and the result may be a panic. Meanwhile, the fire is doing its ghastly work, and the delay caused by confusion may result in heavy loss-of-life.

If a man is killed by an explosion, he may be killed instantly. He has no time to react. He has no opportunity to save himself. It is already too late.

Our figures indicate that there is no increase in the frequency of fires during our periods of instability but there is an increase in the death rate. Let us restrict ourselves to a study of those fires involving the death of victims who were in unfamiliar surroundings. Our best examples will be fires in hotels and places of amusement because the victims never have been subjected to fire drills. In hospitals, schools and other institutions, fire drills play an important part in overcoming the evil effects of possible confusion.

The following list contains only fires in hotels and places of amusement. It indicates all such fires listed by the N. F.P A. from 1943 to 1949 inclusive, and it includes all such fires listed in the 1950 edition of the *World Almanac* There are 23 fires involving 2702 deaths.

We have numbered each fire for reference purpose. Following the number is the date of the fire, then the title and location of the fire. Following this data is a column showing the number or people who died. The last two columns are headed "NS" and "NU". These two columns indicate the distance in geocentric degrees from the sun to the lunar node (NS), and the distance of the planet Uranus from the lunar node (NU). Here are 23 fires of a certain variety. In each instance, the lunar node was within 15 degrees of being conjunct (0 degrees) or square (90 degrees) the Sun or the planet Uranus. There is no exception to the rule.

What is the probability of these results being due to chance alone?

The probability of the Sun being within 15 degrees of the conjunction, or square, of the node is 1/3. The probabilities of Uranus being in similar relationship is also 1/3.

DATE	NAME AND PLACE OF FIRE	DEAD	NS	NU
1—02-06-92	Hotel Royal, New York, N. Y.	28	86	15
2—07-08-92	St. Johns Hotel, Newfoundland	600	63	12
3—03-17-99	Windsor Hotel, New York, N. Y.	45	82	26
4—02-02-02	Park Ave. Hotel, New York, N. Y.	21	86	42
5—12-12-42	K. of C. Hotel, St. Johns, Newfoundland	100	69	87
6—05-03-44	Modesto Hotel, Modesto, Calif.	2	78	54
7—01-07-45	Milner Hotel, Lima, Ohio	2	1	39
8—02-03-46	Congress Hotel, Chicago, Ill.	1	48	14
9—06-05-46	LaSalle Hotel, Chicago, Ill.	61	7	4
10—06-09-46	Canfield Hotel, Dubuque, Iowa	19	3	3
11—06-21-46	Baker Hotel, Dallas, Texas	10	9	2
12—12-07-46	Winecoff Hotel, Atlanta, Ga.	122	4	9
13—12-08-46	Saskatoon Hotel, Saskatchewan	11	5	9
14—01-30-48	Jesse Weldon Inn, St. Albans, Vt.	3	81	33
15—01-21-49	Orton Hotel, Wilmington, N. Car.	2	89	57
16—12-02-49	Loraine Hotel, Sapula, Okla.	1	57	80
17—12-05-76	Brooklyn Theatre, Brooklyn, N. Y.	289	88	21
18—12-30-03	Iroquoise Theatre, Chicago, Ill.	602	84	85
19—01-13-08	Rhodes Theatre, Boyerton, Penna.	169	8	0
20—03-10-41	Strand Theatre, Brockton, Mass.	12	13	50
21—11-28-42	Cocoanut Grove, Boston, Mass.	491	85	87
22—07-06-44	Ringling Bros. Circus, Hartford, Conn.	107	13	48
23—03-02-47	Chicago Restaurant Fire, Chicago, Ill.	4	85	11

The probability of one or the other of these bodies being in this relationship is: 1/3 plus (1/3 X 2/3), which is 5/9 or .5555. The last 5 in .5555 should actually have a dot above it to signify that 5's can be written to the right of the number to infinity. The 5's do not end there. We could write .5555555555, with dot above the last 5. The number of 5's we write is dependent upon the degree of accuracy we wish to attain. For our purpose, .5555 will be sufficient.

Now, since we have 23 fires with no exceptions, we must raise .5555 to its 23rd power. This is best accomplished through the use of logarithms. When we raise .5555 to its 23rd power, we obtain the figure .000001343. This means that there are 1343 chances in one billion. In other words, the odds against our results being due to chance along are over 700,000 to one. Thus, a causative influence is indicated.

This is a remarkable result by the use of statistical evidence, we have offered scientific proof that there is a connection between loss-of-life in these fires and the path of the Moon. Previous evidence of our intervals of instability was of a nature which did not enable us to tie it down to a definite mathematical expression. In this brief but spectacular bit of evidence, we have mathematically evaluated our results. Our conclusions as to the manner in which these deaths occur may still be questioned if anyone wants to do so. We have not proved our right to the use of the words instability and confusion. Here a factor of judgment is involved, but we have illustrated that fires involving people in unfamiliar surroundings do result in heavy loss of life if the fires occur during what we have termed our intervals of instability. We must emphasize that there have been vast numbers of fires in hotels and places of amusement at other times, but there was no loss-of-life.

From our same large body of data, we now select 13 more fires involving public buildings, but not involving hotels and places of amusement.

DATE	NAME AND PLACE OF FIRE	DEAD	NS	NU
1—04-21-30	Ohio State Penitentiary	320	3	21
2—03-08-50	Albuquerque, N. Mex. Prison	14	22	82
3—03-04-08	Lake View School, Collingwood, Ohio	176	62	04
4—05-17-23	Cleveland Rural School, Camden, S. C.	76	68	0
5—03-13-47	Cazenovia Dormitory, Cazenovia, N. Y.	3	73	11
6—02-27-49	Kenyon College Dormitory	9	49	58
7—12-03-49	University of Oklahoma Dormitory	3	58	80
8—05-15-29	Cleveland Clinic Hospital	124	3	42
9—12-24-45	Ranson County Home & Hosp., Pittston, Pa.	1	11	17
10—03-10-48	Highland Hospital, Asheville, N. C.	9	57	36
11—01-07-50	St. Elizabeth's Hospital, Davenport, Iowa	38	86	81
12—03-30-50	Bella Vista Mental Sanitarium, Philadelphia, Pa.	9	2	84
13—12-24-45	Niles St. Convalescent Hospital (Maine)	19	3	15

In these 13 additional fires of a slightly different variety, all but two have the node within 15 degrees of the conjunction or square of Sun or Uranus. When considered in the light of our previous list of fires, this again is remarkable. What are the odds that this could be due to chance?

The answer to this question will be the addition of three figures. Eleven out of 13 fires conform. We must add the probability of having exactly 11 conform, to the probability of having exactly 12 conform, and then add the probability of having all 13 conform. We have stated the case in this fashion to avoid using a calculus symbol, which would mean the addition of these three quantities.

In mathematics, we use "n" to represent the number of trials. We refer to the cases that conform as "successes," and we use the symbol "r" to represent them. We use "p" to represent the probability of "success" and "q" to represent the probability of "failure." Therefore, "q" is always "1-p." To determine the probability of getting *exactly* "r" "successes" out of "n" trials, we use the following standard formulae, but please note our use of the word *exactly*:

$$\frac{n!}{r!\,(n-r)!}\, p^r\, q^{n-r}$$

The exclamation mark is the symbol of the factorial number, and it means multiply the number by all lesser numbers. If the number were "6 !", it would mean: 6 X 5 X 4 X 3 X 2 X 1.

As in our previous list of fires, "p" will be 5/9 or .5555. In this instance "n" will be 13, and we have to work out the above problem using 11, 12, and 13 as "r." The results will be as follows:

Probability of exactly 11 successes .02395
Probability of exactly 12 successes .00498
Probability of exactly 13 successes .00047
Probability of 11 out of 13 successes .0294

This means that the odds are 34 to 1 against these results being due to chance. These odds are not to be compared with those of our first experiment. There we found odds of 700,000 to 1.

Theoretically, we can explain why we should obtain so much more pronounced results in our first experiment. It is a more selected list. In schools, dormitories and hospitals, fire drills have played an important part in overcoming confusion and reducing loss-of-life resulting from fire. When we included all large-loss fires as recorded by the N.F.P.A., we obtained poorer results, because all types of buildings were included, sometimes buildings like warehouses which were unoccupied in so far as people were concerned.

Now we can add these two lists of loss-of-life fires together. We will have 36 fires in public buildings, out of which 34 conform in that they occurred during either the Sun-to-lunar-node or the Uranus-to-lunar-node intervals of instability. What is the probability of 34 out of 36 "successes" when the probability of one "success" is .5555? We can apply the same formulae already expressed in connection with our second list of 13 fires, and we will find that the odds against these results being due to chance are over 26 million to one. If there is anyone who is skeptical of these results, he should study mathematics. **The odds are 26 million to one that the Moon does have its effect upon people residing on planet earth.**

The evidence appears to indicate that people are less stable when the Sun or Uranus is near or square to the lunar node, and that was the theory we set forth before any of this evidence relative to fires became available. In a way, we have only confirmed a theory that goes back into antiquity. The same ancients who gave us our basis for modern mathematics, those who gave us the important zero without which modern mathematics could not have developed, claimed that great events and often catastrophe accompanied eclipses of the Sun and Moon. Two ancient Chinese astronomers, for this reason, were executed for their failure to predict an eclipse of the Sun. Although confirming the ancient theory in one respect, our evidence also questions it from another point of view. Eclipses only occur when the Sun is near a lunar node, and we find the indication of instability also when the Sun is angular or square to the node. There are no eclipses at such times. **The position of the actual body of the moon has played no part in this evidence pertaining to fires. Only the path of the Moon has been involved. Therefore, the conception that eclipses themselves are a cause has not been confirmed by our evidence.**

On the other hand, however, we are not justified in saying that there is no effect from an eclipse. We can only state that our evidence has not substantiated any effect. **If the angular relationship of Sun to node (the square or 90 degree relationship) is sufficient in itself to produce human instability, then it is reasonable to assume that the conjunction of Sun and node could do likewise without including the eclipse factor.** In these calculations, we have ignored the eclipses, despite the fact that we know there are eclipses when the Sun is near the lunar node.

<u>**This discussion is important from a particular point of view. Astrologers have speculated on effects having to do**</u>

with the cutting off of light, but no light is cut off when the Sun is square the lunar node. On the other hand, there is the possibility that some electrical or other type of phenomena is associated with the path of the Moon. We do not know what makes the Moon move. We have only unsubstantiated theories. Those theories may be wrong.

We can think of a path through the woods as a reality. Our great highways are modernized and conditioned paths. Our great cross-continental railroads are paths. The path of an airplane is very real when the plane is following a radio beam. Who knows? The path of the Moon may be something just as substantial. It may have electrical qualities, if that were so, we can understand that its relationship to the Sun might prove very important. Our evidence indicates that it is very important. If it has contributed to the deaths of thousands of people, it is time we looked into the matter seriously.

Fires in Hospitals and Institutions

In 1945 the National Fire Protection Association published a booklet under the title, *Fires in Hospitals and Other Institutions*. Before discussing the contents of this booklet, let us call attention to another factor that should not be overlooked. Of the 36 fires mentioned in prior chapter, not one occurred between July 8th and November 28th, an interval of 42 consecutive days out of the 365 days in a year.

Fire losses are greater in the winter than in the summer. To what extent are they greater? For the three-year period 1941 to 1943 inclusive, estimates of the National Board of Fire Underwriters indicated that U.S. fire losses averaged $929,798 per day. In the table that follows, after allowing for the fact that there are more days in some months than in others, we have presented an average daily-loss figure for each month of the year based on the NBFU estimate for the 1941-43 period. The table also shows the plus or minus deviation from the mean average and it shows the ratio of deviation.

In presenting these figures, it is our desire to establish an empirical probability with which we can compare the facts and approximate whether the absence of the period. July 8th to November 28th, from the list of fires given maybe accounted for by the normal infrequency of fires in the summer. The winter ratio of 'fires is normally increased by the use of heating devices. The summer ratio is decreased by the closing of many buildings such as school houses, etc. Let us view the following table:

The months from July to November inclusive show an average deficiency of $108,137 per day, a ratio of 11.6%.

We have 142 consecutive days during which there are no fires in our Chapter 22 list. Thus, were it not for

AVERAGE PER DAY FIRE LOSS BY MONTHS OF THE YEAR

Month	Loss Per Day	Deviation	Ratio of Deviation
January	$ 965,247	Plus $ 35,449	Plus 3.81%
February	1,072,571	Plus 142,773	Plus 15.36
March	1,088,064	Plus 158,266	Plus 17.03
April	1,017,011	Plus 87,213	Plus 9.38
May	840,505	Minus 89,293	Minus 9.61
June	824,522	Minus 105,276	Minus 11.33
July	749,570	Minus 180,228	Minus 19.40
August	784,892	Minus 144,906	Minus 15.59
September	795,544	Minus 134,254	Minus 14.45
October	893,709	Minus 36,089	Minus 3.88
November	884,588	Minus 45,210	Minus 4.86
December	1,241,354	Plus 311,556	Plus 33.53

the normal summer deficiency of fires, the probability of fires during this period would be 142/365. We can now establish an empirical probability by multiplying this number by .884, which is 100% minus 11.6%. Thus, we have an empirical probability of 142/365 x .884, which is .34391.

What is the probability of all of our 36 fires skipping this 142-day interval? The probability of one fire skipping the period will be 1 minus .34391, or .65609. The probability of all 36 fires skipping this interval will be .65609 carried to its 36th power, or .000000258. This means 25.8 chances in one hundred million, or we can say that **the odds are over 3,800,000 to one against these results being due to chance alone.**

Of course there are other factors to be considered. More people are out of doors in summer. We cannot evaluate these factors, and· so we are forced to leave this affair in mid-air. Yet we feel that we should call the facts to the reader's attention, for they may prove of some value in future research.

If you are going to be burned, our empirical probability indicates that you are much more likely to be burned in winter and fall.

Now, we come to a new list of fires in hospitals and other institutions. There are 65 fires in this list after omitting all fires where no loss-of-life occurred. To be fair, we are including all 65 loss-of-life fires despite the fact that some of these fires are of rather insignificant importance when compared to others. There are a few cases where one person died as the result of an oxygen explosion. We were forced to eliminate two fires where no exact date was given, and two fires where a death had no actual connection with the fire.

Our record is becoming voluminous, and because this list is of secondary importance, we are going to present only dates of the fires with no description of the fire itself. Full details can be obtained from the published booklet from which this, data was taken, and the booklet itself can be obtained from the N.F.P.A.

In listing the 65 fires, we will give the date of the fire, the number of people killed by the fire, the distance from the Sun to the nearest lunar node (designated "NS") and the distance from Uranus to the nearest lunar node (designated "NU").

Please bear in mind that we do not expect results comparable to those found in Chapter 22, because we are now dealing with buildings where, in most cases, precautions such as fire drills have been taken to prevent possible loss-of-life. There are exceptions to this rule, but in most hospitals the problem of confusion during a fire has been anticipated, and employees are trained in what they should do. Now, our table:

FIRES IN HOSPITALS AND OTHER INSTITUTIONS

Date	Dead	"NS"	"NU"
1-31-45	17	24	38
1-31-43	32	14	85
2-07-41	13	46	48
3-24-34	22	45	69
2-20-34	10	13	66
7-24-31	48	68	11
5-15-29	125	4	42
2-18-23	27	22	9
12-26-23	18	62	9
12-14-27	37	3	71
2-11-30	7	15	28
12-22-17	5	1	49
10-06-34	3	66	84
11-16-33	1	90	60
11-11-32	1	66	37
2-11-43	7	3	85
12-16-41	8	83	70
11-30-41	1	80	69
12-07-38	7	29	2
2-16-36	1	47	68
10-06-34	1	67	84
4-13-44	8	81	56
11-09-43	1	84	63
2-16-43	7	1	85
12-14-41	1	85	70
3-31-41	2	10	52
1-03-36	2	0	71

Date	Dead	"NS"	"NU"
2-20-34	10	13	66
12-28-32	3	62	38
2-24-43	35	11	84
10-08-40	10	5	45
6-20-34	1	44	78
1-30-43	1	15	85
11-10-42	1	77	87
11-18-41	7	67	69
1-25-36	4	23	70
11-16-34	1	71	84
3-01-34	1	22	66
2-09-43	8	5	85

Date	Dead	"NS"	"NU"
7-12-40	5	86	40
12-18-39	5	59	22
11-24-35	2	43	72
11-09-35	5	59	73
11-21-34	1	65	84
9-15-33	2	25	59
4-03-33	1	38	47
2-04-33	1	24	41
2-05-45	2	30	37
1-01-35	5	22	85
4-13-34	1	67	71
2-03-33	9	25	41
12-14-31	8	81	14
11-02-31	9	36	13
12-22-42	3	58	86
11-07-41	1	56	39
4-28-41	1	39	56
12-15-40	4	76	45
4-15-40	1	6	31
1-11-40	1	86	24
12-16-37	1	19	25
9-07-37	1	86	27
6-01-37	1	4	34
11-26-36	1	21	49
1-27-36	2	24	70
11-14-34	1	73	84

We might again examine the seasonal factor before progressing further. The following table shows how these fires and deaths were distributed seasonally:

Month	Fires	Deaths
January	8	64
February	13	137
March	3	25
April	5	12
May	1	125
June	2	2
July	2	53
August	0	0
September	2	3
October	3	14
November	14	33
December	12	100

We will let these figures speak for themselves without attempting to further interpret them Weather and seasonal habits can of themselves play an important part in seasonal fluctuations, so let us return to a consideration of our intervals of instability 1/3 of the time, making mean expectancy 21 2/3 out of 65 cases. Actually 27 fires fall within the Sun-node areas of instability--slightly more than expectancy. However, 332 or 58.4% of the deaths occurred in these 27 fires, against an expectancy of 189 or 33.3%. Turning to Uranus, 21 of these fires occurred during Uranus-node unstable areas, as near to mean expectancy as we could hope to come, but these 21 fires involved 224 deaths against a mean expectancy of 183.

Although these 65 fires do show some evidence of our cycles of instability, the important consideration lies in the fact that they do not show the same kind of results obtained in Chapter 22, when we confined ourselves to fires in hotels and places of amusement, where strangers do not have the advantage of fire drills.

While our evidence indicates loss-of-life caused by our cycles of instability, it also indicates the effects of caution and ingenuity on the part of Man. It shows that the negative influence can be overcome. If we are correct in assuming that the high death rate from fire during our intervals of instability is due to confusion and a lack of clear thinking, and if we are correct in assuming, from evidence heretofore presented, that history is altered by confusion on the part of public officials, then we may assume that future knowledge of these cycles may alter the course of history for the improvement of mankind. At any rate, it is something to think about, and meanwhile, we have more evidence to present.

INVADING THE PRIVACY OF A TRADITION

To do any job well, one must stay within certain limitations. Otherwise, one risks the danger of scattered efforts. Therefore, throughout this work, we have endeavored to confine our efforts to determining whether we are influenced by the Moon. We have attempted to keep away from any possible planetary influences, but broke away from our original purpose to the extent of studying a relationship involving the planet Uranus and the lunar path.

During the serialization of our chapters dealing with fires, we received letters from a number of astrologers who urged us to investigate the planet Mars. Various astrologers have associated **the planet Mars with fire. Sepharial, for example, claimed that conjunctions of Mars and Jupiter caused conflagrations. We are not certain that the ancient astrologers associated the planet with physical fire. They may have spoken of fire as a quality of the emotions. Plato warned that the fire that burns buildings should not be mistaken for the "real fire."**

As we studied our data on great fires, our own curiosity did not permit us to ignore the matter of Mars altogether, but as we tabulated our fires we saw no evidence of any connection. On general observation, we convinced ourselves that there was no increase in the frequency of fires when other planets lined up with Mars. We received more letters, however, and we realized that a great many astrologers were firmly convinced of some connection between fires and Mars, and we ultimately decided to invade the privacy of the tradition and either prove or disprove, if possible, whether any such connection might exist. We had detected nothing that appeared visible to the eye, but often that which cannot be otherwise detected is revealed by broad statistical investigations. By now, we had a record of 1,527 fires of over $250,000 loss per fire, covering all such fires in the United States, Canada and Alaska over an interval of eight years.

Such an investigation presented new problems. Because astrology makes its calculations from a geocentric point of view (i.e., with the earth as the central point of observation) it was decided to base the investigation on geocentric measurements.

This brought about serious complications. From such a geocentric point of view, planetary cycles are highly irregular. We have the problem of determining what is normal, and what a mean expectancy should be. A mean expectancy which might be true for long intervals of time, hundreds of thousands of years, would not be applicable for such a short interval as eight years. This problem had to be overcome. This was accomplished by counting the actual number of days that the planet Mars did spend in any given relationship. If we let any such figure be represented by "d," and let "D" represent the total number of days in the eight year period utilized, then "d/D" becomes the probability of a fire occurring at the time of any given relationship of the planet Mars.

It was decided to check the relationship of Mars to the other planets on the day of each fire and tabulate the results. Mars was compared with Neptune, Uranus, Saturn, Jupiter, Venus, Mercury, the Sun and the lunar node. In the plane of the ecliptic, the distance from Mars to the other planets was measured. This distance could be anything from 0 to 180 degrees. We divided these 180 degrees into twelve parts of 15 degrees each, and then checked the number of fires that occurred with Mars in each one of these 15 degree areas as measured from each of the other planets.

The first part of this experiment covered a period of six years, from 1943 to 1948 inclusive. Thereafter, the experiment was continued for two more years, but only as Mars related to the planets Mercury and Saturn, because nothing in our results indicated any effect from the other planets. However, we want to report completely the facts relating to these other planets.

First, we want to present a table showing the number of days spent by Mars in each one of the relationships above mentioned. In this table, we have excluded Mercury and Saturn, and we will return to those two planets later.

DAYS SPENT BY MARS IN RELATIONSHIP TO OTHER PLANETS 1943 TO 1948

DISTANCE MARS TO:	NEP-TUNE	URAN-US	JUP-ITER	VEN-US	SUN	LUNAR NODE (Nearest)
00 to 15 Degrees	142	307	187	292	213	282
15 to 30 "	153	154	160	235	288	411
30 to 45 "	238	271	142	237	343	325
45 to 60 "	235	260	133	240	300	395
60 to 75 "	245	266	239	279	266	377
75 to 90 "	245	154	299	226	200	402
90 to 105 "	206	140	308	216	152	
105 to 120 "	218	133	191	156	120	
120 to 135 "	162	123	193	108	97	
135 to 150 "	113	126	116	74	78	
150 to 165 "	117	134	110	65	68	
165 to 180 "	118	124	114	64	67	

A glance at the above figures will illustrate how much more probable are some relationships. Venus was within a 15-degree relationship of Mars for 292 days, but it was within the 165-to-180 degree relationship for only 64 days. The former relationship, therefore, would be far more probable. The table itself illustrates why such a table is necessary before any such investigation can be made.

Our next table will establish a probability for each relationship by dividing each of the above figures by 2192, the number of days in the interval from 1943 to 1948 inclusive. This is our "d/D" formulae. We have carried this table to the fourth decimal point, which was not necessary, but it supplies us with more than the desired accuracy.

PROBABILITY OF MARS BEING IN VARIOUS RELATIONSHIPS WITH OTHER PLANETS DURING 1943 THROUGH 1948

DISTANCE MARS TO:	NEP-TUNE	URAN-US	JUP-ITER	VEN-US	SUN	LUNAR NODE (Nearest)
00 to 15 Degrees	.0648	.1400	.0853	.1332	.0972	.1287
15 to 30 "	.0698	.0702	.0730	.1072	.1314	.1875
30 to 45 "	.1086	.1236	.0648	.1081	.1565	.1482
45 to 60 "	.1072	.1187	.0607	.1095	.1369	.1802
60 to 75 "	.1118	.1214	.1090	.1273	.1213	.1720
75 to 90 "	.1118	.0703	.1364	.1031	.0913	.1834
90 to 105 "	.0939	.0639	.1405	.0985	.0693	
105 to 120 "	.0994	.0607	.0871	.0712	.0548	
120 to 135 "	.0739	.0561	.0882	.0492	.0442	
135 to 150 "	.0516	.0574	.0529	.0338	.0356	
150 to 165 "	.0534	.0611	.0501	.0297	.0310	
165 to 180 "	.0538	.0566	.0520	.0292	.0305	

Measurements are made to the nearest of the two lunar nodes. Therefore, the figures run only up to 90 degrees, since Mars can be no more than 90 degrees from the nearest node.

There were 1066 major fires in the six-year period under consideration. In our next table, we will multiply each of the above probability figures by 1066, and this will supply us with a mean expectancy-the average number of fires we should expect while Mars was in each of the above relationships to each of the other planets. With this table established, we are prepared to compare our observations with our mean expectancy. In the following table, we have omitted fractions, and each figure is accurate to within a fraction of one.

MEAN EXPECTANCY OF MARS BEING IN VARIOUS RELATIONSHIPS WITH OTHER PLANETS DURING 1943 THROUGH 1948

DISTANCE MARS TO:	NEP-TUNE	URAN-US	JUP-ITER	VEN-US	SUN	LUNAR NODE (Nearest)
00 to 15 Degrees	69	149	91	142	104	137
15 to 30 "	75	75	78	114	140	200
30 to 45 "	116	132	69	115	167	158
45 to 60 "	114	127	65	117	146	192
60 to 75 "	119	127	116	136	129	183
75 to 90 "	119	75	145	110	97	196
90 to 105 "	100	68	150	105	74	
105 to 120 "	106	65	93	76	58	
120 to 135 "	79	60	94	52	47	
135 to 150 "	55	61	56	36	38	
150 to 165 "	57	65	53	32	33	
165 to 180 "	57	60	56	31	33	

Now, we have something tangible with which to compare our actual observations of fires and their frequency. If there is no influence from Mars, our figures should approximate the above table. We are in a position to determine whether there is any increased frequency of fires when Mars is within a 15-degree range of the zero, 90 or 180-degree distance from the other planets.

It should be pointed out that no experiment of this kind has ever been previously conducted from a geocentric point of view, and we are forced to develop our own methods as we go along. Thus this experiment is a test of our methods as well as a test of the possible influence of Mars. Actually, it will bring forth other problems that we will face as we go along.

Our next table will show the actual results of our test. It will show the actual number of fires which did occur while Mars was in each of the above relationships to the other planets. Then, we will be in a position to make our comparisons.

RELATIONSHIP OF MARS TO OTHER PLANETS DURING 1066 FIRES (1943-48)

DISTANCE MARS TO:	NEP-TUNE	URAN-US	JUP-ITER	VEN-US	SUN	LUNAR NODE (Nearest)
00 to 15 Degrees	58	108	100	112	108	127
15 to 30 "	83	61	69	117	159	223
30 to 45 "	169	139	59	130	149	160

DISTANCE MARS TO:	NEP-TUNE	URAN-US	JUP-ITER	VEN-US	SUN	LUNAR NODE (Nearest)
45 to 60 "	126	120	67	121	124	132
60 to 75 "	109	166	89	132	114	215
75 to 90 "	141	73	127	109	83	209
90 to 105 "	102	56	188	113	71	
105 to 120 "	104	61	137	54	63	
120 to 135 "	48	72	105	41	46	
135 to 150 "	48	65	41	43	57	
150 to 165 "	40	83	46	47	55	
165 to 180 "	38	62	38	47	37	

The differences between this table and the last table supply us with the net result. We want to know the manner in which this table varies from the previous table. Therefore, the next table shows us just what those differences or deviations are in terms of plus or minus deviations from mean expectancy.

OBSERVED DEVIATIONS FROM MEAN EXPECTANCY ("P" EQUALS "PLUS")

DISTANCE MARS TO:	NEP-TUNE	URAN-US	JUP-ITER	VEN-US	SUN	LUNAR NODE (Nearest)
00 to 15 Degrees	−11	−41	P 9	−30	P 4	−10
15 to 30 "	P 8	−14	− 9	P 3	P19	P23
30 to 45 "	P53	P 7	−10	P15	−18	P 2
45 to 60 "	P12	− 7	P 2	P 4	−22	−60
60 to 75 "	−10	P37	−27	− 4	−15	P32
75 to 90 "	P22	− 2	−18	− 1	−14	P13
90 to 105 "	P 2	−12	P38	P 8	− 3	
105 to 120 "	− 2	− 4	P44	−22	P 5	
120 to 135 "	−31	P12	P11	−11	− 1	
135 to 150 "	− 7	P 4	−15	P 7	P19	
150 to 165 "	−17	P18	− 7	P15	P22	
165 to 180 "	−19	P 2	−18	P16	P 4	

In these figures, we find no tendency for the frequency to mount when Mars is conjunct (0 Degrees), square (90 Degrees) or opposed (180 Degrees) to the other mentioned planets. We do get some wide and interesting deviations, but these deviations are not placed right to lead us to believe that the relationship between the mentioned planets had anything to do with it. We find that we had an excess of 53 fires when Mars was from 30 to 45 degrees away from Neptune, and we had a deficiency of 60 fires when the node was from 45 to 60 degrees away from Mars. Something caused these deviations, and it would seem that the most likely cause would be that we had in some way tuned into the seasonal cycle. Remember that there are still two planets on which we have not reported.

Next, we decided to check upon the frequency of fires when Mars was in each of the zodiacal signs. We had not checked possible relationship between Mars and Pluto, but if there was any connection we could detect this by a test of Mars in the zodiacal signs, because the motion of Pluto would be very slow. If we were to find any evidence of a possible Pluto relationship, we could check the matter further.

Our next table will show the number of fires that occurred with Mars in each of the zodiacal signs. It also shows the number of days that Mars spent in each of these signs, and from this column of figures, the probability of Mars being in each sign is computed. These figures appear in the next column. The column entitled "mean expectancy" is arrived at by multiplying the total number of fires by the probability figure for each sign. Thereafter, we have a column showing the actual number of fires which did occur with Mars in each zodiacal sign. Thereafter is given the deviation from the mean. For this experiment we used 1527 fires covering all large-loss fires occurring from 1943 to 1950 inclusive.

MARS IN THE ZODIACAL SIGNS DURING 1527 FIRES—1943 TO 1950 INC.

ZODIACAL SIGN	DAYS	PROBABILITY	MEAN EXPECT- ANCY	NUMBER OF FIRES	DEVIATION
Aries	161	.0551	84	61	Minus 23
Taurus	171	.0585	89	62	Minus 27
Gemini	350	.1198	183	137	Minus 46
Cancer	332	.1136	174	169	Minus 5
Leo	362	.1239	189	201	Plus 12
Virgo	366	.1253	191	236	Plus 45
Libra	291	.0996	152	161	Plus 9
Scorpio	176	.0603	92	96	Plus 4
Sagittarius	190	.0650	99	96	Minus 3
Capricorn	198	.0677	103	138	Plus 35
Aquarius	171	.0585	90	96	Plus 6
Pisces	154	.0527	81	74	Minus 7

These figures show a sizeable deviation from the mean. We have a deficiency of 96 in the first three signs. Virgo and Capricorn show a considerable excess. The deficiency of 96 in the first three signs is equal to 5.8 times Standard Deviation, which is far beyond anything we might anticipate due to chance. However, we are still faced with the possibility that the seasonal cycle may have influenced our results. It just happened that during these particular years, when Mars passed through this area, it was usually summer, and we should expect the figures to be low. We could almost dispose of the matter here, except for the fact that during the winter of 1944 Mars passed through this area, and there was a drop in the number of fires.

We find ourselves in a position where we cannot be certain about these fires until more years are tested. It may be necessary to wait for another ten years of records before we can be sure. The presence of the seasonal cycle confuses our efforts and sets up an obstacle.

However, we have come this far. **We can say quite definitely that our results show no apparent connection between fires and the relationship of Mars to Neptune, Uranus, Jupiter, Venus, the Sun and the Lunar Node.**

We have still to report on the planets Saturn and Mercury and their relationship to Mars. We will present figures on these two planets in briefer form. We will merely give the mean expectancy, the actual number of fires and the deviation. In these next two tables, all large loss fires from 1943 through 1950 are included.

RELATIONSHIP OF MARS TO MERCURY DURING 1527 FIRES—1943-1950

DISTANCE MARS TO MERCURY	MEAN EXPECTANCY	NUMBER OF FIRES	DEVIATION
00 to 15 Degrees	200	229	Plus 29
15 to 30 "	243	248	Plus 5
30 to 45 "	169	152	Minus 17
45 to 60 "	183	143	Minus 40
60 to 75 "	159	144	Minus 15
75 to 90 "	123	109	Minus 14
90 to 105 "	101	91	Minus 10
105 to 120 "	121	127	Plus 6
120 to 135 "	83	85	Plus 2
135 to 150 "	59	64	Plus 5
150 to 165 "	36	44	Plus 8
165 to 180 "	50	91	Plus 41

These figures are impressive because there is a peak at either end. They are open to doubt however. First, because there is no peak at 90 degrees. Secondly, because again, we may have happened to have tuned into the seasonal cycle. Third, the low point is not at the center. From the zero point, there is a sharp drop, then a gradual rise to 180 degrees. The low point is from 45 to 60 degrees. This suggests a time factor, because when Mercury is near Mars, it passes Mars at a relatively low speed, but it crosses the opposition quickly. The reason for this is that Mercury is always near the Sun, and when the Sun is in opposition to Mars, Mars appears to travel backwards because the earth is passing it. From the conjunction of Mars with the Sun to the opposition of Mars to the Sun takes an interval not too far removed from one year. Therefore, over a short period of years such as this, these conjunctions and oppositions tend to fall during the same season of the year. Mercury, being close to the Sun. is likely to reflect this condition. We do not say definitely that this is the factor that has caused the results we have obtained, but we do say that such is likely to be the case. As we see it now only a broader experiment over a longer period of time will solve the problem.

Now let us look at similar figures for Mars and Saturn.

RELATIONSHIP OF MARS TO SATURN DURING 1527 FIRES—1943-1950

DISTANCE MARS TO SATURN	MEAN EXPECTANCY	NUMBER OF FIRES	DEVIATION
00 to 15 Degrees	366	413	Plus 47
15 to 30 "	233	232	Minus 1
30 to 45 "	128	114	Minus 14
45 to 60 "	120	103	Minus 17
60 to 75 "	112	86	Minus 26
75 to 90 "	103	99	Minus 4
90 to 105 "	98	89	Minus 9
105 to 120 "	86	75	Minus 11
120 to 135 "	82	81	Minus 1
135 to 150 "	66	64	Minus 2
150 to 165 "	67	94	Plus 27
165 to 180 "	66	77	Plus 11

Here we have a similar result to that found in the Mars-Mercury test. The plus deviations are at the two ends. Here again, however, we find that Mars was often in these relationships to Saturn in the winter rather than in the summer. Despite this fact, we cannot declare these results as negative. After all, there are great fluctuations in the seasonal cycle of fires, and we are unable to say that these fluctuations are not actually caused by the relationship of Mars to Mercury and Saturn. We can only close this chapter without drawing any final conclusions. We; have opened a door to permit three factors to be tested further in the future with new data. We have succeeded in some eliminations, and to that extent we have narrowed down the possibilities. We have also introduced a method for such investigations. We hope that future work can improve upon our methods, because there is sadly needed a practical means of successfully separating one cycle from another. There is one further piece of information that we would like to add. Originally, the work on Mercury and Saturn was carried out for the six year period, 1943 through 1948. When interesting results were discovered, the experiment was continued through 1949 and 1950. The two extra years did not tend to confirm earlier findings, and this weakened the case for Mercury and Saturn.

Some may express the wish that we had narrowed down the 15-degree areas **explored to smaller divisions. In that connection, let us state that we had an opportunity of observing our data very closely as these tabulations were made, and we were unable to find any tendency for the frequency of fires to rise at the time of exact planetary aspects of any kind. Had we observed any such tendency, we would have tested these smaller areas with greater care.**

PLANES CRASH AND BURN

It didn't take long to write the prior chapter but all the writer's evenings and spare time for two months were taken up in tabulating the data necessary to write it. After that amount of labor, it is disappointing to present the data and not draw a more definite conclusion. The matter bothered the writer.

And then, a forgotten file was remembered. From the records of the National Fire Protection Association, we had carefully recorded the dates of plane crashes, where a plane had crashed and burned with a resultant loss of over $250,000. After the data had been recorded, it found its way into a file cabinet for future reference, and there it had been overlooked and forgotten. The original purpose had been to check the data to see whether plane crashes might occur with greater frequency during our so-called periods of instability. Now, it was remembered in connection with our Mars experiments, and so here was an opportunity, not only to carry out our original purpose, but to check the data and see how we might conform with our other data fires and the planet Mars. It was enthusiasm that we searched for the and after finding it, we spent more evenings and weekends making further tabulations. The results were interesting and held promise.

We are going to present for the record a table showing the dates of these plane crashes. Plane crashes do not follow same seasonal cycle that we find were fires are concerned. These crashes actually shown a minimum in winter and spring. There are 102 crashes in the list that will follow. There were 35 in August and September, against 18 colder months of December, January February. This can perhaps be accounted for by the fact that the airlines take cautions to keep their planes on ground when the weather is unusually severe. It might also be taken to indicate that weather is not a primary cause of these disasters. First let us note the months in which these crashes did occur.

102 PLANE CRASHES

Month	Number of crashes
January	6
February	7
March	9
April	5
May	7
June	5
July	10
August	12
September	13
October	9
November	14
December	5

As we will see later, it is important to make note of the fact that we do not have an excess of crashes in the winter months. In the next table, we will present the dates of these 102 crashes. We will show in a column headed "SN" the distance in degrees from the sun to the nearest lunar node. We will show in a column headed "UN" the distance in degrees from the planet Uranus to the nearest lunar node. We will also give in a column headed "Mars" the zodiacal position of Mars at the time of each crash. Thereafter, we will be able to tabulate our results and see in just what manner they may bear out our previous observations.

In our prior chapter experiment, we faced the danger of having our results distorted by the seasonal cycle of fires, but in this case, we do not encounter the same cycle. This can have an important bearing on our conclusions

DATA ON 102 PLANE CRASHES, 1943 THROUGH 1950

Number	Date	"SN"	"UN"	MARS (Degree)
1	2-18-43	5	84	16 Capricorn
2	5-20-43	82	76	25 Pisces
3	3-06-45	60	36	15 Aquarius
4	7-28-45	28	21	3 Gemini
5	1-13-46	25	14	23 Cancer
6	1-18-46	29	14	21 Cancer
7	3-19-46	88	12	17 Cancer
8	6-12-46	1	3	25 Leo
9	7-07-46	26	0	10 Virgo
10	7-09-46	28	0	11 Virgo
11	7-11-46	30	0	12 Virgo
12	7-18-46	37	1	16 Virgo
13	7-29-46	48	2	23 Virgo
14	8-01-46	51	2	25 Virgo
15	8-05-46	55	3	27 Virgo
16	9-05-46	86	5	17 Libra
17	9-12-46	86	6	22 Libra
18	9-15-46	83	6	24 Libra
19	9-18-46	80	6	26 Libra
20	10-02-46	65	7	5 Scorpio
21	10-03-46	64	7	6 Scorpio
22	10-12-46	55	7	12 Scorpio
23	10-12-46	55	7	12 Scorpio
24	11-13-46	54	7	5 Sagittarius
25	1-06-47	36	9	15 Capricorn
26	1-20-47	51	9	26 Capricorn
27	1-27-47	59	10	1 Aquarius
28	2-28-47	88	10	27 Aquarius
29	5-11-47	13	17	23 Aries
30	5-20-47	3	18	29 Aries
31	5-22-47	1	18	1 Taurus
32	5-29-47	4	19	6 Taurus
33	9-15-47	64	30	1 Cancer
34	10-24-47	24	31	13 Leo
35	11-10-47	6	32	21 Leo
36	11-18-47	2	32	25 Leo
37	11-30-47	15	32	29 Leo
38	12-16-47	33	33	4 Virgo
39	1-27-48	77	33	6 Virgo
40	3-10-48	57	35	20 Leo

Number	Date	"SN"	"UN"	MARS (Degree)
42	8-18-48	43	36	18 Leo
43	4-15-48	20	38	19 Leo
44	6-05-48	83	43	8 Virgo
45	7-17-48	75	48	0 Libra
46	8-12-48	78	51	16 Libra
47	8-12-48	78	51	16 Libra
48	8-13-48	77	51	16 Libra
49	8-20-48	71	51	21 Libra
50	8-24-48	67	51	23 Libra
51	9-20-48	39	54	11 Scorpio
52	9-28-48	31	54	17 Scorpio
53	10-06-48	23	54	22 Scorpio
54	10-21-48	7	55	3 Sagittarius
55	11-13-48	17	56	20 Sagittarius
56	12-12-48	48	56	12 Capricorn
57	3-04-49	44	58	16 Pisces
58	5-26-49	41	66	19 Taurus
59	6-26-49	73	69	11 Gemini
60	7-12-49	89	70	23 Gemini
61	8-11-49	61	74	13 Cancer
62	8-29-49	42	76	24 Cancer
63	8-31-49	40	76	26 Cancer
64	9-12-49	28	77	3 Leo
65	9-15-49	25	77	5 Leo
66	9-15-49	25	77	5 Leo
67	9-26-49	14	77	12 Leo
68	11-03-49	26	79	4 Virgo
69	11-11-49	35	80	8 Virgo
70	11-16-49	40	80	11 Virgo
71	11-18-49	42	80	12 Virgo
72	11-29-49	54	81	18 Virgo
73	12-15-49	71	81	25 Virgo
74	12-22-49	87	81	28 Virgo
75	2-13-50	46	82	11 Libra
76	2-15-50	48	82	10 Libra
77	2-22-50	36	82	10 Libra
78	2-24-50	34	82	10 Libra
79	2-24-50	34	83	10 Libra
80	3-07-50	22	82	7 Libra
81	3-12-50	17	82	5 Libra
82	3-23-50	5	84	1 Libra
83	4-05-50	8	84	26 Virgo
84	4-07-50	11	85	26 Virgo
85	4-11-50	15	85	25 Virgo
86	4-26-50	31	86	22 Virgo
87	5-14-50	48	87	22 Virgo
88	6-01-50	67	89	26 Virgo
89	6-22-50	87	82	4 Libra
90	7-13-50	71	85	14 Libra
91	7-13-50	71	85	14 Libra
92	8-05-50	48	83	27 Libra
93	8-14-50	39	83	2 Scorpio
94	9-01-50	22	81	13 Scorpio
95	9-21-50	0	79	27 Scorpio
96	10-06-50	16	78	7 Sagittarius
97	10-13-50	23	77	12 Sagittarius
98	11-07-50	50	76	1 Capricorn
99	11-13-50	56	76	5 Capricorn
100	11-16-50	59	76	8 Capricorn
101	11-22-50	66	76	12 Capricorn
102	12-13-50	88	75	23 Capricorn

In the above list, whenever a date appears twice, it represents two separate and. independent disasters on the same day.

If we check the figures in the column the "SN", we find that 30 of these plane crashes occurred during our so-called sun-to-lunar-node periods of instability. Mean expectancy would be 1/3 X 102, or 34. Thus, there is no excess of plane crashes during these intervals.

On the other hand, when we check the column "UN", **we find that most of the crashes occurred during the Uranus-to-lunar-node intervals of instability**. Again a mean expectancy of 34, we have 67 out of 102 of these crashes within these periods. This is near 8 times Standard Deviation. This is not likely to be a matter of chance, but what other causes might there be?

It takes about 3.75 years to go from one high point in this cycle to the next. Therefore, 8 years is not a very long test, and we must be extremely careful in our judgments. We must realize that during these years, the price trend was up. In 1943, there were less planes worth $250,000. Planes worth less than $250,000 wouldn't get into this list.

On January 1st, 1943, Uranus was 86 degrees west of the north node. On December 31st, 1948, Uranus was 105 degrees east of the north node. One factor moved 191 degrees in relation to the other. This is too short a term for definite judgment, but we cannot get away from the fact that **when the node reached a conjunction with Uranus, the ratio of plane crashes increased substantially**, and as it left the node, they decreased. And then, when it reached the square, there was a substantial rise. Insofar as this period is concerned, these plane crashes were certainly following this cycle. This could be coincidence, but we cannot pass it off as coincidence until the matter has been tested further.

Meanwhile, let us look at these figures in another way. Let us see the frequency with which these crashes occurred in each 15-degree area:

DISTANCE URANUS TO NODE	PLANE CRASHES
0 to 15 Degrees	24
15 to 30 "	5
30 to 45 "	13
45 to 60 "	13
60 to 75 "	4
75 to 90 "	43

These are impressive figures. They cannot be ignored. Even a constant increase in the number of planes valued at over $250,000 over the 8-year period would not account for a 10 to 1 ratio of difference between the last two figures.

The figures indicate a possible connection between these crashes and the Uranus-to-node cycle, but no association with the Sun-to-node cycle. How can we account for this discrepancy? I don't know that we need to account for intelligent speculation. It suggests, however, that the two cycles may operate differently. If we are dealing with energy, it may be of an unknown variety. In studying the death rate caused by fires, both of these cycles appeared to operate. We assumed the possibility of a psychological or emotional reaction, possibly resulting from a biological condition, which may have been caused by cycles relating to the lunar path. The local cause of many of these plane crashes is unknown. It is a mystery. A plane crashes. Everyone is killed. There are no witnesses. No one knows what happened. Was it a human failing, or could the motors have been, in some way, affected? Could one of these cycles have a biological and resultant psychological and emotional effect, while the other cycle has both a similar effect plus an effect upon a delicate motor? Perhaps if we investigate long enough, we might learn something.

Next, let us turn again to the position of Mars. In a prior chapter, we set up a table showing the probability of Mars being in each of the zodiacal signs during the years 1943 through 1948. We can make use of these probabilities, but we will later discuss whether we have a right to do so, and we will consider the matter from a different point of view. In studying Mars and fires, our efforts were complicated and confused by what appeared to be a seasonal cycle. In this respect, we might say that we have a fortunate "break" in our air-crash data, because the plane crashes do not follow the same cycle. There is no evidence of any excess of plane crashes in the winter months. In fact, if anything, it is the other way around. We have more plane crashes in the summer. Therefore, if we find similar to those present in the prior chapter, we can rule out the possibility of those results being due to a seasonal cycle.

In our next table, we show the frequency with which Mars appeared in each zodiacal sign as compared with a 'mean expectancy' based on the probability figures (1943-1948) established in the previous chapter.

FREQUENCY OF MARS IN THE ZODIACAL SIGNS AT TIME OF 102 AIR CRASHES

ZODIACAL SIGN	MEAN EXPECTANCY	FREQUENCY	DEVIATION	
Aries	5.6	2	MINUS	3.6
Taurus	6.0	3	MINUS	3.0
Gemini	12.2	3	MINUS	9.2
Cancer	11.6	7	MINUS	4.6
Leo	12.6	13	PLUS	.4
Virgo	12.8	23	PLUS	10.2
Libra	10.2	22	PLUS	11.8
Scorpio	6.1	10	PLUS	3.9
Sagittarius	6.6	5	MINUS	1.6
Capricorn	6.9	9	PLUS	2.1
Aquarius	6.0	3	MINUS	3.0
Pisces	5.4	2	MINUS	3.4

We find our excess in the same position as found in our 1527 fires. We also find a minor peak in Capricorn, exactly as in the case of fires. With fires we thought that a seasonal cycle might have been the cause. In this case, such could not be true. The seasonal factor is different.

Now, let us question our "mean expectancy." Actually, only four these crashes occurred prior to 1946. Was this because of fewer planes of $250,000 valuation in the air prior to 1946? Let us consider the matter from that point of view. Let us make up a new table eliminating these four cases, cutting our total down to 98, and eliminating 1943, 1944 and 1945 from our computed probabilities, This will leave us the five years from 1946 through 1950. Our next table will show: the number of days that Mars spent in each of the signs during these years; the probability of Mars being in each sign; a new mean expectancy for 98 cases; the frequency with which our crashes occurred; and the deviation from the mean.

FREQUENCY OF MARS IN THE ZODIACAL SIGNS AT TIME OF 98 AIR CRASHES (1946 THROUGH 1950)

ZODIACAL SIGN	DAYS	PROBABILITY	MEAN EXPECTANCY	FREQUENCY	DEVIATION	
Aries	80	.0438	4.3	2	Minus	2.3
Taurus	82	.0449	4.4	5	Minus	1.4
Gemini	86	.0471	4.6	2	Minus	2.6
Cancer	206	.1128	11.0	7	Minus	4.0
Leo	266	.1457	14.3	13	Minus	1.3
Virgo	318	.1742	17.1	23	Plus	5.9
Libra	246	.1347	13.2	22	Plus	8.8
Scorpio	133	.0729	7.1	10	Plus	2.9
Sagittarius	123	.0673	6.6	5	Minus	1.6
Capricorn	117	.0641	6.3	8	Plus	1.7
Aquarius	93	.0509	5.0	2	Minus	3.0
Pisces	76	.0416	4.1	1	Minus	3.1

It will be noted that the general pattern has not changed. We have our excess in Virgo, Libra and Scorpio, with Capricorn pushing its way above the mean. We find this general curve regardless of any seasonal factor. It applied to fires which had their seasonal excess in winter, and it applies to plane crashes, with their seasonal excess in summer.

On the basis of the evidence at hand, it is indicated that fires and plane crashes show an increased frequency when Mars is near the autumnal equinox, a decreased frequency when Mars is near the vernal equinox. This is not a perfect up-and-down symmetrical cycle, however. The deficiency in the frequency cycle is greater to the east of the vernal equinox than to the west, and we have the peculiar secondary peak after Mars passes the winter solstice.

(Before closing this chapter, we might, mention that 55 train wrecks covering the period from 1856 to 1950 did not indicate any conformance with this cycle. The list was taken from the 1950 *World Almanac*.)

Moon Wobbles and Eclipse Periods with Uranus 1950-2000

In general, the most dramatic years for eclipses and moon wobbles are when the lunar nodes are in hard aspect (conjunct or square) to Uranus. But of course hard aspects with Pluto and Mars will create extra drama too. Below are all major events found online that correlate to these time periods. At this point I feel it's unnecessary to list every eclipse period since it is a well-studied and established mundane event generator. So these periods are the more dramatic ones since they involve Uranus and sometimes other planets. Only the very most noteworthy events will be accompanied by a horoscope for the reader. But this list could be a good start for statistical research in the future.

I'm well aware that most astrologers use the Sun's degree to measure eclipse periods but this creates the illusion that the Sun's degree is the most important element. With experience, it has become clear that **the better measurement is the degree of the north lunar node.** This makes analysis and measurement much more consistent when the sign and degree of the node is noted for events over longer periods of time. In this list, the degree of the moon wobble during an eclipse period is the listed lunar node degree that is used here since in general, it's the center of an eclipse period. By using this moon's lunar node degree it creates a level of consistency in the listing.

There can be sensitive points within the transit of the north lunar node when it crosses a heliocentric planetary node that can modify the nature of an eclipse or a moon wobble. For example, when the lunar nodes are in Leo/Aquarius, the heliocentric planetary nodes of Mars are at 19-20 Scorpio/Taurus. That is a hidden modifier of Mars becoming involved with that specific eclipse period of a Moon Wobble. Another important modifying degree factor is the heliocentric nodes of Uranus are at 14 Gemini/Sagittarius and the heliocentric nodes of Saturn are 23 at Cancer/Capricorn. The heliocentric nodes of Pluto are at 20 Cancer/Capricorn and the heliocentric nodes of Jupiter are at 10

Cancer/Capricorn. These are hidden modifiers that need to be considered whether it's a natal chart or a mundane event. Charles Jayne and Carl Payne Tobey both noted that **planets crossing their own nodes intensified the nature of the planet.**

In this chapter is a listing of planetary nodes in both tropical and sidereal zodiacs for the reader. The heliocentric planetary nodes move forward in the tropical sign zodiac very, very slowly, about 20-40 minutes in a century. These same nodes in the sidereal constellation zodiac hardly move at all since they are measured against the star constellations from the star of Spica (Lahiri).

The lunar nodes move backwards in the zodiac signs and stay in these signs for 18 months. In 2019-20, the **true** lunar nodes moved into Gemini/Sagittarius on May 5, 2020. The **mean** lunar nodes left Cancer/Capricorn and enter 29 Gemini/Sagittarius on June 4, 2020. This is a month difference so the study of which type of lunar node to use can make a difference in chart calculations. I prefer the mean lunar nodes but many astrologers use the true lunar nodes because of the word 'true' in the description but this is misleading.

Depending on which ephemeris or software is used, the degree measurement of the north lunar node can be off by a day depending on whether the reader is using the **mean north lunar node or the true north lunar node.** The American Ephemeris for the 21st Century (3rd edition) by Neil F. Michelsen uses the true lunar node with notation table to convert the true node into a mean node in the preface. The Astrolabe World Ephemeris 2001-2050 uses the mean lunar node. The two ephemerides are different by one day between them. There is an ongoing debate of which node to use. I personally prefer the mean lunar nodes. The use of the term 'true' node is misleading. The better term is 'osculating'. The lunar nodes are only 'true' when the planetary bodies are aligned.

"Nodes and apsides can also be derived from the osculating orbital elements of a body, the parameters that define an ideal unperturbed elliptic (two-body) orbit for a given time. Celestial

bodies would follow such orbits if perturbations were to cease suddenly or if there were only two bodies (the Sun and the planet) involved in the motion and the motion were an ideal ellipse. This ideal assumption makes it obvious that **it would be misleading to call such nodes or apsides "true"**. *It is more appropriate to call them "osculating". Osculating nodes and apsides are "true" only at the precise moments, when the body passes through them, but for the times in between, they are a mere mathematical construct, nothing to do with the nature of an orbit."*[1]

The list below is chronological so the moon wobbles and eclipses are listed on their exact date. Please remember that these periods can have a span of 15 degrees of the Sun coming into aspect with the lunar nodes since Uranus is involved in these events. It's a magnifier so the orb of events can be expanded a bit greater than normal with ordinary aspects. In general, eclipses and moon wobbles are the strongest of event aspects in astrology. Squaring moon wobbles are weaker than eclipses. However, having **Uranus in hard aspect to the lunar nodes is more powerful and stronger than normal.**

To make this chapter more abbreviated, a listing of terms is given below which can be used by Jyotish or Western astrologers, therefore no glyphs are used.

Events can be used in either system. All zodiacal signs are in the tropical zodiac.

SE	Solar Eclipse	Ar	Aries
LE	Lunar Eclipse	Ta	Taurus
MW	Moon Wobble	Ge	Gemini
NN	North Lunar Node	Ca	Cancer
SN	South Lunar Node	Le	Leo
Mo	Moon	Vi	Virgo
Su	Sun	Li	Libra

Me	Mercury	**Sc**	Scorpio
Ve	Venus	**Sg**	Sagittarius
Ma	Mars	**Cp**	Capricorn
Sa	Saturn	**Aq**	Aquarius
Ur	Uranus	**Pi**	Pisces
Np	Neptune	**Rx**	Retrograde
Pl	Pluto	**Sq**	Square 90
Er	Eris	**OOB**	Out of Bounds
°	Degree	'	Minute of Deg

T-Square: When three planets are 90 degrees from each other and one pair are in opposition.

Grand Square: When four planets are 90 degrees from each other and also 180 degrees from each other.

Cardinal Cross: The signs of Aries, Cancer, Libra and Capricorn.

Fixed Cross: The signs of Taurus, Leo, Scorpio, and Aquarius.

Mutable Cross: The signs of Gemini, Virgo, Sagittarius and Pisces.

The Planetary Nodes

Planet	North Node 2010	North Node 2000	North Node 1900	Annual Movement
Mercury	18TA 27'54"	18TA 20'48"	17TA10'48"	42.6"
Venus	16GE46'52"	16GE41'28"	15GE45'36"	32.4"
Mars	19TA48'59"	19TA44'22"	18TA57'22"	27.7"
Jupiter	10CN35'31"	10CN28'24"	9CN28'12"	36.7"
Saturn	23CN43'39"	23CN38'25"	22CN47'05"	31.4"
Uranus	14GE02'24"	13GE59'24"	13GE29'24"	18.0"
Neptune	11LE53'05"	11LE46'31"	10LE40'51"	39.4"
Pluto	20CN26'49"	20CN18'41"	18CN57'21"	48.8"
Eris	06TA12'	06TA07'	04TA21'	30.0"

Sidereal-Lahiri Zodiac Positions
(1deg 23min 15sec precession for 100 yr)

Planet	North Node 2010	North Node 2000	North Node 1900	100 yr Movement
Mercury	24AR24'40"	24AR37'43"	24AR42'49"	-05'06"
Venus	23TA03'38"	22TA58'23"	23TA17'47"	-01°19'24"
Mars	26AR05'45"	26AR01'17"	26AR29'23"	-28'06"
Jupiter	17GE53'17"	16GE45'19"	17GE00'13"	-14'54"
Saturn	00CN00'25"	29GE55'20"	29GE19'04"	+36'16"
Uranus	20TA19'10"	20TA16'09"	21TA01'25"	-45'16"
Neptune	18CA09'51"	18CA03'26"	18LE12'52"	+09'26"
Pluto	26GE43'35"	26GE35'36"	26GE29'29"	+00'30"
Eris	12AR29'	12AR24'	11AR54'	+00'30"

(The backward motion of precession versus the forward motion of planetary nodes creates almost stationary positions sidereally compared to the tropical placements.)

1950

Capricorn Sun, Moon Wobble 12 Aries
Jan 2 1950
NN 12 Ar, Su 12 Cp, Ur 2 Ca, Ma 2 Li
Mars Rx in Libra 1950

Dec 07 1949 The government of the Republic of China finishes its evacuation to Taiwan and declares Taipei its temporary capital city.
Dec 15 1949 A typhoon strikes a fishing fleet off Korea, killing several thousand.
Jan 07 1950 Mental health wing of Mercy Hospital burns, kills 41 in Davenport, Iowa
Jan 12 1950 Swedish tanker rams British submarine Truculent in Thames, 64 die
Jan 26 1950 Constitution of independent India comes into effect, Rajendra Prasad elected India's first president
Jan 31 1950 US President Harry Truman publicly announces support for the development of a hydrogen bomb

Feb 09 1950 Senator Joseph McCarthy charges State Department infested with 205 communists
Feb 17 1950 31 die in a train crash in Rockville Center NY

Eclipse Period Mar 7 Aries
SE Mar 15 1950, MW Mar 29 7 AR, NN 8 Ar, Ur 0 Ca, Ma Rx 3 Li
LE Apr 2 1950, NN 7 Ar, Ur 1 Ca, Ma Rx 27

Mar 12 1950 Llandow, Ireland Air disaster at 3:05 pm with Rugby team, 80 dead

T- Square Cancer Sun, Moon Wobble 2 Aries
Jun 24 1950
NN 2 Ar, Su 5 Ca, Ur 5Ca, sq Ma 5 Li

Jun 12 1950 2 Air France DC-4s crash near Bahrain, about 100 die
Jun 23 1950 Plane disappears over Lake Michigan, 22:51 CST Benton Harbor, MI, 58 dead
Jun 25 1950 North Korea invades South Korea, beginning the Korean War
Jun 27 1950 US sends 35 military advisers to South Vietnam
Jun 27 1950 North Korean troops reach Seoul, UN asks members to aid South Korea, Harry Truman orders US Air Force & Navy into Korean conflict
Jul 5 1950 First battle with No. Korea, Battle of Osan starts 8:16 am
Jul 8 1950 General Douglas MacArthur named commander-in-chief of UN forces in Korea

T-Square Eclipse Period 28 Pi
SE Sep 11 1950, MW Sep 22, NN 28 Pi, Ur 9 Ca, Sa 22Vi
LE Sep 26 1950, NN 27 Pi, Su 2 Li, Ur 9 Ca

Aug 15 1950 8.6 earthquake in India kills 20,000 to 30,000
Sep 01 1950 Plane crash lands, leaves Cairo at 23:35, last contact at 23:55, 55 dead

Sep 04 1950 Heavy typhoon strikes Japan, kills about 250
Sep 11 1950 33 die in a train crash in Coshocton Ohio
Oct 21 1950 Chinese forces occupy Tibet
Oct 26 1950 Mother Teresa founds Missionaries of Charity in Calcutta, India

Sagittarius Sun, Moon Wobble 23 Pisces
Dec 16 1950
NN 23 Pi, Su 23 Sg, Ur 8 Ca

Nov 22 1950 79 die in a train crash in Richmond Hills, NY
Nov 30 1950 US President Harry Truman threatens China with atom bomb
Dec 19 1950 Tibet's Dalai Lama flees Chinese invasion
Dec 22 1950 2 self-propelled trains of Long Island RR collide, killing 77
Dec 28 1950 Chinese troops cross 38th Parallel, into South Korea

1954

Eclipse Period 24 Cancer
SE Jan 5 1953, MW Jan 15, NN 24 Cp, Su 14 Cp, Ur 21Ca
LE Jan 19 1950, NN 23 Cp, Su 28 Cp, Ur 20 Ca

Jan 07 1954 Georgetown-IBM experiment, 1st public demonstration of a machine translation system, is held at IBM's head office in New York
Jan 08 1954 Elvis Presley pays $4 to a Memphis studio & records his 1st two songs
Jan 10 1954 A Comet jet airliner crashes in the Mediterranean. 35 people are missing
Jan 11 1954 2 ton locomotive swept into ravine by avalanche 10 die (Austria)
Jan 11 1954 Austria's worst avalanche-kills 200; 9hrs later 2nd one-kills 115

Feb 02 1954 Pres. Eisenhower reports detonation of 1st H-bomb (done1952)
Feb 10 1954 Eisenhower warns against US intervention in Vietnam
Feb 18 1954 The first Church of Scientology is established in Los Angeles, Californi
Feb 23 1954 1st mass inoculation against polio with Salk vaccine (Pittsburgh)
Mar 01 1954 US explodes Castle Bravo, 15 megaton hydrogen bomb at Bikini Atoll - most powerful nuclear device ever detonated by the US
Mar 09 1954 Edward R Murrow criticizes Sen. Joseph McCarthy

Aries Sun, Moon Wobble 19 Capricorn
Apr 19 1954
NN 19 Cp, Su 19 Ar, Ur 19 Ca, Ma 29 Sg

Apr 01 1954 Earthquake/tsunami ravage Aleutians, 200 killed
Apr 05 1954 Elvis Presley records his debut single "That's All Right"
Apr 18 1954 Colonel Gamal Abdal Nasser seizes power & becomes Prime Minister of Egypt
Apr 25 1954 Bell Labs announces the 1st solar battery made from silicon. It has about 6% efficiency.
May 17 1954 US Supreme Court unanimously rules on Brown v Topeka Board of Education reverses 1896 "separate but equal" Plessy v Ferguson decision
May 24 1954 1st rocket attains 150 mi (241 km) altitude, White Sands, New Mexico
May 24 1954 IBM announces vacuum tube "electronic" brain that could perform 10 million operations an hour
Jun 17 1954 CIA exile army lands in Guatemala. Organized by John Foster Dulles and United Fruit Co.
Jun 27 1954 First atomic power station opens - Obninsk, near Moscow in Russia
Jun 27 1954 CIA-sponsored rebels overthrow elected government of Guatemala

Eclipse Period 14 Capricorn
SE Jun 20 1954, MW Jul 7, NN 15 Cp, Su 7 Ca, Ur 22 Ca, Np 23 Li
LE Jul 15 1954, NN 14 Cp, Su 22 Ca, Ur 23 Ca, Np 23 Li

Jul 12 1954 Pres. Eisenhower put forward a plan for an interstate highway system
Jul 14-15 1954 118°F (48°C), Warsaw & Union, Missouri (state record) Heat wave in Illinois, Virginia
Jul 17 1954 Construction of Disneyland commences
Jul 20 1954 Armistice for Indo-China signed, Vietnam separates into North and South
Jul 27 1954 Armistice divides Vietnam into two countries
Aug 11 1954 Formal peace treaty ends over 7 yrs of fighting in Indochina between the French and the Communist Viet Minh
Aug 30-Sep 1 Hurricane Carol kills 68 on the US East Coast, 210 dead
Sep 9-10 1954 Earthquake strikes Orleansville, Algeria: 1,400 killed
Sep 14 1954 Hurricane Edna (2nd of 1954) hits NYC, $50 million damage
Sep 26 1954 Typhoon hits Japan - 5 ferryboats sink killing about 1,600

Libra Sun, Moon Wobble 10 Capricorn
Oct 3 1954
NN 10 Cp, Su 10 Li, Ur 27 Ca, Ma 18 Cp

Oct 05 1954 Hurricane Hazel forms in the Caribbean, killing 400-1000 people in the Bahamas and Haiti
Oct 14 1954 Israeli act of revenge in Qibiya Jordan, kills 53
Oct 15 1954 Hurricane Hazel makes landfall in the US in North Carolina as a category 4 hurricane, 195 die in US and Canada
Oct 18 1954 Texas Instruments Inc. announces the first transistor radio.
Oct 19 1954 Egypt and Great Britain sign treaty; British troops depart

Oct 24 1954 Pres. Eisenhower pledges United States' support to South Vietnam
Oct 30 1954 US Defense Department announces elimination of all racially segregated regiments
Oct 31 1954 Algerian Revolution against French begins
Nov 01 1954 US Senate admonishes Joseph McCarthy because of his slander campaigns
Nov 23 1954 For the first time, the Dow Jones Industrial Average closes above the peak it reached just before the 1929 crash.

Eclipse Period 5 Capricorn
SE Dec 25 1954, MW Dec 28, NN 5 Cp, Su 2 Cp, Ur 26Ca

Dec 02 1954 Taiwan (ROC) & US sign the Mutual Defense Treaty, preventing Mainland China (PRC) from taking Taiwan between 1955-1979
Dec 02 1954 US Senate censures Joseph McCarthy (Sen-R-Wis) for "conduct that tends to bring Senate into dishonor & disrepute"
Dec 23 1954 The first human kidney transplant is performed by Dr. Joseph E. Murray at Peter Bent Brigham Hospital in Boston, Massachusetts

1957

T-Square Aquarius Sun, Moon Wobble 24 Scorpio
Feb 13 1957
NN 24 Sc, Su 24 Aq, Ur 4 Le, Ma 9 Ta, Np 2 Sc

Jan 22 1957 Mad Bomber (George P Metesky) accused of 30 explosions, arrested
Feb 02 1957 UN adopts a resolution calling for Israeli troops to leave Egypt
Feb 17 1957 A fire at a home for the elderly in Warrenton, Missouri kills 72 people.

T-Square Eclipse Period 19 Scorpio

SE April 29 1957, MW May 10, NN 20 Sc, Su 9 Ta, Ur 2 Le, Np 1 Sc
LE May 13 1957, NN 19 Sc, Su 21 Ta, Ur 3 Le, Np 0 Sc

Mar 08 1957 Egypt reopens the Suez Canal after Israel withdraws from occupied Egyptian territory
May 17 1957 Presidential plane crashes on Mt. Manunggal in Cebu, Philippines killing 25 including Filipino President Ramon Magsaysay
May 29 1957 Algerian rebels kill 336 collaborators

Leo Sun, Moon Wobble 15 Scorpio
Aug 8 1957
NN 15 Sc, Su 15 Le, Ur 7 Le, Np 0 Sc

July 24 1957 US performs nuclear Test at Nevada Test Site
Jul 08 1957 Heavy rain and a mudslide in Isahaya, western Kyushu, Japan, 992 dead
Sep 01 1957 Excursion train crashed into a ravine killing 175, injuring 400
Sep 23 1957 White mob forces 9 black students who had entered a Little Rock high school in Arkansas to withdraw
Sep 24 1957 Pres. Eisenhower orders US troops to desegregate Little Rock schools
Oct 04 1957 USSR launches Sputnik I, 1st artificial Earth satellite
Oct 10 1957 A fire at the Windscale nuclear plant in Cumbria, England becomes the world's first major nuclear accident.
Oct 19 1957 Sputnik launched.

Uranus Squaring Eclipse Period 10 Scorpio
SE Oct 23 1975, MW Nov 3, NN 11 Sc, Su 29 Li, Ur 11 Le, Np 1 Sc
LE Nov 7 1975, NN 10 Sc, Su 14 Sc, Ur 11 Le, Np 2 Sc

Dec 04 1957 2 commuter trains collide in heavy fog killing 92 (St John's, England)
Dec 06 1957 1st US attempt to launch a satellite fails-Vanguard rocket blows up

Dec 18 1957 World's 1st full scale nuclear power plant begins to generate electricity, at the Shipping port Atomic Power Station in Pennsylvania

1961

Mutable Eclipse Period 6 Virgo
SE Feb 15 1961, MW Feb 25, NN 6 Vi, Su 26 Aq, Pl 7 Vi
LE Mar 2 1961, NN 6 Vi, Su 11 Pi, Pl 6 Vi

Jan 11 1961 Racial riot at University of Georgia
Jan 17 1961 Pres. Eisenhower orders assassination of Congo's Patrice Lonumba
Jan 29 1961 Robert Frost recites "Gift Outright" at JFK's inauguration
Mar 13 1961 Landslide in USSR, kills 145
Mar 27 1961 Black demonstrators in Charleston staged ride-ins on street cars
Apr 11 1961 Trial of Nazi Adolf Eichmann in Israel
Apr 12 1961 Russian cosmonaut Yuri Gagarin becomes the first person to orbit Earth (Vostok 1)
Apr 17 1961 1,400 Cuban exiles land in Bay of Pigs in a doomed attempt to overthrow Fidel Castro

Gemini Sun, Moon Wobble 1 Virgo
May 23 1961
NN 1 Vi, Sun 1 Ge, Ur 21 Le

May 01 1961 First US plane hijacked to Cuba
May 14 1961 First Freedom Riders bus burned and bombed
May 20 1961 White mob attacks "Freedom Riders" in Montgomery, Alabama
May 25 1961 JFK announces intent to put first man on the moon
May 30 1961 Dictator Rafael Trujillo is assassinated in Santo Domingo, Dominican Republic

Eclipse Period 27 Leo
SE Aug 11 1961, MW Aug 21 NN 27 Le, Su 18 Le, Ur 25 Le, Pl 7 Vi
LE Aug 26 1961, NN 26 Le, Su 2 Vi, Ur 26 Le, Pl 7 Vi

Jun 23 1961 Antarctic Treaty to keep it international
Jun 25 1961 Iraq announces that Kuwait is a part of Iraq (Kuwait disagrees)
July 05 1961 80 die in collisions in Algiers
July 06 1961 Portuguese ship explodes near Mozambique, kills 300
Jul 24 1961 US commercial plane is hijacked to Cuba
Aug 01 1961 German DR limits traffic to West Berlin
Aug 05 1961 118°F (48°C), Ice Harbor Dam, Washington (state record)
Aug 10 1961 UK applies for membership of the European Common Market
Aug 13 1961 Construction of the Berlin Wall begins in East Germany
Aug 16 1961 Martin L King protests for black voting right in Miami
Aug 20 1961 Last Spanish troops leave Morocco
Sep 01 1961 USSR performs nuclear test at Eastern Kazakh/Semipalitinsk USSR
Sep 05 1961 JFK begins underground nuclear testing
Sep 5-20 1961 USSR multiple nuclear tests

Scorpio Sun, Moon Wobble 22 Leo
Nov 15 1961
NN 22 Le, Su 22 Sc, Ur 0 Le, Pl 9 Vi

Oct 01 1961 US nuclear test in Nevada (blamed for John Wayne's cancer)
Oct 06 1961 JFK advises Americans to build fallout shelters
Oct 09 1961 US members of communist party obliged to report to police
Oct 17 1961 Battle of Paris-police kill 210 Algerians

Oct 30 1961 Soviet Union tests a 58 megaton hydrogen bomb named Tsar Bomba
Nov 08 1961 Plane Crash 21:321 EST, Richmond, VI with 75 dead
Nov 23 1961 Plane Crash 5:38 am, San Paulo, Brazil

Nov 22 1963 President JF Kennedy assassination, 12:30 pm Dallas, Tx (*out of range but too important*)

1964-65

Grand Mutable Square
Eclipse Period 22 Gemini
SE Dec 4 1964, MW Dec 14, NN 23 Ge, Su 11 Sg, Ur 14 Vi, Pl 16 Vi, Ma 13 Vi
LE Dec 19 1964, NN 22 Ge, Su 27 Sg, Ur 14 Vi, Sa 0 Pi, Pl 16 Vi, Ma 19 Vi

Nov 03 1964 LBJ elected President (Sun in Virgo)
Nov 15 1964 Plane crash Phoenix, Az 29 dead
Nov 20 1964 Plane crash 8:25 pm, Las Vegas, NV
Nov 20 1964 Plane Crash Helsingborg, Sweden
Nov 28 1964 France performs underground nuclear test at Ecker Algeria

Grand Mutable Square
Pisces Sun, Moon Wobble 18 Gemini
Mar 9 1965
NN 18 Ge, Sun 18 Pisces, Ur 12 Vi, Sa 8 Pi, Pl 14 Vi, Ma Rx 18 Vi

Feb 12 1967 Nuclear test at Pacific Ocean
Feb 21 1965 Malcolm X murdered in NYC
Feb 27 1965 Malcolm X funeral
Mar 01, 1965 Gas explosion kills 28 in apartment complex in La Salle, Quebec
Mar 03 1965 US and USSR perform nuclear tests

Mar 07 1965 Bloody Sunday Selma, Ala 600 protestors
Mar 09 1965 Second Selma March
Mar 18 1965 Russian first cosmonaut to walk in space
Mar 19 1965 Indonesia nationalizes all foreign oil companies
Mar 21 1965 Third Selma March
Mar 23 1965 Moroccan army shoots on demonstrators, about 100 killed
Mar 30 1965 Car bomb explodes in front of the U.S. Embassy in Saigon, killing 22 and wounding 183 others
Mar 31 1965 Plane crashes into the sea on approach to Tangier killing 47

Mutable Grand Square Eclipse Period 13 Gemini
SE May 30 1965, MW Jun 4, NN 14 Ge, Su 8 Ge, Ur 10 Vi, Ju 6 Ge, Sat 15 Pi,
Pl 13 Vi, Ma 12 Vi, Ve 2 Gi
LE Jun 14 1965, NN 13 Ge, Su 13 Ge, Ur 10 Vi, Ju 9 Ge, Sa 16 Pi,
Pl 13 Vi, Ma 18 Vi, Me 3 Ge

May 11 1965 First of 2 cyclones in less than a month kills 35,000 (India)
May 11 1965 Bangladesh windstorm kills 17,000
May 14 1965 2nd Chinese atom bomb explodes
May 20 1965 Pakistani Boeing 720-B crashes at Cairo Egypt, killing 121
May 25 1965 Ali vs. Liston heavyweight fight
Jun 01 1965 Coal mine explosion in Fukuoka Japan kills 236
Jun 07 1965 Morocco King Hassan suspends constitution, grabs power

Virgo Sun, Moon Wobble 9 Gemini
Sep 2 1965
NN 9 Ge, Su 9 Vi, Ur 14 Vi, Pl 15 Vi

Aug 06 1965 Voting Rights Act by LBJ
Aug 09 1965 Titan missile Silo Fire, 53 dead
Aug 14 1965 Beatles are on Ed Sullivan TV

Aug 11-15 1965 Los Angeles Watts Riots
Aug 27 1965 Hurricane Betsy in Louisiana, 76 dead
Sep 01 1965 Indo-Pakistani conflict - Pakistani counter-attack
Sep 06 1965 India invades West Pakistan - official beginning Indo-Pakistani War
Sep 12 1965 Hurricane Betsy kills 75 in Louisiana & Florida
Sep 28 1965 Taal Volcano explodes on Luzon Philippines killing around 100

Eclipse Period 4 Gemini
SE Nov 23 1965, MW Nov 27, NN 4 Ge, Ur 19 Vi, Pl 18 Vi

Oct 30 1965 Fireworks explosions kill 50 in Cartagena, Colombia
Nov 03 1965 Several U.S. states and parts of Canada are hit by a series of blackouts lasting up to 13 hours
Nov 25 1965 Congo military coup under Gen Mobutu, Pres. Kasavubu overthrown
Nov 27 1965 15-25,000 demonstrate against war in Vietnam in Washington, D.C.
Dec 06 1965 Two trucks crashed into a crowd in Sotouboua Togo, kills 125
Dec 15 1965 3rd cyclone of year kills 15,000 at the mouths of the Ganges River in Bangladesh

1969

Mutable Grand Square
Gemini Sun, Moon Wobble 25 Pisces
June 17 1969
NN 25 Pi, Sun 25 Vi, Ur 29 Vi, Pl 22 Vi, Ma 4 Sg

May 30 1969 Riots on the Caribbean island of Curaçao
Jun 05 1969 Race riot in Hartford, Connecticut
Jun 20 1968 Jimi Hendrix 200,000 attend Newport '69'
Jun 28 1969 Stonewall Riots
Jul 01 1969 Lennon and Ono car crash
Jul 08 1969 US troop withdrawal begins in Vietnam

Jul 18 1969 Chappaquaddick, MA Ted Kennedy car crash, woman dies
Jul 21 1969 First Moon Walk at 2:56:15 AM (GMT)

Eclipse Period 21 Pisces
SE Sep 11 1969, MW Sep 14, NN 21 Pi, Su 18 Vi, Ur 2 Li, Pl 24 Vi

Aug 08 1969 Manson family commits Tate-LaBianca murders
Aug 15 1969 Woodstock Music & Art Fair opens in New York State
Aug 18 1969 Mike Jagger accidentally shot while filming
Aug 30 1969 Racial disturbances in Fort Lauderdale Florida
Sep 01 1969 Gaddafi deposes King Idris in the Libyan revolution

1970

MW May 29 1970, Nov 20 1970

May 31 1970 8.0 mag earthquake 35 km off coast of Peru at 15:23, 66,000 dead
Nov 01 1970 Club Cinq-Sept Club fire, 1:40 am Grenoble, France, 145 dead
Nov 13 1970 Bhola cyclong in Ganges delta in Bangladesh, 500,000 – 1 M dead.

SE Aug 31 1971
Aug 1971 Heavy rains and sever flooding around Hanoi, Vietnam, 100,000 dead

1972-73

Taurus Sun, Moon Wobble 0 Aquarius
Apr 20 1972
NN 0 Aq, Su 0 Ta, Ur 15 Li

May 02 1972 Sunshine Mine Fire 11:35 am, Kellogg, ID, 91 dead
May 15 1972 Assassination attempt on US Governor Wallace

Eclipse Period 26 Capricorn
SE Jul 10 1972, MW July 19, NN 26 Cp, Su 17 Ca, Ur 14 Li
LE Jul 26 1972, NN 26 Cp, Sun 3 Le, Ur 14 Li

Jun 06 1972 US bombs Haiphong, North-Vietnam; 1000s killed
Jun 23 1972 US Pres. Nixon & Haldeman agree to use CIA to cover up Watergate
Jul 01 1972 First issue of NOW magazine
Jul 01 1972 The first Gay Pride march in England
Jul 19 1972 Herd of stampeding elephants kills 24, Chandka Forest India
Jul 21 1972 In New York 57 murders occur in 24 hours
Jul 21 1972 Bloody Friday in Belfast, 130 injured
Jul 31 1972 Operation Motorman: the British Army use 12,000 soldiers against IRA

Libra Sun, Moon Wobble 21 Capricorn
Oct 15 1972
NN 21 Cp, Su 21 Li, Ur 18 Li, Pl 2 Li, Ju 2 Cp

Sep 01 1972 American chess Bobby Fischer beats Russian Boris Spassky
Sep 5-6 1972 Olympic Munich Massacre at 4:30 am
Sep 19 1972 Parcel bomb sent to Israeli Embassy in London kills one diplomat.
Sep 21 1972 Marcos declares martial law in Philippines
Sep 30 1972 Passenger train derails killing 48 (Rust Stasie South Africa)
Oct 02 1972 Aeroflot Il-18 crashes near Black Sea resort of Sochi, kills 105
Oct 06 1972 22-car train carrying 2,000 pilgrims derails, kills 208 in Mexico
Oct 11 1972 Prison uprising at Washington, D.C. jail
Oct 12 1972 46 sailors injured in race riot on American aircraft carrier

Oct 12 1972 Aeroflot Il-62 crashes in large pond outside Moscow, 176 die
Oct 30 1972 Worst US rail accident in 14 years; 45 die in Chicago, IL

T-Square Eclipse Period 16 Capricorn
SE Jan 4 1973, MW Jan 7, NN17 Cp, Sun 13 Cp, Ur 22 Li, Ju 18 Cp

Dec 18 1972 Joe Biden's wife and daughter die in car wreak
Dec 29 1972 Plane Crash 23:41 Miami, Fl with 101 dead
Jan 09 1973 Joe Biden becomes a senator in Congress
Apr 17 1973 Bangladesh tornado 681 dead
Jan 07 1973 Mark Essex's mass shooting New Orleans, 9 dead
Jan 27 1973 End of Viet Nam War ends by Pres. Nixon

Aries Sun, Moon Wobble 12 Capricorn
April 2 1973
NN 12 Cp, Sun 12 Ar, Ur 21 Li, Pl 2 Li

Aug 05 1975 Massive flooding Yangtze River, China, 60 dams fail, 85,000 dead
Apr 08 1973 Thirty-two terrorist bombings in Cyprus
Apr 28 1973 Over 6000 Mk. (82) 500 pound bombs detonate over 18 hrs in a rail yard in northern California. 5500 structures damaged, town of Antelope destroyed, with every building reduced to foundations. Leads to Transportation Safety Act (1974)

1976

Capricorn Sun, Moon Wobble 18 Scorpio
Feb 7 1976
NN 17 Sc, Su 17 Aq, Ur 7 Sc

Jan 11 1976 Military coup in Ecuador, President Guillermo Lara leaves
Jan 22 1976 Bank robbery in Beirut nets $20-50 million (record)
Feb 04 1976 7.5 earthquake kills 22,778 in Guatemala & Honduras

Opposition Eclipse Period 12 Scorpio
SE Apr 29 1976, MW May 3 1976, NN 12 Sc, Su 8 Ta, Ur 4 Sc, Ju 7 Ta
LE May 13 1976, NN 23 Sc, Su 22 Ta, Ur 4 Sc, Ju 8 Ta, Ve 0 Ta

Apr 01 1976 Apple Computer founded (incorporated 3 Jan 1977)
Apr 11 1976 The Apple I computer released
May 05 1976 Train collision at Schiedam, Netherlands, kills 24
May 06 1976 Earthquake strikes Friuli in Northern Italy, causes 989 deaths
May 14 1976 Oil tanker Urqui Ola explodes off Spanish coast
May 17 1976 Earthquake in Uzbekistan: thousands killed

Leo Sun, Moon Wobble 8 Scorpio
July 31 1976
NN 8 Sc, Su 7 Le, Ur 3 Sc, Sa 6 Le

Jul 10 1976 Chemical factory in Seveso, Italy explodes covering area with dioxin
Jul 15 1976 36-hr kidnap of 26 school children and their bus driver in California
Jul 21 1976 First Legonnaire's Disease
Jul 27 1976 Tangshan China double earthquake 7.8 mag, 03:43 and 18:45 Peking time
Jul 28 1976 Great Tangshan Earthquake 7.8 magnitude, 3:42 am Hebei, China, 655,000 dead (19:43:53 UTC 27 July 1976)
Aug 25 1976 Heavy earthquake strikes China, 1,000s die
Aug 31 1976 Mexican peso devalued

T-Square Eclipse Period 3 Scorpio

SE Oct 23 1976, MW Oct 27, NN 3 Sc, Su 29 Li, Ur 6 Sc,
Sa 15 Le, Ma 9 Sc

Sep 10 1976 Two airliners collide over Yugoslavia, kills all 176 aboard
Sep 10 1976 Five Croatian terrorists capture TWA-plane at La Guardia Airport, NY
Oct 06 1976 Cubana Flight 455 crashes into the Atlantic from CIA bomb, 76 dead
Oct 13 1976 A Bolivian cargo jet crashes in Santa Cruz, Bolivia killing 100
Oct 20 1976 70 die as Norwegian tanker Frosta collides with George Prince

SE Apr 18 1977, LE Sep 16 1978

May 28 1977 Beverly Hills Club Fire 8:56 pm in Southgate, KY, 165 dead
Aug 20 1978 Cinema Rex Fire in Abadan, Iran at 20:21, 430 dead (Shah was blamed)

1979-1980

Sagittarius Sun, Moon Wobble 3 Virgo
Nov 26 1979
NN 3 Vi, Su 3 Sg, Ur 22 Sc, Ma 2 Vi

Nov 04 1979 American hostages taken in US Embassy Tehran, Iran

Eclipse Period 29 Leo
SE Feb 16 1980, MW Feb 19, NN29 Le, Su 26 Aq, Ur 25 Sc

Jan 09 1980 63 beheaded in Mecca, Saudi Arabia
Mar 21 1980 Elevator in Vaal Reefs gold mine, South Africa plunges, 23 dead

Mar 27 1980 Mount St Helens becomes active after 123 years 12:36 pm

Taurus Sun, Moon Wobble 24 Leo
May 15 1980
NN 24 Le, Su 24 Ta, Ur 23 Sc, Ju 0 Vi, Ma 3 Vi

May 17 1980 Major race riot in Miami Florida - 16 killed, 300 injured
May 18 2018 Mount St Helens erupts at 8:32 am PDT, becomes active after 123 years, 57 dead

Eclipse Period 19 Leo
SE Aug 10 1980, MW Aug 12 1980
NN 20 Le, Su 17 Le, Ur 21 Sc

Jul 07 1980 The Safra massacre in Lebanon
Jul 09 1980 7 die in a stampede to see Pope in Brail
Jul 25 1980 Train crash at Winsum, 9 die
Aug 01 1980 Buttevant, Ireland Rail Disaster kills 18 and injures dozens
Aug 04 1980 Hurricane Aline, kills 272 in Texas & Caribbean
Aug 12 1980 IBM PC released
Aug 07 1980 Hurricane Allan Cat 5, kills 70
Aug 19 1980 Riyadh,Saudi Arabia plane fire 10 pm, 301 dead
Aug 28 1980 Hotel Bombing, Lake Tahoe, NV
Sep 12 1980 Hostage Crisis negotiation and release
Sep 19 1980 Titan II missile explosion (Damascus, AR)
Sep 22 1980 Iraq invades Iran
Sep 26 1980 Bomb attack on Octoberfest in Munich, 12 killed
Oct 10 1980 4,500 die when a pair of earthquakes strikes NW Algeria

Scorpio Sun, Moon Wobble 15 Leo
Nov 8 1980
NN 15 Le, Su 15 Sc, Ur 25 Sc

Nov 09 1980 Iraqi Pres. Saddam Hussein declares holy war against Iran
Nov 21 1980 MGM Grand Hotel fire 84 dead
Nov 23 1980 7.0 earthquake Irpenia, Italy
Dec 08 1980 John Lennon shot 10:50 pm NYC

Feb 14 1981 Stardust Fire in Dublin, Ireland apprx 1am, 48 dead (out of orb)

1983-1984

Virgo Sun, Moon Wobble 20 Gemini
Sep 14 1983
NN 20 Ge, Su 20 Vi, Ur 5 Sg

Aug 07 1983 Some 675,000 AT&T employees strike
Aug 08 1983 Military coup in Guatemala
Aug 14-19 1983 Hurricane Alicia, kills 17 in Texas
Aug 26 1983 Floods destroy most of the old town of Bilbao, Spain
Sep 01 1983 Korean palne strays into Siberia & is shot down by a Soviet jet
Sep 21 1983 11 killed in anti Marcos demonstrations in Manila

Square Eclipse Period 15 Gemini
SE Dec 4 1983, MW Dec 8
NN 15 Ge, Su 11 Sg, Ur 9 Sg, Ju 18 Sg

Nov 04 1983 Bomb attack on Israeli headquarter in Tyrus Lebanon, 60 killed
Nov 07 1983 Bomb explodes in US Capitol, causing heavy damage but no injuries
Nov 12 1983 4 die in a train crash in Marshall Texas
Nov 27 1983 Colombian jetliner Boeing 747 crashes in Madrid killing 181
Dec 06 1983 Bomb planted on a bus in Jerusalem explodes, kills 6 Israelis

Dec 07 1983 Two jets collided at Madrid Airport killing 93

Pisces Sun, Moon Wobble 11 Gemini
March 2 1984
NN 11 Ge, Su 11 Pi, Ur 15 Sg,

Feb 15 1984 500,000 Iranian soldiers move into Iraq
Feb 25 1984 Oil fire in Cubatao Brazil kills 500
Mar 18 1984 Mobil oil tanker spills 200,000 gallons into Columbia River

Squaring Eclipse Period 6 Gemini
MW May 28 1984, SE May 30
NN 6 Ge, Su 8 Ge, Ur 11 Sg, Ve 4 Ge

May 26 1984 Floods kill 14 in Tulsa, Oklahoma
Jun 06 1984 1,200 die in Sikh "Golden Temple" uprising India

 5 die in a train crash in Williston, Vermont
Jul 12 1984 A car bomb set off by the military wing of the ANC
Jul 19 1984 21 dead and 19 injured in a massacre in San Ysidro, Ca
Aug 6 1984 203.05 million shares traded in NYSE

Dec 2-3 1984 Bhopal, India Gas Leak Disaster 1am

T-Square Virgo Sun, Moon Wobble 2 Gemini
Aug 24 1984
NN 2 Ge, Su 2Vi, Ur 9 Sg, Ma 3 Sg

Jul 19 1984 21 Dead and 19 injured in a massacred in San Ysidro, Ca
Aug 06 1984 203.05 millions shared traded on NYSE

Dec 2-3 1984 Bhopal, India gas leak disaster at 1am (*out of range but important*)

Eclipse Period 8 Taurus
LE May 4 1985, SE May 20 1985, MW Aug 6 1985,

SE Nov 12 1985

May 11 1985 Bradford City, UK Stadium Fire Panic at 3:43 pm, 2,000 dead
Jun 23 1985 Ireland Terrorist Bomb on Plane, 439 dead, Libya blamed
Aug 12 1985 JAL plane crash, 520 dead
Nov 13-14, 1985 Volcano mudslide near Armero, Colombia, 25,000 dead

1986-87

Aquarius Sun, Moon Wobble 4Ta
MW Jan 25 1986
NN 4 Ta, Su 4 Aq , Pl 7 Sc

Jan 28 1986 Challenger Explosion at 1:38 am

Eclipse Period 29 Aries with Pluto
SE April 9, MW Apr 21, 1986, LE Apr 24 1986
NN 29 Ar, Sun 0 Ta, Pl 6 Sc

Apr 26 1986 Chernobyl, USSR Meltdown at 1:23 am, 10,000 dead of radiation

Capricorn Sun Moon Wobble
Jan 8 1987
NN 16 A, Sun 16 Ta, (Ma NN 18 Ta)

Dec 31 1986 Puerto Rico Hotel Fire at San Juan starting 15:30, 97 dead

1987-88

T- Square Eclipse Period 2 Aries
SE Sep 23 1987, MW Sep 16, NN 2 Ar, Sun 29 Vi,
Ur 22 Sg, Sa 15 Sg

LE Oct 7 1987, NN 1 Ar, Su 13 Li, Ur 22 Sg, Sa 15 Sg

Aug 16 1987 Plane Crash 20:46 EDT Detroit, MI, 154 dead
Oct 15-16 1987 The Great Storm of 1987 hits France and England., 175-kph winds cause blackout in London
Oct 19 1987 Stock Market Crash
Nov 8 1987 11 are killed in an IRA bomb attack in Enniskillen, Northern Ireland
Nov 15 1987 28 of 82 aboard Continental Airlines DC-9, die in crash at Denver
Nov 18 1987 King's Cross Flash Fire London at 19:45, 31 dead

**T-Square Sagittarius Sun, Moon Wobble 27 Pisces
Dec 20 1987
NN 27 Pi, Su 27 Sg, Ur 26 Sg, Sa 24 Sg**

Nov 25 1987 Super typhoon Nina pummels the Philippines with cat 5, 1,030 dead
Nov 28 1987 South African Airways Boeing 747 crashes into Indian Ocean, 159 die
Nov 29 1987 N. Korea Plane Bomb, 115 dead
Dec 07 1987 Plane Crash, Pilot shot, Cayucos, Ca, 43 dead
Dec 08 1987 First Intifada Palestine vs. Israel
Dec 20 1987 Two Oil Tankers explode, 1750 dead
Jan 02 1988 Guerrillas ambush a train near Mozambique's western border
Jan 18 1988 Airliner crashes in SW China, killing all 108 on board
Jan 31 1988 Barge sinks near Anacortes, WA, spills 70,000 gallons of oil

**T- Square Eclipse Period 23 Pisces
LE Mar 3 1988, MW Mar 14, NN 23 Pi, Su 13 Pi, Ur 0 Cp, Sa 1 Cp
SE Mar 18 1988, NN 23 Pi, Su 27 Pi, Ur 0 Cp, Sa 2 Cp**

Feb 20 1988 500 die in heavy rains in Rio de Janeiro, Brazil

Mar 06 1988 Orville Moodey shoots 63 at Seniors golf tournament
Mar 16 1988 US sends 3,000 soldiers to Nicaragua's neighbor Honduras
Mar 16 1988 Chemical attack on Halabja by Iraqi forces kills 5000 civilians

T- Square Gemini Sun, Moon Wobble 18 Pisces
June 9 1988
NN 18 Pi, Su 18 Ge, Ur 29 Sg, Sa 0 Cp

Apr 20 1988 US accuses Renamo of killing 100,000 Mozambiquians
Apr 28 1988 Aloha Airlines 737 roof tears off in flight; kills stewardess
Jun 01 1988 Train crash kills two in Zeeland, Netherlands
Jul 04 1988 US Navy shoots down Iranian civilian jetliner over Gulf, kills 290

Sagittarius Sun, Moon Wobble 9 Pisces
MW Dec 1 1988
NN 9 Pi, Su 9 Sg

Nov 30 1988 Cyclone lashes Bangladesh, Eastern India; 317 killed
Dec 07 1988 Spitak earthquake 6.9 mag, 11:42 AMT in Armenia, 50,000 dead

1990-1991

Eclipse Period 16 Aquarius
SE Jan 26 1990, MW Feb 6, LE Feb 9 1990
NN 16 Ta, Su 16 Aq, (Ma NN 19 Ta)

Jan 04 1990 307 dead and 700 injured after overloaded passenger train

Mar 03 1990 Los Angeles police officers severely beat Rodney King (LA Riots)
Mar 25 1990 Happyland Fire at 3:00am, in Bronx, NY, 87 dead

Taurus Sun, MW May 3 1990 12 Aquarius
NN 12 Aq, Su 12 Ta, Pl 16 Sc

Jun 12 1990 Manjil-Rudbar earthquake 7.7 Iran at 00:31 IRST, 50,000 dead

Eclipse Period 28 Capricorn
SE Jan 15 1991, MW Jan 19
NN 28 Ca, Su 24 Cp, Sa 27 Cp

Jan 12-16 1991 Desert Storm, Kuwait Gulf War begins
Jan 22 1991 Kuwaiti oil facilities are destroyed by Iraqi forces

Aries Sun, Moon Wobble 23 Capricorn
April 14 1991
NN 23 Cp, Su 23 Ar, Ur 13 Cp, Ne 16 Cp

Mar 03 1991 United Airlines 737 crashes near Colorado Springs, kills 25
Mar 21 1991 20 Tornadoes kill 5 in Tennessee
Apr 05 1991 Southeast Airlines crashes in Georgia, killing 23
Apr 10 1991 Boat rams a tanker in Livorno Italy fog, killing about 138
Apr 25 1991 Earthquake strikes Costa Rica & Panama, kills 95
Apr 26 1991 23 killed in Kansas & Oklahoma by tornadoes
Apr 29 1991 Bangladesh Cyclone and flooding, 139,000 dead
Apr 29 1991 Earthquake in Georgia, kills 100

Eclipse Period 18 Capricorn
SE Jul 11 1991, MW Jul 12, NN 19 Ca, Su 18 Cp, Ur 11 Cp, Ne 15 Cp

Jul 10 1991 L'Express Airlines crashes in Alabama, killing 13

Jul 11 1991 Nigeria Airways crashes at Jeddah, Saudi Arabia, killing all 261
Jul 15 1991 Mt. Pinatubo Volcano Eruption Manila, Philippines, 800 dead
Aug 04 1991 The Greek cruise ship Oceanos sinks off of South Africa
Aug 06 1991 WWW available, World Wide Web
Aug 11 1991 400,000 demonstrate for democracy in Madagascar, 31 killed
Aug 19 1991 Conservative members of the Communist Party of the Soviet Union attempt to depose Gorbachev in a coup d'état

Libra Sun, Moon Wobble 14 Capricorn
Oct 14 1991
NN 14 Cp, Su 14 Li, Ur 9 Cp, Ne 14 Cp, Ma 24 Li

Sep 03 1991 Plant Fire Hamlet, NC 8:30 am, 25 dead
Sep 11 1991 14 die in a Continental Express commuter plane crash near Houston
Oct 05 1991 Military transport plane crashes at Jakarta, 133 dies
Oct 11 1991 Anita Hill sexual harassment testimony against Charles Thomas
Oct 15 1991 Clarence Thomas is confirmed as Supreme Court Justice
Oct 20 1991 6.1-7.1 earthquake in Uttar Kashi, India, about 670 die

Cardinal Eclipse Period 9 Capricorn
MM Jan 1 1992, SE Jan 4, NN 9 Cp, Sun 12 Cp, Ur 13 Cp, Ne 16 Cp

Jan 09 1992 Pres. HW Bush gets ill & vomits on Japanese prime minister's lap
Jan 20 1992 Plane Crash 87 dead

Aug 16-17 1992 Hurricane Andrew Cat 5, $27B damage, 58 dead.

Mar 12-15 1993 'Storm of the Century' paralyzed Eastern US, 243 dead
Jun 12 1994 Nicole Simpson killed by OJ Simpson

1995

Jan 17 1995 Kobe earthquake at 5:46:53 JST, Osaka, Japan, 6,000 dead (*out of range but important*)

Fixed Grand Square Eclipse Period 6 Scorpio
LE Apr 15 1995, MW Apr 26, NN 6 Cp, Su 24 Ar, Ur 0 Aq, Ma 15 Le
SE Apr 29 1995, NN 5 Sc. Su 8 Ta, Ur 0 Aq, Ma 19 Le

Mar 02 1995 Ferry boat sinks off Sumbe Angola, 42+ killed
Mar 10 1995 Car bomb explodes in Karachi at shiite mosque, 17+ killed
Mar 20 1995 Poison Gas released in Tokyo subway 12 killed, 4,700 injured
Apr 19 1995 Oklahoma City Bombing at 9:02 am, 168 dead, 500 injured
Apr 28 1995 Gas explosion in South Korean metro, 103 die
Apr 28 1995 Sri Lankaan plane crashes at Palaly, 52 die
May 01 1995 Croatian starts Ops Flash during Croatian War of Independence
May 06 1995 Zaire Ebola outbreak 245 dead
May 10 1995 In South Africa, 104 miners killed in an elevator accident
May 27 1995 Christopher Reeve is paralyzed from the neck down after horse fall

Leo Sun, Moon Wobble 0 Scorpio
July 24 1995
NN 0 Sc, Su 0 Le, Ur 28 Cp, Ne 23 Cp

Jun 26 1995 Gunmen ambush Egyptian President Mubarak who escapes
Jul 11 1995 7,000 Bosnian Muslim men are massacred

Jul 18 1995 DC3 crashes at Antananarivo, Madagascar, 34 die
Jul 25 1995 A gas bottle explodes in Saint Michel station. Paris

Squaring Eclipse Period 26 Libra
MW Oct 20 1995, SE Oct 24
NN 26 Li, Su 26 Li, Ur 26 Cp, Ne 22 Cp, Pl 29 Sc, Ma 29 Sc

Sep 24 1995 Emillio & Gloria Estefan's boat hits & kills a jet skier
Sep 24 1995 Volcano Mount Ruapehu (North Island, NZ) erupts
Oct 03 1995 OJ Simpson found not guilty of the murder
Oct 16 1995 Million May March
Oct 17 1995 Paris Subway bomb
Oct 21 1995 Prison Riots in Greenville, IL
Oct 28 1995 Baku Metro Fire in Azerbaijan 18:00, 265 injured, 289 dead
Nov 13 1995 National Guard Bomb
Nov 13 1995 Car Bomb in Riyadh, Saudi Arabia
Nov 19 1995 Egypt Embassy Bomb in Islamabad, Pakistan

1996-97

T-Square Capricorn Sun, Moon Wobble 21 Libra
Jan 12 1996
NN 21 Li, Su 21 Cp, Ur 29 Cp, Pl 2 Sg, Ma 2 Aq

Dec 20 1995 Plane Crash 21:42 EST Miami, Fl, 152 dead
Dec 26 1995 Thousands protest in Belgrade
Jan 3 1996 US govt shutdown
Jan 6 1996 Plane Crash 13:00, Simbazikita, 297 dead
Jan 6 1996 US government suspended, Pres. Clinton vs Congress
Jan 7-8 1996 Giant NE snow storm
Jan 7-8 1996 DJ drops 125 pts in 2 days
Jan 8 1996 Sri Lanka suicide bomber, 74 dead
Feb 17 1996 8.2 Earthquake Biak Island, Indonesia at 14:59 local time, 166 dead

Mar 18 1996 Ozone Disco Fire, Manila Philippines just past midnight, 150 dead
Jul 17 1996 Prince Charles-Princess Di divorce agreement
Sep 10-12 1996 Palatine 200 dead
Dec 26 1996 Jon Ramsey Child Murder

Pisces Sun, Eclipse Period 28 Virgo
SE Mar 9, MW Mar 19, LE Mar 24 1997
NN 28 Vi, Su 28 Pi, Sa 8 Ar, Ma 29 Vi, Ve 24 Pi

Mar 22 1997 Heaven's Gate mass suicide (Hale-Bopp comet)
Apr 13 1997 Tiger Woods wins the Masters Gold Tournament at 18

Gemini Sun, Moon Wobble 24 Vi
June 16 1997
NN 24 Vi, Su 24 Ge, Ma 28 Vi

Jun 13 1997 Timothy McVeigh sentenced to death

Virgo Sun, Eclipse Period 19 Vi
SE Sep 1, MW Sep 12, LE Sep 16 1997
NN 19 Vi, Su 19 Vi,

Aug 31 1997 Princess Di car crash in Paris, France at 12:23 am
Sep 05 1997 Mother Teresa dies

Sagittarius Sun, Moon Wobble 15 Virgo
Dec 8 1997
NN 15 Vi, Su 15 Sg, Ur 5 Aq, Ma 22 Cp (NN Sa 23 Cp)

Nov 2 1997 Typhoon Linda kills at least 208 in southern Vietnam
Nov 17 1997 Luxor, Egypt, 62 people are killed by 6 Islamic militants
Nov 27 1997 Twenty-five are killed in the second Souhane massacre in Algeria
Dec 1, 1997 14 yr boy kills 3 at school, starts at 7:45 am in West Paducah, KY

Dec 12 1997 SWAT team shoots John E Armstrong in Fla, freeing 2 hostages
Dec 26 1997 Orville Lynn Majors, 36, arrested for many deaths

1998-99

Eclipse Period 10 Virgo
SE Feb 26 1998, MW Mar 1 1998
NN 10 Vi, Sun 7 Pi, Ur, 10 Aq, Pl 8 Sg, Ma 20 Pi

Jan 21 1998 Pres. Clinton sex scandal under oath
Feb 2 1998 Philippine DC-9 crashes, 104 dead
Feb 4 1998 Earthquake 6.1 in northeast Afghanistan kills 5,000
Feb 12 1998 250-car Italy pile-up due to fog, 4 die & 50 hurt
Feb 23 1998 Tornadoes in Florida kills at least 31
Feb 23 1998 Osama bin Laden fatwa against all Jews and Crusaders
Mar 03 1998 Bill Gates testifies to Senate about Microsoft monopoly
Mar 24 1998 A tornado in Dantan, India killing 250 people, injuring 3000

Mutable T-Square Gemini Sun, Moon Wobble 5 Virgo
May 27 1998
NN 5 Vi, Su 4 Ge, Ur 12 Aq, Pl 6 Sg, Ma 2 Ge

May 11-12 1998 India 3 atomic tests
May 29-30 1998 Pakistan stages five nuclear test
May 28 1998 Phil Hartman Murder-Suicide 3:00 am, Encino, CA
May 30 1998 6.6 earthquake hits northern Afghanistan, killing 5,000
Jun 07 1998 Eschede train disaster, derails in Lower Saxony, Germany, dead 101

Fixed T-Square Eclipse Period 1 Virgo
SE Aug 22 1998, MW Aug 24
NN 1 Vi, Su 28 Le, Ur 10 Aq, Ne 0 Aq, Sa 3 Ta, Ma 0 Le

Aug 17 1998 Pres. Clinton Grand Jury testimony
Aug 15 1998 Omagh bombing in Northern Ireland, 29 dead, 220 injured
Sep 02 1998 Swissair plane crashes near Peggys Cove, Nova Scotia, 229 dead
Sep 09 1998 Ken Starr report
Sep 15 1998 Google.com is registered as a domain name
Sep 23 1998 Hedge fund Collapse
Oct 2-8 1998 Stock Market Panic
Oct 08 1998 Fed bailout of Capital Holding

Grand Square Scorpio Sun, Moon Wobble 26 Leo
Nov 19 1998
NN 26 Le, Su 26 Sc, Ur 8 Aq, Ne 29 Cp, Sa 28 Ar

Oct 29 1998 Gothenburg Disco Fire in Sweden at 23:42 CET, 63 dead.
Oct 29 1998 Hurricane Mitch, the second deadliest Atlantic hurricane in history
Nov 09 1998 Newt Gingrich steps down as House Speaker (staffer affair)
Dec 12 1998 Pres. Clinton orders Iraq airstrikes.
Dec 19 1998 Pres. Clinton Impeachment
Dec 24 1998 Conviction of Carlos the Jackal
Dec 1998 Osama bin Laden plans to attack the USA. Foiled attempt on Jan 3 2000

Fixed Grand Square Eclipse 1 Vi

LE Aug 8, SE Aug 22, MW Aug 24, LE Sep 6 1998
NN 1 Vi, Su 1 Vi, Pl 5 Sg, Np 0 Aq, Sa 3 Ta, Ma 2 Le, Ur 9 Aq

Jul 24 1998 Man bursts into the United States Capitol killing two police officers.
Aug 15 1998 Omagh bombing in Northern Ireland, kills 29 people and injures 220.

Aug 17 1998 Monica Lewinsky scandal, Pres. Clinton testifies under oath.
Aug 20 1998 U.S. embassy bombings: US military launches attacks against al-Qaida
Sep 02 1998 Swissair Flight 111 Nova Scotia. 229 dead
Sep 02 1998 Google is incorporated.
Sep 11 1998 Clinton investigation report sent to the U.S. Congress to impeach him.
Sep 18 1998 ICANN formed

Scorpio Sun Moon Wobble 26 Leo
Nov 19 1998
NN 26 Le, Su 26 Sc, Ur 9 Aq

Nov 09 1998 Brokerage houses are ordered to pay 1.03 B to NASDAQ investors to compensate for price-fixing

Eclipse Period 22 Leo
MW Feb 12 1999, SE Feb 16
NN 21 Le, Su 26 Aq, Ur 13 Aq, Ne 3 Aq, Ma7 Sc

Jan 02 1999 Brutal snowstorm smashes into the Midwest. 68 dead
Jan 04 1999 Gunmen fires on Shiite Muslims in an Islamabad mosque, 16 dead, 25 injured
Jan 04 1999 Rainbow Bridge Collapse, 7pm Chomqqina, Qijiang County, China 1000 dead
Jan 25 1999 Earthquake hits Colombia, South America, 300 dead, 1000 injured
Feb 12 1999 US Pres. Clinton acquitted by the Senate
Feb 23 1999 Avalanche destroys the Austrian village of Galtür, killing 31
Feb 24 1999 A China Southern Airlines crashes at Wenzhou airport, China, 61 dead
Mar 24 1999 Dr Jack Kevorkian convicted of murder in assisted suicide

Fixed T-Square Taurus Sun, Moon Wobble 17 Leo

May 9 1999
NN 17 Le, Su 17 Ta, Ur 16 Aq, Ne 4 Aq, Sa 8 Ta

Apr 20 1999 Columbine High School student shooting at 11:19 am in Colorado, 15 dead, injured 25
May 03 1999 Tornadoes in Okla and Kans, 46 dead, 500 injured
May 07 1999 NATO bombs Chinese Embassy midnight in Belgrade, Yugoslavia
May 09 1999 Bus Crash Kills 23 in LA.
May 20 1999 Student wounds six at Conyers, Ga school
Jun 19 1999 At about 4:30 pm Stephen King is hit by a car on in Lovell, Maine.

Grand Square Eclipse Period 12 Leo
LE Jul 28 1999, MW Aug 5, NN 13 Le, Su 4 Le, Ur 15 Le, Ne 2 Aq, Ju 3 Ta, Ma 8 Sc
SE Aug 11 1999, NN 12 Le, Su 17 Le, Ur 14 Aq, Ne 2 Aq, Ju 4 Ta, Ma 13 Sc

Jul 3-24 1999 Lance Armstrong Tour de France (doping scandal)
July 16 1999 JFK, Jr. as pilot dies in plane crash, 2 others
July 22 1999 Day trader kills 9 in Atlanta brokerage
Aug 10 1999 Holy war declared against Russia
Aug 16 1999 Izmit, Turkey Earthquake 7.6 magnitude, 00:01:39 UTC, 45,000 dead
Aug 17 1999 Japanese earthquake, few dead
Sep 07 1999 Athens, Greece quake, 2:56 pm, 143 dead
Sep 15 1999 Shooting ramage in Ft. Worth, Texas church near 7pm, 8 dead
Sep 21 1999 ChiChi, Taiwan quake 1:47 am, 2,000 dead
Sep 30 1999 Tokai-Mura, Japan nuclear accident at 20:35 am, radiation, 2 dead

Fixed Scorpio Sun, Moon Wobble 8 Leo
Nov 1 1999
NN 8 le, Su 8 Sc, Ur 12 Aq, Ne 1 Aq, Sa 14 Ta

Oct 12 1999 Military coup overthrows Pakistani government

Oct 13 1999 Tobacco companies admit harn by smoking
Oct 25 1999 Plane crash with 6 pro golfers
Oct 21 1999 Chechnya Bombing at market, 143 dead
Oct 29 1999 Cyclone in India, 10 Million homeless, 7,500 dead
Oct 31 1999 Plane Crash, 1:50 EST, Nantucket Island, Mass
Nov 01 1999 Plane crash from New York, liftoff 1:29 am, crash 1:50 am, 217 dead
Nov 02 1999 Xerox employee shoots coworkers in Honolulu, Hawaii
Nov 05 1999 Microsoft declared a monopoly
Nov 12 1999 US and UN buildings attacked in Pakistan (Osama bin Laden)
Nov 12 1999 Turkish earthquake 7.2 mag, 547 dead
Nov 15 1999 China and USA landmark trade agreement
Nov 18 1999 Texas A&M bonfire, students killed
Nov 28 2999 USA and Yeltsin clash over Chechnya
Nov 21 1999 China launches first spacecraft
Nov 23 1999 Hilary Clinton declares to run for NY Senate seat
Nov 25 1999 Elian Gonzales – Cuba custody battle
Dec 24 1999 Terrorist hijack Indian Air with 189 on board
Dec 31 1999 Russian Pres. Yelstin resigns and gives reins to Vald. Putin

2000-2001

T-Square Eclipse Period 3 Leo
LE Jan 21 2000, MW Jan 24
NN 4 Le, Su 0 Aq, Ur 15 Aq, Ne 3 Aq, Sa 10 Ta

Jan 31 2000 Alaska Airlines plane off the coast of Point Mugu, Ca, 88 dead

Libra Sun, Moon Wobble 1 Cancer
MW Sep 24 2001
NN 1 Ca, Su 0 Li, Ma 7 Cp, Sa 17 Ge (SN Uranus)

Sep 11 2001 Osama bin Laden attacks World Trade Center and the Pentagon

2003

Pisces Sun Moon Wobble 4 Ge
Feb 24 2003
NN 4 Ge, Su 4 Pi, Ur 29 Aq

Feb 1 2003 Space Shuttle Columbia Disaster The Space Shuttle Columbia disaster disintegrated over Texas and Louisiana during re-entry at 8:59 am Dallas, Tx.

Feb 17 2003 E2 Nightclub Stampede The E2 nightclub stampede occurred on February 17, 2003, at the in Chicago, Illinois, in which 21 people died and more than 50 were injured in a crowd of 1500 people when panic ensued.

Feb 18 2003 Daegu Subway Fire As the train left Daegu Station around 9:53 a.m. The Daegu subway fire of February 18, 2003 killed at least 198 people and injured at least 147. An arsonist set fire to a train stopped at the station.

Feb 19 2003 Passengers of Islamic Revolutionary Guard Die in Plane Crash
The 284 members of Iran's Islamic Revolutionary Guard and 18 crew members on the plane were confirmed and 18 crewmembers crashed at approximately 2:30 p.m. GMT on 19 February in the Shahdad area of Kerman Province.

Feb 20 2003 The Station Nightclub Fire 11:07 PM EST, on Thursday, February 20, 2003, at The Station in West Warwick, Rhode Island, it is considered to be the fourth deadliest nightclub fire in US history, killing 100 people.

Pisces Sun, Moon Wobble 4 Gemini
Feb 23 2003 MW
NN 4 Ge, Ur 29 Aq, Ma 24 Sg, Sa 22 Ge, Pl 19 Sg

Mar 19 2003 9:34PM The US-led Invasion of Iraq Begins At approximately 02:30 UTC, or about 90 minutes after the lapse of the 48-hour deadline, at 5:30 am local time, explosions were heard in Baghdad.

Mar 20 2003 to May 1 2003 USA Invades Iraq The 2003 invasion of Iraq, from March 20 to May 1, 2003, was spearheaded by the United States, backed by British forces and smaller contingents from Australia, Spain, Poland and Denmark.

Eclipse Period 29 Taurus
LE May 15 2003 , MW May 20 2003 , SE May 30 2003
NN 29 Ta, Ur 2 Pi

May 1 2003 President Bush Declares "Mission Accomplished" in Iraq on aircraft carrier in the Persian Gulf
May 12 2003 The Riyadh compound bombings, carried out by Al Qaeda, kill 26
May 16 2003 In Casablanca, Morocco, 33 civilians are killed and more than 100 people are injured in terrorist attacks

Leo Sun, Moon Wobble 24 Taurus
August 18 2003
NN 24 Ta, Su 24 Le, Ur 1 Pi, Ma 7 Pi, Ju 28 Le

Aug 3 2003 French Heat Wave of 2003 Between August 3 and August 13, temperatures regularly exceeded 40 C (104 F). Doctors said typically about 30 people a day die in the Paris area. This year, that number has climbed to more than 180 a day. Temperatures rose to over 40C in the first two weeks of the month. In France, there were 14,802 heat-related deaths (mostly among the elderly).
Aug 19 2003 The Canal Hotel Bombing - At Least 22 Killed in Baghdad
The Canal Hotel Bombing in Baghdad, Iraq, in the afternoon of August 19, 2003, killed at least 22 people and wounded over 100.
Aug 22 2003 Alcântara VLS Accident On August 22, 2003, at 13:30 (local time) an explosion destroyed a Brazilian rocket as it stood on its launch pad at the Alcântara Launching Center in the state of Maranhão in northern Brazil. 21 people, standing on the launch pad, died.

Eclipse Period 19 Taurus (NN Mars)
LE Nov 8 2003, MW Nov 12 2003, SE Nov 23 2003
NN 19 Ta , Su 16 Sc, Ur 29 Aq, Ma 17 Pi, Pl 19 Sg

Dec. 26 2003 An earthquake devastated the ancient city of Bam, in central Iran, leaving between 31,000 and 43,000 people dead. [Outside the norm but too big not to list]

2005

Capricorn Sun, Moon Wobble 27 Aries
Jan 17 2005
NN 27 Ar, Su 27 Cp, Sa 24 Ca, Ur 4 Pi

Dec 26 2004 Indonesia Tsunami with 275,000 dead (too big not to list)
Jan 10 2005 A mudslide occurs in La Conchita, California, killing 10 people.
Jan 15 2005 An intense solar flare blasts X-rays across the solar system.
Jan 21 2005 Belmopan, Belize, riots over new taxes
Jan 25 2005 Stampede kills 258 at temple in Mandhradevi, India kills 258
Jan 26 2005 Glendale, Ca. train crash: Two trains derail killing 11 and injuring 200 .

Cancer Sun, Moon Wobble 18 Aries
July 10 2005
NN 18 Ar, Ma 19 Ar

July 7 2005 London Terrorist bomb blasts strike London's public transport system during the morning rush hour killing 52 and injuring 700

Eclipse Period 13 Aries
SE Oct 5, MW Oct 8, LE Oct 17 2005

NN 13 Aries sq helio Jupiter node, Me and Ve OOB

Oct 8 2005 At least 80,000 people were killed and three million left homeless after a quake struck the mountain-ous Kashmir district in Pakistan.

2006-2007 (Uranus conjunct NN)

Eclipse Period 25 Pisces (Ur square Pl)
LE Sep 7 2006, MW Sep 19, SE Sep 22 2006
NN 25 Pi, Su 25 Pi, Ur 12 Pi, Pl 24 Sg

Aug 24 2006 The International Astronomical Union (IAU) redefines the term "planet" such that Pluto is considered a Dwarf Planet.
Aug 27 2006 Comair Flight 5191 crashes on takeoff from Blue Grass Airport in Lexington, Kentucky, bound for Hartsfield-Jackson International Airport in Atlanta, Georgia killing 49 of 50 on board
Sep 4 2006 Tiger Woods matches the lowest final round of his career.
Sep 19 2006 Thai military stages a coup in Bangkok. The Constitution is revoked.
Sep 22 2006 A German maglev train crashes, killing 23.

Sagittarius Sun, Moon Wobble 20 Pisces
Dec 12 2006
NN 20 Pi, Su 20 Sg, Ur 11 Pi, Pl 26 Sg

Jan 9 2007 Apple Computer, Inc. Changes Name to Apple, Inc. 30 Years After Founding and unveils the iPhone.
Jan 20 2007 Hillary Rodham Clinton announces a presidential exploratory committee

Eclipse Period 15 Pisces
LE Mar 3 2007, MW Mar 6 2007, SE Mar 18 2007
NN 15 Pi, Ur 15 Pi, Pl 28 Sg

Feb 23 2007 Train derails near Grayrigg, Cumbria, England, one dead, 22 injured.
Mar 1 2007 Tornadoes across the southern United States, killing at least 20.
Mar 23 2007 Burnley Tunnel catastrophe occurs in Melbourne, Australia

Gemini Sun, Moon Wobble 11 Pi
June 2 2007
NN 13 Pi, Su 11 Ge, Ur 18 Pi

May 4 2007 Greensburg, Kansas is almost completely destroyed by a 1.7m wide EF-5 tornado
May 5 2007 Kenya Airways Flight 507 Crashes in Camaroon, Killing 114
May 12 2007 Riots in Karachi, Pakistan 48 killed

Mutable Grand Square Eclipse Period 6 Pisces
LE Aug 28 2007, MW Aug 30 2007, SE Sep 11 2007
Uranus Square Mars, Nodes square Saturn
NN 6 Pi, Ur 16 Pi, Sa 1 Vi, Ma 21 Ge

Aug 1 2007 I-35W Mississippi River Bridge Collapse
About 6:05 p.m. CDT on August 1, 2007, the eight-lane, 1,907-foot-long I35W highway bridge over the Mississippi River in Minneapolis, Minnesota collapsed,
falling 108 feet into the 15-foot-deep river. A total of 111 vehicles, 17 recovered 13 died, and 145 injured.
Aug 1 2007 Benaleka Train Crash At least 100 people have died following the derailment of a goods train near Benaleka, 140 miles northwest of Kananga, Congo, a further 200 have been injured.
Sep 12 2007 Sumatra Earthquake The magnitude 8.4 and 7.8 southern Sumatra earthquakes of September 12, 2007.
Sep 26 2007 Can Tho Bridge Collapse The collapse of bridge accident occurred at 8 am local time (GMT+7) on the morning of September 26, 2007. There were 250 engineers and workers

working on and under the span at the time it collapsed. As of September 27 there were 52 dead and 140 injured.

2008-2009

2008 Taurus Sun, Moon Wobble 23 Aquarius
May 13 2008
NN 23 Aq, Su 23 Ta, Nep 24 Aq

May 2 2008 Burma: Cyclone Nargis, when 100,000 were killed.
May 12 2008 China: Sichuan Earthquake killed nearly 100,000, leaving 4.5 million homeless.
May 13 2008 India: 80 people killed in serial bomb blasts in Jaipur.

Libra Sun, Moon Wobble 28 Capricorn
Oct 21 2009
NN 28 Cp, Ma 2 Le, Me opp Ur, Su sq Pl,
Sa contra Ur, Me sq Pl, Ma conj SN

Sep 28 2009 Philippines: 90 die around Manila in flooding caused by Tropical Storm Ketsana
Sep 2 2009, Samoa: hundreds die, thousands left homeless in tsunami caused by Magnitude 8.0 undersea quake
Oct 10 2009 Pakistan: climax of weeklong violence, attack on Pak GHQ Rawalpindi; 11 soldiers & 4 Taliban die, many wounded.
Oct 10 2009 Nigeria: over 70 killed as fuel tanker flips & explodes in Anambra.
Oct 10 2009 Haiti: UN plane crashes killing 11 on border of Dominican Republic, 45 km from Port-au-Prince
Oct 11 2009 Cambodia: 17 killed after river ferry capsizes on a tributary of the Mekong.
Oct 12 2009 Pakistan: car bomb in Shangla marketplace kills 41. Pakistani jets bomb Taliban camps kill 17.
Oct 13 2009 Nepal: 4,000 families displaced; 152,000 affected, 62 die; houses, crops destroyed in W. Nepal floods, landslides.
Oct 15 2009, Pakistan: coordinated series of terror attacks focusing mainly on Lahore kill 39. Pakistani jets bomb Taliban,

kill 60.
Oct 16 2009 Iraq: 12 killed, 70 injured by suicide bomber in Sunni mosque at Tal Afar, near Mosul.
Oct 18 2009, India: At least 33 killed in Tamil Nadu as explosion sets fire to firecracker warehouse.
Oct 18 2009 Mexico: Hurricane Rick, massive cat. 5 $100 million damage to crops, property.
Oct 19 2009 Yala, Thailand: Remotely detonated motorcycle bomb injures 24.

April 2010 – 2011 Uranus Square Nodes

Eclipse Period
SE Dec 31 2009, MW Jan 11 2010, LE Jan 15 2010
NN 21 Cp, Su 21 Cp

Jan 12 2010 A 7.0 Earthquake Strikes Haiti, Severe Damage 4:53PM The 2010 Haiti earthquake was a magnitude 7.0 earthquake 10 miles (16 km) from Port-au-Prince, Haiti. 230,000 people were killed

Grand Square Uranus oppose Saturn square Pluto
Aries Sun, Moon Wobble 16 Capricorn
April 6 2010
NN 16 Ca, Ur 27 Pi, Sa 0 Li, Pl 5 Cp

Apr 5 2010 Upper Big Branch Mine Disaster 3:27 pm
The Upper Big Branch Mine disaster occurred on April 5, 2010 at Upper Big Branch coal mine at Montcoal, West Virginia. 29 miners were killed.
Apr 4 2010 Mexico: Mg 7.2 quake 19 miles SE of Mexicali, on US/Mex border; biggest in region in 18 years. Major damage, 2 killed in Calexico 1000 aftershocks & "triggered" quakes on both sides of border.
Apr 5 2010 Pakistan: Taliban suicide bombers kill 8 at US Consulate in Peshawar; earlier suicide attack kills 41 in NW

Province.
Apr 5 2010 USA: Explosion rocks coalmine in Montcoal, W. Virginia; kills 12 & traps at least 10 thousands of feet underground in worst U.S. mine disaster since 2006.
Apr 5 2010 Brazil: Worst rains in Rio's history bring floods, mudslides, kill over 100; 300,000 homeless.
Apr 6 2010 Indonesia: Mg 7.8 quake at 5:15 AM 125 miles northwest of Sibolga in Sumatra. Tsunami warnings later withdrawn.
Apr 6 2010 Iraq: Wave of terror bomb attacks kill 100, wound 160 in Baghdad & across country.
Apr 6 2010 India: 73 police killed as 700 Maoist guerrillas in Chhattisgarh (East Central India) ambush 120 personnel with bombs & gunfire.
Apr 2010 Kyrgyzstan: 100 killed, 400 wounded in as police open fire on thousands of protesters at Bishkek.
Apr 2010 Brazil: Mudlsides bury 200 in worst rains in Brazil, destroying homes in Niteroi near Rio.
Apr 10 2010 Crash of Polish Air Force Plane kills the Polish president and dozens of the country's top political and military leaders.
Apr 11 2010 Solomon Is: Mg 7.1 quake hit south-west of Kira Kira island in the South Pacific, about 130 miles south-east of the capital Honiara.
Apr 11 2010 Thailand: Tourists warned after worst political violence in two decades kills 21, injures 874.
Apr.11 2010 Ireland: IRA dissidents detonate bomb, 50 evacuated.
Apr 11 2010 Italy: Landslide derails train in Northern Italy, kills 9, injures 28. Cascade of rocks, debris slam into train near Austrian border
April 14 2010 Icelandic Volcano Eyjafjallajökull begins erupting from the top crater in the centre of the glacier
Apr 15 2010 Closure of airspace over most of Europe from volcanic ash from the eruption of Eyjafjallajökull in Iceland.
Apr 14 2010 Yusku Earthquake 7:49 am About 400 people have died and 10,000 others were injured after a 7.1 in Yushu, Qinghai,

China. 2,698 people have been confirmed dead, 270 missing, and 12,135 injured of which 1,434 injured.
Apr 20 2010 10:00 pm Tuesday (0300 GMT Wednesday),
Offshore Oil Rig 'Deepwater Horizon' Explodes Off the Gulf of Mexico
The Deepwater Horizon drilling rig explodes, killing 11 and causing the rig to sink, causing a massive oil discharge into the Gulf of Mexico and an environmental disaster. 126 people escaped, 11 dead, 3 injured. A continuous disaster until Jun 16.

Events Outside of Normal Range

May 6 2010 Flash Crash The May 6, 2010 Flash Crash also referred to as The Crash of 2:45, the 2010 Flash Crash or just simply, the Flash Crash, was a stock market crash on May 6, 2010 involving U.S. corporate stocks, followed by an almost immediate rebound.
May 8 2010 Ice Crystals Form Inside of Gulf Spill Containment Dome, Leading to Its Removal. Chief operating officer Doug Suttles said Saturday.
May 10 2010 to Aug 16 2010 China Floods of 2010 As of Wednesday, flooding in China has killed 392 people this year, with 143 still missing which have affected 72.97 million people and 4.63 million hectares of farmland.
May 12 2010 Crash of Afriqiyah Airways Flight 771, 6:00 am crashed while landing at the airport in Tripoli, Libya, killing 92 passengers and 11 crew members.
May 17 2010 Pamir Airways Flight 112 Crash over 44 people aboard
May 20 2010 Five Paintings Worth 100 Million Euros are Stolen From Musée d'Art Moderne de la Ville de Paris.
May 22 2010 Crash of Air India Express Flight 812 from Dubai. Around 06:30 local time.
May 23 2010 Jiangxi Train Derailment at 02:10. The death toll of 17. 71 people were injured.
May 28 2010 Gyaneshwari Express Derailment A day after a major train accident involving the Howrah-Kurla Jnaneswari Express the death count rose to 141, 80 injured in Kolkata.

Grand Square Eclipse Period 11 Capricorn
LE June 26, MW July 4 2010, SE July 11
NN 11 Ca, Su 11 Ca, Ur 00 Ar, Ju 2 Ar, Pl 3 Cp

Jun 3 2010 Dhaka Fire The 2010 Dhaka fire was a fire in the city of Dhaka, Bangladesh that killed at least 117 people.
Jun 7 2010 Natural Gas Pipeline Explodes in Cleburne, Tx, killing three people and injuring at least eight at 2:40 pm.
Jun 16 2010 Bill Gates, Melinda Gates, and Warren Buffett Announce 'The Giving Pledge' Bill Gates, Melinda Gates, and Warren Buffett are asking the nation's billionaires to pledge to give at least half their net worth to charity
Jun 16 2010 BP Agrees to $20 Billion Escrow Fund for Spill Victim
Jun 16 2010 North Korea Threatens UN With War If rhetoric could kill, the Korean Peninsula would have been strewn with corpses of nuclear war.
Jun 18 2010 Convicted Murderer Ronnie Lee Gardner Is Executed By Firing Squad Gardner, 49.
Jun 19 2010 Internal BP Document Released Showing Estimate of 100,000 Barrels (4.2 Million Gallons), Almost Double Earlier Assessments
Jun 21 2010 Yanga Train Derailment Georges Moyen, the health minister, warned the death toll 16 from Pointe-Noire and was headed to the capital, Brazzaville, Republic of Congo
Jun 23 2010 Spain: 12 killed, 14 injured in rail accident at Castelldefels, south of Barcelona.
Jun 24 2010 Australia: Prime Minister Kevin Rudd overthrown in "palace coup" by his deputy, Julia Gillard and treasurer Wayne Swan.
Jun 25 2010 China: Deathtoll from floods in South climbs to 377. Millions displaced, hundreds missing; $11 billion in damages so far.
Jun 25 2010 Bangladesh: Lancet documents "largest mass poisoning in history" as 77 million in Bangladesh exposed to toxic levels of arsenic.
Jun 25-26 2010 Widespread OD's, Arrests, and One Death at the Electric Daisy Carnival Police initiated a temporary ban on raves.

Jun 25 2010 Pensacola Beach Officials Lift Swimming Ban, 400 People Fall ill.
Santa Rosa Island officials flew the double-red flag – no swimming – over Pensacola Beach in Florida
Jun 26 2010 India: 23 killed, 25 injured as bus collides with truck in Bihar, east of country.
Jun 27 2010 Mexico: 9 killed in attack by gunmen on rehab centre in Gomez Palacio, north of country. Drug cartel suspected.
Jun 28 2010 China: 100 buried in landslide at Dazhai, Guizhou prov. Rains & floods kill hundreds, displace millions this month in S. China.
Jun 29 2010 India: 26 police killed in Maoist Naxalite rebel attack in central Chhattisgarh. Follows death of hundreds from attacks in April, May.
Jun 28 2010 Supreme Court Affirms Right to Bear Arms advancing a recent trend by the John Roberts-led bench to embrace gun rights.
Jun 30 2010 Reports Surface that Tiger Woods to Pay at Minimum $750 Million in Divorce Settlement
Jul 1 2010 Pakistan: 41 killed, 174 wounded in suicide terrorist attack on Sufi shrine in Lahore.
Jul 1 2010 Japan: Toyota recalls 270,000 vehicles over engine fault. Follows 8 million recalled earlier this year over accelerator fault.
Jul 1 2010 Mexico: 21 killed in battle 12 miles south of Mex/US border between rival groups associated with drugs & people-trafficking. Police arrest 9.
Jul 2010 to Sep 2010 Russian Wildfires Wildfires in Russia have killed 50 people to date as record heat and drought continue to plague the heartland.
Jul 2 2010 South Kivu Truck Explosion At least 230 people were killed and 190 injured when an oil tanker flipped over and exploded in the Democratic Republic of Congo, and set fire to a village in eastern Democratic Republic of Congo, killing at least 221 people and injuring almost an equal number.
Jul 7 2010 Iraq: Bomb attacks kill 50, wound 100 Shia pilgrims converging on shrine in northern Baghdad, say police.
Jul 9 2010 Pakistan: Suicide motorcycle bomber kills 102,

wounds 115 in Yakaghund village in Mohmand tribal region, bordering Afghanistan.

Jul 9 2010 Afghanistan: Gunmen kill 11 wound 3 in ambush of Pak bus carrying Shia tribesmen on detour to avoid danger.

Jul 10 2010 Spain: 1.1 million demonstrators march in Barcelona to claim Catalan autonomy, as Spain is gripped with World Cup fever.

Jul 11 2010 Uganda: 64 killed, 65 injured in twin blasts in capital Kampala. Rugby club & restaurant bombed as fans watch World Cup final.

Jul 12 2010 Haiti: 1700 displaced, some injured as electrical storm hits Corail-Cesselesse refugee camp north of Port-au-Prince.

Jul 13, Russia: 233 drown, scores die from heat in past week. Many drown taking
swim after too much vodka. Worst drought in 100 years; 19 regions declare state of emergency. Roads melting; crops shriveling.

Jul 13 2010 Philippines: 68 killed, 84 missing in Typhoon Conson, north of Manila. Manila blacked out; 3 vessels sink including LPG tanker.

Jul 13 2010 Japan: 2 killed, 3 injured in severe storms & landslide near Hiroshima.

Jul 13 2010 China: 41 die in rain-triggered landslides in Western China; over 100 killed by flooding this month so far.

Jul 13 2010 Germany: 3 killed, 11 injured in tornados & extreme weather; heavy rain & winds unroof houses.

Jul 14 2010 Iran: 30 killed, 100 wounded in twin suicide blasts at Grand Mosque in SE city, Zahedan. Wahabi extremists blamed.

July-August 2010 Floods triggered by heavier-than-normal monsoon rains hit northwest Pakistan. By the time the waters began to recede in late August, more than 160,000 square kilometers of land — about one-fifth of the country — was under water. More than 1,700 people were killed and 17.2 million people have been affected.

Jul 12 2010 BP Places New Containment Cap Atop Leaking Gulf Oil Well

Jul 17 2010 Puerto Rico: Mosquito-borne Dengue Fever

epidemic kills dozens, sickens thousands across entire Caribbean. Hospitals overloaded. Authorities fear increase as rainy season advances. US secure so far.

Jul 18 2010 China: At least 38 miners killed in 3 separate accidents in dangerous coal mines. Lax safety blamed.

Jul 18 2010 Mexico: Pre-dawn gun attack on birthday party in Torreon kills 17, injures 10. Drug runners suspected.

Jul 18 2010 Argentina: 9 die in cold snap; more die in Bolivia, Chile, Paraguay & Uruguay. Patagonia temp: −14°C. Snow in Buenos Aires.

Jul 19 2010 India: At least 40 killed, 100 injured as passenger train ploughs into another at Sainthia station, W. Bengal.

Jul 20 2010 China: Flood update – 701 killed, 347 missing, 645,000 houses lost, 131 million people affected; 7 million hectares crops destroyed; $21 billion direct damage.

Jul 21 2010 The Dodd-Frank Wall Street Reform and Consumer Protection Act Is Signed Into Law At 5:08 a.m.

Jul 24 2010 Love Parade Disaster 16:00 Nineteen people were crushed to death on Saturday Duisburg, north of Dusseldorf, police said. Another 340 people were injured in the mass panic.

Jul 25 2010 WikiLeaks Publishes the Afghan War Diary **Jul 27 2010 to Aug 16 2010** Pakistan Floods of 2010 The 2010 Pakistan floods began in July 2010 after record heavy monsoon rains. The Khyber Pakhtunkhwa province of Pakistan at least 1,600 people were killed, thousands homeless, and fourteen million people affected. The death-toll may reach 3,000 victims. According to the UN, people suffering exceeds 13.8 million

Jul 28 2010 Pakistan Airbus A321 Crash An Airblue Airbus A321 crashed (04:41 UTC) into the hills overlooking Islamabad, Pakistan, in rainy weather Wednesday, killing all 152 people on board, according to an Associated Press report.

Cardinal Grand Cross Libra Sun, Moon Wobble 7 Capricorn
Sep 20 2010
Uranus & Jupiter oppose Pluto sq Saturn
NN 7 Cp, Ur 28 Pi, Ju 28 Pi, Pl 2 Cp, Sa 7 Li

Sep 9 2010 San Bruno, Ca Pipeline Explosion 6:11 pm PDT A San Bruno man who suffered serious injuries when a gas line exploded and spread flames through the Crestmoor neighborhood, a suburb of San Francisco, killing four and injuring nearly 60 others.
Oct 13 2010 33 Chilean Miners Rescued After Being Trapped For 68 Days, entombed for 10 weeks.
Oct 13 2010 Benoit Mandelbrot Dies Benoît B. Mandelbrot, a maverick mathematician who developed the field of fractal geometry and applied it to physics, biology, finance and many other fields, died on Thursday in Cambridge, Mass. Benoît Mandelbrot enjoyed the rare distinction of having his name applied to a feature of mathematics that has become part of everyday life – the Mandelbrot set. He had a visionary, maverick approach, harnessing computer power to develop a geometry that mirrors the complexity of the natural world. He used the geometry of fractals to explain how galaxies cluster, how wheat prices change over time and how mammalian brains fold as they grow. He was born on Nov. 20, 1924 in Warsaw, Poland. Professor Peitgen said, "he is one of the most important figures of the last 50 years." [Ed. Important to astrology as a form of fractal geometry]

2011

Cardinal Grand Square Eclipse Period
LE Dec 21 2010, LE, MW Dec 24 2010, LE Jan 4 2011
NN 2 Cp, Ur 27 Pi, Ju 27 Pi, Pl 5 Cp, Sa 16 Li

Nov 22 2010 Phnom Penh Stampede 10:00 pm Thousands of Cambodians were on the streets to mark the end of the festival when the crowd rushed onto a bridge connecting the capital city to an island. 378 people had been killed and 755 injured [outside of normal range]
Dec 2 2010 to Dec 5 2010 Mount Carmel Forest Fire A 14-year-old boy from the Carmel region admitted Monday Reporting from Jerusalem northern Israel killed at least 37 prison guards The 82-

hour fire claimed the lives of 41 people, burnt dozens of homes, destroyed thousands of acres of land,

Dec 7 2010 Julian Assange Is Arrested By London Metropolitan Police
Swedish prosecutors had issued an arrest warrant for the 39-year-old Australian, who is accused of sexual misconduct with two women.

Dec 9 2010 A car containing Prince Charles and the Duchess of Cornwall has been attacked amid violence

Dec 11 2010 Bernard Madoff's Son Mark Commits Suicide The Saturday morning suicide of Mark Madoff, found hanging by a dog leash from a pipe in the ceiling of his New York apartment, by the Bernard L. Madoff bankruptcy.

Dec 17 2010 Mohamed Bouazizi sets himself on fire, triggering mass anti-government protests across, his act of protest cemented a revolt.

Dec 18 2010 US Senate Votes To Repeal 'Don't Ask, Don't Tell'

Dec 28 2010 Protesters Clash with Police in Algiers Over Housing Shortages
At least 53 people have been injured.

Jan 8 2011 Shooting of U.S. Rep. Gabrielle Giffords, Following Inclusion on Sarah Palin's 'Hit List' In March of last year, Giffords Tucson office was vandalized   She was one of 20 House Democrats targeted with gun sights on Sarah Palin's election map.

Jan 8 2011 Surgeon Optimistic Giffords Will Survive Arizona congresswoman Gabrielle Giffords is out of surgery

Jan 9 2011 Jared Loughner Charged in Tucson Shooting Federal prosecutors today charged Jared Lee Loughner of murder.

Jan 11 2011 Sales of Glock Pistols Surge After Use in Tucson Shooting

Jan 11 2011 Floods and Landslides Kill Hundreds in Rio de Janeiro Floods and landslides triggered by heavy rains have killed at least 270 people in southern Brazil.

Jan 13 2011 400 Dead in Brazilian Flooding and Mudslides The death toll from Brazil's mudslides in the mountain towns north of Rio rose to 381 today,

Jan 13 2011 Arrest of Prominent Human-Rights Lawyer Sets off protests in Libya The anti-government protest wave unleashed in Tunisia and Egypt in the past few weeks swept into Libya.
Jan 14 2011 Tunisian government ousted After 23 years of iron-fisted rule, the president of Tunisia was driven from power.
Jan 20 2011 US Mob Crackdown Ninety-one members and associates of seven organized crime families of La Cosa Nostra (LCN), including the New England LCN family, all five New York-based families and the New Jersey-based Decavalcante family. The arrests of nearly 130 organized crime the largest mob sweep

Pisces Sun, Moon Wobble 29 Sagittarius
March 18 2011
NN 28 Sg, Ur 0 Ar, Ma 18 Pi, Mo OOB, Ma sq NN of Ur @ 15 Ge

Mar 11 2011 9.0 Earthquake, Tsunami Slams Japan 14:26 JST A tsunami rammed the coast of Japan following a powerful 8.9-magnitude the tsunami took not more than 30 minutes after the earthquake, rather than the several hours. Six minutes of shaking, 230K dead.
Mar 12 2011 Walls of Nuclear Reactor Explode in Wake of Earthquake, Tsunami An explosion at a nuclear power station today destroyed a building housing the reactor amid fears that it was close to a disastrous meltdown.
Mar 14 2011 Third Explosion Strikes Dai-ichi Nuclear Plant A third explosion in four days rocked the earthquake-damaged Fukushima Dai-ichi nuclear plant in northeast Japan early Tuesday, the country's nuclear safety agency said.
Mar 15 2011 Bahrain Declares State of Emergency Bahrain's king declared a three-month state of emergency to battle a Shiite-led protest movement that has threatened the Sunni monarchy.
Mar 18 2011 Radiation from Damaged Japanese Reactor Reaches US West Coast
Mar 19 2011 Elevated Levels of Radiation Discovered in Japan's Water
Mar 23 2011 Elizabeth Taylor Dies
Apr 5 2011 Tepco Announces Radioactive Water Leak into Pacific Stopped

Leakage of highly radioactive water into the Pacific Ocean from the crippled Fukushima Daiichi nuclear power plant has halted after Tokyo Electric Power Co. (9501.TO) injected a chemical agent. Tepco earlier injected 1,500 liters of "water glass," or sodium silicate, and another agent near a seaside pit where the water had been seeping through. [A global danger for decades]

Cardinal Grand Cross Eclipse Period 25 Sagittarius
SE Jun 1 2011, MW June 14 2011, SE June 15 2011
NN 25 Sg, Ur 3 Ar, Pl 6 Cp, Sa 10 Li

May 1 2011 US Forces Kill Osama Bin Laden was killed in a firefight with US forces in Pakistan on Sunday

May 13 2011 80 Killed in Pakistani Taliban Bombing in Retaliation for bin Laden Killing The bombing in Charsadda, Pakistan, on Friday morning.

May 13 2011 Dominique Strauss-Kahn Arrested on Allegations of Sexual Assault in NYC. The chief of the International Monetary Fund was ordered jailed without bail Monday on charges of trying to rape a maid.

Jun 3 2011 Jack Kevorkian Dies

Jun 6 2011 Arizona Towns Begin Evacuations as Fire Spreads A forest fire continues to rage in Arizona, now covering 287 square miles with some 2,300 firefighters on the scene.

Jun 15 2011 Wallow Fire Officially Largest in Arizona History The bad news: Arizona's Wallow wildfire is now the state's largest-ever.

Jun 17 2011 Scuffle Breaks Out Over Casey Anthony Trial Seats The spectators screaming as more than 100 people jockeyed for position in line.

Jun 22 2011 FBI Captures James "Whitey" Bulger in Santa Monica, Ca
Fugitive South Boston gangster James "Whitey" Bulger, wanted for 19 murders, was captured last night in Southern California.

Jul 22 2011 Norway Attacks Norwegian authorities early Saturday dramatically increased the death toll in a gun attack at a youth camp on the Norwegian island of Utoya to at least 80,

bringing the total number dead in a pair of apparently related attacks Friday to 87.
Jul 23 2011 Amy Winehouse found dead at 27 in London
Jul 26 2011 Heavy Rainfalls Trigger Deadly Flash Floods in South Korea
historic flooding and extensive landslides, heaviest in 100 years around Seoul, 51 dead.

Virgo Sun, Moon Wobble 19 Sagittarius
Sept 18 2011
NN 18 Sg, Ur 3 Ar, Pl 4 Cp, Sa 16 Cp

Sep 6 2011 Deadly Wildfires Rage Across Central Texas One of the most devastating wildfire outbreaks in Texas history left more than 1,000 homes in ruins Tuesday and stretched the state's firefighting ranks to the limit, confronting Gov.
Sep 6 2011 Gunman Opens Fire on Police, Bystanders at Nevada Restaurant
At least three people have been killed and six wounded in South Carson City, Nev., on Tuesday morning.
Sep 16 2011 Plane Crashes at Reno, Nevada Air
Sep 17 2011 Approximately 1,000 People Attend First 'Occupy Wall to protest that 40 per cent of the wealth in the U.S. is held by one per cent of the people.
Sep 30 2011 Anwar al-Awlaki Killed
Oct 5 2011 Steve Jobs Dies at 56.

Eclipse Period 14 Sagittarius
SE Nov 25 2011 , MW Dec 7 2011, LE Dec 10 2011
NN 14 Sg, Ur 0 Ar, Pl 6 Cp, Ma 6 Vi

Nov 9 2011 Joe Paterno Fired Following Child Sex Abuse Scandal Joe Paterno's head coaching career at Penn State began on Sept. 17, 1966The Penn State assistant football coach who said he saw a former assistant coach in a shower with a young boy and reported it to head coach Joe Paterno.
Nov 10 2011 Penn State Students Riot After Firing of Joe Paterno

More than 1,000 Penn State University students clashed with police after one of the most famous football coaches in American sport was sacked amid a child abuse scandal.

Nov 14 2011 Jerry Sandusky Claims innocence in interview as a sexual predator.

Dec 15 2011 Iraq War Officially Ends After nearly nine years of war, the loss of more than 100,000 lives and hundreds of billions spent

Dec 17 2011 Kim Jong-il Dies, the North Korean died of a heart.

2014

Aquarius Sun, Moon Wobble 3 Scorpio
23 Jan 2014
NN 3 Sc, Ur 9 Ar, Pl 12 Ca

Protests in Ukraine Continued massive protests in Ukraine continue thru January.

Jan. 16 2014 Parliament hastily passes sweeping measures that stifle protesters and demonstrations. The protests then turn violent, with demonstrators attacking police.

Cardinal Grand Square Eclipse Period 28 Libra
LE April 15 2014, MW April 19 2014, SE April 29 2014
NN 28 Li, Ur 13 Ar, Ju 14 Ca, Pl 13 Cp

Apr 7 2014 Pistorius Murder Trial Testimony: Olympic runner Oscar Pistorius takes the stand to testify in his murder trial. Pistorius says he shot Steenkamp by mistake, believing she was an intruder in the bathroom.

Apr 12 2014 Pro-Russian Movement Continues in Ukraine: Pro-Russian protesters and armed militants in the eastern cities of Donetsk, Kharkiv, Luhansk, and Mariupol take over several government buildings and police stations.

Apr 14 2014 Mass Kidnapping in Nigeria Sparks International Outrage: Islamist militant group Boko Haram is accused of kidnapping about 280 girls and making them sex slaves.

May 2 2014 Mudslide Kills Thousands in Afghanistan: As many as 2,100 people are killed in a mudslide in Abi Barak, a village in northern Afghanistan.

**Cancer Sun, Moon Wobble 23 Libra
16 July 2014
NN 23 Li, Ur 16 Ar, Pl 12 Cp**

Jul 1 2014 ISIS Declares Territory in Iraq: ISIS changes its name to the Islamic State and declares the territory in Iraq.
Jul 16 2014 U.S., EU Place New Sanctions on Russia: President Obama announces new sanctions against Russia due to Ukraine.
(July 29): The European Union imposes broad sanctions on Russia. Sanctions are the toughest by the EU against Russia since the Cold War.
Jul 17 2014 Passenger Jet Crashes in Eastern Ukraine: Malaysia Airlines Boeing 777 en route from Amsterdam to Kuala Lumpur, Malaysia, crashes in eastern Ukraine near the Russian border killing all 298 passengers and crew members.
Jul 31 2014 Ebola Outbreak Hits West African Countries: The death toll from the Ebola virus in West Africa is 672, with the total number of confirmed, infected patients at 1,323, making this outbreak the worst since the virus was first identified almost forty years ago.

**Eclipse Period 18 Libra
LE 8 October, MW 13 Oct 2014, SE 23 Oct 2014
NN 18 Li, Ur 13 Ar, Pl 11 Cp, Mars OOB**

Sep 1 2014 Fleeing ISIS, Refugees Pour into Turkey: About 130,000 mostly Kurdish refugees from north-central Syria flood into Turkey. More than 1 million refugees had already entered Turkey from Syria creating a humanitarian crisis.
Sep 10 2014 Pakistan, India floods in Kashmir Valley kills 441
Sep 28 2014 Police Attempt to Crack Down on Protests in Hong Kong: Protests in Hong Kong intensify throughout September

with tens of thousands of demonstrators shutting down the heart of the business district

Sep 30 2014 First U.S. Ebola Case Confirmed: Officials from the Centers for Disease Control announce that a man who recently arrived in Dallas, Tx from Liberia.

Oct 22 2014 Gunman Attacks Canada's Parliament: A Canadian soldier is shot and killed while guarding the National War Memorial in Ottawa, Canada. It is the second assault in three days. On Oct. 20, a car strikes two people. One is a uniformed member of Canada's armed forces.

Nov 16 2014 Missing College Students Spark Protests in Mexico: Thousands of protestors take to the streets in Mexico City, setting fires and blocking highways. The protests are over the 43 college students from Iguala who were abducted and presumed killed after clashing with police on Sept. 26.

2015

Capricorn Sun, Moon Wobble 14 Libra
Jan 5 2015
NN 14 Li, Ur 12 Ar, Pl 13 Ca

Jan 7 2015 Twelve Are Killed in Terrorist Attack at Newspaper in Paris: Two masked gunmen storm the office of Charlie Hebdo that satirized the Prophet Muhammad **(Jan. 9):** The Kouachi brothers take a hostage at a printing facility outside Paris. Meanwhile, in another incident in Paris, Amedy Coulibaly allegedly takes several hostages at a kosher supermarket. **(Jan. 11):** About 1.5 million people and more than 40 heads of state march in Paris.

Jan 14, 2015 Russia Cuts Off Ukraine Gas Supply To 6 EU Countries Putin ordered the Russian state energy giant Gazprom to cut supplies to and through Ukraine. Gazprom cut gas exports to Europe by 60%, plunging the continent into an energy crisis.

Jan 18 2015 Argentine prosecutor Alberto Nisman, found dead, a high-profile Argentine prosecutor, was found dead in Buenos Aires. He was set to release a report that would condemn the government of a cover-up in the 1994 bombing of a Jewish centre that killed 85 people

Grand Square in Cardinal Eclipse Period 10 Libra
SE March 20 2015, MW April 1 2015, LE April 4 2015
NN 10 Li, Ur 5 Ar, Ma 21 Ar, Pl 13 Cp

March 11 2015 Ferguson police chief quits after racism report after a scathing US Justice Department report of black teenager Michael Brown

March 12 2015 Police seek suspects in Ferguson, MO police 'ambush'
The shooting of two police officers during a protest rally in Ferguson, Missouri, sparked an intense manhunt

Mar 14 2015 Category Five Cyclone Hits Vanuatu: Tropical cyclone Pam

Mar 16 2015 Cincinnati, Ohio Mother Accused of Decapitating Baby

Mar 17 2015 Deadly train accident in Bachhrawan, India in Rae Bareli, Uttar Pradesh, India 20 March 2015. At least 30 people were killed and 50 injured

Mar 18 2015 Pregnant Colorado woman stabbed, A 26-year-old pregnant woman in Longmont, CO was beaten and stabbed by the 34-year-old woman. The attacker "removed" the fetus from her victim's body, according to police.

March 19 2015 Nearly all fuel in Fukushima reactor has melted, says TEPCO

Mar 19 2015 Islamic State responsible for Tunnis, Tunisia attack The group claimed responsibility Thursday for the attack that killed 21.

March 20, 2015 Houston Woman Shot in the Head During Road Rage Incident, Police Say The woman who was shot in the back of this morning.

March 20 2015 Children killed in Brooklyn fire A fire apparently caused by a malfunctioning hotplate left on for the Sabbath leaving seven children from the same Orthodox Jewish family dead

March 20 2015 5.3 Quake Shakes Central Mexico; Some Evacuations in Capital
A moderate 5.3-magnitude earthquake shook central Mexico and Mexico City. The U.S. Geological Survey said the quake hit at 4:30 p.m. local time in the state of Puebla near Tulcingo del Valle.

March 20 2015 Three suicide bombings target Shiite rebel mosques in Aden Yemen Quadruple suicide bombers on Friday hit a pair of mosques controlled by Shiite rebels in the Yemeni capital, Sanaa, that killed at least 137 people and wounded around 350.

Mar 24 2015 German Jetliner Carrying 150 Passengers Crashes: Germanwings Flight 9525 crashes into the French Alps while on a routine flight from Barcelona, Spain All 144 passengers and six crew members are killed.

Mar 26 2015 Using evidence from a cockpit voice recorder, investigators determine that the co-pilot deliberately crashed Flight 9525 into the French Alps. The co-pilot has been identified as 28-year-old German Audreas Lubitz. Investigators conclude that Lubitz locked the pilot out of the cockpit before taking the aircraft into its descent.

Mar 18 2015 Gunmen Open Fire at Tunis Museum: At least 20 people are killed when two gunmen go on a shooting spree in Tunis, Tunisia.

Apr 2 2015 Iran Agrees to Nuclear Deal Despite Interference by Congress, Netanyahu: Iran the U.S., and the four other permanent members of the UN Security Council plus Germany agree on a detailed, compre-hensive framework for the future of Iran's nuclear program.

Apr 27 2015 Nigerian Army Frees Boko Haram Hostages: Forces in Nigeria advance into the Sambisa Forest and begin freeing the women and children who have been held as hostages by Boko Haram. **(Apr. 28)** Almost 300 hostages are freed.

Apr 19 2015 Ship Capsizes in Mediterranean Hundreds of migrants are missing and feared dead after their ship 850 people and only 28 survived.

Apr 21 2015 President Morsi sentenced to 20 years in jail Egyptian court sentenced Mohammed Morsi to 20 years in prison.

Apr 25 2015 Earthquake Kills Thousands, A 7.8 earthquake strikes central Nepal near the capital, Katmandu, killing nearly 4,000 people, injuring tens of thousands.

Cancer Sun, Moon Wobble 5 Libra
June 27 2015
NN 5 Li, Ur 20 Ar, Ma 0 Ca

June 1, 2015 Jianli, China   A cruise ship listed heavily amid pounding rain on the Yangtze River. capsized in the storm Monday night with 458 people aboard.

Jun 2 2015 More than 2,000 killed in Indian heat wave - The death toll from the
heat wave in peak summer in India crossed 2,300, according to a report on June 2. Of these, more than 1,700 died in the worst-affected Andhra Pradesh state in the south. In neighboring Telangana, about 600 people died. Temperatures as high as 45.5 degrees Celsius were recorded. Many of the dead are believed to be daily-wage casual labor who are forced to work. This was the world's fifth deadliest recorded heat wave. The most lethal heat wave occurred in Europe in 2003, claiming 71,310 lives. India's deadliest heat wave claimed 2,541 lives in 1998.

June 3 2015 FBI operates fleet of spy planes Flights equipped with cameras, cell phone tracking.

Jun 7 2015 Erdogan Loses Majority in Turkey's Elections: President Erdogan's Justice and Development Party (AKP) loses its majority

June 26 2015 Marriage Equality: The Supreme Court decision for gay rights

Jun 26 2015 Gunman Kills Dozens at Beach Resort in Tunisia: A guman opened fire in a beach hotel in the town of Sousse. 38 dead and 20 injured.

Jun 29 2015 Greece Misses Debt Payment: Greece misses a critical debt payment of 1.5 billion euros to the IMF. Greece's international creditors refuse to extend the country's bailout program.

Jun 30 2015 143 killed in plane crash in Medan, Indonesia: A C-130 Hercules aircraft crashed, killing all 121 people on board and 22 people on the ground.

Aug 12 2015 Five people killed in Boston shootings - Five people were killed in four separate shooting incidents in Boston, Cambridge and Everett on August 12. Three victims were killed in Boston.

August 18 2915 More than 300,000 taxpayers affected by a hack.
In a series of scattered cyber attacks from February to May, hackers believed to be tied to a Russian crime syndicate gained access to 334,000 private records, bypassing several layers of security. The hack generated roughly $50 million in stolen funds.

Sep 11 2015 Mecca Crane Crash: the Holy city of Mecca witnessed a major tragedy as 118 people were killed when a crane, involved in a construction work, fell on the Masjid al-Haram, the Grand Mosque in Mecca.

Eclipse Period 1 Libra
SE Sep 13, MW Sep 24, LE Sep 28 2015
NN 1 Li, Ur 19 Ar, Pl 13 Li

Sep 24 2015 1,453 worshipers killed in stampede near Mecca: The Hajj stampede that took place near the holy city of Mecca is one of the deadliest recorded incidents during Hajj. The tragic incident sparked a diplomatic row between Iran and Saudi Arabia. Iran, which lost 465 citizens in the tragedy, blamed Saudi Arabia for failing to protect worshipers.

Oct 29 2015 China Ends One-Child Policy after Decades: In a landmark decision, the China ended its decade-old one child policy. With the new policy in place, all married couples can have two children.

Nov 13 2015 Terrorist attack in Paris: The French capital witnessed bloodbath and mayhem on 13 November 2015 as terrorists allegedly armed with AK-47s and some with bombs strapped to them attacked six locations in and around Paris. A total of 128 deaths have been reported in the shootings and bombings.

Nov 20 2015 27 killed in Mali attack: Gunmen attacked a hotel in Bamako, killing 27 and taking 170 hostage.
Nov 22 2015 Shootout at park in New Orleans injures 16: Sixteen people were injured in a gun battle between two groups in a park in New Orleans. Multiple suspects fired into a crowd of over 300 people, reports said
Dec 3 2015 Britain carries out first air strikes in Syria: Britain launched its first airstrikes against ISIS targets in Syria, hours after lawmakers voted to authorize military action.
May 17 2017 Robert Mueller appointed Special Counsel to investigation Russia interference in the 2016 Presidential Election

2018

Eclipse Period 15 Leo
LE Jan 31 2018, MW Feb 3 2018, SE Feb 15 2018
NN 15 Le, Ur 25 Ar

Jan 1 2018 Initiative of 300 Hollywood women called "Time's Up" announced to fight sexual harassment
Jan 1 2018 Iranian President Rouhani says recent unrest "is nothing" after 30 people killed in 5 days of anti government demonstrations
Jan 2 2018 Bus crash in Pasamayo, Peru, kills 51 on notorious "Devil's Curve" road.
Jan3 2018 Landslide and flooding caused by heavy rains in Kinshasa, Democratic Republic of Congo, kills at least 37
Jan 3 2018 Lawyers of Pres Trump try to stop the publication of book on Trump's administration "Fire and Fury" by Michael Wolff
Jan 4 2018 'Bomb Cyclone' hits US Northeast prompting flooding and snow in New York subway system
Jan 7 2018 It snows in the Sahara desert - 15 inches reported in Aïn Séfra, Northwest Algeria
Jan 7 2018 Sydney, Australia has its hottest day for 80 years as Penrith reaches 47.3 degrees

Jan 9 2018 Former White House strategist Steve Bannon leaves Breitbart News after his criticism of the White House in "Fire and the Fury" book

Jan 9 2018 Mudslides sweep away 100 houses in Montecito, California, killing at least 20, on land stripped bare by recent fires

Jan 13 2018 Early-morning ballistic missile alert sent across Hawaii in error, revoked after 38 minutes

Jan 15 2018 US Gynmnast Simone says she is one of more than 130 women sexually abused by former team doctor Larry Nassar

Jan 16 2018 A California couple have been arrested after police found their 13 children allegedly held captive at home, some "shackled to their beds with chains and padlocks".

Jan 22 2018 US government ends three-day shutdown after an agreement in Congress to extend funding

Jan 24 2018 Former US Olympic team doctor Larry Nassar found guilty of molesting over 150 girls, sentenced up to 175 years in prison

Jan 26 2018 At least 37 people have been killed and about 130 injured in a fire at a hospital in South Korea.

Jan 27 2018 Bomb in an ambulance kills over 100 people in Kabul, Taliban claim responsibility

Jan 29 2018 Toronto police arrest landscaper Bruce McArthur for murder after remains of at least 5 people found in potted plants

Jan 31 2018 trump administration formally suspends the Clean Water Act

Feb 1 2018 The Indian government announces plan to give 500 million people free healthcare.

Feb 2 2018 All 955 miners rescued from the Beatrix gold mine in Welkom town, South Africa, after 2 days underground.

Feb 3 2018 Moscow has its heaviest snowfall in a day on record, killing one and bringing down 2,000 trees

Feb 6 2018 6.0 magnitude earthquake strikes Hualien County, Taiwan, leaving 10 dead and over 50 missing

Feb 11 2018 Russian airliner crashes south-east of Moscow, killing all 71 on board

Feb 12 2018 Tropical cyclone Gita strikes Tonga as a category four cyclone causing widespread damage

Feb 13 2018 South Africa declares a three-year drought a National Disaster, though pushes Cap Town's "Day Zero" to June 4
Feb 13 2018 Israeli Police report recommends PM Benjamin Neytanyahu be prosecuted on bribery, fraud and breach-of-trust charges
Feb 14 2018 Ex-student Nikolas Cruz guns down 17 people at Marjory Stoneman Douglas High School, Florida, before being captured Never Again Movement
Feb 18 2018 Aseman Airlines flight crashes in the Zagros mountains, Iran, killing all 66 on board
Feb 18 2018 Syrian government forces begin a new offensive on Eastern Ghouta in Syria's civil war killing over 100 civilians
Feb 19 2018 At least 17 killed when a garbage mound collapses in Maputo, Mozambique
Feb 19 2018 Nigeria says 110 girls missing, presumed kidnapped by Boko Haram after attack on school in Dapchi,
Feb 26 2018 7.5 earthquake in central Papa New Guinea kills at least 100

Taurus Sun, Moon Wobble 10 Leo
May 1 2018
NN 10 Le, Ur 29 Ar, Pl 21 Cp, Ma 23 Cp

Apr 17 2018 Protests across India at the rape and murder of an 8-year old Muslim girl in Kathua, Bengalu
Apr 18 2018 Protests begin in Managua, Nicaragua, over proposed changes to social security, protesters beaten by suspected pro-government gangs
Apr 20 2018 Commonwealth countries decide Prince Charles will succeed Queen Elizabeth as the next head of the Commonwealth
Apr 22 2018 Gunman opens fire at Waffle House in Nashville, Tennessee, killing four with James Shaw Jr. wrestling rifle from gunman's hands
Apr 22 2018 Bus crash in North Korea kills 36, with most Chinese tourists
Apr 23 2018 Van deliberately driven into pedestrians in Toronto, Canada, killing 10 and injuring 13

Apr 26 2018 Serial killer "Golden State Killer" identified after 40 years as a former police officer, responsible for 12 killings, 50 rapes in California

Apr 26 2018 Bill Cosby Found Guilty of Three Counts of Sexual Assault

Apr 27 2018 Mass protests across Spain after 5 men convicted of sexual abuse but not rape of teenage girl during Running of the Bulls festival in Pamplona

Apr 27 2018 More than 40 Tuareg killed over two days by suspected jihadists in Menaka region, Mali

Apr 27 2018 Historic Korean summit, the North's Kim Jong-un and Moon Jae-in of South Korea agree to officially end Korean war and rid peninsula of nuclear weapons

April 28 2018 North and South Korea declare the Korean war is over.

Apr 30 2018 Etienne Terrus art museum in Elne, France, reveals half of its collection are fakes

Apr 30 2018 Coordinated double suicide attack kills 36 in Kabul, Afghanistan, including nine journalists

Apr 30 2018 Pakistani city of Nawabshah sets global record for an April temperature, recording high of 50.2C

May 2 2018 Rudy Guiliani said to Hannity of Fox News that Trump knew about Cohen paying off Stormy Daniels at 21:39 NYC.

May 3 2018 Kilauea, Hawaii lava flow Thursday, midday Friday: A 5.6-magnitude quake hit south of the volcano about 11:30 a.m., followed about an hour later by a 6.9-magnitude temblor, according to the Geological Survey.

May 5 2018 E-cigarette explodes killing a man in St. Petersburg, Florida, first death from a vaping product

May 7 2018 Mudslides in Rwanda kill 18 people bringing the year's death toll to 200

May 9 2018 Iranians and their president Rouhani react angrily to Trump pulling the US out the Iran Nuclear deal

May 9 2018 Dam bursts after heavy rains near Solai, Kenya, killing at least 41

May 9 2018 Nicaraguan anti-government protests involving tens of thousands take place in Managua and Matagalpay Chinandega

May 11 2018 Mass murder-suicide in Margaret River, Australia, grandfather shoots six members of his family and himself
May 12 2018 63rd Eurovision song contest won by Netta from Israel in Lisbon, Portugal
May 12 2018 Insurgent group attacks the town of Muse, Myanmar, killing at least 19 people, Ta'ang National Liberation Army claim responsibility
May 12 2018 Family of six carry out 3 church bombings in Surabaya, Indonesia, killing at least 13. Islamic State claims responsibility.
May 14 2018 Melania Trump is treated in hospital for a benign kidney condition
May 15 2018 58 Palestinians killed by Israeli forces and 1700 hospitalized on the Gaza border protesting opening of US embassy in Jerusalem and 70 year founding of Israel
May 15 2018 Flyover collapses in Varanasi, India, killing at least 18
May 15 2018 North Korea threatens to pull out of summit with US and South Korea saying it can "not hide our feeling of repugnance" towards US security advisor John Bolton

Fixed Grand Square Eclipse Period 6 Leo
SE July 13, LE July 26, SE Aug 11 2018
NN 6 Le, Ur 2 Ta, <u>Ma 7 Aq</u> <u>Rx OOB</u>, Pl 20 Cp, Su 20 Ca

Jul 5 2018 At least 24 killed in explosions at pyrotechnics workshops in Tultepec, Mexico
Jul 5 2018 Heatwave in southern Quebec, Canada, kills 33
Jul 6 2018 Floods and landslides begin in south-western Japan, killing at least 200 people with more missing. Evacuation orders for nearly 2 million.
Jul 9 2018 US President Trump names Brett Kavanaugh as his Supreme Court nominee
Jul 10 2018 The final 4 boys and their coach are rescued from Tham Luang Nang Non cave, Thailand after being trapped there for 18 days by monsoon flooding

Jul 13 2018 Suicide bombing in Baluchistan, Pakistan, targeting election campaign event kills 128, Islamic State claims responsibility

Jul 14 2018 More than 300 people now reported killed in protests against government of President Daniel Ortega of Nicaragua

Jul 14 2018 Civilians killed in Afghan war reaches record high with 1,692 killed in first six months of 2018 says UN

Jul 14 2018 Russian covert agent Maria Butina arrested by the FBI in Washington, D.C., charged with being unregistered foreign agent

Jul 18 2018 44 Forest fires in Sweden as far north as the Arctic Circle prompt Swedish government to request extra assistance, with drought and warm weather to blame

Jul 18 2018 Turkey ends its two-year State of Emergency

Jul 18 2018 New Earth geological age announced, the Meghalayan Age 4,200 years ago to the present, by the International Commission on Stratigraphy

Jul 18 2018 Seventeen men charged with the gang-rape of a 12-year old girl in Chennai, India

Jul 18 2018 Lava from Kilauea volcano eruption has now destroyed 700 homes and added 700 acres to Big Island confirms Hawaii National Guard

Jul 19 2018 Duck boot sinks in Table Rock Lake, Missouri, drowning 17 people

Jul 22 2018 Heatwave in Japan kills 11 in one day

Jul 22 2018 Lone gunman shooting kills 3 including gunman and injures 13 in Toronto, Canada

Jul 23 2018 Japan records its highest ever temperature at 41.1 degrees (105.98F) in Kumagaya

Jul 23 2018 Dam collapses while under construction in Attapeu province, Laos, killing at least 20 with more than 100 missing

Jul 24 2018 Wildfires near Athens, Greece, kill 91 with 104 injured, over 600 rescued from the coast by boats

Jul 25 2018 Multiple suicide bombings and attacks by the Islamic State in Sweida and surrounding areas of Syria kill more than 200

Jul 26 2018 Authorities in Stung Treng province, Cambodia, evacuate 25,000 below collapsed Laos dam as waters rise
Jul 26 2018 Over 700 immigrant children still separated from their parents in the US as court-imposed deadline to reunite them passes
Jul 28 2018 Longest "blood moon" eclipse of the 21st century, lasting 1 hour 43 minutes
Jul 29 2018 6.4 magnitude earthquake strikes island of Lombok, Indonesia, killing at least 14
Jul 31 3018 Aeroméxico flight 2431 crash lands in Durango, Mexico, all 103 on board survive
Aug 1 2018 Swedish crown jewels stolen in heist from Strängnäs Cathedral, Stockholm
Aug 4 2018 President Nicolás Maduro of Venezuela survives an assassination attempt by drone, live on TV
Aug 5 2018 Vintage Junkers Ju-52 plane crashes near Flims, Switzerland, killing all 20 on board
Aug 5 2018 6.9 magnitude earthquake on island of Lombok, Indonesia, kills at least 460 people and displaces 350,000
Aug 7 2018 Mendocino Fire becomes the largest recorded fire in California's history at 290,600 acres, overtaking 2017 Thomas Fire
Aug 9 2018 Saudi-led air coalition strikes a school bus in Sada Province, Yemen, killing 43, many of them children
Aug 12 2018 US man steals a plane from Seattle-Tacoma International Airport, flies for an hour chased by military jets before crashing on Ketron Island
Aug 12 2018 More than 200 Afghan soldiers reported killed after 3 days of attacks by taliban insurgents over multiple fronts including Ghazni city
Aug 14 2018 2.3 million estimated Venezuelans have left crisis-hit Venezuela since 2015 according to the UN
Aug 14 2018 Italy's Morandi Bridge collapses in Genoa, taking 30 vehicles with it and killing 43
Aug 14 2018 Pennsylvania grand jury alleges 300 "predator priests" abused over 1000 children over 30 years and Catholic leaders covered it, up after 2-year investigation

Aug 15 2018 Boat overturns in floods near the Nile in Northern Sudan, leaving 25 dead, most of them school children
Aug 15 2018 Suicide bomber attacks tuition centre in Kabul, Afghanistan, killing 48 and injuring 67
Aug 15 2018 US President Trump revokes security clearance of former CIA Director and Trump critic John Brennan
Aug 16 2018 Unprecedented flooding and landslides in Kerala, India, reported to have killed 106 people with 150,000 homeless
Aug 16 2018 British Columbia, Canada, declares State of Emergency with 566 wildfires burning, prompting evacuation of 3,000 people
Aug 19 2018 Monsoon rains finally ease in Kerala State, India, with flooding taking 350 lives with 200,000 in relief camp
Aug 19 2018 Two more earthquakes hit Lombok in Indonesia killing 14 two weeks after previous earthquakes
Aug 19 2018 Rudy Giuliani, US President Trump's lawyer claims in interview with NBC Chuck Todd that "truth isn't truth"
Aug 19 2018 Weinstein accuser Asia Argento is alleged to have sexually assaulted a 17-year old in article by "The New York Times"
Aug 20 1018 Measles cases reach record high in Europe with 41,000 infected first six months of 2018 with 37 deaths according to WHO
Aug 20 2018 Pope Francis releases letter to all Catholics condemning sexual abuse atrocities and clerical cover-ups "We showed no care for the little ones; we abandoned them"
Aug 20 2018 Colorado man Christopher Lee Watts is charged with the murder of his wife and two daughters
Aug 21 2018 Michael Cohen, President Trump's personal lawyer, pleads guilty to charges including illegal payment at direction of Trump to women Trump had affairs with
Aug 21 2018 Australian PM Malcolm Turnbull calls for and wins a leadership vote 43-35 over Home Affairs Minister Peter Dutton
Aug 21 2018 Paul Manafort, former Trump campaign chairman, is convicted on eight counts of fraud in a federal court in Alexandria, Virginia

Grand Square Fixed, Scorpio Sun, Moon Wobble 1 Leo

Oct 24 2018
NN 1 Le, Ur 0 Ta, Mo 4 Ta SU 1 Sc, Ve 4 Sc

Oct 2 2018 Saudi American journalist Jamal Khashoggi enters the Saudi consulate in Istanbul, never to be seen again prompting a diplomatic crisis
Oct 6 2018 Brett Kavanaugh is confirmed and sworn onto the US Supreme Court amid protests and after an FBI investigation
Oct 7 2018 Limousine crash kills 20 people, including two pedestrians in Schoharie, New York
Oct 10 2018 Hurricane Michael makes landfall near Mexico Beach, Florida, as a category 4 hurricane with winds of 155 mph (250 km/h), going on to kill 27, having killed 15 in Central America.
Oct 10 2018 Flash floods kills at least 10 in Sant Llorenç des Cardassar, Majorca, Spain
Oct 12 2018 US air strike in central Somalia kills about 60 al-Shabab militants
Oct 14 2018 Flash floods in Aude region, France kill at least 10 people
Oct 15 2018 Caravan of up to 4,000 Central American migrants that started in Honduras reaches Guatemala, heading for Mexico and the US
Oct 15 2018 American retailer Sears files for bankruptcy
Oct 15 2018 At least 180,000 migrants driven out of Anglo and back into the Democratic Republic of Congo
Oct 16 2018 Saudi Arabian Crown Prince Mohammed Bin Salman denies knowledge of the death of journalist Jamal Khashoggi according to President Trump
Oct 17 2018 Canada legalizes the sale of recreational cannabis, the second country after Uruguay
Oct 21 2018 Train derails in Yilan County, Taiwan, killing 18 and injuring 178
Oct 21 2018 Sectarian fighting between Muslim and Christian youths kill 55 at Kasuwan Magani, Nigeria
Oct 24 2018 Pipe bombs sent to prominent US Democrats including the Obamas, Clintons, John Brennan and CNN, but safely defused

Oct 25 2018 Flash floods near the Red Sea in Jordan kill 17 as a school bus is washed away

Oct 25 2018 Super Typhoon Yutu strikes the Northern Mariana Islands of Saipan and Tinian with winds of 180mph (290km/h)

Oct 25 2018 Google says it has fired 48 people for sexual harassment after New York Times reveals Android creator Andy Rubin got $90 package when let go for sexual harassment

Oct 26 2018 Trump supporter Cesar Sayoc arrested for sending 14 pipe bombs to prominent US Democrats

Oct 25 2018 Google says it has fired 48 people for sexual harassment after New York Times reveals Android creator Andy Rubin got $90 package when let go for sexual harassment

Oct 26 2018 Trump supporter Cesar Sayoc arrested for sending 14 pipe bombs to prominent US Democrats

Oct 29 2018 Storms in Italy kill at least 11 with 75% of Venice flooded and two tornadoes striking Terracina

Oct 29 2018 Lion Air flight JT 610 crashes into the sea just after takeoff near Jakarta, Indonesia, with the loss of all 189 on board

Oct 30 2018 Boston mob boss James "Whitey" Bulger killed in prison at the Penitentiary Hazelton in Bruceton Mills, West Virginia

Nov 1 2018 Google employees stage mass walkout to protest the company's handling of sexual harassment

Nov 3 2018 Truck loses control hitting 31 cars and killing at least 15 people near a tollbooth in Lanzhou, China

Nov 4 2018 Death toll from week-long storm in Italy rises to 29 with death of nine people in floods in Casteldaccia, Sicily

Nov 5 2018 More than 80 students and teachers kidnapped from a boarding school in Bamenda, Cameroon

Nov 6 2016 In US Midterm elections Democrats retake control of the House of Representatives after eight years, the Senate is held by Republicans

Nov 7 2018 US President Donald Trump fires Attorney General Jeff Sessions

Nov 8 2018 Deadliest fire in Californian history, the Camp Fire starts at Plumas National Forest spreads in Butte County destroying town of Paradise, more than 7,600 buildings and killing at least 70, 1000 missing.

Nov 8 2018 Woolsey Fire starts near Thousand Oaks, California with Malibu and Calabasas evacuated, kills two
Nov 9 2018 Mudslide after heavy rain in Rio de Janeiro state, Brazil kills 10
Nov 9 2018 Three car bombs explode in Mogadishu, Somalia, killing 52 people and injuring 100

2019

Eclipse Period 27 Cancer
SE Jan 5 2019, MW Jan 17 2019, SE Jan 21 2019
NN 27 Ca, Ur 28 Ar, Pl 20 Cp

Jan 1 2019 Initiative of 300 Hollywood women called "Time's Up" announced to fight sexual harassment
Jan 2 2019 Bus crash in Pasamayo, Peru, kills 51
Jan 3 2019   Landslide and flooding caused by heavy rains in Kinshasa, Democratic Republic of Congo, kills at least 37
Jan 4 2019   Truck hits a train near Kroonstad city, South Africa killing 19 passengers
Jan 6 2019   Oil tanker Sanchi collides with a freighter off the coast of Shanghai with 32 probable deaths
Jan 9 2019   Mudslides sweep away 100 houses in Montecito, California, killing at least 20
Jan 17 2019   Senate interviews Wm Barr for Attorney General, confirmed Feb 14
Jan 25 2019 Roger Stone indicted and arrested by FBI
Jan 27 2019   Bomb in an ambulance kills over 100 people in Kabul, Taliban
Jan 28 2019 USA indicts Huawei and CFO
Feb 10 2019   Sexual abuse investigation into US Southern Baptist churches reveals 400 church members implicated with over 700 victims
Feb 10 2019   Number of women alleging sexual assault by former Costa Rica President Óscar Arias Sánchez grows to nine. He resigns.
Feb 12 2019 Hotel fire in New Delhi, India, kills 17

Moon Wobble 22 Cancer
April 13 2019
NN 22 Ca, Sa 20 Cp, Pl 23 Cp
(Sa on Pluto Nodes, Pluto on Sa Nodes)

Apr 1 2019 Japanese government announces the name of a new era 'Reiwa' for the next Emperor, Crown Prince Naruhito.
Apr 2 2019 70 villages evacuated in Khuzesta province, Iran, after at least 45 killed in flooding
Apr 3 2019 Brunei brings into force new Sharia laws punishing gay sex and adultery with death by stoning
Apr 8 2019 Actress Allison Mack pleads guilty to sex-trafficking charges.
Apr 8 2019 Protests in Sudan against the government, 7 killed, 2,500 arrested
Apr 10 2019 First home delivery service by drone begins in Canberra, Australia by Wing
Apr 10 2019 New York declares health emergency and compulsory vaccinations, measles outbreak in Brooklyn with 285 cases
Apr 11 2019 WikiLeaks Julian Assange is forcibly removed from the Ecuadorian embassy
Apr 11 2019 Sudanese President Omar a--Bashir overthrown and arrested
Apr 14 2019 11 tornadoes hit US southern states killing eight
Apr 15 2019 Paris cathedral Notre Dame catches fire
Apr 23 2019 54 jade miners buried by a mudslide in Myanmar
Apr 25 2019 2019 Former US VP Joe Biden announces his campaign for president
Apr 25 Cyclone Kenneth strikes Mozambique killing at least 38 people
Apr 26 2019 Six suspected militants connected to Sri Lankan terror attacks killed along with ten others in a shootout
Apr 29 2019 Over 300 people declared to have died due overwork in Indonesia's election on April 17th, with over 2,000 fallen sick
Apr 30 2019 Japanese Emperor Akihito declares his abdication

May 1 2019 Wikileaks Julian Assange sentenced to 50 weeks in jail

Eclipse Period 17 Cancer
SE Jul 2 2019, MW Jul 10 2019, LE Jul 16 2019
NN 17 Ca, Sa 17 Cp, Ve 15 Ca

Jun 16 2019 Massive unprecedented power cut affects all of Argentina and Uruguay and parts of Paraguay
Jun 16 2019 Three suicide bomb attacks kill 30 people in Konduga, north east Nigeria
Jun 17 2019 Former Egyptian President Mohamed Morsi dies
Jun 18 2019 US Pres. Trump announces his campaign for reelection
Jun 1 2019 8 Two 14 year-old boys become the youngest in Irish history to be convicted of murder when found guilty of the murder and sexual assault of 14 year-old girl in Dublin
Jun 19 2019 US Nxivm sex cult leader Keith Raniere found guilty in New York court of racketeering, sex trafficking and child pornography
Jun 20 2019 Iran shoots down a US drone over the Straits of Hormuz
Jun 21 2019 UK police called to house of leader contender Boris Johnson over alleged altercation with his girlfriend
Jun 22 2019 Seven-story building collapses in Sihanoukville, Cambodia, 25 dead
Jun 2 2019 Russian volcano Raikoke erupts from 700m-wide-crater
Jun 24 2019 US Presi. Trump imposes sanctions on Iran
Jun 24 Mysterious sickness affects 718 children with 152 deaths around Muzaffarpur, Indian
Jun 26 2019 Highest ever June temperatures recorded during week-long heatwave in Europe
Jun 30 2019 Large protests in Khartoum, Sudan, against continuing military rule, kill seven and injure 181
Jul 02 2019 Air strike kills at least 40 people at Libyan migrant

Jul 03 2019 Heavy monsoon rains strike Mumbai and surrounding Maharashtra state in India killing at least 43, worst flooding in a decade
Jul 04 2019 Largest earthquake in California in 20 years 6.4 magnitude near Ridgecrest
Jul 04 2019 Record temperatures in Alaska as Anchorage reaches 90F
Jul 05 2019 Second stronger earthquake in Southern California at 7.1 magnitude
Jul 08 2019 US financier Jeffrey Epstein indicted
Jul 11 2019 US stock markets reach new records, the Dow tops 27,000 points
Jul 17 2019 Irrigation canal system collapses near Fort Laramie, Wyoming parching 100,000 acres
Jul 22 2019 Air strikes have killed at least 31 people in Syria, with Russian planes
Jul 17 2019 Mexican drug cartel head "El Chapo" Guzmán sentenced to life in prison
Jul 19 2019 Heat wave begins across America affecting 100 million people and killing 6
Jul 21 2019 Puerto Rico's governor Ricardo Rosselló says he won't seek re-election after widespread protests over misogynistic and homophobic comments in his leaked online chats
Jul 23 2019 Boris Johnson chosen the new British Prime Minister
Jul 23 2019 Investigation launched after no girls born in 3 months in 132 villages in Uttarkashi district, India, with sex-selective abortions
Jul 23 2019 36 people killed by a mud landslide in Guizhou province, China
Jul 24 2019 Second heatwave of the summer in Western Europe sets record temperatures
Jul 24 2019 Facebook agrees to pay $5 billion fine
Jul 25 2019 Scandal-hit Governor of Puerto Rico Ricardo Rosselló resigns
Jul 25 2019 Worst Mediterranean migrant drownings, capsized boat carrying 250 people over 100 feared drowned

Jul 27 2019 At least 65 mourners killed in a gun attack at a funeral near Maiduguri

Jul 29 2019 Prison riot kills 58, with 16 decapitated in battle Altamira prison in Brazil

Jul 31 2019 Russian President Putin orders army to help put out huge wildfires in Siberia

Jul 31 2019 American officials Osama bin Laden's son, Hamza bin Laden killed

Libra Sun Moon Wobble 12 Cancer
Oct 6, 2019
NN 12 Ca, Sa 14 Cp

Sep 21 2019 Skies turn red over Jambi province, Indonesia, as worst illegal forest fires since 2015 burn more than 800,000 acres

Sep 22 2019 US Pres. Trump i admits he spoke to Ukrainian President about Joe Biden's son

Sep 23 2019 violence in West Papua region, Indonesia, leaves 27 dead

Sep 24 2019 UK Supreme Court rules suspension of UK parliament for 5 weeks by PM Boris Johnson unlawful

Sep 24 2019 House Speaker Pelosi announces formal impeachment inquiry into US President Trump

Sep 24 2019 5.8 magnitude earthquake in northern Pakistan kills10, injures 300

Sep 28 2019 Elon Musk unveils SpaceX spacecraft Starship

Sep 29 2019 Houthi rebels from Yemen claim they have killed 500 Saudi soldiers and captured 2,000

Sep 30 2019 315 billion-tonne iceberg named D28 calves from Antarctica

Oct 01 2019 Bernie Sanders taken to hospital after suffering a heart attack

Oct 02 2019 Prince Harry and Meghan, Duchess of Sussex sue British newspaper The Mail

Oct 04 2019 Fuel subsidies end in Ecuador after four decades, prompting nationwide protests

Oct 06 2019 99 Iraqis have died and 4,000 injured in protests over 5 days against living conditions
Oct 09 2019 Nearly 1 million people in northern California have their power cut by Pacific Gas and Electric to prevent wildfires
Oct 10 2019 3,500 women are the first to be allowed to attend a football match in Iran
Oct 12 2019 Typhoon Hagibis makes landfall near Tokyo, Japan, record rainfall, killing 56 people
Oct 13 2019 Kurdish forces make a deal with Syrian army
Oct 14 2019 Hundreds of forest fires break out in western Lebanon, killing three
Oct 17 2019 UK PM Boris Johnson announces new Brexit deal with the EU
Oct 17 2019 Mick Mulvaney, acting WH chief of staff says the White House withheld nearly $400 million in military aid from Ukraine
Oct 22 2019 Russian Presi Putin and Turkish Pres. Erdogan agree deal to jointly control former Kurdish territory in Northern Syria
Oct 22 2019 Top US diplomat in Ukraine, Bill Taylor, testifies Pres. Trump tied aid to Ukraine
Oct 23 2019 Lorry containing 39 bodies of Vietnamese nationals found in Essex, England
Oct 26 2019 US raid kills ISIS founder Abu Kakr al-Baghdadi in Syria

2020

Eclipse Period 8 Cancer
SE Dec 26 2019, MW Dec 31 2020, LE Jan 10 2020
NN 8 Ca, Ju 8 Cp

Dec 04 2019 58 migrants drown after a boat sinks off the coast of Mauritania
Dec 08 2019 Fire in an illegal bag factory in Delhi, India, kills 43
Dec 09 2019 Chilean Air Force plane lost on flight to Antarctica with presumed loss of 38 lives

Dec 10 2019 Shooting at a New Jersey cemetery and a kosher supermarket leaves six dead
Dec 11 2019 Wuhan, China identifies first cases of Covid-19
Dec 12 2019 British General Election won by PM Johnson's Conservative Party
Dec 15 2019 6.8 Earthquake Philippines
Dec 17 2019 Australia has its hottest day ever with average temperature of 40.9 across the country
Dec 18 2019 House votes Two articles of Impeachment against Trump
Dec 18 2019 Indian Ocean Dipole, extreme weather
Dec 22 2019 Las Vegas Apt Fire kills 6
Dec 22 2019 69 Car Pileup injures many, Williamsberg, Va
Dec 25 2019 Wuhan Covid-19 cases identified
Dec 27 2019 Extreme weather and fires in Australia
Dec 28 2019 Plane crash kills 5, Lafayette, Ga
Dec 28 2019 Truck bomb in Somalia kills 76
Dec 30 2019 Scientist globally spread news of Covid-19 while China covers up truth
Dec 30 2019 Carlos Goshn, Nissan CEO escapes Japan
Jan 04 2020 Australian bushfires death toll reaches 23
Jan 04 2020 torrential rain in Jakarta, Indonesia, kill at least 53
Jan 07 2020 6.4 magnitude earthquake in Puerto Rico
Jan 08 2020 Ukrainian Boeing 737-800 crashes just after take-off from Tehran, Iran, killing all 176
Jan 11 2020 China releases the genome to WHO
Jan 12 2020 Taal volcano, 70km (45 miles) south of Manila in the Philippines
Jan 13 2020 Queen Elizabeth II issues a statement saying she reluctantly supports Prince Harry and Meghan Markle's wish to live a more independent life
Jan 16 2020 Impeachment trial of US Pres. Trump begins in the Senate
Jan 20 2020 Science considers this the last day to contain Covid-19 worldwide
Jan 23 2020 China locks down city of Wuhan and its 11 million people at 10:00 am.
Jan 23 2020 Rape NYC trial for Harvey Weinstein

Jan 23 2020 Trump informed of contagious spread of Covid-19
Jan 25 2020 Severe rainstorms landslides and floods in Brazil killing at least 30
Feb 5 2020 Trump acquitted by Senate

Aries Sun Moon Wobble 3 Cancer
Mar 25, 2020
NN 3 Ca, Ma 25 Cp, Ju 25 Cp, Sa 0 Aq, Pl 19 Cp

Mar 03 2020 storm producing multiple tornadoes rips through central Tennessee killing at least 25
Mar 03 2020 Iran releases 54,000 people from prison to avoid spread of Covid-19 as country reports 77 deaths
Mar 03 2020 Heavy rain and landslides hit coastal areas of São Paulo and Rio de Janeiro states, Brazil, killing at least 18 people
Mar 04 2020 "Once in a century" winter in Moscow the hottest in 140 years
Mar 08 2020 Italy announces it is locking down northern region of Lombardy, including Milan, with 16 million people, as CONVID-19 cases reach 5,800 with 233 deaths
Mar 08 2020 America registers 521 cases of COVID-19 with 21 deaths across 33 states
Mar 09 2020 US country due to spike in COVID-19 cases with 10,040 cases and 630 deaths
Mar 10 2020 Russian lower house of Parliament passes legislation to allow Putin to hold office of President for life
Mar 11 2020 COVID-19 declared a pandemic by the head of the WHO
Mar 11 2020 Harvey Weinstein is sentenced to 23 years in prison
Mar 11 2020 11-year bull market ends as the Dow Jones industrial average falls more than 20%
Mar 12 2020 US Pres. Trump bans travel with 26 European countries
Mar 13 2020 US Pres. Trump declares a national emergency
Mar 15 2020 European countries impose restrictions on gatherings and borders as . COVID-19 deaths rates rise dramatically – Italy 1,809, Spain 288, France 120

Mar 15 2020 US Federal Reserve slashes interest rates to near zero

Mar 17 2020 European Union announces a 30-day ban on entering its 26 countries

Mar 18 2020 US Pres. Trump and Canadian PM Trudeau agree to close the US-Canada border

Mar 20 2020 Smoke from Australian bushfires killed more people than the fires – 417

Mar 22 2020 2020 2020 India puts 1 billion people under a daytime curfew

Mar 23 New York confirmed as center of the COVID-19 pandemic in the US with 20,875 cases (5,707 in the last day) and 157 deaths

Mar 23 2020 WHO says the COVID-19 pandemic is increasing, 1st 100,000 cases took 67 days, 2nd 100,000 cases 11 days, 3rd 100,000 cases 4 days

Mar 24 2020 Indian PM Modi orders a 21 day lockdown

Mar 25 2020 UK Prince Charles tests positive for COVID-19

Mar 26 2020 Record number of Americans file for unemployment – 3.3 million

Mar 27 2020 UK P M Johnson announces he has contracted the Covid-19

Mar 28 2020 US Pres. Trump makes grim projection that 240,000 American could die from COVID-19

Mar 29 2020 CDC Dr. Antony Fauci warns America may see between 100,000 – 200,000 deaths from COVID-19

Apr 01 2020 US Pres. Trump id says the US Strategic National Stockpile is almost depleted amid widespread shortages of medical equipment

Apr 02 2020 Number of COVID-19 cases worldwide passes 1 million, with 1,002,159 cases and 51,485 deaths reported

Apr 03 2020 US aircraft carrier captain Brett Crozier cheered off his ship after being fired

Apr 03 2020 27 people swept off a ferry and feared dead in the Solomon Islands during Cyclone Harold

Apr 06 2020 British PM Johnson admitted to hospital

Apr 06 2020 US COVID-19 death toll passes 10,000 in six weeks, with more than 356,000 American infected, New York deaths 4,758

Eclipse Period 29 Gemini
LE Jun 5 2020 , MW Jun 20 2020, SE Jun 21 2020,
LE Jul 5, 2020
NN 29 Ge, Su 29 Ge, Ma 25 Pi, Ne 20 Pi, Ju 25 Cp,
Pl 24 Cp
(Sun square Mars all month, Ju & Pl on NN of Sa)

May 07 UK economy heading for its' worst crash in 300 years (-14%), since 1706

May 07 Toxic leak at Indian chemical factory near Visakhapatnam kills at least 13 and injures many

May 14 Global death toll from COVID-19 passes 300,000 with 4.4 million confirmed infections

May 20 Cyclone Amphan comes ashore in West Bengal, East India and Bangladesh, with winds of 185 km per hour (115 mph) killing at least 84 people

May 22 Pakistan International Airlines flight crashes near Jinnah International Airport in Karachi killing 97

May 25 Video of African American George Floyd's arrest and murder while restrained in Minneapolis police custody (start of world protests)

May 27 America's COVID-19 death toll passes 100,000

May 27 Locust swarms in western and central India worst since 1993

Jun 01 US Pres. Trump threatens to employ the military to quell protests across the country sparked by the death of George Floyd then walks with staff to St. John's Church

Jun 04 Memorial for George Floyd led by Rev. Al Sharpton, killed in police custody, in Minneapolis, as 10th night of protests

Jun 04 State of Emergency declared after 20,000 tons of diesel oil spills near Russian city of Norilsk, Siberia within the Arctic Circle

Jun 07 Black Lives Matter Protests continue worldwide in large numbers

Jun 07 COVID-19 global death toll passes 400,000 with confirmed cases at 6,973,195
Jun 08 World Bank says the COVID-19 pandemic will shrink the global economy by 5.2%
Jun 08 Lockdowns for COVID-19 in Europe saved 3 million lives
Jun 10 Statues of Confederate figures and explorers become focus of #BlackLivesMatter protests, with many removed
Jun 11 Bodies of 46 migrants recovered off the coast of Tunisia
Jun 12 African American Rayshard Brooks shot dead in drive-through carpark in Atlanta leading to further protests
Jun 14 India reports surge of nearly 12,000 a day confirmed COVID-19 cases (320,922 overall), the world's fourth-affected country, as death toll hits 9,195
Jun 16 At least 20 Indian soldiers killed in 1st deadly clash on the Chinese Indian border in 45 years
Jun 18 Global COVID-19 death toll passes 450,000 (451,118) with 8,421,357
Jun 20 Pres. Trump controversially holds his first re-election rally in Tulsa, Oklahoma, only 6,200 people
Jun 20 Arctic circle record its highest-ever temperature of 38C (100F)
Jun 20 Historic dust cloud from the Sahara desert reaches the Caribbean
Jun 22 US government data shows African Americans four times more likely than whites to be hospitalized for COVID-19 highlighting racial disparities for the pandemic
Jun 23 COVID-19 cases rise sharply again in America as country records its 3rd highest daily total, more than 35,000
Jun 24 World Monetary fund predicts a deeper global recession with contraction of 4.9%
Jun 25 US Center of Disease Control estimates 20 million people in America have been infected with Covid-19, 10 times higher than confirmed cases
Jun 26 New York Times says Russia secretly offered bounties to Taliban-linked forces to kill US and coalition troops in Afghanistan
Jun 28 Global death toll from COVID-19 passes 500,000

Jun 29 Golden State Killer and former police officer Joseph DeAngelo Jr pleads guilty to 12 murders and dozens of rapes
Jul 01 WHO says Middle East at "critical threshold" with COVID-19 cases over 1 million, 80% of deaths in Egypt, Iran, Iraq, Pakistan and Saudi Arabia
Jul 02 Nationwide unrest killed over 80 people In Ambo, Ethiopia
Jul 02 More than 160 people die after a landslide at a jade mine in north Myanmar
Jul 04 Record rain in Kyushu, Japan causes flooding killing a least 37
Jul 07 Texas records more than 10,000 daily cases of COVID-19 for the 1st time
Jul 07 Brazilian Pres. Bolsonaro announces he has tested positive for COVID-19
Jul 08 Americans and Polynesians made contact around 1200 A.D. according to new genomic study in "Nature", people from eastern Polynesia had DNA from indigenous Colombia
Jul 15 Heavy monsoon flooding in NE Indian n affects more than 2 million people, kills more than 50

Moon Wobble 24 Gemini
Sep 17, 2020
NN 24 Gi, Ne 19 Pi, Ma Rx 27 Ar, Sa 25 Cp, Pl 22 Cp
(Pl on NN of Sa)

Sep 3 2020 More healthcare workers have died of COVID-19 in Mexico than any other country - 1320 deaths vs 1077 (US) and 649 (UK)
Sep 5 2020 More than 50 arrested as Portland, Oregon, marks 100 days of protests
Sep 7 2020 India overtakes Brazil to record the second-highest number of COVID-19 cases with 4.2 million
Sep 7 2020 Wildfires have burnt a record 2 million acres in California 2020 fire season
Sep 9 2020 Global death toll from COVID-19 passes 900,000 with the US the most deaths at 190,589

Sep 10 2020 California's August Complex wildfire becomes largest recorded in state history at 471,000 acres
Sep 17 2020 More than 15,000 fires have caused widespread devastation in Brazil's Pantanal wetlands in 2020
Sep 18 2020 Supreme Court Justice Ruth Bader Ginsburg Dies
Sep 19 2020 US President Trump vows to swear in a new Supreme Court judge.
Sep 22 2020 America's COVID-19 death toll passes 200,000
Sep 23 2020 President Trump refuses to commit to a peaceful transfer of power.
Sep 23 2020 President Trump nominates Judge Amy Coney Barrett for the US Supreme Court (Appointed in 4 days)
Sep 27 2020 Details of President Trump's tax returns released by the NYT.
Sep 29 2020 First debate between US President Trump and Joe Biden.

Eclipse Period 19 Gemini
LE Nov 30, MW Dec 11, SE Dec 22, LE Dec 30 2020
NN 19 Gi, Ju 27 Cp, Ma 21 Ar, Sa 29 Cp, Pl 23 Cp
(Pl on NN Sa, Ur on NN Eris)

Nov 15 2020 US President Trump tweets [Biden] "won because the election was rigged,"
Nov 16 2020 US drugmaker Moderna says its COVID-19 vaccine is 94.5%
Nov 19 2020 Floods and landslides effect more than 3 million people, killing at least 70 in wake of Typhoon Vamco, Philippines
Nov 18 2020 US COVID-19 death toll passes 250,000, recorded cases at 11.5 million
Nov 23 2020 AstraZeneca is the third drugmaker to report an effective vaccine for COVID-19
Nov 25 2020 US President Trump pardons former security advisor Michael Flynn guilty of lying to the FBI
Nov 26 2020 Turkey gives life sentences to 337 military officers
Nov 28 2020 At least 110 people killed in attack on Koshobe village in north-east Nigeria by Boko Haram

Dec 11 2020 America's FDA authorizes the Pfizer/BioNTech COVID-19 vaccine for emergency use

Dec 14 2020 America begins its first COVID-19 vaccinations using the Pfizer/BioNTech vaccine on the same day it records over 300,000 deaths

Dec 14 2020 US Attorney General William Barr resigns

Dec 15 2020 Russia revealed to have been behind massive cyberattack on US government agencies and private companies

Dec 16 2020 Moderna COVID-19 vaccine granted emergency authorization

Jan 3 2021 US President Trump says to Georgia's secretary of state Brad Raffensperger "I just want to find 11,780 votes, which is one more than we have," in recording released by the Washington Post

Jan 6 2021 Supporters of President Trump storm the US Capitol in Washington

Jan 7 2021 US Congress completes the ceremonial certification of Joe Biden's presidential victory

Jan 13 2021 President Trump is impeached by the US House of Representatives voting 232-197.

References

www.astro.com "Osculating nodes and apsides"
https://worldhistoryproject.org
http://www.disaster-report.com
https://www.infoplease.com/world
https://www.mapsofworld.com
https://www.onthisday.com/events
http://www.astrologycom.com/moonwobble.html
http://www.cbc.ca/news/world/the-world-s-worst-natural-disaster-1.743208

Major Squaring Moon Wobble Events and Famous People

I have selected only the most dramatic Moon Wobble events that have timed charts so that astrological houses can be used. In my prior book, Foundations of Astrology, I explain why I used equal houses, how I interpret the houses and the use of heliocentric nodes. These additional elements add to chart interpretation, but their use will not be further explained in this book about Moon Wobbles. They can be referenced in the prior book.

Some examples have a wide orb of 15 degrees between the Sun and Lunar Nodes. This wide orb is used in mundane events* and I use it if there is another planet involved. The squaring Moon Wobble of the Paradise Camp Fire involved Uranus or the Indonesia tsunami because Saturn was involved too. These are examples of intensity events that are modified by slow transits to the Nodes but close enough to the Sun degree to still be in the orb of a Moon Wobble.

The second section will be of famous persons who were born under an eclipse or Moon Wobble periods to show how this affects their life. This is especially true for Prince Charles, Donald Trump and Joe Biden. There are many more examples that will be given but the intention is to give the reader an idea of how these aspects influence their lives because transits to these points can indicate dramatic turning points in the future of those born with these aspects.

Dramatic World Events with Squaring Moon Wobbles

Paradise, Ca Camp Fire, Nov 9, 2018 at 7:23 am, MW on Oct 24

This was a raging fire caused by PG&E electrical transmission lines. It killed 85 people and destroyed 18,800 buildings. The entire town of Paradise had only one road out of the blaze.

The Lunar Nodes were square the Sun, Venus and Uranus to create a grand square. Uranus is especially associated with electricity and explosions. In that early morning, the Moon was near the Ascendant (representing the public) and squaring Mars down in the 4th house, indicating real estate, physical buildings and homes. Astrologically, the grand square indicated these kinds events for several weeks but it was the Moon square Mars that set the trigger for the fire that day. The Sun was 16 degrees from the Lunar Nodes but it was Uranus to the Nodes that set the electrical transformer to explode that day with Moon squaring Mars.

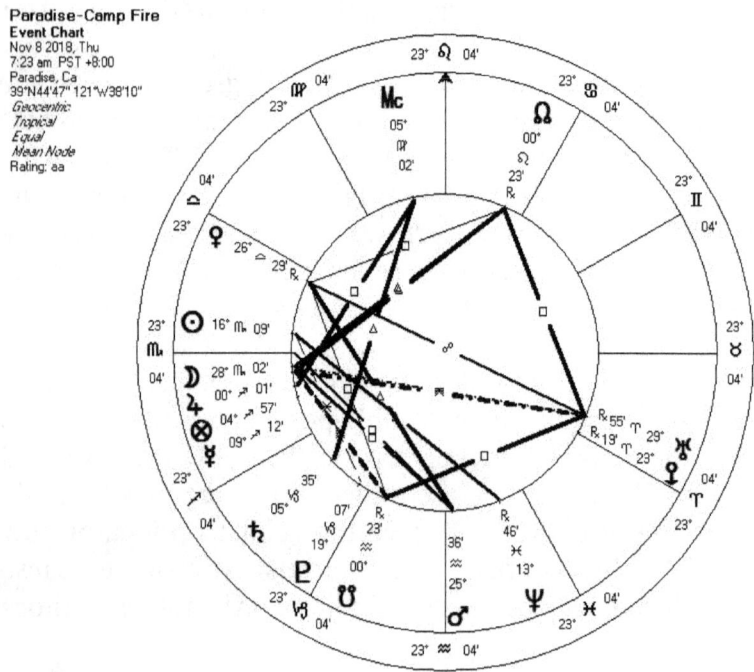

Paradise-Camp Fire		Paradise, Ca
Event Chart		39°N44'47" 121°W38'10"
Nov 8 2018, Thu	Equal	Geocentric, Tropical
7:23 am PST +8:00		Mean Node

Pt	Decl.	Long.	L.E.Dec
♀	-02°10'	23°♈19	24°♓30
♆	-07°17'	13°♓46	11°♓22
☿	+09°39'	05°♍02	05°♍02
♅	+10°55'	29°♈55	28°♈27
♀	-13°14'	26°♎29	05°♏10
♂	-14°50'	25°♒36	19°♒54
☽	-15°24'	28°♏02	11°♏54
☉	-16°40'	16°♏09	16°♏09
⊗	-16°46'	04°♐57	16°♏29
As	-18°32'	23°♏04	23°♏04
♃	-19°29'	00°♐01	27°♏00
☊	+20°03'	00°♌23	00°♌23
☋	-20°03'	00°♒23	00°♒23
♇	-22°05'	19°♑07	18°♑57
♄	-22°45'	05°♑35	13°♑28
☿	-24°34'	09°♐12	12°♐37

Kilauea Eruption and 5.6 Quake, May 3, 2018 at 11:30 am Hawaii, MW May 1st

Just three days after a squaring Moon Wobble, Kilauea started erupting with an earthquake and then spewed lava for weeks, devouring entire communities. Transiting Uranus was at the end of Aries and proceeded to move into Taurus, the sign of fixed earth. Uranus, the disturber, was within the orb of the Sun and the nodes to induce this eruption. That week, transiting Mars was forming a square to Uranus that is highly associated with violence and destruction. Pluto was still within range of a separating square to Uranus. So this Moon Wobble had a double trigger. Uranus in Taurus is symbolic of earthly destruction in the form of earthquakes and volcanoes or explosions.

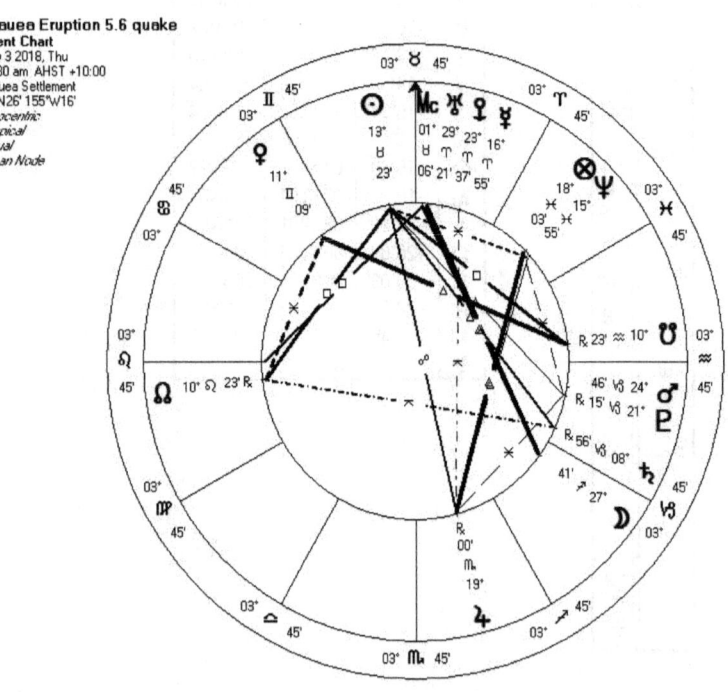

Kilauea Eruption 5.6 quake			Kilauea Settlement
Event Chart			19°N26' 155°W16'
May 3 2018, Thu		Equal	Geocentric, Tropical
11:30 am AHST +10:00			Mean Node

Pt	Decl.	Long.	L.E.Dec
⊗	-01°36'	18°♓03	25°♓56
♀	-01°56'	23°♈37	25°♓05
☿	+03°53'	16°♈55	09°♈50
♆	-06°24'	15°♓55	13°♓42
♅	+10°45'	29°♈21	27°♈58
Mc	+11°51'	01°♉06	01°♉06
☉	+15°51'	13°♉23	13°♉23
♃	-16°14'	19°♏00	14°♏41
☊	+17°38'	10°♌23	10°♌23
☋	-17°38'	10°♒23	10°♒23
As	+19°18'	03°♌45	03°♌45
☽	-20°02'	27°♐41	29°♏29
♇	-21°29'	21°♑15	22°♑56
♄	-22°14'	08°♑56	17°♑49
♂	-22°34'	24°♑46	15°♑09
♀	+23°05'	11°♊09	20°♊18

Fukushima Nuclear Explosion, March 12, 2011 at 3:36 pm, MW March 19

Japan suffered a 133-foot high tsunami on March 11th from a 9.0 earthquake at 14:46 JST. By the next day, the seawater had flooded the three Fukushima nuclear power towers and a meltdown was happening. The first explosion released massive amounts of radiation into the air. Later the meltdown went into the ground and released more radiation into the ocean. Today it is barely discussed, but this is a continuing disaster of epic proportions that isn't resolved even in 2020.

The very day of this nuclear explosion Uranus had just entered Aries (which I believe is ruled by Pluto). Both are associated with nuclear events and radiation. The sun was squaring the Lunar Nodes along with Uranus. The planet Pluto was with the north lunar node in the fifth house of risk-taking. Neptune, the planet of the sea and the deep unknown, was on the Descendant representing water and the tsunami. The Moon was on the heliocentric nodes of Uranus, sign of explosion and sudden change, and it was OOB (Out of Bounds). In this case it represents the people of the world being profoundly changed by this event. The new planet Eris (which I believe is the ruler of fixed earth) sits squaring on the heliocentric nodes of Saturn for long-term consequences. I would not be surprised if we will see a rise in thyroid cancer and other cancers in the years to come, along with a continuous low level of radiation in seafood.

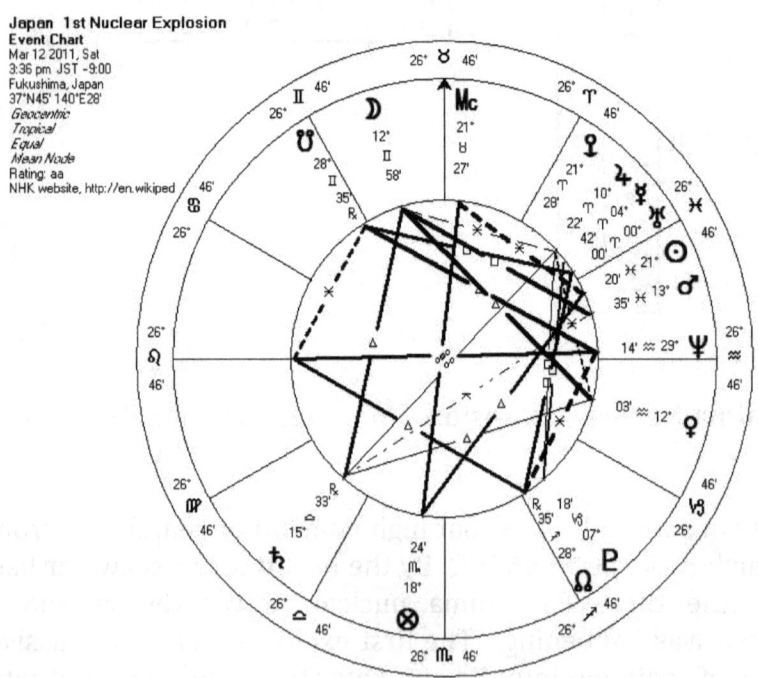

Japan 1st Nuclear Explosion		Fukushima, Japan	
Event Chart		37°N45' 140°E28'	
Mar 12 2011, Sat	Equal	Geocentric, Tropical	
3:36 pm JST -9:00		Mean Node	

Pt	Decl.	Long.	L.E.Dec
♅	-00°38'	00°♈00	28°♓23
☿	+01°58'	04°♈42	04°♈58
♃	+03°05'	10°♈22	07°♈48
☉	-03°26'	21°♓20	21°♓20
♄	-03°38'	15°♎33	09°♎10
♀	-04°00'	21°♈28	19°♓52
♂	-07°23'	13°♓35	11°♓06
♆	-12°11'	29°♒14	27°♒54
As	+12°35'	26°♌46	26°♌46
⊗	-16°00'	18°♏24	13°♏52
♀	-17°00'	12°♒03	12°♒40
℞	+18°07'	21°♉27	21°♉27
♇	-18°45'	07°♑18	06°♒04
☋	+23°25'	28°♊35	28°♊35
☊	-23°25'	28°♐35	28°♐35
☽	+23°42'	12°♊58	21°♊36

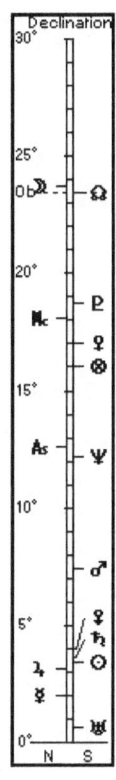

China Sichuan 8.0 Earthquake on May 12, 2008 at 6:28 UT in Chengdu, China, MW May 14

This was the deadliest earthquake this century so far with loss of life estimated at 69,000 people and many more thousands were injured and homeless.

The transiting Out of Bounds Moon had just risen with the South Lunar Nodes and Saturn when this earthquake started. Neptune was opposing these points in Aquarius and the Sun squared them all. This time Uranus was in sextile, not in a hard aspect to the Sun. The Moon and the Sun with the nodes were the triggers, but Saturn and Neptune played their part as the

Chinese tried to not let the world know how large the loss of life was for some time. This earthquake has an exact time that placed the nodes of Uranus squaring the Ascendant-Descendant axis of strength and power. There was a cluster of declinations for Saturn-Lunar Nodes-Neptune-Moon that added power to these alignments.

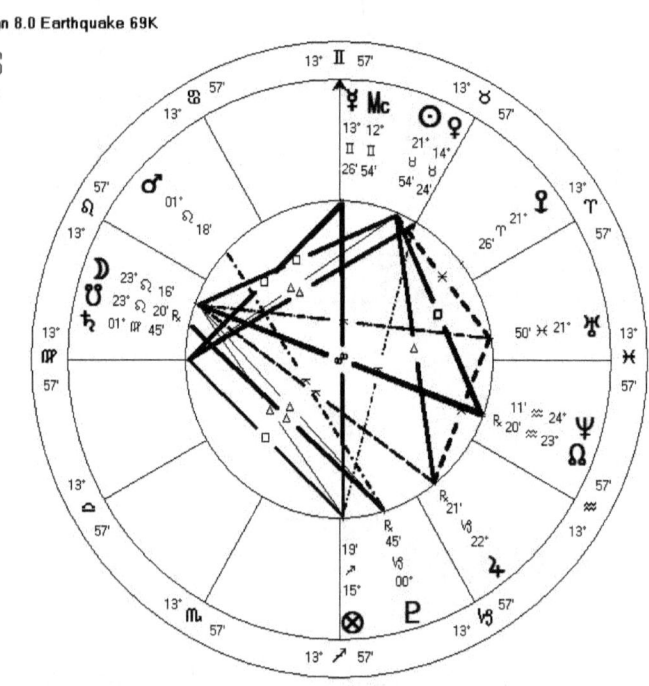

China Sichuan 8.0 Earthquake 69K		chengdu, China
Event Chart		30°N39' 104°E04'
May 12 2008, Mon	Equal	Geocentric, Tropical
6:28 am UT +0:00		Mean Node

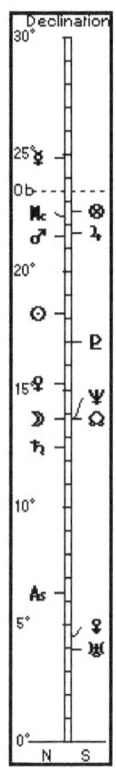

Pt	Decl.	Long.	L.E.Dec
♅	-03°55'	21°♓50	20°♓04
♀	-04°31'	21°♈26	18°♓34
As	+06°18'	13°♍57	13°♍57
♄	+12°30'	01°♍45	27°♌00
☊	-13°44'	23°♒20	23°♒20
☋	+13°44'	23°♌20	23°♌20
♆	-13°45'	24°♒11	23°♒17
☽	+13°45'	23°♌16	23°♌15
♀	+15°13'	14°♉24	11°♉19
♇	-17°01'	00°♑45	12°♒37
☉	+18°14'	21°♉54	21°♉54
♂	+21°32'	01°♌18	22°♋37
♃	-21°38'	22°♑21	22°♑02
Mc	+22°20'	12°♊54	12°♊54
⊗	-22°37'	15°♐19	15°♐15
☿	+24°52'	13°♊26	10°♊28

London Subway/Bus Bombing, July 7 2005 at 8:50 am in London, MW July 10

Four terrorists separately detonated three homemade bombs in quick succession aboard in the subway trains across the city and, later, a fourth on a double-decker bus. 52 died and 700 were injured.

The Sun was near the Moon and Saturn in a wide conjunction that was squared by the Lunar Nodes with Mars and Jupiter. Uranus, the planet associated with explosions, was on the Descendant. The positions of the Moon and Saturn in Cancer put them on the heliocentric nodes of Saturn and the Moon was

OOB. The Moon represents the public in mundane charts, so the loss of life was great.

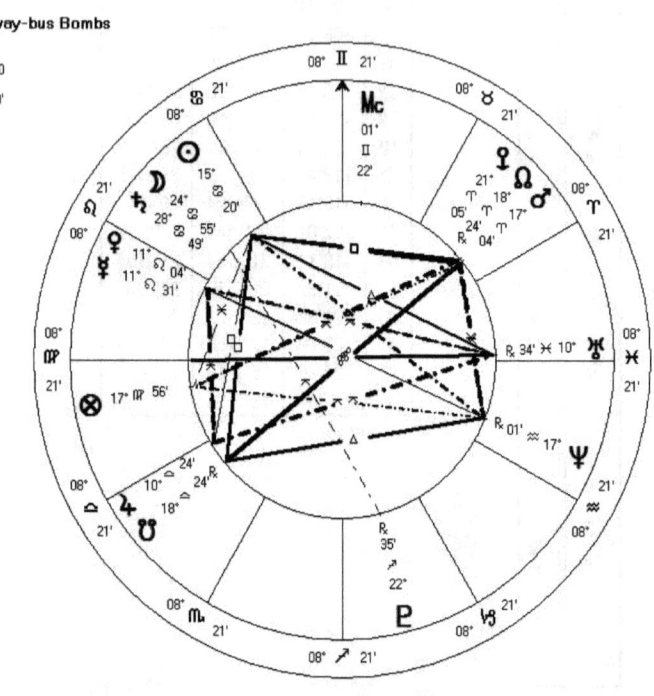

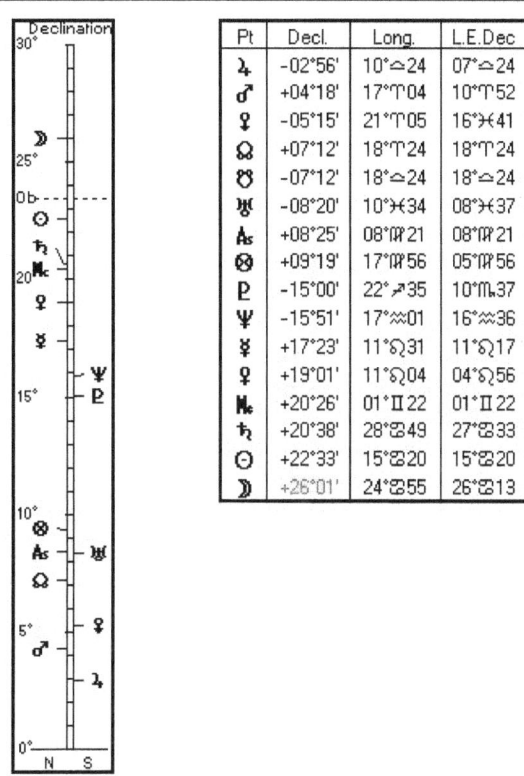

Indonesia Tsunami, December 26 2004 at 7:58 am in Indonesia, MW Jan 17 2005

This was one of the greatest losses of life with at least 275,000 dead, swept away into the ocean in a very large area after an earthquake.

The Sun was in a very wide (out of aspect) square to the Lunar Nodes since the exact squaring Moon Wobble was 24 days away and therefore 24 degrees apart from the square. However, Saturn was close to the nodes and sitting very close to its own heliocentric node of Saturn. Saturn was on the Descendant, giving it power and strength. The major trigger for that day was the Moon being OOB at 26 degrees north in extreme declination and at 28 Gemini. It was in opposition to Pluto (associated with massive pandemics and loss of life). In addition, Mars squared Uranus that week - inducing enough energy for an earthquake along with the extreme Moon.

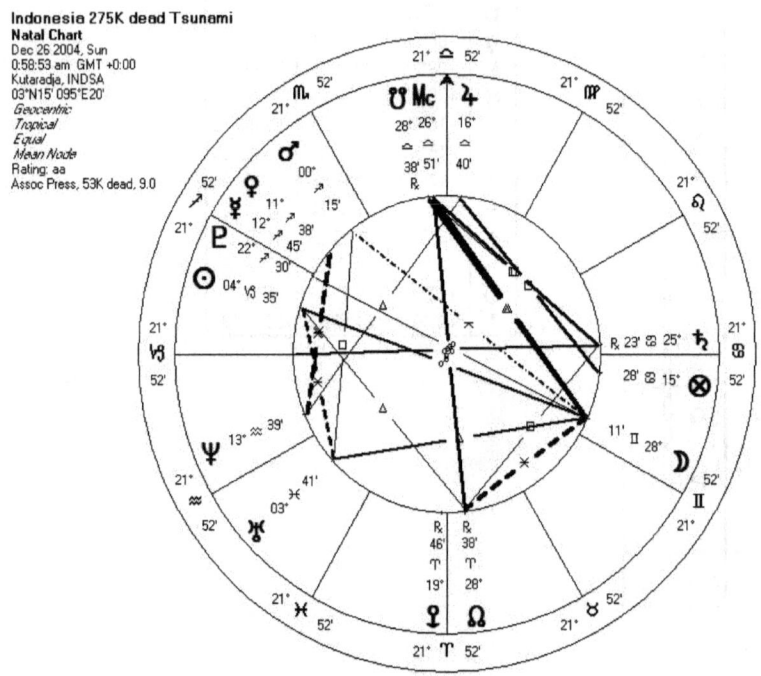

Indonesia 275K dead Tsunami	Kutaradja, INDSA
Natal Chart	03°N15' 095°E20'
Dec 26 2004, Sun Equal	Geocentric, Tropical
0:58:53 am GMT +0:00	Mean Node

Pt	Decl.	Long.	L.E.Dec
♃	-05°22'	16°♎40	13°♎37
♀	-05°52'	19°♈46	15°♓05
☾	-10°21'	26°♎51	26°♎51
♅	-10°51'	03°♓41	01°♓45
☋	-10°59'	28°♎38	28°♎38
☊	+10°59'	28°♈38	28°♈38
♇	-15°11'	22°♐30	11°♏11
♆	-16°48'	13°♒39	13°♒21
☿	-19°54'	12°♐45	28°♏50
♂	-19°59'	00°♐15	29°♏14
♄	+21°02'	25°♋23	25°♋30
♀	-21°12'	11°♐38	05°♐27
As	-21°39'	21°♑52	21°♑52
☉	-23°21'	04°♑35	04°♑35
⊗	+26°47'	15°♋28	29°♋54
☽	+27°42'	28°♊11	26°♉13

Columbia Explodes, February 1 2003 at 7:59 am at Huntsville, Tx, MW Feb 22

The Columbia Space Shuttle exploded across Texas and Louisiana as it attempted to return to earth. Seven crewmembers perished. The damaged tiles allowed hot atmospheric gases to penetrate the heat shield and destroy the internal wing structure, which caused the spacecraft to become unstable and break apart. It was a disaster that resonated around the world for the rest of the month.

The New Moon and the Sun were in Aquarius and conjunct Neptune (ruled by Uranus-Aquarius), right on the south node of Neptune (planet of the unknown and mysterious). Jupiter in Leo was on the north node of Neptune (the unknown) and opposing the Moon-Sun-Neptune. Uranus was very close to the Ascendant, representing the explosion. They all widely squared the Lunar Nodes while Mars (planet of mistakes and fevers/heat) was conjunct the Nodes and the MC. There was a long chain of declinations of Venus, Moon, Mercury, Lunar Nodes, Mars and Saturn that brought a tighter closeness to this wide square between the Lunar Nodes and Mars. Declinations can increase the linkage of planetary aspects that have wide longitude orbs. At the time of the explosion was 22 days before the squaring Moon Wobble but the power of Mars with the Nodes and the cluster of planets in Aquarius activated this Moon Wobble early with the Moon near the Ascendant.

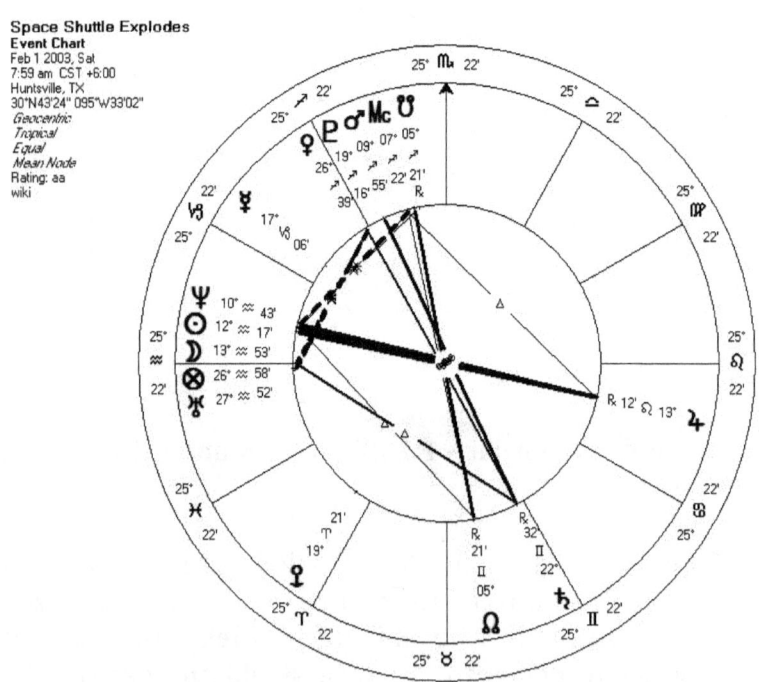

Space Shuttle Explodes				Huntsville, TX
Event Chart				30°N43'24" 095°W33'02"
Feb 1 2003, Sat		Equal		Geocentric, Tropical
7:59 am CST +6:00				Mean Node

Pt	Decl.	Long.	L.E.Dec
♀	-06°16'	19°♈21	14°♓03
⚷	-12°52'	27°♉52	25°♒55
As	-13°03'	25°♒22	25°♒22
♇	-13°47'	19°♐16	06°♏48
⊗	-16°53'	26°♒58	13°♒04
☉	-17°06'	12°♒17	12°♒17
♆	-17°30'	10°♒43	10°♒50
♃	+17°40'	13°♌12	10°♌14
☿	-20°40'	26°♐39	02°♐36
☽	-21°06'	13°♒53	25°♑06
⚷	-21°07'	17°♑06	25°♑01
☋	-21°11'	05°♐21	05°♐21
☊	+21°11'	05°♊21	05°♊21
Mc	-21°32'	07°♐22	07°♐22
♂	-21°34'	09°♐55	07°♐32
♄	+22°02'	22°♊32	10°♊37

World Trade Center Attack on September 11, 2001 at 8:46 am in New York City, MW Sept 24th

Four planes took off with terrorists organized by Osama bin Laden of Saudi Arabia. Two hit the World Trade buildings that collapsed, one hit the Pentagon, and the last one, intended for the White House, crashed in a field. This is the chart for the first plane. Many astrologers have written on this but few (only Frances McEvoy) discussed the planetary nodes in this event. It is my belief that astrology was used for the timing because chart is almost too perfect for success. That day, the Moon was conjunct the north lunar nodes and opposed by Mars (action, war). Venus was opposite Uranus at 18 and 21 degrees of Leo-

Aquarius, which places them exactly square the heliocentric nodes of Mars. Saturn was in opposition to Pluto and they were both on the heliocentric nodes of Uranus. The time of impact places the Midheaven at 16 Cancer on the heliocentric nodes of Pluto (cold military planning). Pluto has opposing Saturn and they were both on the heliocentric nodes of Uranus (unexpected, original, explosive). Mars, the planet of war, revenge and attack was OOB in extreme declination and the declinations of the Lunar Nodes with Jupiter and the Moon were tight.

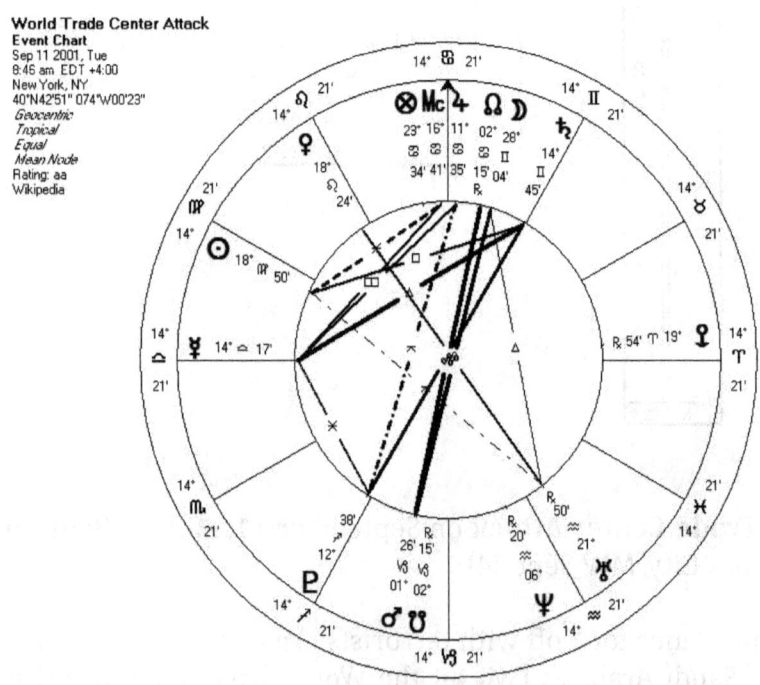

World Trade Center Attack		New York, NY
Event Chart		40°N42'51" 074°W00'23"
Sep 11 2001, Tue	Equal	Geocentric, Tropical
8:46 am EDT +4:00		Mean Node

Pt	Decl.	Long.	L.E.Dec
☉	+04°24'	18°♍50	18°♍50
As	-05°39'	14°♎21	14°♎21
♀	-06°29'	19°♈54	13°♓29
☿	-07°12'	14°♎17	18°♎23
♇	-12°12'	12°♐38	02°♏05
♅	-14°56'	21°♒50	19°♒35
♀	+15°47'	18°♌24	16°♌49
♆	-18°33'	06°♒20	06°♒51
♄	+20°47'	14°♊45	03°♊09
⊗	+20°56'	23°♋34	26°♋01
☾	+22°23'	16°♋41	16°♋41
♃	+22°44'	11°♋35	13°♋41
☽	+22°58'	28°♊04	18°♊58
☊	+23°25'	02°♋15	02°♋15
☋	-23°25'	02°♑15	02°♑15
♂	-26°47'	01°♑26	29°♑56

Columbine HS Shooting 13 Dead, April 20 1999 at 11:19am Littleton, Co, MW May 8th

This day two students killed 13 other students and wounded 24 out of resentment of others. Eric Harris was born on April 9, 1981 in Wichita, Kansas and Dylon Klebold was born on September 11, 1981 in Lakewood, Colorado.

The Sun was conjunct with Saturn in early Taurus, squaring the lunar nodes and Uranus. In addition, Mars was exactly opposing Saturn in a wide square to Uranus. This wide grand square involved the Sun, Saturn, Mars, Uranus, Nodes and Neptune, all in fixed signs. This points to determined actions that were volatile and impulsive. Strangely, Venus was OOB describing extreme attitudes toward friends and piers.

The tight declination of Pluto, Saturn, Sun and Mars helped to intensify that t-square between 10-12 degrees of declination. The lunar nodes themselves were exactly square the heliocentric nodes of Mars, increasing the likelihood of violent acts.

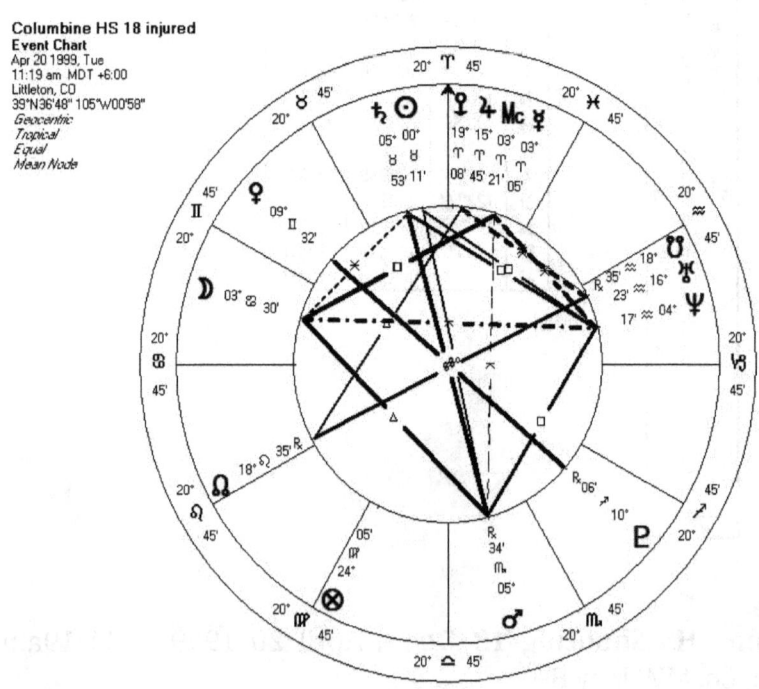

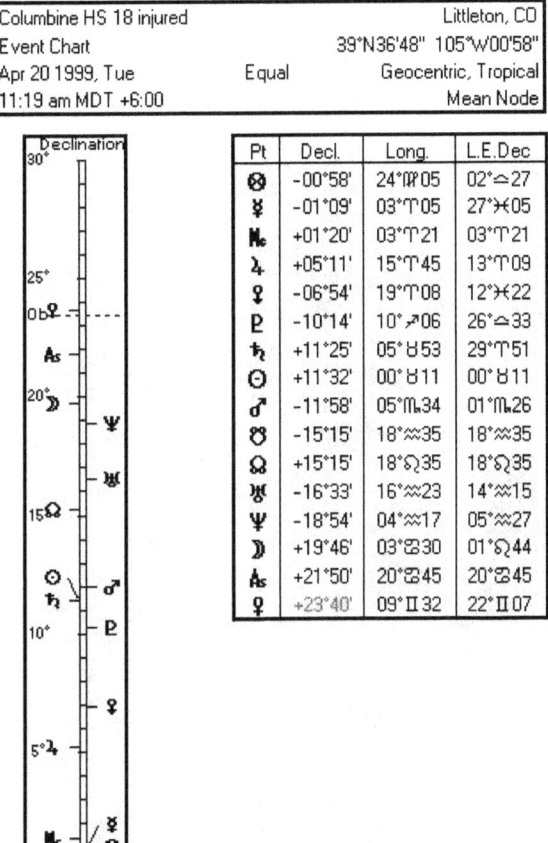

People with Squaring Nodes

This section is of famous persons born under a squaring Moon Wobble to show how this affects their life. This is especially true for Queen Elizabeth II and Joe Biden. These are examples to give the reader an idea of how these aspects influence their lives because transits to these points can indicate dramatic turning points in the future of those born with these aspects.

Amy Winehouse born September 14, 1983 at 10:23 pm in London. MW Sept 14

Amy Winehouse was a noted singer with great emotionality and musicality. Sadly, she had a serious addiction problem that led to her overdose death on July 25, 2011. She is one of the many young deaths around the age of 27 at the one and one-half cycle of the lunar nodes. Amy was born with the nodes on her Ascendant-Descendant axis along with Neptune and the Moon (which happened to be Out of Bounds). All this was square to her Sun and Mercury in Virgo. It was the Moon OOB-Neptune combo that points to her addiction problems and great emotionality.

333

Amy singer Winehouse
Female Chart
Sep 14 1983, Wed
10:23 pm BST -1:00
London, England
51°N30' 000°W10'
Geocentric
Tropical
Equal
Mean Node
Rating: aa
BC online

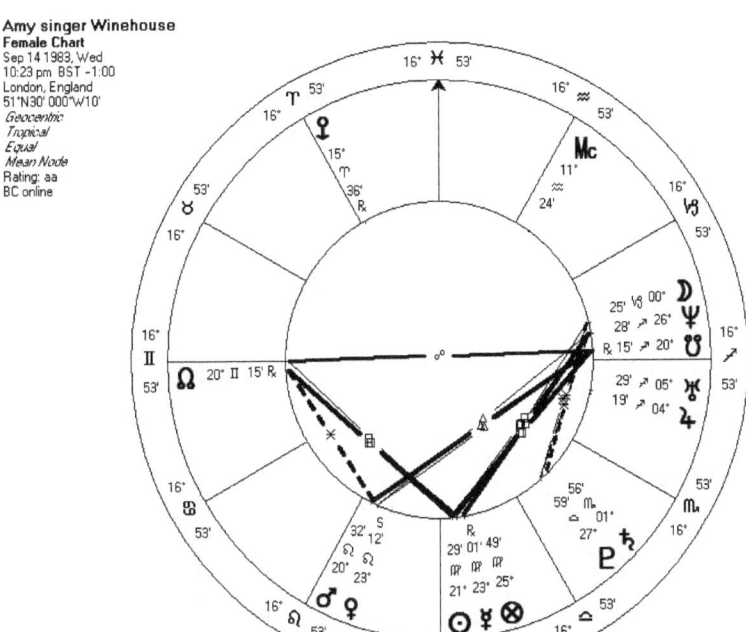

Amy singer Winehouse		London, England
Female Chart		51°N30' 000°W10'
Sep 14 1983, Wed	Equal	Geocentric, Tropical
10:23 pm BST -1:00		Mean Node

Pt	Decl.	Long.	L.E.Dec
☿	-00°25'	23°♍01	01°♎03
⊗	+00°51'	25°♍49	27°♍49
☉	+03°22'	21°♍29	21°♍29
♇	+04°40'	27°♎59	18°♍10
♀	+07°16'	23°♌12	11°♍27
♄	-10°01'	01°♏56	25°♎58
♀	-11°10'	15°♈36	00°♓49
♂	+15°46'	20°♌32	16°♌52
☽c	-17°21'	11°♒24	11°♒24
♃	-20°28'	04°♐19	01°♐33
♅	-21°08'	05°♐29	05°♐05
♆	-22°10'	26°♐28	11°♐35
As	+22°47'	16°♊53	16°♊53
☋	-23°04'	20°♐15	20°♐15
☊	+23°04'	20°♊15	20°♊15
☽	-24°18'	00°♑25	15°♑07

At the time of death, transiting Mars and the transiting lunar nodes had come to her lunar nodes to aspect her T-square of Sun-Mercury-Nodes-Neptune-Mars. She made a fatal mistake coming out of rehab that cost her life. It didn't help that transiting Pluto in early Capricorn had been conjuncting her Moon -- likely making her more emotional and obsessive-compulsive.

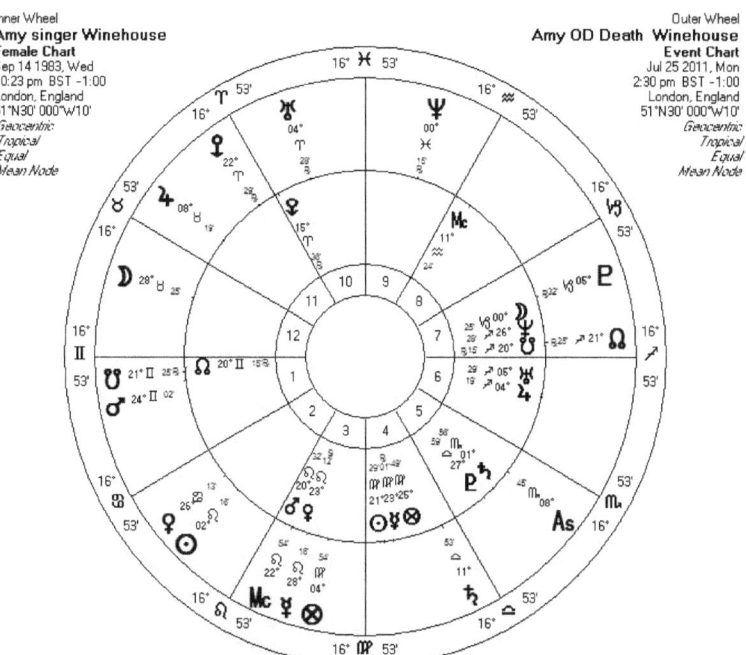

Winehouse on the inside ring, her death on the outside ring

Charlie Sheen born September 3, 1965 at 10:48 pm in New York City, MW Sept 2

Charlie Sheen is a well-known actor who has had constant addiction problems, serial sex episodes and anger problems. After many run-ins and difficulties, he was finally terminated from CBS on March 7, 2011. Sheen was born one day from a squaring Moon Wobble with an OOB Moon. He had Sun-Uranus-Pluto all opposed to Saturn. Here is the bad boy who needs to have it his way, is a rebel in confronting limitations and responsibilities.

337

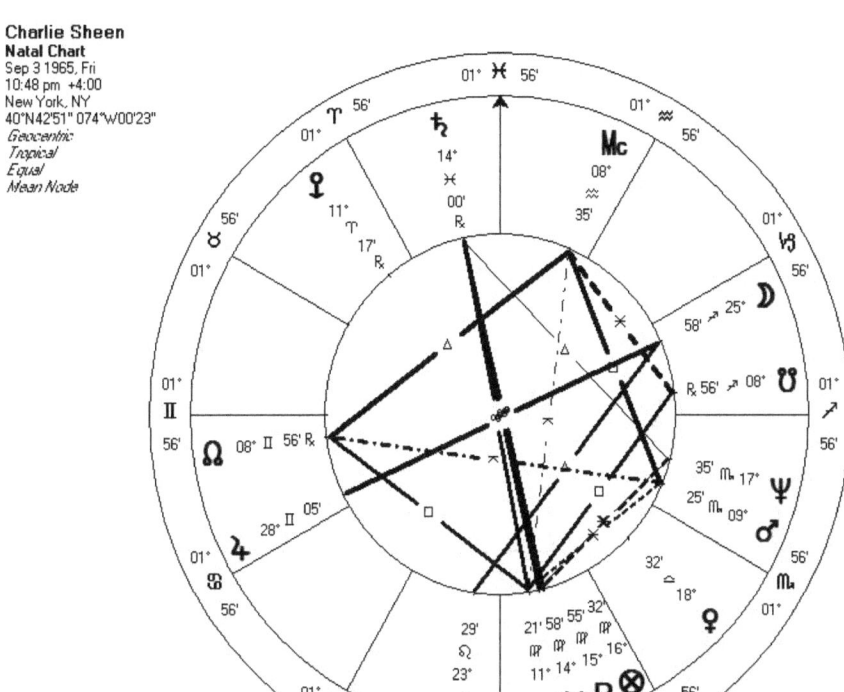

Charlie Sheen			New York, NY
Natal Chart			40°N42'51" 074°W00'23"
Sep 3 1965, Fri		Equal	Geocentric, Tropical
10:48 pm +4:00			Mean Node

Pt	Decl.	Long.	L.E.Dec
⊗	+03°58'	16°♍32	19°♍58
♅	+06°35'	14°♍58	13°♍13
♀	-07°14'	18°♎32	18°♎28
☉	+07°18'	11°♍21	11°♍21
♄	-08°15'	14°♓00	08°♓49
☿	+14°03'	23°♌29	22°♌23
♂	-15°16'	09°♏25	11°♏26
♆	-15°24'	17°♏35	11°♏55
♀	-15°46'	11°♈17	16°♒52
Mc	-18°07'	08°♒35	08°♒35
♇	+18°22'	15°♍55	07°♌36
As	+20°33'	01°♊56	01°♊56
☋	-21°47'	08°♐56	08°♐56
☊	+21°47'	08°♊56	08°♊56
♃	+22°56'	28°♊05	18°♊25
☽	-24°50'	25°♐58	10°♐46

When transiting nodes crossed his Moon-Jupiter opposition, his luck and money source ended. The termination was also near a squaring Moon Wobble on March 19th with the transiting Sun on Sheen's Saturn (consequences) opposing all his Sun-Uranus-Pluto. Transiting Neptune (drug addiction) was very near his 10th house cusp of career. Transiting Mars (anger and mistakes) was on the other side of his 10th cusp (authorities over you) so CBS was sick of dealing with him. Transiting was Uranus squaring his Moon-Jupiter opposition so there was an abrupt change of income. Management was finally fed up with his out of control behaviors despite the money he brought into the network.

339

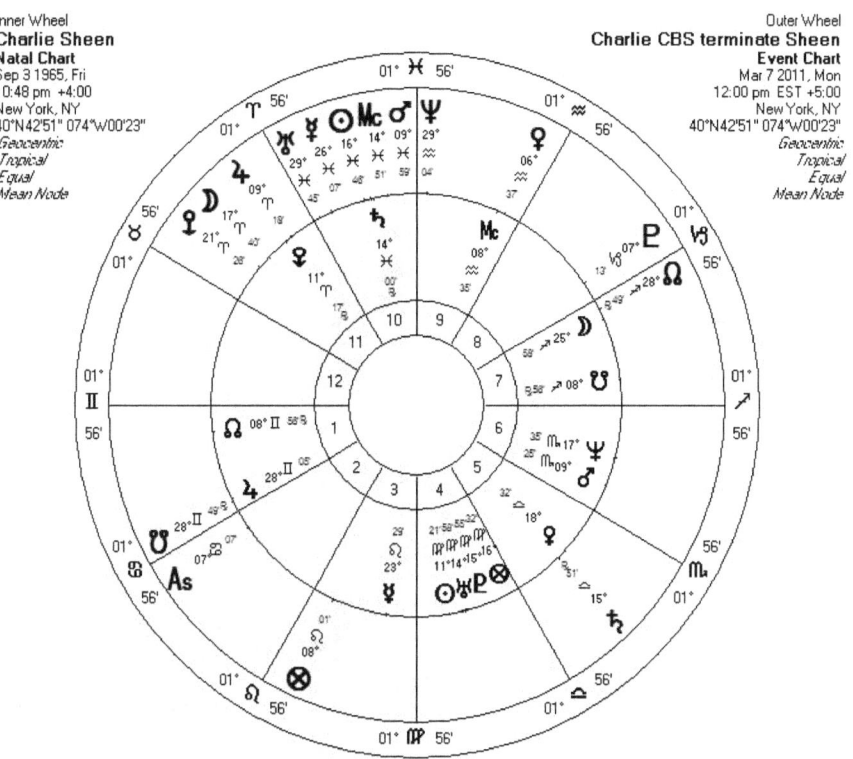

Sheen in the inner ring, CBS firing in the outer ring

Jimi Hendrix born November 27, 1942 at 10:15 am in Seattle, WA, MW Nov 22

One of the greatest rock guitar musicians, Hendrix was another of the 27 Club that died too young at the 1.5 nodal return. He had a dramatic t-square cluster of six planets that were also in very close declination; this simply increased the intensity of his Mercury-Sun-Venus conjunction (creative, talented guitarist), squared by the Nodes and opposed by the Saturn-Uranus conjunction.

341

Jimi Hendrix
Natal Chart
Nov 27 1942, Fri
9:45 am PWT +7:00
Seattle, WA
47°N36'23" 122°W19'51"
Geocentric
Tropical
Equal
Mean Node

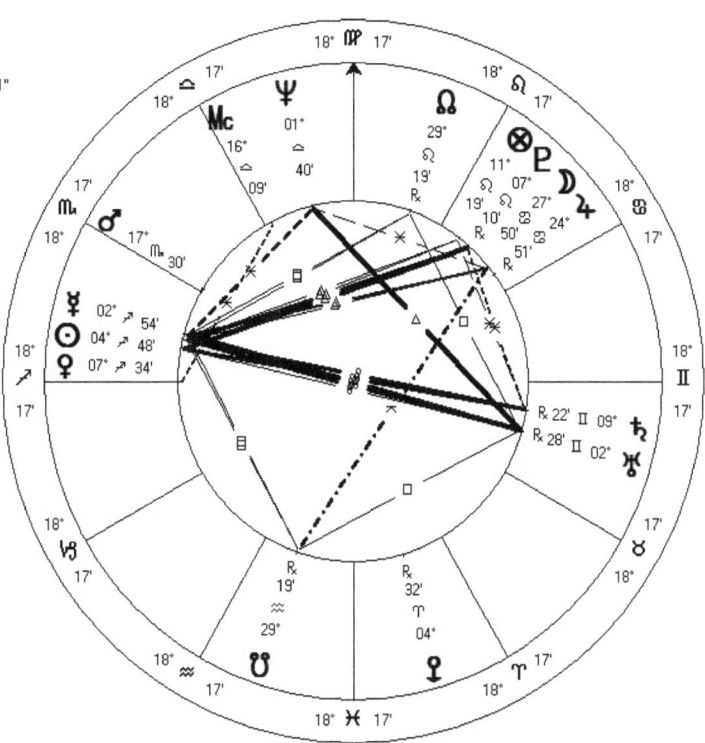

Jimi Hendrix		Seattle, WA
Natal Chart		47°N36'23" 122°W19'51"
Nov 27 1942, Fri	Equal	Geocentric, Tropical
9:45 am PWT +7:00		Mean Node

Pt	Decl.	Long.	L.E.Dec
♆	+00°32'	01°♎40	28°♍38
☿	-06°21'	16°♎09	16°♎09
☋	-11°42'	29°♒19	29°♒19
☊	+11°42'	29°♌19	29°♌19
⊗	+14°53'	11°♌19	19°♌44
♂	-16°49'	17°♏30	16°♏39
☽	+18°03'	27°♑50	08°♌48
♄	+19°56'	09°♊22	28°♉58
♅	+20°30'	02°♊28	01°♊41
☉	-21°06'	04°♐48	04°♐48
☿	-21°10'	02°♐54	05°♐12
♃	+21°19'	24°♋51	23°♋53
♀	-21°27'	07°♐34	06°♐50
♀	-21°54'	04°♈32	20°♑17
As	-22°55'	18°♐17	18°♐17
♇	+23°19'	07°♌10	05°♋31

We again see transiting Mars coming to the square of this six-planet cluster and the transiting Nodes approaching the opposition to his Lunar Nodes. The fact that transiting Saturn had been opposing his Mars pointed to some depression or limitation that might have added to his addictions. Transiting Jupiter, his ruling planet, was approaching the square to his natal Pluto at the time, likely intensifying whatever else was going on in his life.

343

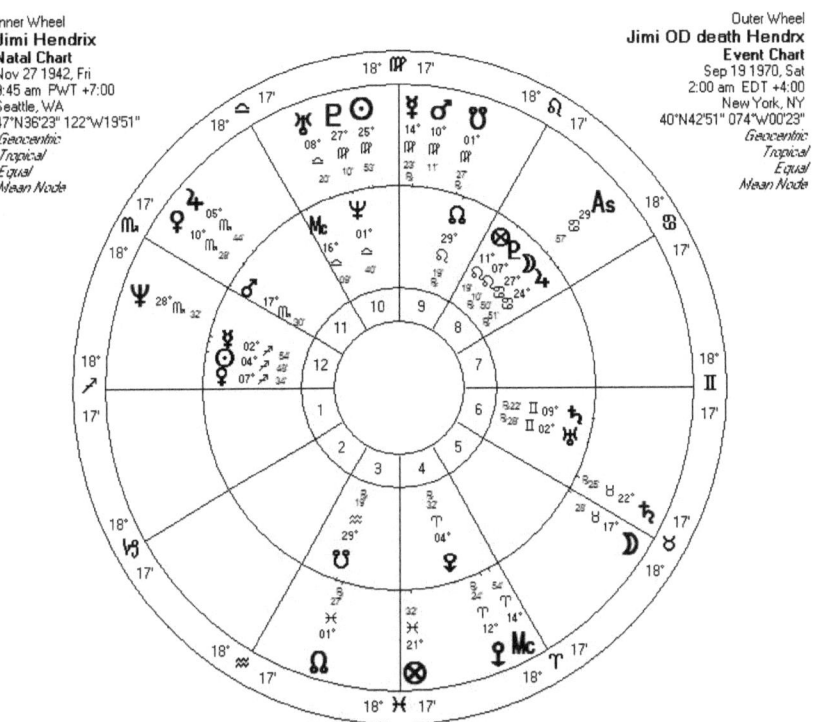

Hendrix in the inner ring, his Death in the outer ring

Roseanne Barr born November 3, 1952 at 1:21 pm in Salt Lake City, UT, MW Nov 9

Roseanne Barr has been a controversial comedienne with a strong voice that put her on TV with her own sitcom. She has an extreme chart with Mars, Moon and Venus all OOB. With a declination chain of six planets, Pluto-Uranus-Mercury-Venus-Mars-Moon, her energy and talent is original and intense. She tends to be highly impulsive and perhaps reckless with natal Mars opposing Uranus, suggesting possible problems with self-control.

345

Roseanne Barr
Natal Chart
Nov 3 1952, Mon
1:21 pm MST +7:00
Salt Lake City, Utah
40°N45' 111°W53'
Geocentric
Tropical
Equal
Mean Node

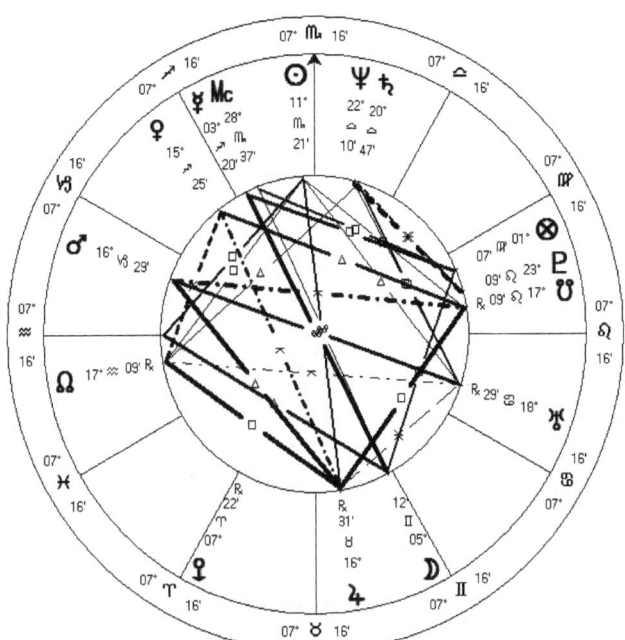

Roseanne Barr		Salt Lake City, Utah	
Natal Chart		40°N45' 111°W53'	
Nov 3 1952, Mon	Equal	Geocentric, Tropical	
1:21 pm MST +7:00		Mean Node	

Pt	Decl.	Long.	L.E.Dec
♄	-06°01'	20°♎47	15°♎16
♆	-07°08'	22°♎10	18°♎11
☉	-15°14'	11°♏21	11°♏21
♃	+15°30'	16°♉31	12°♉13
⊗	+15°32'	01°♍07	17°♌41
☊	-15°41'	17°♒09	17°♒09
☋	+15°41'	17°♌09	17°♌09
As	-18°27'	07°♒16	07°♒16
♀	-19°19'	07°♈22	03°♒41
Mc	-19°51'	28°♏37	28°♏37
♇	+22°28'	23°♌09	16°♋04
♅	+22°34'	18°♋29	15°♋10
☿	-23°21'	03°♐20	25°♐03
♀	-24°04'	15°♐25	17°♐00
♂	-24°08'	16°♑29	13°♑34
☽	+25°52'	05°♊12	04°♊36

She had a famous episode when she sang the Star-Spangled Banner badly on July 25, 1990 under a Moon Wobble that squared her natal Sun (while transiting Pluto was close to her Sun). This formed a t-square between the transits and her natal placements.

347

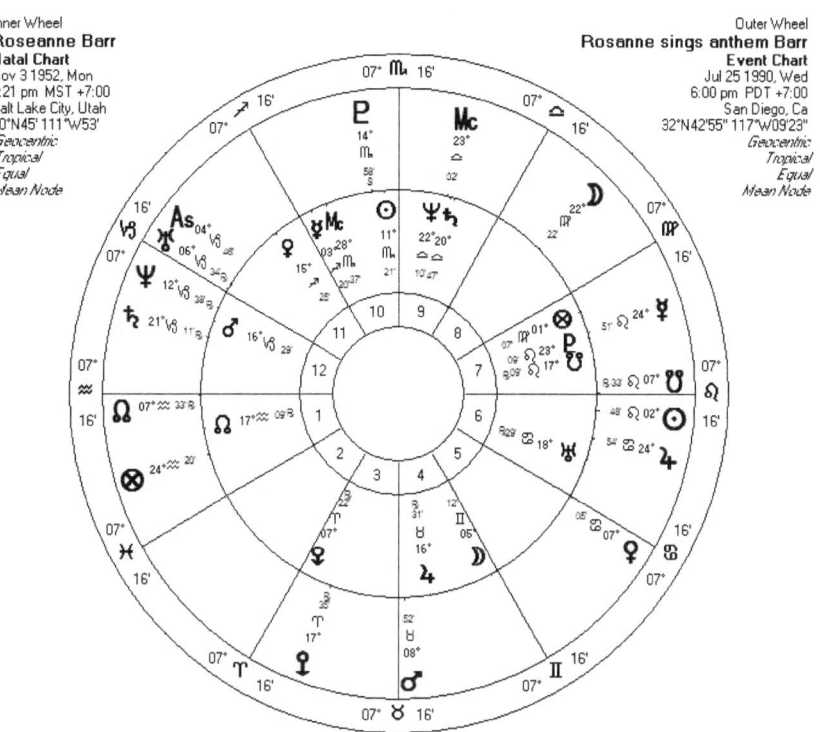

Rosanne in inner ring, Anthem Controversy in outer ring

She was finally terminated from TV on May 28, 2018 after a racist tweet. That transit had Mars and the Nodes crossing her Ascendant. With transiting Pluto on her natal Mars-Uranus opposition, she just went too far too quickly to recover from another mistake.

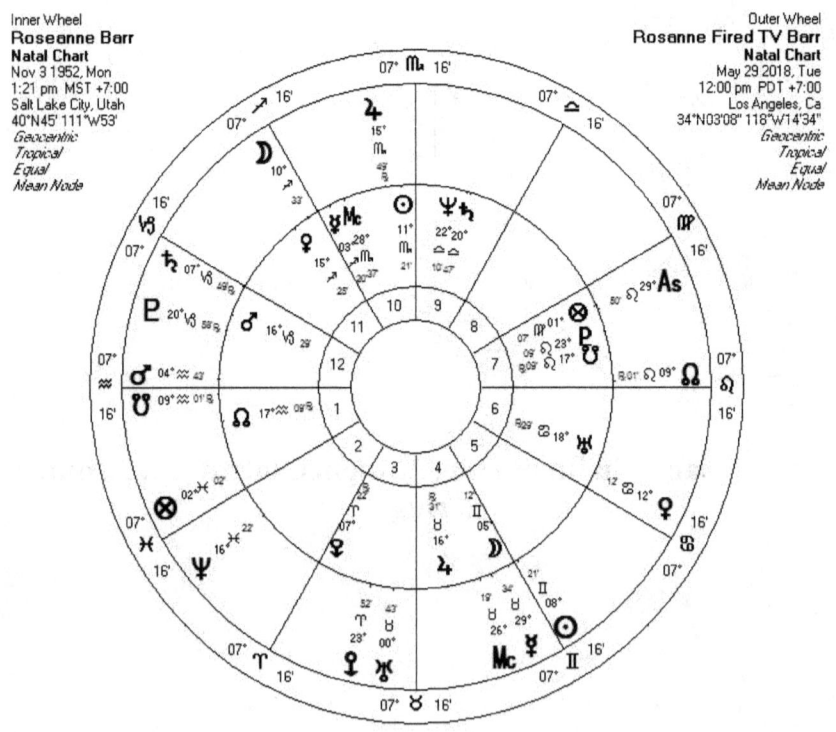

Rosanne Barr in inner ring, fired from TV in outer ring

Johnny Carson born October 23 1925 at 7:14 am in Corning, IW, MW Oct 24

Carson was considered one of the great TV personalities who dominated and defined late-night television for over 20 years. He was born one day from a squaring Moon Wobble and with Venus OOB. He was also famous for his multiples marriages and divorces that cost him lots of money. That OOB Venus was in his 2nd House of liquid assets. Carson said he had a cold, critical mother and he was known to be a very controlling executive. This is seen with Moon-Jupiter opposed by Pluto and squared by Mars that gives an intense attraction to women, stern mothers, executive ability and a very strict leader.

Johnny Carson
Natal Chart
Oct 23 1925, Fri
7:15 am +6:00
Corning, Iowa
40°N59'24" 094°W44'26"
Geocentric
Tropical
Equal
Mean Node
Rating: AA

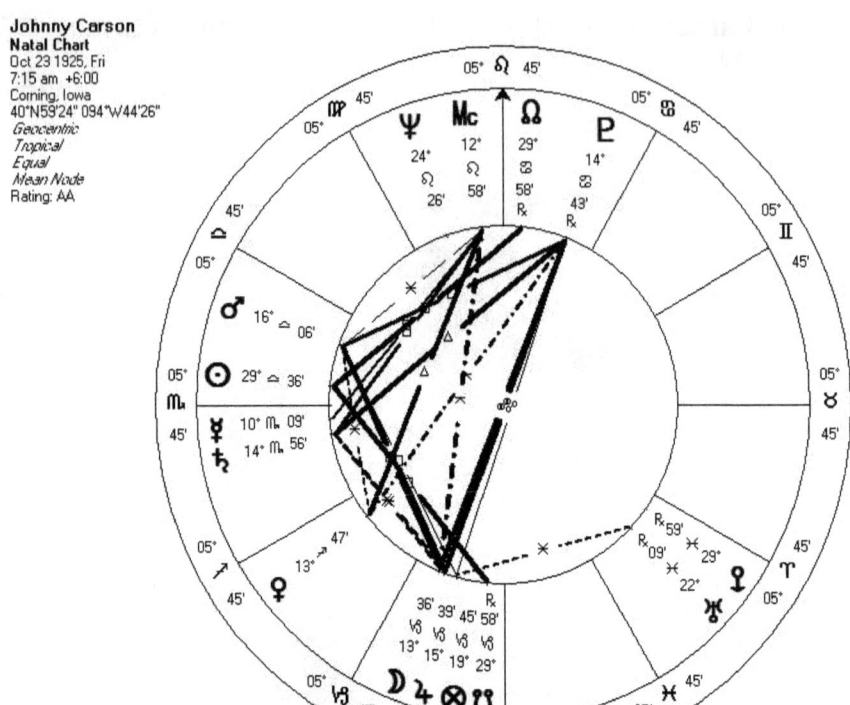

Johnny Carson			Corning, Iowa
Natal Chart			40°N59'24" 094°W44'26"
Oct 23 1925, Fri	Equal		Geocentric, Tropical
7:15 am +6:00			Mean Node

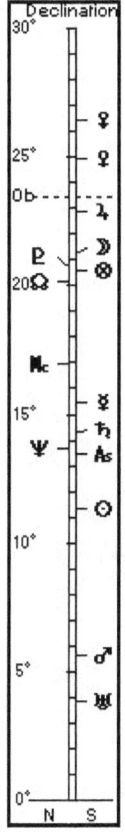

Pt	Decl.	Long.	L.E.Dec
♅	-03°50'	22°♓09	20°♓18
♂	-05°37'	16°♎06	14°♎16
☉	-11°20'	29°♎36	29°♎36
As	-13°26'	05°♏45	05°♏45
♆	+13°42'	24°♌26	23°♌25
♄	-14°20'	14°♏56	08°♏28
☿	-15°28'	10°♏09	12°♏05
Mc	+16°55'	12°♌58	12°♌58
☊	+20°09'	29°♋58	29°♋58
☋	-20°09'	29°♑58	29°♑58
⊗	-20°34'	19°♑45	27°♑57
♇	+20°49'	14°♋43	26°♋41
☽	-21°19'	13°♑36	23°♑54
♃	-22°53'	15°♑39	12°♑08
♀	-24°56'	13°♐47	10°♐07
☿	-26°24'	29°♓59	28°♑04

He had a major heart attack on March 19, 1999 that caused him to retire before he really wanted. Transiting T-square of Uranus-Nodes-Mars-Saturn all aligned to Carson's Saturn.

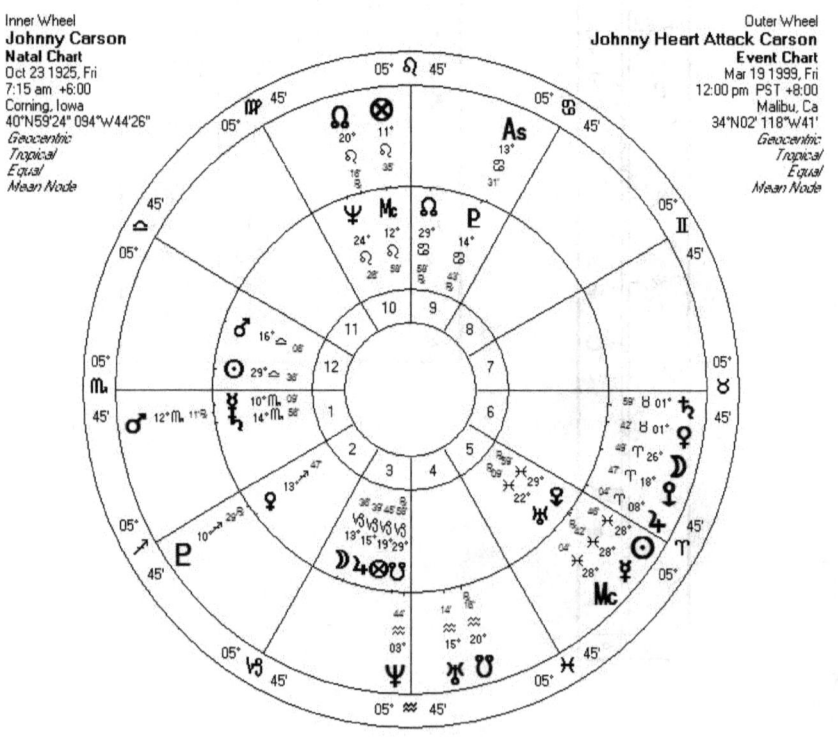

Carson in inner ring, Heart Attack in outer ring

His death occurred on January 23, 2005 under a squaring Moon Wobble. This time the Nodes were on his Sun with the transiting Sun on his Nodes. Again, transiting Mars was conjunct Pluto and squaring Carson's natal Uranus (sudden, fatal events).

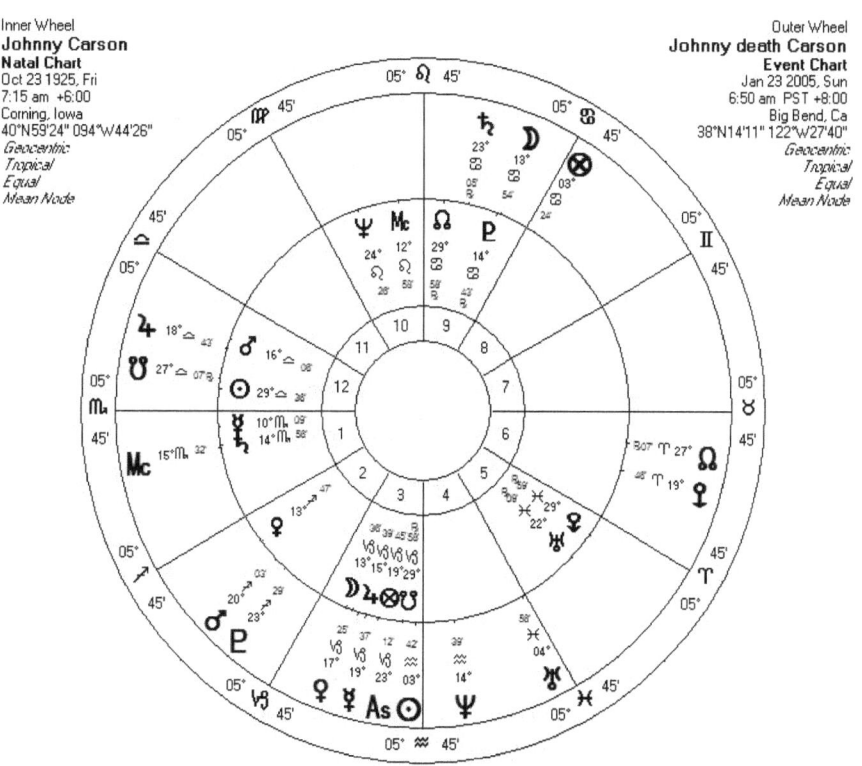

Carson in inner ring, his Death in the outer ring

354

Queen Elizabeth II born April 21, 1926 at 2:40 am in London, MW April 11

England's current monarch has been written about extensively but I want to concentrate on how Eclipses and Moon Wobbles with transits have turned her life around. She was born after a squaring Moon Wobble on April 11th and the lunar nodes are prominent in her chart since they are on her Ascendant-Descendant axis. Her Taurus Sun is in the 4th house of fixed assets, family heredity and real estate. She is the richest woman in the world. It's interesting that she has Eris (the natural ruler of Taurus-Fixed Earth) is OOB when she owns so many fixed assets of real estate.

Queen II, Elizabeth
Natal Chart
Apr 21 1926, Wed
2:40 am -1:00
London, England
51°N30' 000°W10'
Geocentric
Tropical
Equal
Mean Node
Rating: AA

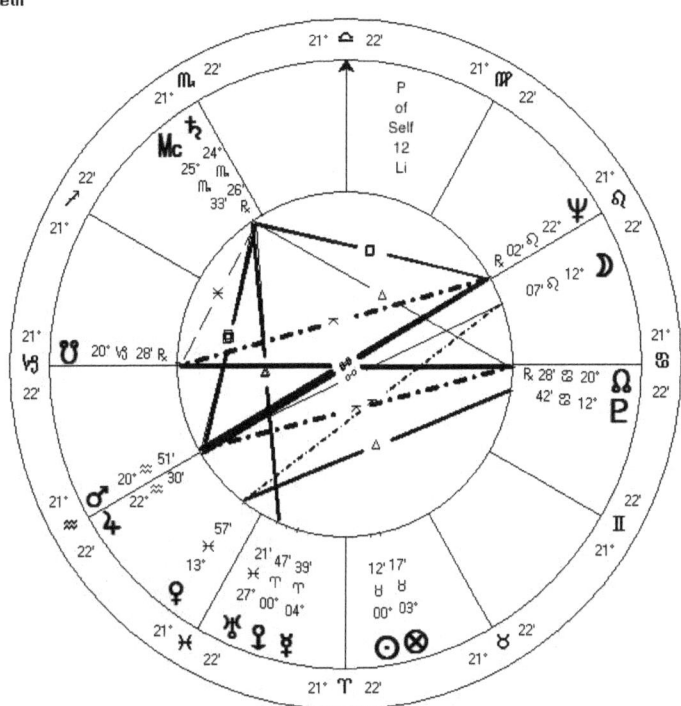

Queen II, Elizabeth		London, England
Natal Chart		51°N30' 000°W10'
Apr 21 1926, Wed	Equal	Geocentric, Tropical
2:40 am -1:00		Mean Node

Pt	Decl.	Long.	L.E.Dec
☿	+00°04'	04°♈39	00°♈12
♅	-01°43'	27°♓21	25°♓40
♀	-06°14'	13°♓57	14°♓08
☉	+11°32'	00°♉12	00°♉12
⊗	+14°24'	03°♉17	08°♉41
♆	+14°32'	22°♌02	20°♌51
♃	-14°38'	22°♒30	20°♒34
♂	-15°54'	20°♒51	16°♒29
♄	-16°33'	24°♏26	15°♏45
☽	+18°59'	12°♌07	05°♌08
Mc	-19°09'	25°♏33	25°♏33
♇	+21°13'	12°♋42	24°♋30
As	-21°44'	21°♑22	21°♑22
☊	+21°53'	20°♋28	20°♋28
☋	-21°53'	20°♑28	20°♑28
⚷	-25°33'	00°♈47	23°♑42

At the tender age of 10, her uncle abdicated (January 20, 1936) his role as king which put her in line to the throne. Transiting Uranus was on her Sun in the 4th house for this major change of hereditary duties. Edward VIII abdicated the day near a lunar eclipse on January 8th. It's interesting to note that transiting Eris (family duties) had joined her Mercury (work and service). The transiting nodes were on her natal Pluto and squaring her important Part of Self** at 12 Libra in the 9th house of religion (she would become the head of the Church when crowned queen).

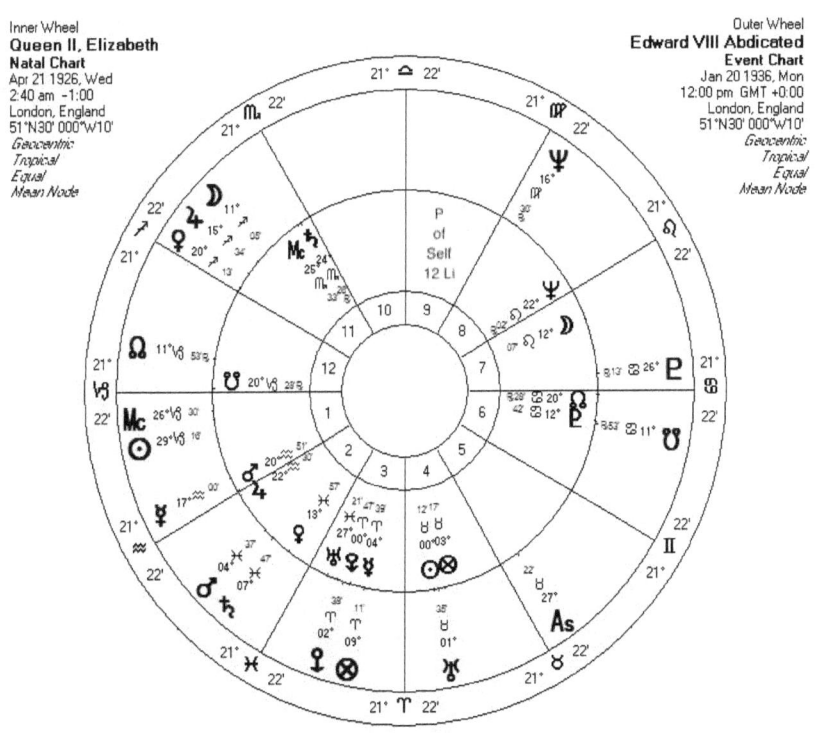

The Queen in inner ring, the Abdication in the outer ring

Her marriage to Prince Phillip was on November 20, 1947 in the month of a solar eclipse on November 12th. The transiting Nodes and Sun were on the Queen's Saturn and Midheaven (public prominence), and the transiting Mars-Saturn conjunction was on her Neptune. This formed a potent t-square involved five transiting planets to her natal powerhouse of fixed five planets: of Mars-Jupiter in Aquarius opposing Neptune in Leo, all squared by Saturn-Midheaven in Scorpio.

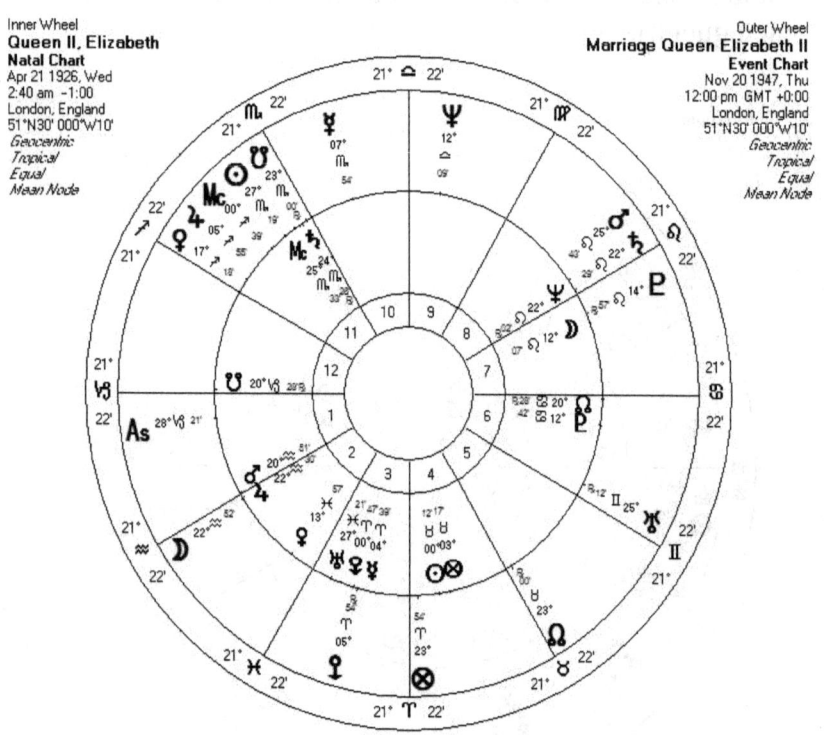

The Queen in inner ring, her Marriage in the outer ring

Her own father died on February 2, 1952 during an eclipse period with the North Lunar Node at 1 Pisces. Importantly, transiting Uranus had moved up to join her Pluto at 10 Cancer and transiting Jupiter was at 10 Aries reinforcing her Part of Self** at 12 Libra again in the 9th house. Transiting Saturn was at 14 Libra suggesting the responsibilities of office she was about to hold.

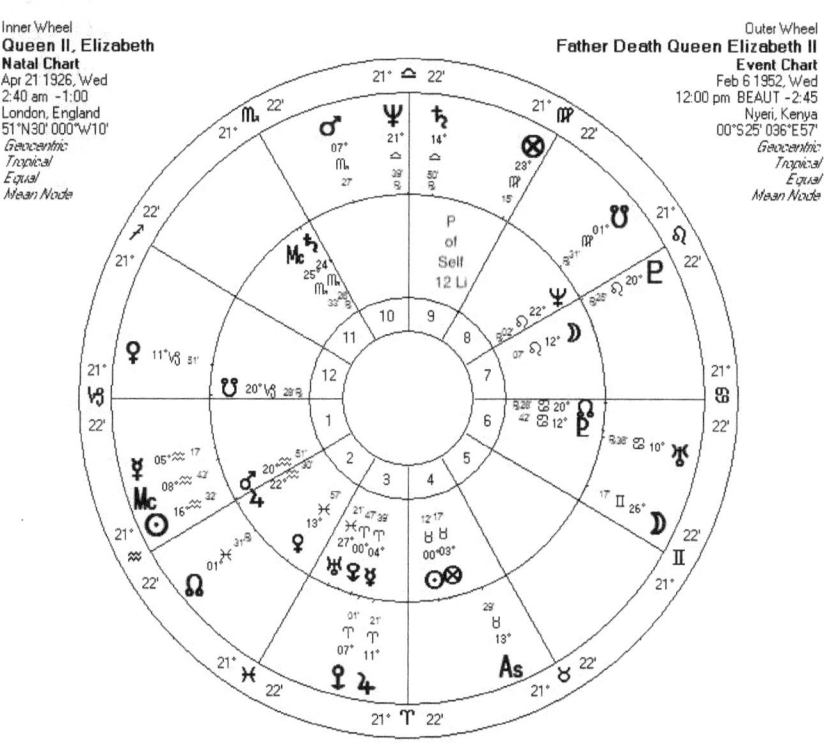

**The Queen in inner ring
Father's death in outer ring**

Skipping to 1992, she named this year Annus Horribillis. Prince Charles and Princess Di had a very public divorce that embarrassed the Family and then Windsor Castle caught fire on her wedding anniversary on November 20,, 1992. The fire didn't involve an eclipse or Moon Wobble but transiting Neptune and Uranus were opposing her Pluto (children and drastic events) and widely aspecting her natal Lunar Nodes and her Ascendant. Transiting Pluto had been sitting on her Saturn and the night of the fire, the Sun had just passed Pluto and was near the Queen's Midheaven for this public event. Curiously transiting Eris (fixed earth, homes and real estate) was squaring the transiting Neptune-Uranus conjunction close to her fourth house cusp (real estate and buildings). The transiting Nodes were squaring her Uranus of shocking events and were on her 6th-12th cusp axis of servants and workers. The fire cost 36 million pounds to repair. Workers had been in the chapel restoring art when a spotlight ignited a curtain. The fire spread across the attic.

361

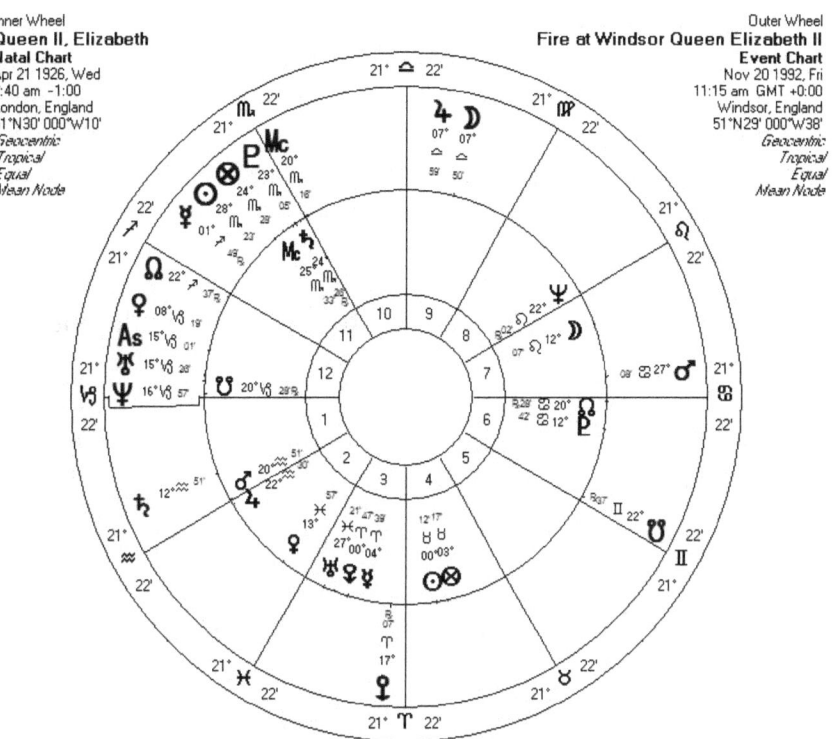

The Queen in inner ring
Windsor Fire in outer ring

Princess Di was killed in a car accident in Paris on August 31, 1997. The solar eclipse was the next day on September 1st and the Queen was highly criticized on how the royal family handled her funeral. That week transiting Mars was squaring Uranus, an edgy aspect that can bring accidents. Transiting Saturn was close to her 4th house cusp of family and she was keeping the family cloistered in Balmoral. The Prime Minister finally got them to attend Di's public funeral (the family had wanted a private funeral) in London to satisfy the public and save the Crown.

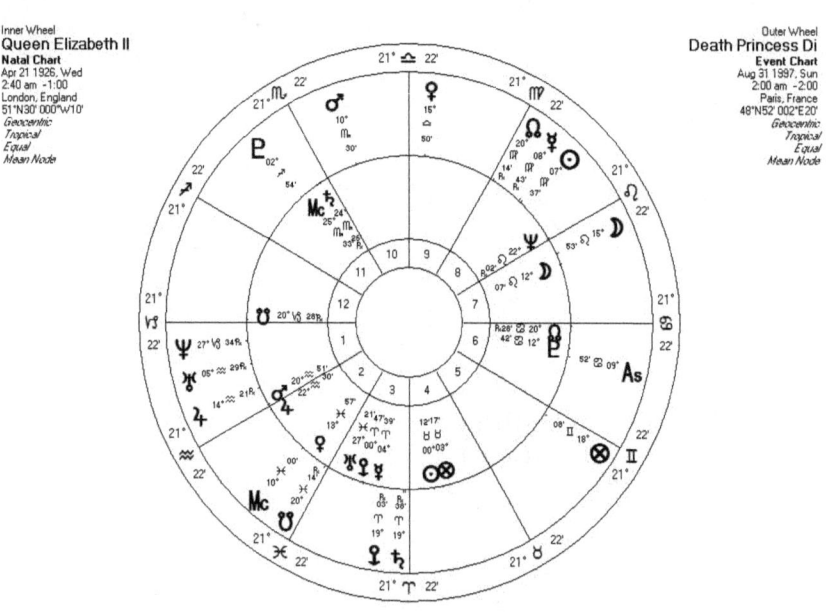

The Queen in inner ring
Death of Princess Di in outer ring

Joe Biden born November 20, 1942 at 8:30 am in Scranton, PN, MW Nov 22

Biden was born just two days from a squaring Moon Wobble that involves his Sun-Venus conjunction and its opposition to Uranus. These planets are very close to the Ascendant-Descendant axis. Natal Saturn is just six degrees further into his 7th house of partners. Seven degrees between Uranus and Saturn is wide but they straddle the Descendant so that cusp ties them together.

Joe Biden
Natal Chart
Nov 20 1942, Fri
8:30 am EWT +4:00
Scranton, Pennsylvania
41°N24'32" 075°W39'46"
Geocentric
Tropical
Equal
Mean Node

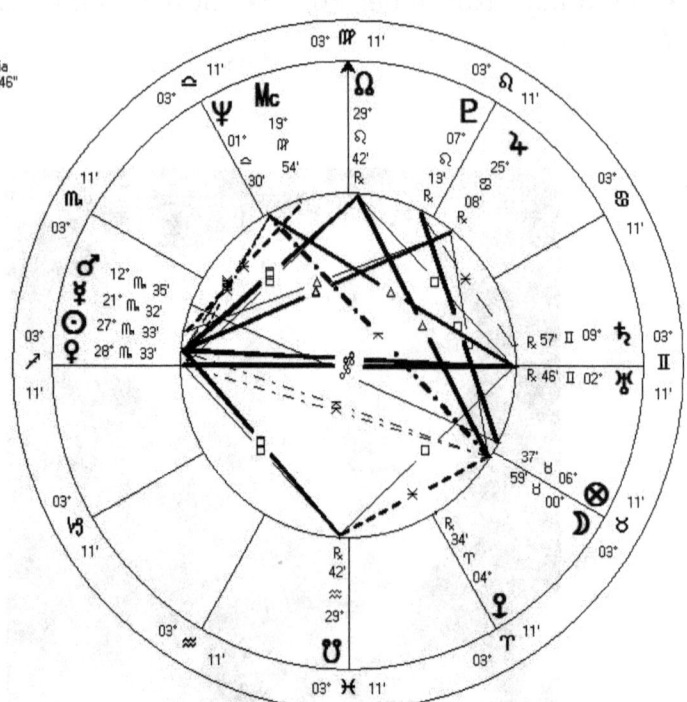

Joe Biden		Scranton, Pennsylvania
Natal Chart		41°N24'32" 075°W39'46"
Nov 20 1942, Fri	Equal	Geocentric, Tropical
8:30 am EWT +4:00		Mean Node

Pt	Decl.	Long.	L.E.Dec
♆	+00°36'	01°♎30	28°♍29
Mc	+03°59'	19°♍54	19°♍54
☽	+07°43'	00°♉59	19°♈43
⊗	+09°35'	06°♉37	24°♈46
☋	-11°34'	29°♒42	29°♒42
☊	+11°34'	29°♌42	29°♌42
♂	-15°19'	12°♏35	11°♏36
☿	-17°47'	21°♏32	20°♏10
♀	-19°27'	28°♏33	26°♏48
☉	-19°37'	27°♏33	27°♏33
♄	+20°00'	09°♊57	29°♉20
♅	+20°33'	02°♊46	01°♊58
As	-20°48'	03°♐11	03°♐11
♃	+21°15'	25°♋08	24°♋16
♀	-21°55'	04°♈34	20°♑12
♇	+23°17'	07°♌13	06°♋19

His wife and young daughter were killed in a car accident on December 18, 1972. His two sons were hospitalized but survived. He had just been elected a Senator and hadn't taken office yet in January 1973. This event marked his life with transiting Uranus squaring the Lunar Nodes in the 8th house of death. At the same time transiting Neptune was on his Ascendant and opposing his Uranus-Saturn conjunction straddling the 7th cusp - pointing to deep grief and depression. He was sworn into office at his sons' hospital beds.

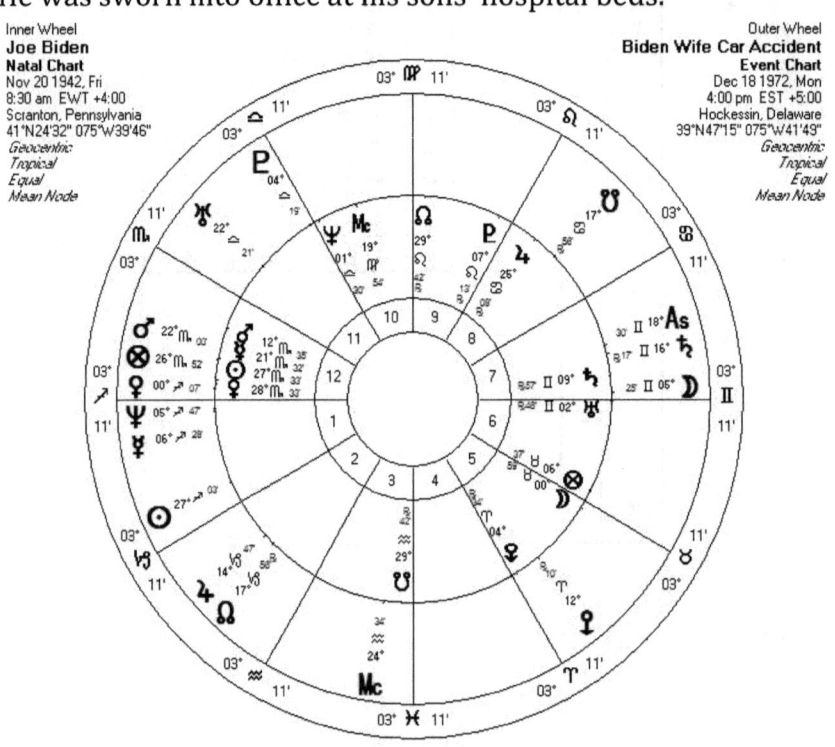

Biden inner ring, Wife's Death outer ring

In February 12, 1988 he experienced a brain aneurysm and had immediate surgery. This time the transits of Moon-Mars-Saturn-Uranus (all in Sagittarius in his first house) were squaring the transiting Lunar Nodes. Transiting Pluto was on his Mars (ruler of his Sun in Scorpio) at the same time and transiting Sun was on his personal Lunar Nodes near the 4th cusp. The Pluto transit created a life-death crisis but it took the transiting Sun to reach his natal Lunar Nodes to get him to the hospital for emergency surgery.

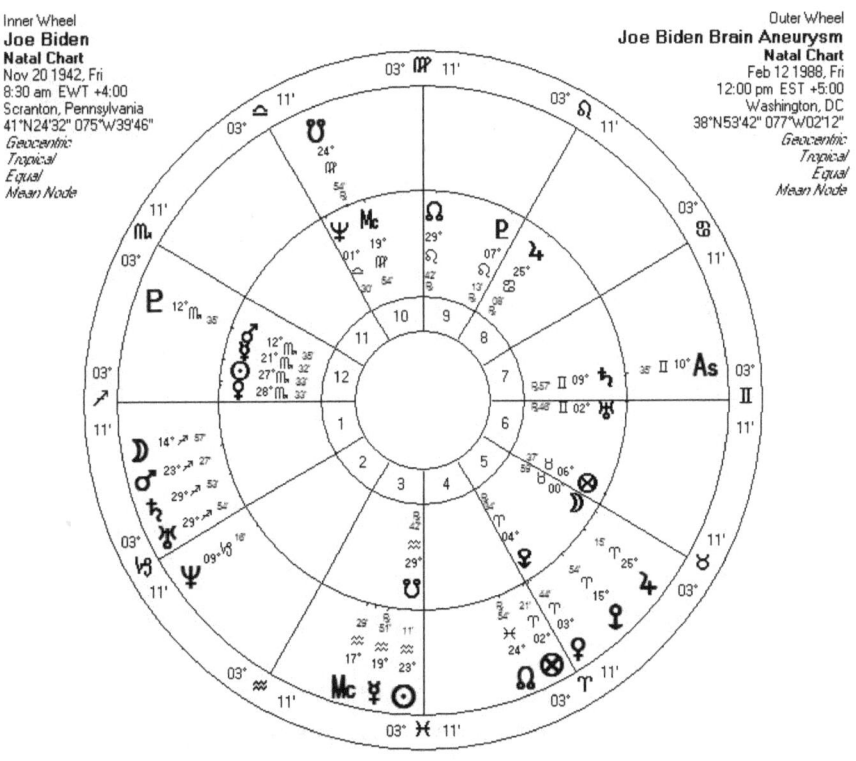

Biden in inner ring
Brain Aneurysm in outer ring

That Pluto transit wasn't done with him. He again had surgery for another brain aneurysm on May 8, 1988. Transiting Pluto was still on his natal Mars but this time transiting Jupiter and the Sun were opposing Pluto to activate another near death experience for Biden. The transiting Lunar Nodes were on his Midheaven for another life changing experience.

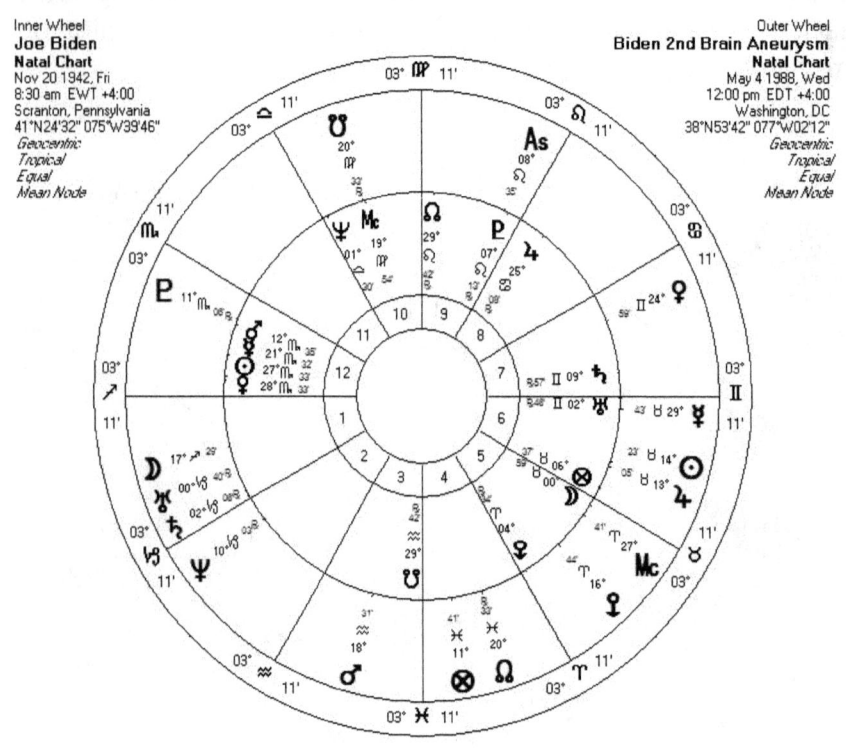

Biden in inner ring
Second Aneurysm in outer ring

Biden was greatly affected by the death of his oldest son Beau on May 30, 2015. Transiting Saturn was on his Ascendant and hitting his grand square. The transiting Sun was opposing transiting Saturn but it also landed on Biden's Uranus-Saturn so the week was a crisis point of grief and depression for him again.

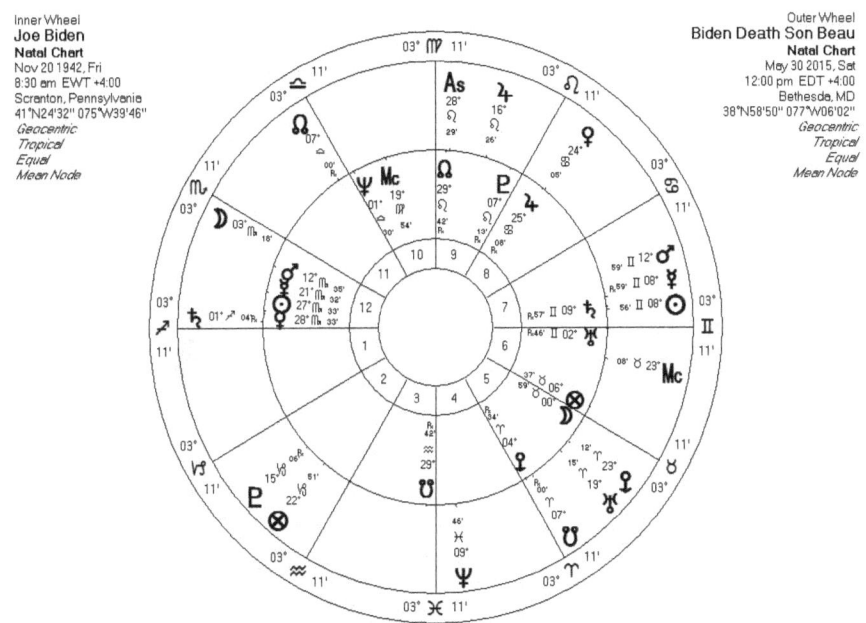

**Biden in inner ring
Death of Beau in outer ring**

As this is written, Biden is running for President against Donald Trump. Biden is likely to win this election but the results may take days for a winner to be announced because of the pandemic. His chances are good with the transiting Sun on his natal Mars which rules his Sun. Transiting Jupiter-Pluto opposes his Jupiter, sextiles his Sun-Venus and trines his Midheaven. He has luck with him, people like him and the public want stability. Transiting Venus is in Libra and transiting Mars is in Aries. They both sextile and trine his Ascendant and Part of Self* at 8 Sagittarius which is another plus. Transiting Uranus is on his Part of Fortune for luck and a dramatic change but the Moon in

Gemini is not in his favor that day. The transiting Lunar Nodes are in his First-Seventh houses which is good for a competition between opponents and public exposure. Transiting Mercury is squaring Saturn all that week and the election results are slow and tedious.

[Ed. Biden did win but Trump disputed the election. He encouraged a riot on the Capitol on January 6, 2021 and was impeached a second time on Jan 14, 2021. Trump left office without ever acknowledging Biden's win.

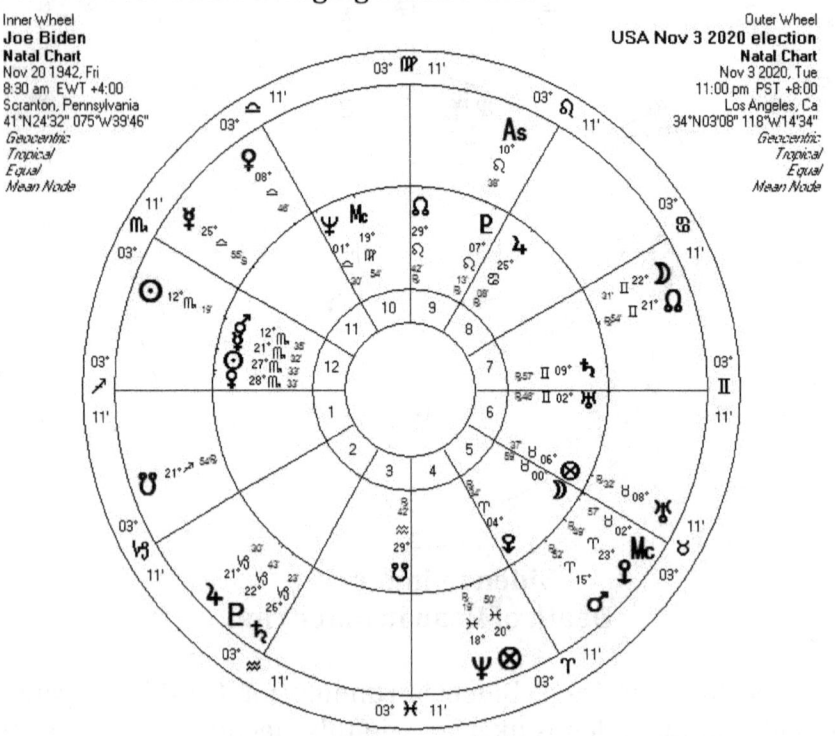

Biden in inner ring
US election in outer ring

The 2020 Pandemic has affected early voting and mail-in ballots that will take a week or more to be counted. This chart is for the closing of the polls on the west coast since Hawaii and Alaska never determine an election.

The year 2021 looks very difficult for him with an economic depression and a pandemic to manage. It will likely strain his health and greatly wear on him. He has wanted this all of his life in his service to America and he still tries to be a bridge between the two political parties.

2020 Pandemic

This book has been completed January 2021 during the 2nd wave of the Great Pandemic of 2020. Vaccines are being produced but the end of the pandemic is not sure since production and distribution are problems. This past year was dominated by slow heavy planets in the sign of Capricorn which is associated stagnation, restriction, old age and death. One could say this was a year when the world stayed home, the elderly were most severely affected with hospitalizations and death. The world economy dropped and governments had to help support people with money and food distributions. All governments under reported 2020 deaths by about 25% below the averaged death rates in cities.

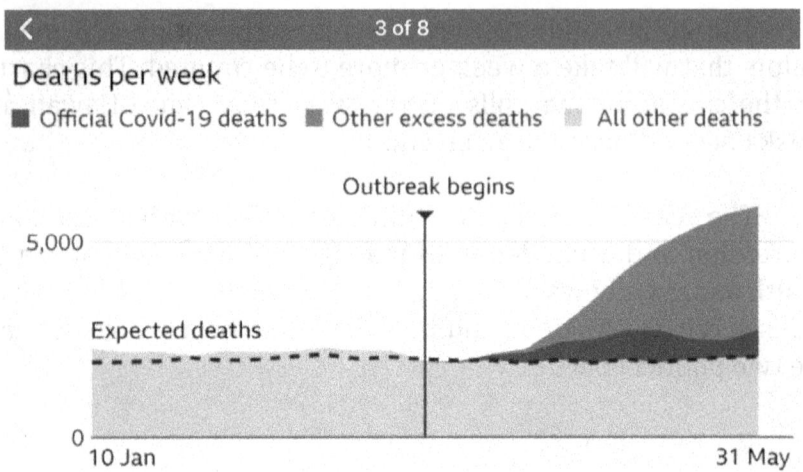

Excess Deaths in USA by NYT

During the 1918 pandemic that lasted 15 months, there were three waves with the second wave being the most lethal. Pluto and Jupiter were together in Cancer with a total of 670,000 US death, most of them in the prime of their life. The most deathly part was August – December of 1918. There was also a Saturn in Leo opposing Uranus in Aquarius during this second wave. During this entire period, the north lunar was in Sagittarius (sign of globalization and foreign travel), the south lunar node in Gemini (rules of lungs).

In 2019, Wuhan, China discovered Covid-19 in mid-December 2019 but actively covered it up and didn't release the genome sequence until January 11th. By then it had spread around the world and major outbreaks happened in cities with dense populations. This all occurred during an eclipse period that say Trump impeached and put on trial.

Astrologically the signatures between these pandemics had similarities. This time Pluto, Saturn and Jupiter were all in Capricorn, the sign of restriction, old age and death. 85% of deaths from Covid-19 were ages 60-90+. This time Eris (ruler of Taurus, home) squaring the big three of Pluto, Saturn and Jupiter. The world was sent home to isolate from each other. The lunar nodes started in Cancer-Capricorn but by June they had moved into Gemini (lungs)-Sagittarius. This time Mars stayed extra long in Aries because every two years it goes retrograde. From the end of June 2020 to January 6, 2021, Mars was continuously in Aries (sign of youth, aggression, war and risk-taking). All summer the US had #BLM Black Lives Matter protests and the growth of QAnon, Proud Boys and the Three Percent militant groups. There was a summer spike of Covid-19 but the major death toll was November 2020 through February 2021 when the USA averaged 3-4,000 dead each day. So the combination of Pluto-Jupiter conjunctions and the lunar nodes in Gemini-Sagittarius repeated themselves in each pandemic but they were six signs apart by the nodes being reversed and the two heavies being in the opposite signs of Cancer vs Capricorn. The famous French astrologer, Andre Baubault predicted this pandemic years earlier.

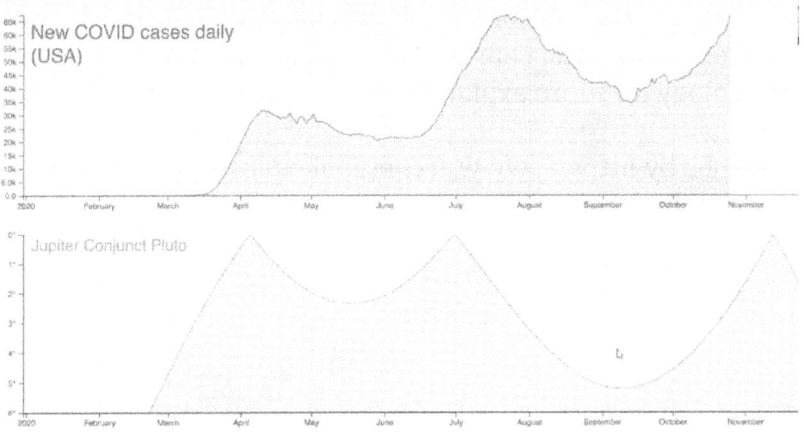

Deaths plotted against Pluto-Jupiter 2020***

References

Paradise Fire: https://abc7news.com/camp-fire-video-bodycam-of-evacuations/4850913/

Astrodatabank.com and Frank Clifford databases for famous persons. Only timed birth charts were used.

* Cosmos and Psyche by Richard Tarnas uses a wide 15 degree or more orb for long slow transits in mundane work.

**The Part of Self is calculated Ascendant + Ascendant – Sun = Part of Self. In astrology software Solar Fire, this must be added to the Arabic Parts Editor. Halloran Software will calculate Solar Arabic Parts and Sirius Software will calculate these points under Tobey's Secondary Ascendant. It acts as another Ascendant that is hidden in the natal chart. Also reference my book, Foundations of Astrology for more explanation.

***Graphs by https://www.archetypalexplorer.com and The Astrology Podcast 2020.

Memories of Former Students of Tobey

My Experience with Carl Payne Tobey
By Diane Elizabeth Clarke

One of the most profound turning points in my life took place the day I was introduced to Carl Payne Tobey's "clockwise house system". At a holiday party in early December 1971, I serendipitously struck up a conversation with a fellow astrology aficionado, Wayne Cowdrey. He was studying at *Prosperos*, a metaphysical institute in Los Angeles founded by Thane, one of Tobey's long-time friends & supporters. Wayne enthusiastically shared Tobey's ideas with me and proceeded to draw up the Leo 1st house design on a cocktail napkin.

Instantly, bells & whistles started going off in my head! All the issues I'd had with the traditional house/sign/planet associations had suddenly cleared up upon seeing the image of the reversed wheel. At last, the pieces all came together! It was as though some great truth had just been revealed to me, one that was so compelling that I knew that there was no turning back. I was so excited! Little did I know at the time that Pluto had just crossed my ascendant and Uranus was in exact trine to my natal Uranus. It was certainly a significant initiation – one that was to send me off on the major journey of my life!

My interest in astrology had awakened in the spring of '67, just a month prior to my graduation from UCSB, when on a blind date with a fellow Virgoan. His uncanny insights into my sign, as well as those of mutual friends, immediately piqued my *mercurial* interest. From there on, I embarked upon my astrological quest – reading any book I could get my hands on, taking any class available, attending conferences, networking & studying with other astrologers, interpreting charts for my friends and doing mini-readings at psychic fairs.

But as much as I was enthralled with astrology, the discrepancies between what I had been taught or read in books —and what I was learning from firsthand feedback—confused & baffled me. The so-called *astrological alphabet*, based on the commonly-used flat chart (which begins with Aries and goes counter-clockwise), left me cold. The correlations of the signs with houses made no sense at all based on my observations. I'd learned to set up horoscopes using the *Placidus* system, but along the way, I was introduced to the *equal house system*. After comparing the various house systems amidst the 200 charts of friends & family I'd collected at the time, it became obvious that the equal houses were the most accurate. This was a great improvement, but there were still too many lingering questions. Something was missing from the equation. And as a result, my astrology studies remained only a part-time hobby.

And then—in that magical instant—my passion for astrology was reawakened! It was time to delve deeper. I started taking classes at *Prosperos,* where I met Marcy Nelson, a serious student of Tobey's correspondence course. She shared the course materials with me, and for the next several years, we met regularly to go over charts and test out his theories. By November 1972, it became clear that my obsession with astrology was first & foremost in my life and—with Pluto now back on my ascendant and conjunct my Jupiter—walked away from my job as a social worker and took a flying leap into the great unknown! I had never had an official reading and didn't know what an astrologer actually did, but I was determined to figure it out and be the best astrologer I could be!

I was fortunate to finally met Tobey in person in January 1975, after having two years of astrological practice under my belt. Marcy and I drove to Tucson together to spend a day with him, pick his brain and share our research with him. It was definitely a pilgrimage! A true hospitable Taurus, he welcomed us to his book & manuscript-strewn abode and generously shared hours of his time with us. He felt like a long-lost grandfather (no surprise, considering that his Moon in Capricorn was conjunct my South Node). Earthy & straightforward, he talked and smoked non-stop, shared lots of tidbits and opinions and was actually interested in our findings. It was such a thrill to be in his presence.

When I asked him if there was some aspect of his research that required further development, he encouraged us to dig deeper into the subject of future & past dynamics. He obviously enjoyed the company of younger individuals and was particularly intrigued by those of us in the "Neptune in Libra" generation. Although we only spent a day together, I came away with a deeper appreciation of his contribution to astrology – and an even stronger commitment to share the truths that he had uncovered. And after nearly 50 years of astrological counseling, teaching, researching and writing about Tobey's concepts (www.dianeclarke.com), I continue to be excited and inspired by his research. I attribute my success as an astrologer to the fact that my work is based on Tobey's amazing "clockwise house system"!

At the time, I didn't realize what a challenging path I'd put myself on. Already out-of-step with the mainstream due to my passion for astrology, the fact that I used both equal house and Tobey's system also set me apart from the other astrologers. We just didn't speak the same language – and very few were comfortable looking at things from a different perspective. However, my compulsion to follow what was *truth* for me won out over my desire for peer acceptance. I started teaching astrology so that I could have others to talk with!

I am grateful to have connected with Naomi Bennett – a fellow traveler on this mission to spread the word and keep the work of Carl Payne Tobey alive & well! Her publications of his correspondence course and his collected works, along with her own books explaining his concepts, have been a major gift to the astrological community—and will hopefully inspire new generations to step off the beaten path and put his ingenious theories to the test.

My Astrology Teacher: Carl Payne Tobey
By Susie Cox

Looking back at my life as a serious astrologer, my true beginning happened with the esteemed astrologer, Carl Payne Tobey. Even though I started studying astrology as a young child,

Carl is the one who taught me how to be a professional astrologer. So here is my story about how I met Carl and how he ended up being my mentor.

In my late teens I went to a psychic conference in Phoenix where I attended a talk about the different astrology ordinances and the legalities of getting a business license. The speaker suggested we all check it out where we live, since they are city-wide and specific to each city. So when I returned to Tucson, I went downtown and found the ordinance on astrology. It was a fascinating story that led me to Carl.

The ordinance is called a "Fortune Telling Ordinance", which is still named that to this day. This is the listing from the actual ordinance, which includes, "astrology, palmistry, phrenology, fortunetelling (either of the past, present or future), clairvoyance, clairaudience, crystal gazing, hypnotism, mediumship, prophesy, augury, divination, magic or necromancy".

It seems that there were some questionable gypsies who came through Tucson, so the city created an ordinance to protect the citizens. To practice any of these arts, a business license was required and the fee was $2,400 per year. Depending on the type of business, most licenses cost about $50. - $200. This is where Carl Payne Tobey entered the picture. He made a proposal to the Tucson city council and had the fee reduced to $300 per year, which is still in effect today. That change was made in 1961.

After I found that he was involved, I looked in the phone book and found a listing for Carl Payne Tobey and called him. Of course, I had no idea of what an influential and important astrologer he was at that time. My love of astrology and serendipity led me to him, which totally changed my life as a young, eager and budding astrologer.

Our first meeting lasted about 4 hours and after that he took me under his wing as my mentor. He was about 60 years old at the time and was at a perfect phase in his life to have an energetic astrologer help him with every day projects. I had already started interpreting astrology charts, so I was at a perfect level to help him and learn at the same time. My early twenties were spent visiting Carl several afternoons each week. Looking back, those were some of my most precious memories in my life. I'm getting teary now just thinking about it. I was such a lucky young astrologer.

What did I learn from Carl? Actually, I learned how to be a professional astrologer. Since I already know how to calculate and interpret a chart, Carl didn't have to start from beginning with me. The main thing I did for him was to help him organize his research. Carl was one of the first astrologers who did statistical research, which he started as early as 1936. I remember one of his favorite research projects was what he named "The Aquarian Kids". He had so many of their charts and had me get them more organized. Those born in January and February 1962 had up to seven planets in the sign of Aquarius. He could see that this generation had an important destiny, which was to move humanity forward.

The other thing I learned from Carl was how to handle the media. Reporters seemed to interview him all the time and Carl handled them with dignity and an authoritative voice that couldn't be denied. He was charming and very clever with his words. His background was as a journalist and it showed with how he talked to the media. So often reporters can twist an interview to make astrology look bad and he never let that happen. He was one of the smartest people I've ever known. But his intelligence was one of curiosity that wanted to figure out the big picture. He was one with his ephemeris, which is the book full of numbers showing the degrees of the planets every day. He taught me how to read an ephemeris.

But the main memory I have about Carl was the ongoing dialogue he had with astronomer, Dr. Bart Bok, who was the head of the Astronomy department (1966-70) at the University of Arizona at the time. They had lots of discussions about how astrology worked within the framework of science. I was there for many of the discussions, which I thought were cordial, fascinating and very informative. Both Carl and I thought things were going well with all the dialogues until the paper Objections to Astrology was signed by 186 academics and co-authored by Dr Bok in 1975 that said astrology doesn't work. It was more than a shock for both of us.

I realize that my relationship with Carl was life changing for me. I have to give my immense gratitude to Carl for his insight to guide me at the perfect time in my life as an astrologer. I now teach chart interpretation at Kepler College, lecture internationally, and have written 5 books; so I'm sure Carl is looking down on me now with a big smile. www.susiecox.com

CPT from Kenneth Kaiserman

I first met CPT while I was in high school in Tucson. I was not unfamiliar with 'esoterica', as I had been exposed in my youth to the Theosophy Society, devotees of Madame Blavatsky. Carl was a fascinating persona, clearly a heavyweight in his field. He was an astrologer/mathematician who was often selected as an ex-officio dean of astrologers to scientifically debate sceptics like Dr. Bok, the Harvard astronomer, no friend of astrologers.

I was quite fascinated to discover that there was clearly something to astrology and Carl's work. He was very engaging, and liked to welcome anyone eager to learn, freely sharing the lessons of his correspondence course which gave a firm foundation in astrology to the uninitiated.

I recall he had an Aquarian/Uranian openness to hearing others perspectives, and as our friendship grew we debated politics with gusto, he the Goldwater Conservative, and me the left-leaning Democrat. He liked to hear contrary viewpoints, and felt he learned by not being rigidly doctrinaire. He liked to speak with the youth of the '60's', to learn other points of view. He disapproved of the process of higher education demanding conformity in studies, and thought the brightest were those not shaped to an institutional molding & perspective.

When Tobey was in his 20's, he had become part of a film crowd with the Selznick brothers. He met an actress named Marjorie Daw who first piqued his interest in astrology. Over time he was a close friend with Grant Lewi, the editor for many astrology magazines and author of Heaven Knows What. Carl's investigation into astrology led to research and discovery. He developed an impressive clientele of personal clients, from the business world, and many others. Overtime I was often on hand or aware of consultations with renowned clients. Even the local Chief of Police came for assistance in crime sleuthing and the editor of the Tucson paper was his client and friend. Through Carl, I got to know his good friend and famous astrologer, Sydney Omarr. Many Hollywood people came to Omarr along with Dorothy Chandler, owner of the Los Angeles Times, was one of his clients.

Carl advised a Presidential campaign in 1968 for Alabama's Gov. George Wallace running for the American Independent Party. Wallace had been the target of an assassin and wasn't taking chances. On Saturday evenings I would routinely go to Carl's ranch house and have some supper and a cocktail with him. On the way into town I would drop the brown manila envelopes at the Post Office, addressed to Montgomery, Alabama.

Carl was also the consummate ladies' man, and loved hosting impromptu parties. I recall one of the many attractive women in his circle. In the mode of the times, he had a bar in his home. His was in his first ranch house, a Polynesian themed decor with aquariums set into the walls and beaded curtains. Meyers Rum was the ingredient of choice for Cuba Libra. The 'salons' at his home drew an eclectic group of engaging people. UFO research was a keen interest of his, and the well known Lorenzens' who lived in Tucson were occasional guests. Joanne Clancy, publisher of American Astrology magazine lived in Tucson and Carl wrote for them. For his 70th surprise birthday party, people came in from world-wide.

My Memories of Carl Payne Tobey
Naomi C Bennett

I was 20 when I interviewed him for a college research paper. That first visit impressed me and I became his student. Unknown to me I had a strong Jupiter and Venus transits that made learning astrology very easy, the understanding was just automatic. Within this same year I met my future husband who was also an early Taurus Sun like Carl. Six months later I was debating whether to marry the young Taurus or stay in Tucson to work with the older Taurus mentor. I married the young one and then managed to move to Tucson with my husband, birth a daughter and work for Carl too. Since I was a Psychology major, we did a psychological testing of the Aquarian Children born in early February 1962. The results have been lost to time since Carl was required to move to Texas as he got older and to that, I had already moved to Colorado.

We spent many nights watching the transits of the stars, planets and the Milky Way in the warm Tucson summer nights. He showed me how the ecliptic flips back and forth in the sky in 24 hours, just like the Milky Way does. Every morning he contemplated the ephemeris as he drank his coffee and had a first cigarette. In his era, everyone smoked and drank. He used his Tiki bar as a means to lubricate his visitors to loosen up and tell their personal stories that became his form of research serving Cuba Libras into the night. His house was a bit like a hotel since people drifted in and out on a regular basis. I felt like I got the best from him at the end of his life with so much experience and knowledge gained over 50 years.

I helped edit his last book in 1972 called, Astrology of Inner Space. In the mid 20th century, astrologers did not document their sources. Carl only wrote about part of his discoveries in each book but the entire theory was given in his private astrology lessons that he taught to over 700 people.

Finally in the 1990's I started a quest that lasted a decade to discover the physical evidence behind his astrological discoveries that he did astronomically and mathematically. I studied with the Project Hindsight conferences, and traveled to New York, London, Paris, Cairo and Luxor looking for the proof of how astrology was formed. The result was my book, Foundations of Astrology in 1914.

From that process I researched Tobey's early articles in the astrology magazines of the 1930-50's. The New York City public library stores all of these old magazines under the Science Library since astrology is classified as 'Pseudo-Science'. Later in the 2000's I discovered that the American Federation of Astrologers had a huge collection of old astrology magazines. That discovery has produced this book.

The Tobey System of Astrology

In 1968, I was a university student in Arizona and had the assignment to do a research paper on the subject of my choice. I chose astrology. I couldn't find much information on the subject at my local library but I was allowed to interview people. I discovered one of the best astrologer of the 20th century, Carl Payne Tobey, who lived in Tucson, Arizona. I called him and explained my task and my dilemma. I asked if I could interview him. He accepted my request and graciously invited me to his home. He drew up my chart and asked me: "Was your mother ill when you were young?" I hesitate for a moment and reply: "Why yes, she died when I was 12." He got me right there. How did he know that? My interest was kindled that day and the passion I have for astrology is still with me thanks to Carl becoming my teacher and mentor.

Carl Payne Tobey

Most current American astrologers have forgotten Tobey's name and many of the others from the last century. Copyright law has kept their work out of print, yet their contributions were immense. Tobey was 66 when I met him with an astrological career that spanned 40+ years. He was America's first astrological statistician and researcher since the 1930's. Tobey was part of a group of New York City astrologers that consisted of Grant Lewi, Sydney K. Bennett (Wynn), Charles Jayne, Dane Rudhyar and many others. They were the young astrology turks of their time. They all revolved around Lewi since he was the editor for three major astrology magazines. They were all working to determine what functioned in astrology and what was a myth.

Astrology was re-introduced in the USA by Madam Helena Blavatsky around 1875-90, but she was very esoteric. Sydney Bennett learned Sanskrit, Jayne investigated eclipses, Rudhyar studied psychology and Tobey did statistics and coined the term 'Astrostatisics'. Lewi studied repetitive patterns and at one point only used the angular houses in many of his articles. Lewi and Tobey were best friends and they were both born in 1902. Tobey had Uranus on his Ascendant in Sagittarius. He was an unconventional truth seeker who was ahead of his time. He made friends of astronomers and scientists and then interviewed many of them for several New York astrology magazines.

In Tobey's research, he discovered the personal lunar cycle highs and lows by studying the flow of money into an astrology magazine. Using the owner's chart, he found that more money came into the magazine when the transiting Moon was conjunct the owner's natal Sun and less came in the magazine when the transiting Moon was opposing the owner's Sun. This was consistent over many months. He studied his own gambling wins and losses and found the same personal cycle highs and cycle lows for his gambling wins. Tobey stated "a person reaches his best period of the month, a period of emotional fulfillment, when the Moon crosses the birth Sun position by zodiacal longitude." [1]

Cycle High/Low Data

SPACE SEGMENT	AMOUNT	DAYS	AVERAGE	3-MOVING AVERAGE
1	$1784	24	$73	$78
2	2220	24	92	79
3	1460	20	73	80
4	1587	21	75	72
5	1220	18	68	68
6	1097	18	61	57
7	794	18	42	60
8	1888	24	78	61
9	1357	21	64	80
10	1848	20	97	80
11	2086	26	80	82
12	1634	24	68	74

GRAPH "M"

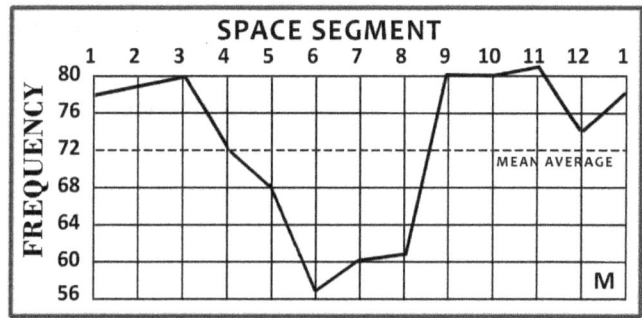

Cycle High and Lows with Income [2]

He also discovered that major loss of life occurred during eclipses and moon wobbles. He called them periods of instability. Moon wobbles are 90 degree aspects between the lunar nodes and the Sun. Eclipses are produced with conjunctions and oppositions but the 90 degree square aspect is effective too. The square of the Sun to the lunar nodes will not produce an eclipse and Charles Jayne noted their effectiveness too. In older astrology texts They were called 'lunar bendings'. Tobey's research was done statistically using US national fire data and then he tracked catastrophic actual events over time. He noticed that the transit of Uranus on the lunar nodes also produced instability and made moon wobbles more dramatic.

DATA OF FIRES 1943 TO 1946

DISTANCE SUN TO MOON'S NODE	NUMBER OF FIRES	FIRES RESULTING IN DEATH	NUMBER KILLED	AVERAGE DEATHS PER FIRE
0-15 degrees	107	20	488	4.560
15-30 "	107	14	89	.831
30-45 "	101	18	147	1.455
45-60 "	87	11	38	.436
60-75 "	69	10	85	1.232
75-90 "	103	16	252	2.446

US National Fire Statistics

DISTANCE SUN TO MOON'S NODE	AVERAGE DEATHS PER FIRE
0-15 degrees	24.4
15-30 "	6.3
30-45 "	8.1
45-60 "	3.4
60-75 "	8.5
75-90 "	15.7

Eclipse and Moon Wobble Deaths in Fires [3]

With his study of eclipses and moon wobbles Tobey concluded:

> "The ancient astrologers, even back in the most ancient civilization of India and China, attributed great significance to the nodes of the

moon. The north node was called the dragon's head; the south node, the dragon's tail. The dragon's head was supposed to be a fortunate influence while the dragon's tail was an unfortunate influence. For the most part, the writer has not found any cause for such conviction, although most the U.S. wars came about with the dragon's tail near the birth-sun position of the United States. For the most part, the writer doubts whether there is any difference in the two nodes. Both seem to bring about instability when near the Sun or Uranus." 4

Tobey did a series of articles called Solar Biology for the American Astrology magazine in 1936 that analyzed 6,788 Physicians' sun-signs. Capricorn dominated the sun-signs and there were 16% more Capricorns than Pisces (the lowest number sun sign). Below is a small sample of his work, but he analyzed many other groups like 5,000 Industrialist and 28,000 in Who's Who.

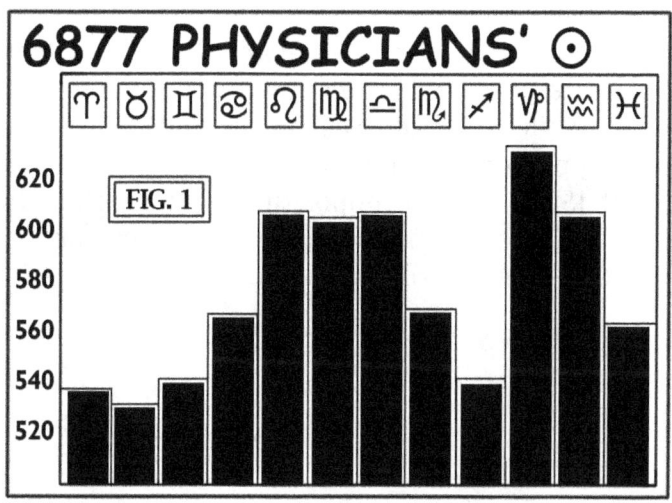

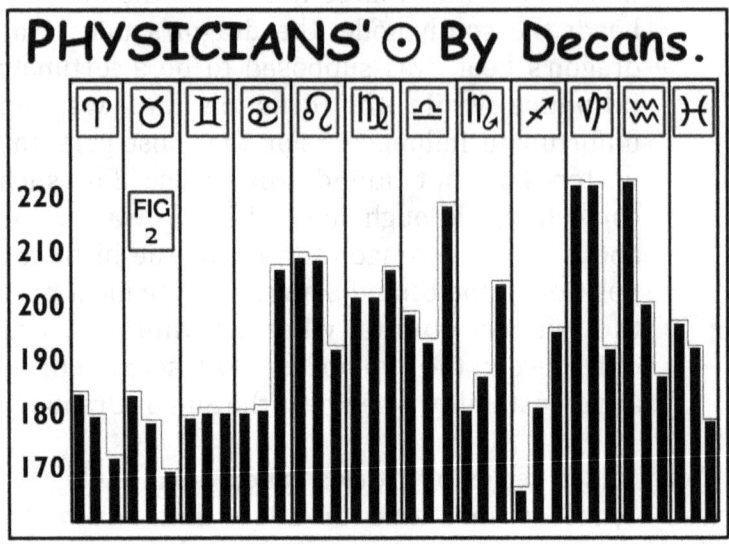

In 1944 Tobey wrote on the Hadaller Divorce Experiment. An attorney had collected birth data on 1,245 couples over 20 years. Major Hadaller was a California divorce attorney and wrote a book called <u>What's Behind Divorce</u>. Tobey used Hadaller's data to analyze it.

> "He found that divorces between couples whose birthdates were within 35 days of each other were rare, while divorce was much more common among persons born a half or a quarter of a year apart [Suns were in opposition or square]. The figures indicated that divorces were few among persons born a third or a sixth of a year apart." [5]

Size of Area	Degrees Between Sun Positions	Number of Divorced Couples	Expectancy	Deviation
35 Degrees	0 to 35	41	242	Minus 201
20 "	35 to 55	211	138	Plus 73
20 "	55 to 75	39	138	Minus 99
35 "	75 to 110	480	242	Plus 238
18 "	110 to 128	19	125	Minus 106
17 "	128 to 145	183	117	Plus 66
20 "	145 to 165	85	138	Minus 53
15 "	165 to 180	187	105	Plus 82
180 "	TOTAL	1245	1245	

Squares and Oppositions dominate Divorces

Tobey then analyzed the birth data collected by Dr. Jacob Levie of 2,161 married couples. Tobey found that natal Sun signs was highest with the 60 degree sextile aspects between the couples. There was an excess of sextile marriages.

> "people are least likely to marry persons of their own solar sign and persons whose sun-sign is trine to their own." ..."it is our general finding that people tend to select mates born two signs away from their own sun-sign." As a footnote by the editor, Grant Lewi, he comments: "the fact that people 'marry on the sextile' is very interesting. Signs in sextile to each other represent the 11th and 3rd Houses of interests and relationships. Thus, if Aries marries Gemini (on the sextile), Aries represents Gemini's 11th [solar] House and Gemini represents Aries' 3rd. Their mutuality of interest is therefore centered in friends and aspirations (11th House); and in mental companionship, family and neighborhood relationships (3rd House)." [6]

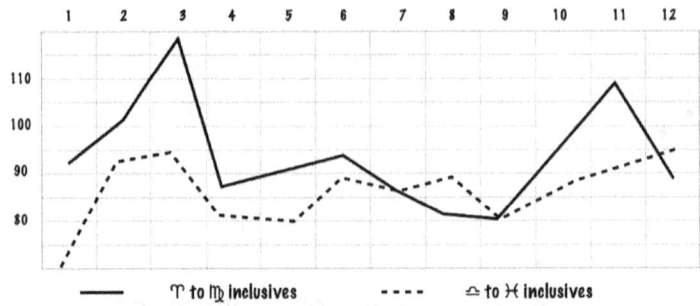

Sextiles are Good for Marriage

Tobey's twin birth study that shows that Gemini has the most twin birth rate but also the lowest birthrate of the year.

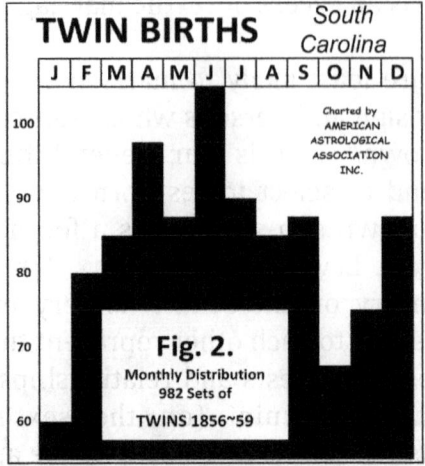

Twin Birth Rates

He wrote for all the major astrology magazines in the past. In the 1970's he had a nationally syndicated column in many major newspapers, but not the standard sun-sign column. It was a half-page in the Sunday comics and was illustrated by the famous southwest artist, Ted DeGrazia. Using the comic strip section bypassed all the fortune telling laws since it was considered entertainment! In his youth, he was a newspaper reporter and he knew the most read section of the newspaper was the Sunday comics.

This Week in Astrology 1969

He was an amateur mathematician and studied abstract design in astrology for most of his life. As early as 1933, he determined that Pluto had to rule Aries. With the discovery of Uranus and Neptune, astrologers had unconsciously followed the ancient pattern of assigning rulership by **Average Mean Distance from Geocentric Earth.** This is seen in traditional Hellenistic Planetary Order with the dual rulership of Mercury to Virgo-Gemini , Venus to Libra-Taurus, Mars to Scorpio-Aries, Jupiter to Sagittarius-Pisces and Saturn to Capricorn-Aquarius. Astrologers assigned Uranus to Aquarius and Neptune to Pisces. To continue this pattern of Average Mean Distance from Earth, Pluto should be assigned to Aries. Tobey did this along with a minority of other astrologers.

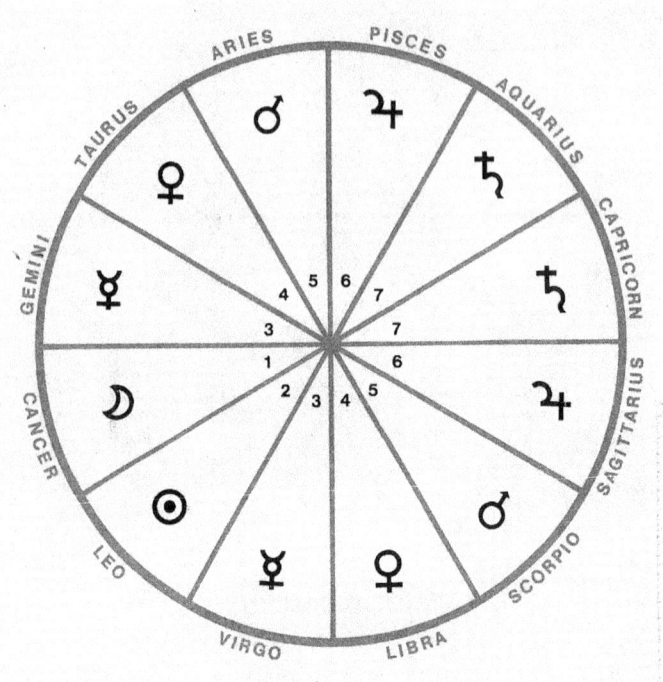

Ancient Planetary Rulerships [7]

I thought the astrological order of Moon, Sun, Mercury, Venus and Mars was crazy when I learned it in the 1970's. The ancient order of Moon, Sun, Mercury, Venus and Mars doesn't make sense to us moderns when we were taught that the solar system is centered around the Sun. From a heliocentric point of view, Venus and Mars are closest to Earth. But astrology's point of view is from Earth, it's geocentric. In 1996, I confirmed Tobey's discovery of sign rulership based on Average Mean Distance from Earth with the help of Cornell University professor Avery Solomon, who taught mathematics. But I didn't have the program he used. In 2013, I discovered an online video that exactly modeled this principle. From Earth, Mercury and Venus spend more time on the far side of the Sun from us. Therefore, the Sun is closer to Earth most of the time. The ancients studied the skies for centuries, they had figured it out long ago. Modern astronomy confirms this order in astrology!

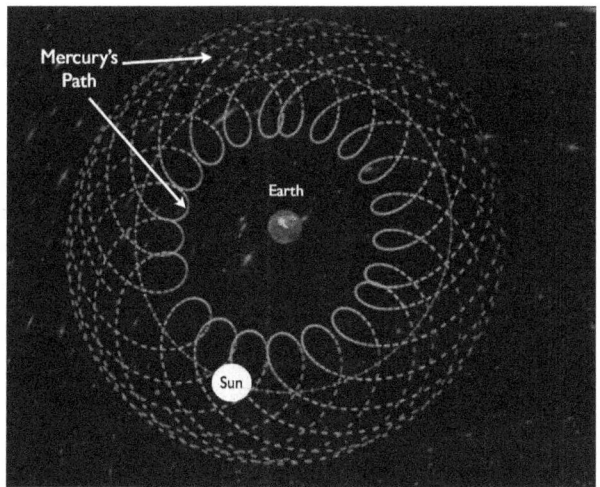

The Sun is Closer to Earth than Mercury [8]

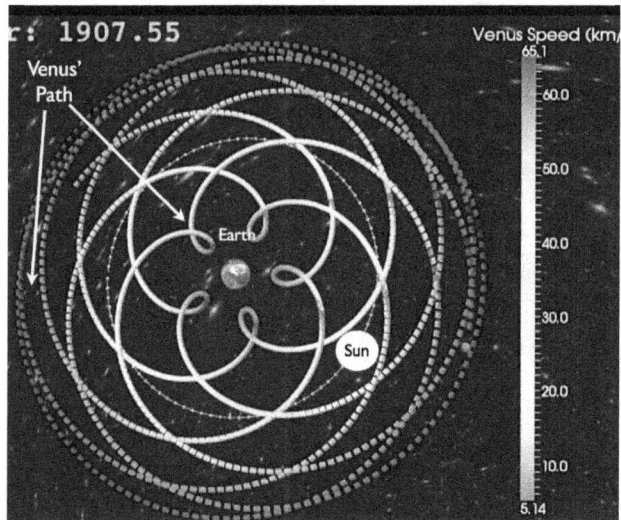

The Sun is Closer to Earth than Venus [8]

After determining that Pluto was the natural ruler of Aries in 1933, it lead Tobey to investigate the original design of astrology's house rulership. His study of geometric design in astrology made him realize that ancient dual rulership had another hidden secret in it. Duality of rulership could be started from the Moon and go in a forward count through the signs for sign rulership **OR** it could be started from the Sun and go backwards in a counter-clockwise count for house rulership! He realized that astrology's original design had a duality of rulership between signs and houses. It was embedded in the astrology's design from the very start with Cancer and the Moon starting the rulership for zodiacal signs. Leo and the Sun start the rulership for the houses. He called it the Counterclockwise House System. He taught his methods to over 700 private students from the 1950's-70's. This was spelled out in his book, <u>Astrology of Inner Space</u>.

The Duality of Signs and Houses

Sign Rulership	Planet	House Rulership
Cancer	Moon-Sun	Leo 1st House
Leo	Sun-Moon	Cancer 2nd House
Virgo	Mercury	Gemini 3rd House
Libra	Venus	Taurus 4th House
Scorpio	Mars	Aries 5th House
Sagittarius	Jupiter	Pisces 6th House
Capricorn	Saturn	Aquarius 7th House
Aquarius	Uranus-Saturn	Capricorn 8th House
Pisces	Neptune-Jupiter	Sagittarius 9th House
Aries	Pluto-Mars	Scorpio 10th House

Taurus	Eris-Venus	Libra House	11th
Gemini	Unkn ??-Mercury	Virgo House	12th

With these two discoveries, he realized that aspects where based on the houses. For example, the sextile aspect is the combination of the nature of the 3rd and 11th houses and the square aspect is the combination of the 4th and 10th houses. All together, the entire design of astrology follows geometric patterns that are perfect in conception and design. These insights were profound and took the confusion out of how and why astrology functioned. He wrote many articles, booklets and two major books, <u>Astrology of Inner Space</u> and <u>Astrology for the Millions</u>.

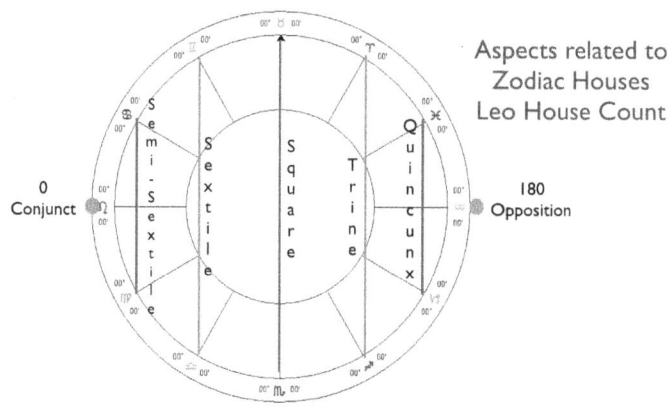

Aspects Related to Houses

The Tobey System was promoted by Thane at The Prosperos Institute in California, Moby Dick in San Francisco, Diane Clarke in Las Vegas, Betty Baxter in Arizona and myself in Austin, Texas; who all became astrology teachers. Now with my own 40+ years of experience, I find that Tobey's system has given me a level of reliability that satisfies both my clients and students.

Mid-twentieth century American astrology books never included footnotes or references. So I spent 20 years finding references in Egyptian horoscopic astrology, fractal geometry, ancient measurements and astronomy to confirm that Tobey's discoveries where based on fact. I gathered these proofs and references in my book, <u>Foundations of Astrology</u>.

In order to keep Tobey's work available, I published <u>The Collected Works of Carl Payne Tobey</u> and <u>Astrology Lessons by Carl Payne Tobey</u>. Tobey's books are very relevant to evolutionary astrology because of his deep psychological insights into human behavior and motivations. Since Tobey addresses the basic design of how astrology is structured, his ideas speak to the traditional astrology movement too as astrologers try to understand it's original structure.

So how did he know that my mother had been ill? In the equal house system, I had my Moon at 2 Virgo conjunct Saturn at 4 Virgo, one degree from the Nonagesimal, (the equal house 10th cusp). These two planets were square to my Mars at 7 Sagittarius, near my Ascendant. Since the Moon represents the mother and it was with Saturn and square to Mars, it indicated a possible illness or serious limits of the mother, especially since my Moon and Saturn were very close to the equal house 10th cusp, which is a major angle associated with parents or authority. Tobey made this his first question. When analyzing a chart, Tobey recommended looking for the strongest point in the natal chart and asking a probing question, a very good technique indeed.

Tobey has been forgotten by our younger generation of astrologers with the current trend back to traditional astrology. But as astrology is redefined in this 21st century, the research by Wynn, Tobey, Lewi and Jayne needs to be integrated into our knowledge base of how and why astrology functions.

Footnotes

Ps. Special thanks must be given to Ehsan Khazeni for re-created the images in this article so they were legible and sharp. More thanks are due to the American Federation of Astrologers for the access to these old astrology magazines and our community recognition to the AFA for saving these precious records of 20th century American astrology.

[1] T*he Astrologer* magazine, July 1946, page 21. I have not included the statistical methods he used in this article. This data was compiled manually before computers. Tobey was aware of statistical methods and used them.

[2] Ibid, June 1950

[3] Ibid, March 1951, page 15-17

[4] Ibid, November 1950, page 68

[5] *Astrological Review* October 1944, p. 117-8 (a reprint from Astrology Guide, editor Dal Lee)

[6] *The Astrologer* magazine, Sept 1946, page 9-12.

[7] Tobey, Carl, Astrology on Inner Space, Omen Press 1972, p. 412.

[8] Bennett, Naomi, Foundations of Astrology, Bonami Publishing 2014, p. 36-37.

About the Authors

Naomi C Bennett is an internationally known astrologer, lecturer and teacher of astrology since 1970. She currently lives in Austin, Tx . She has reproduced works of Tobey as a gift to the astrological community so that his research could be remembered and utilized. After more than 20 years of using astrology, she started to research the history of astrology as inspired by the three Roberts—Robert Zollar, Robert Schmidt and Robert Hand. She expanded her search to Egyptian artifacts that confirmed the astrological design re-discovered by Tobey. The result was her 2014 Book, Foundations of Astrology. She can be found on Facebook, Instagram and Twitter. Her website is http://www.LearnAstrologyNow.com.

Carl Payne Tobey (1902-1980) was a leading astrological researcher from 1930-1975. He started as a Wall Street Trader before the 1929 crash and was a newspaper man too. He was in the heart of the American re-discovery of astrology in the 1930's when all the major astrology magazines were created. As Grant Lewi's best friend, he was asked to come to Tucson. AZ after Lewi's death to save the magazine, The Astrology Magazine. He never left the Southwest and the romance of the West. He taught 700 private students and had a nationally syndicated weekly astrology feature in the Sunday comics in the 1970's.

www.ingramcontent.com/pod-product-compliance
Lightning Source LLC
Chambersburg PA
CBHW071733150426
43191CB00010B/1558